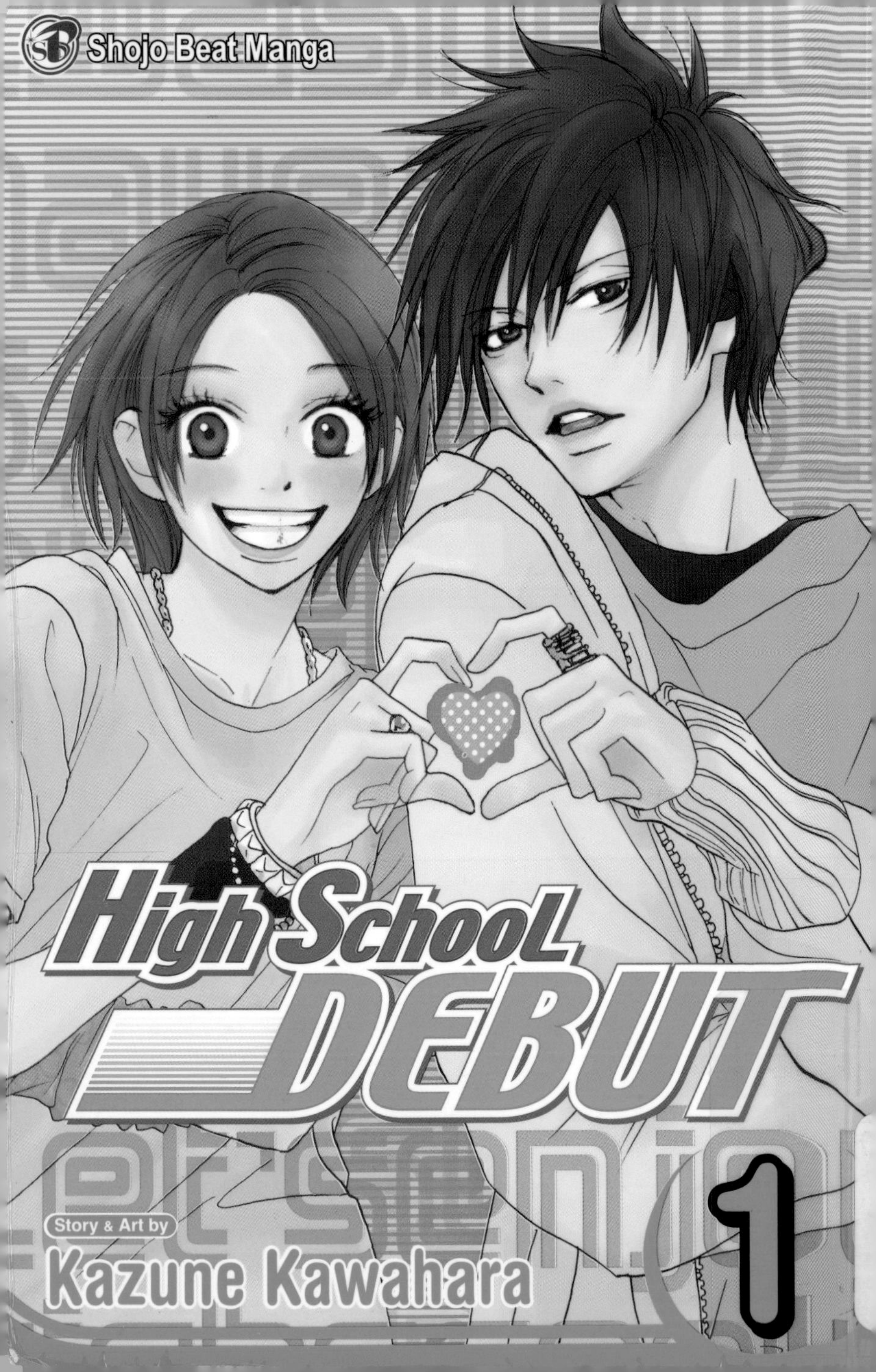
Shojo Beat Manga
High School DEBUT
1
Story & Art by
Kazune Kawahara

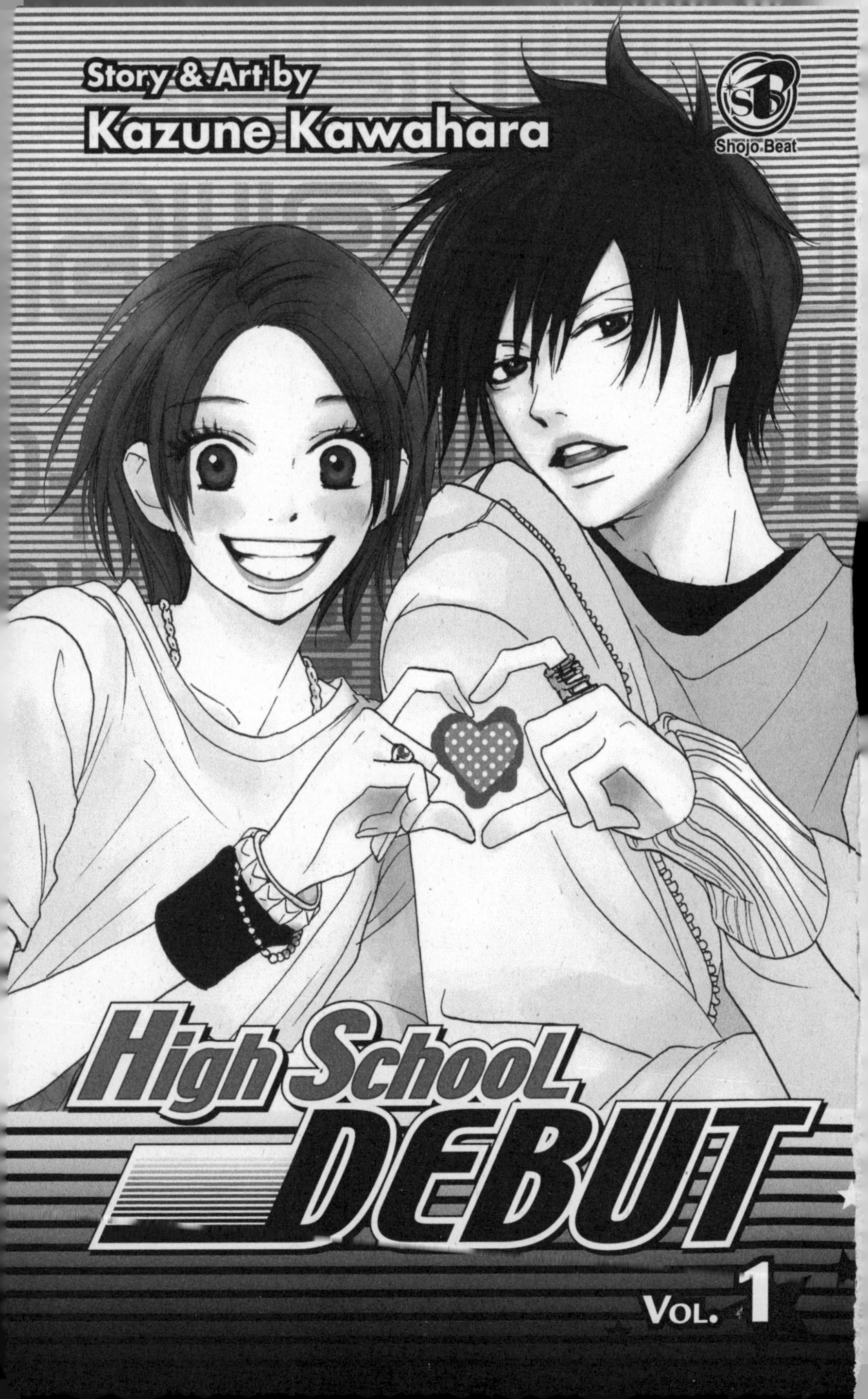
Story & Art by
Kazune Kawahara
Shojo Beat
High School
DEBUT
VOL. 1

High School DEBUT

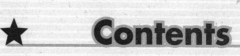

Contents

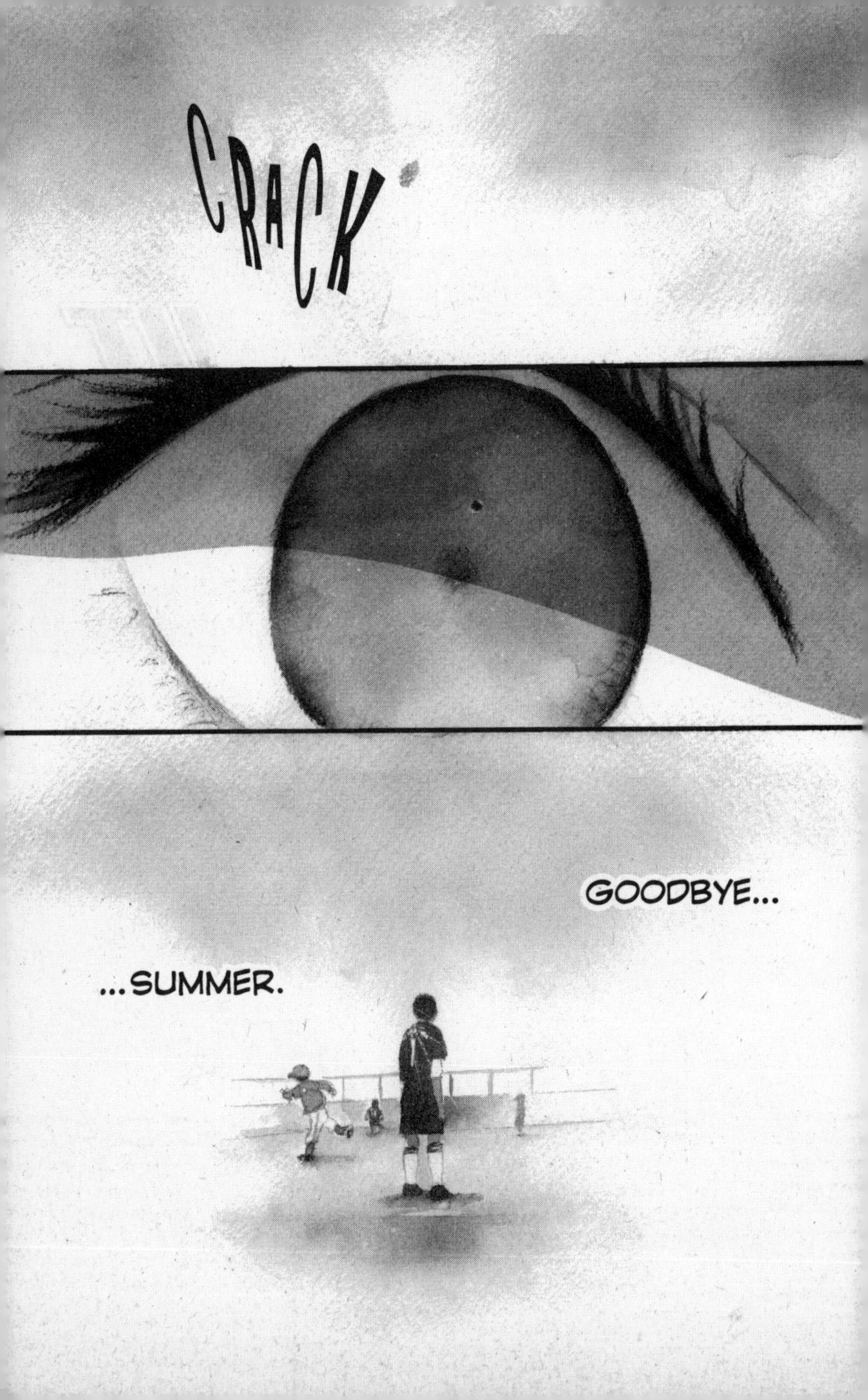

CRACK

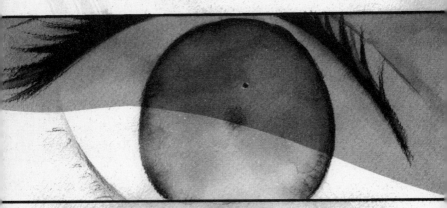

GOODBYE...

...SUMMER.

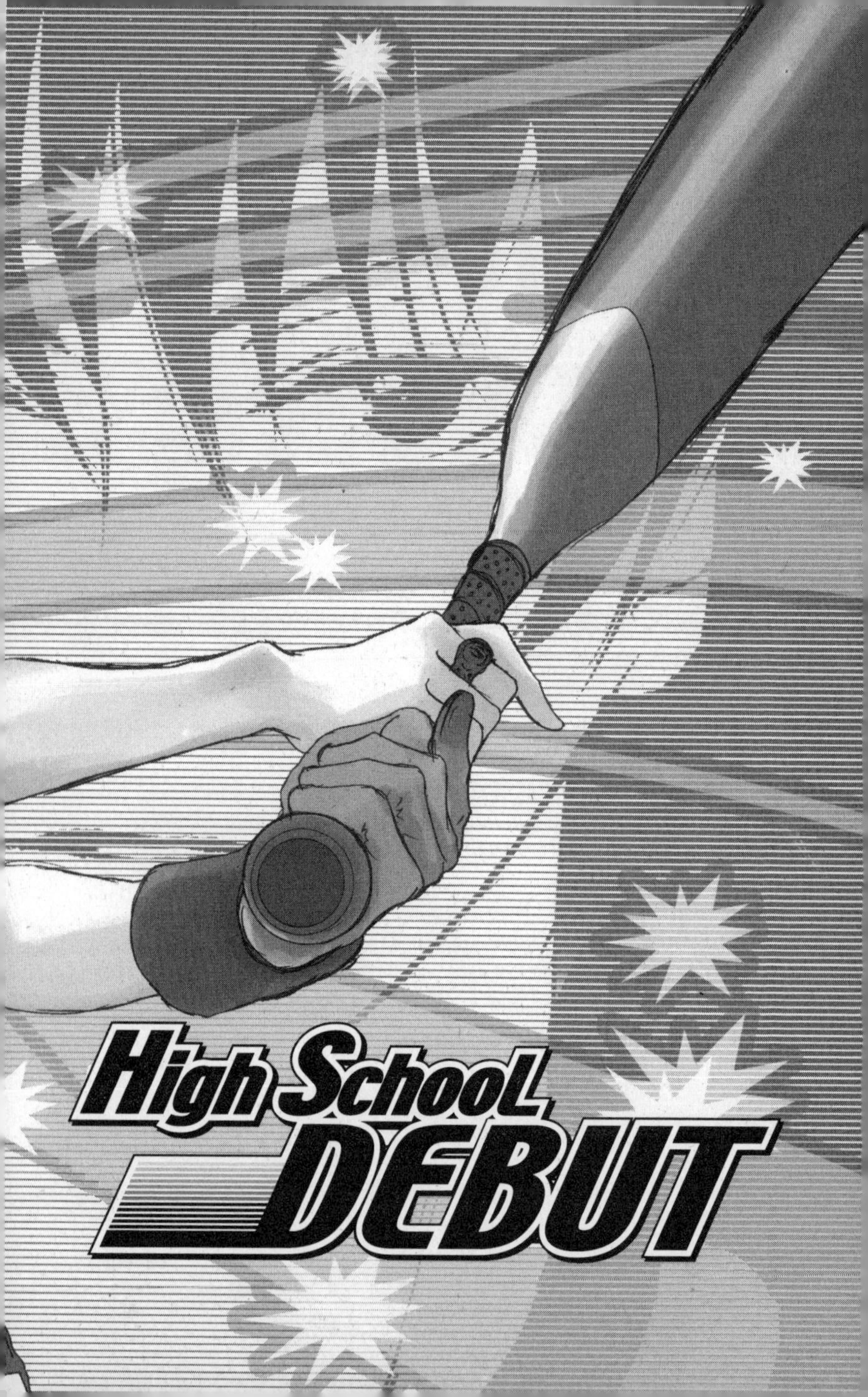
High School
DEBUT

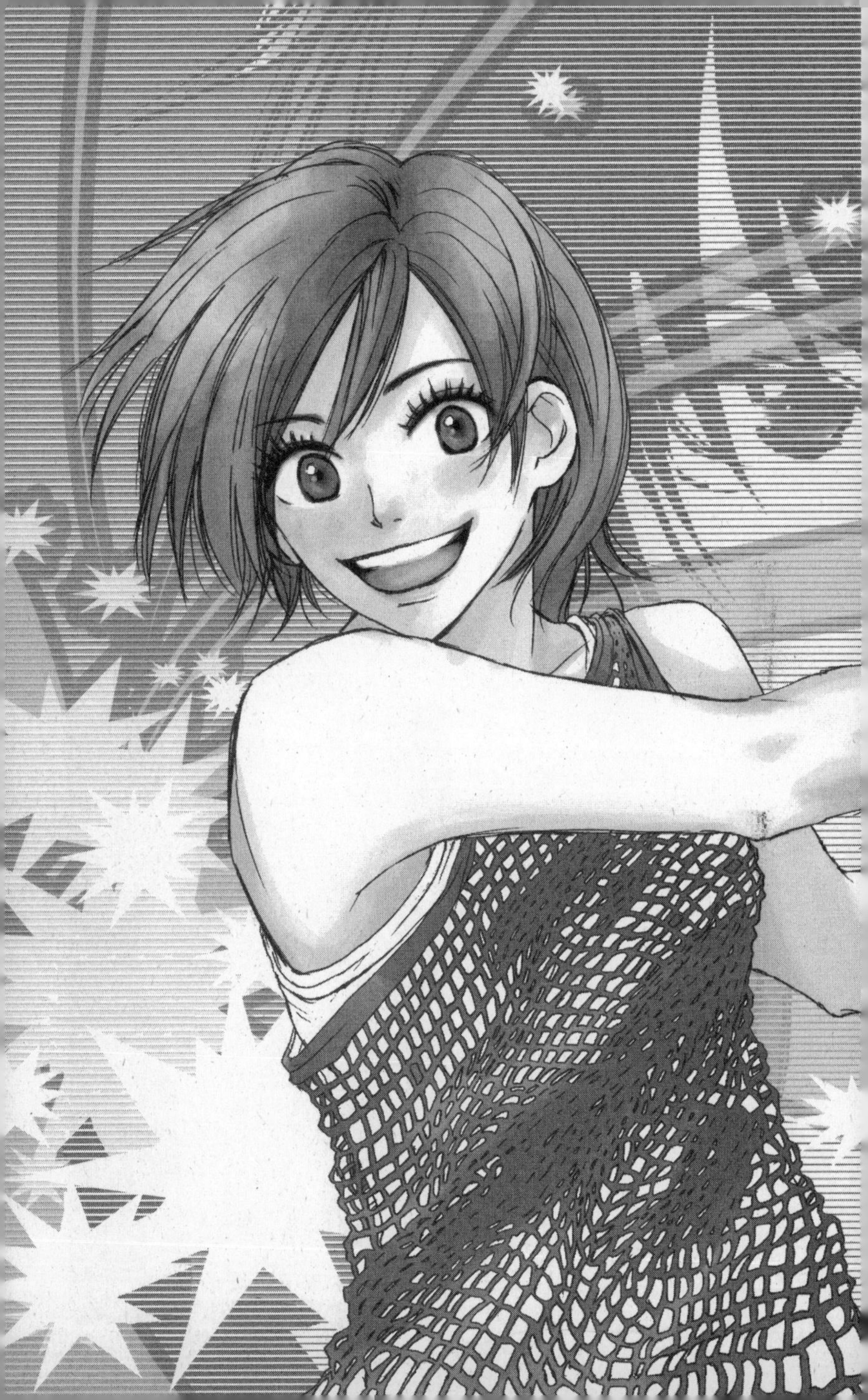

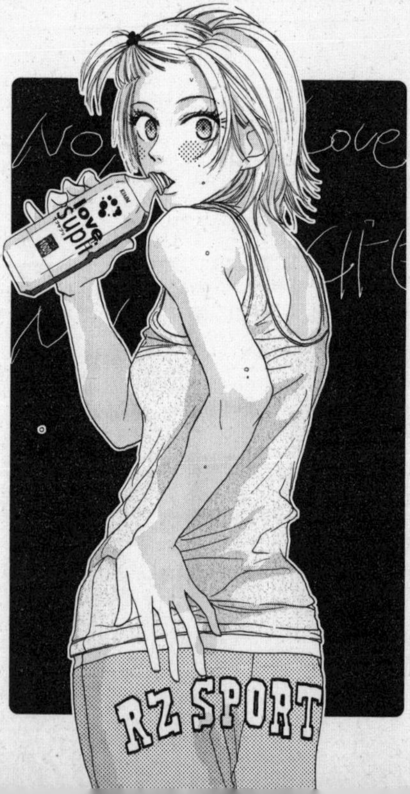
love supli
RZ SPORT

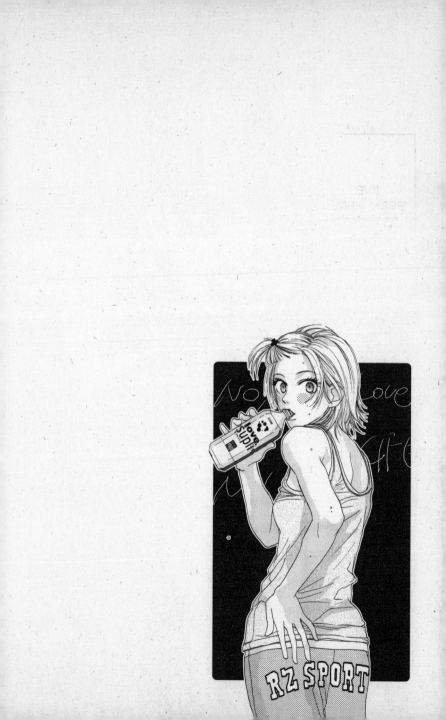

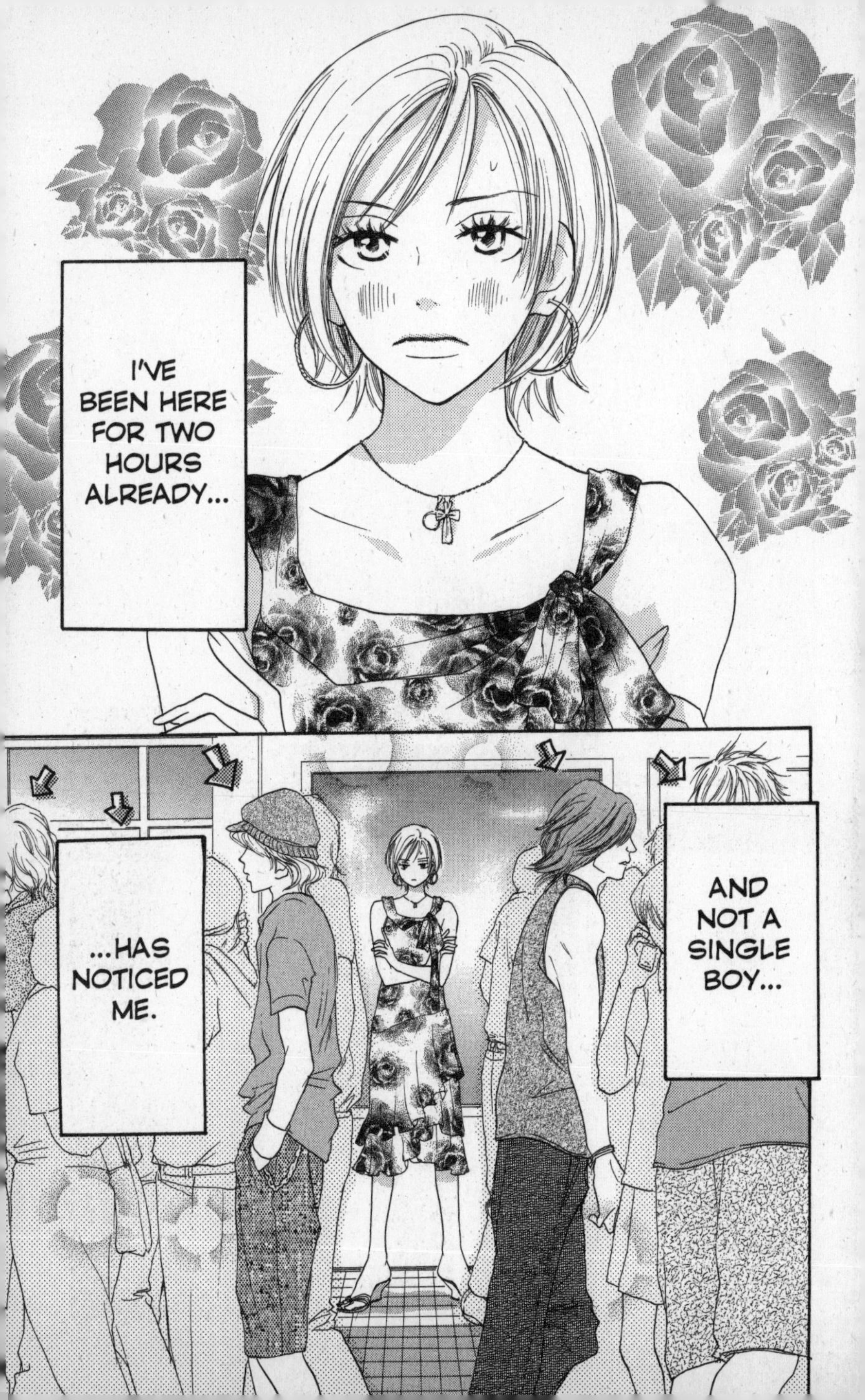
I'VE BEEN HERE FOR TWO HOURS ALREADY...
AND NOT A SINGLE BOY...
...HAS NOTICED ME.

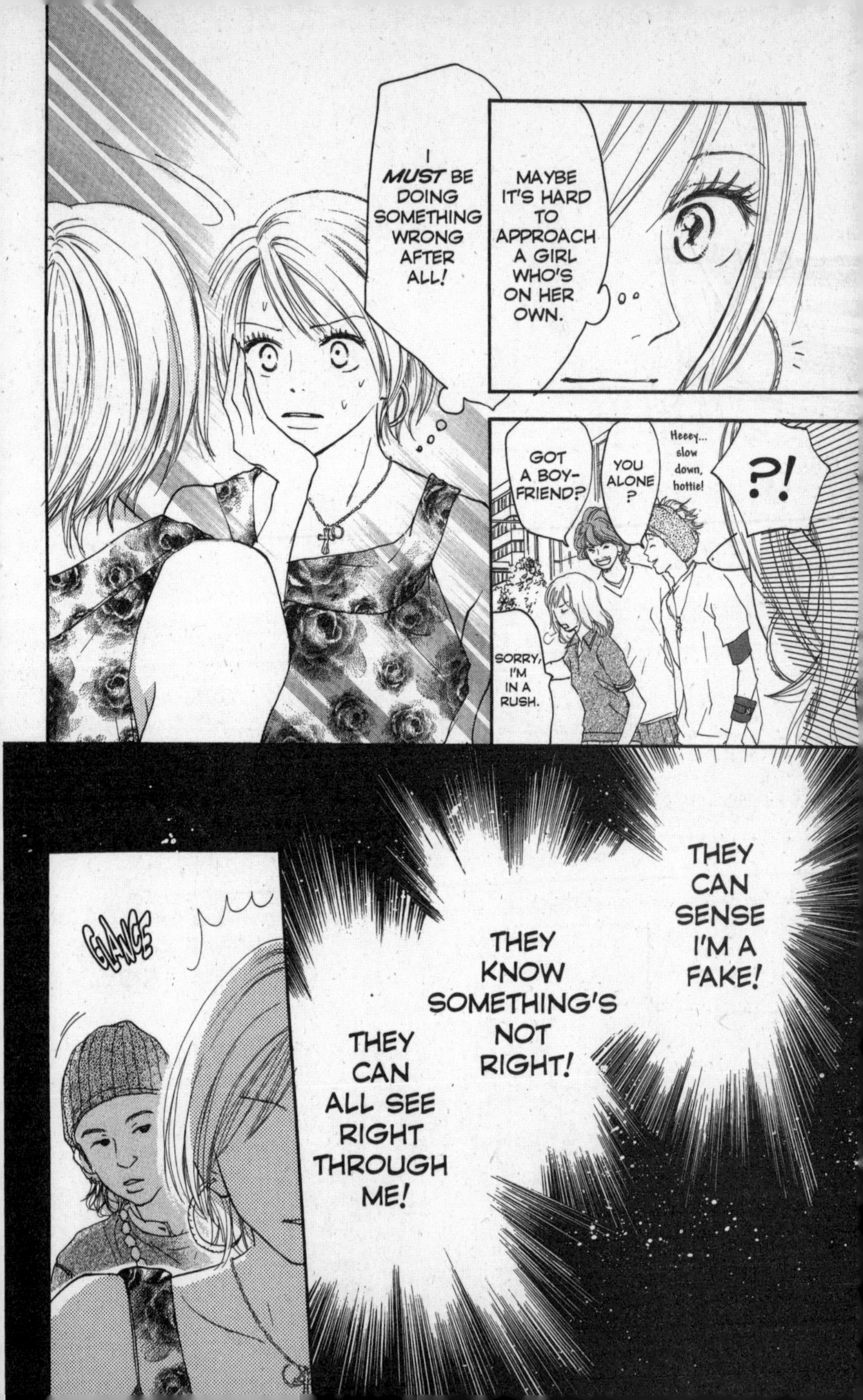
MAYBE IT'S HARD TO APPROACH A GIRL WHO'S ON HER OWN.
?!
Heeey... slow down, hottie!
YOU ALONE?
GOT A BOY-FRIEND?
SORRY, I'M IN A RUSH.
I *MUST* BE DOING SOMETHING WRONG AFTER ALL!
THEY CAN SENSE I'M A FAKE!
THEY KNOW SOMETHING'S NOT RIGHT!
THEY CAN ALL SEE RIGHT THROUGH ME!
GLANCE

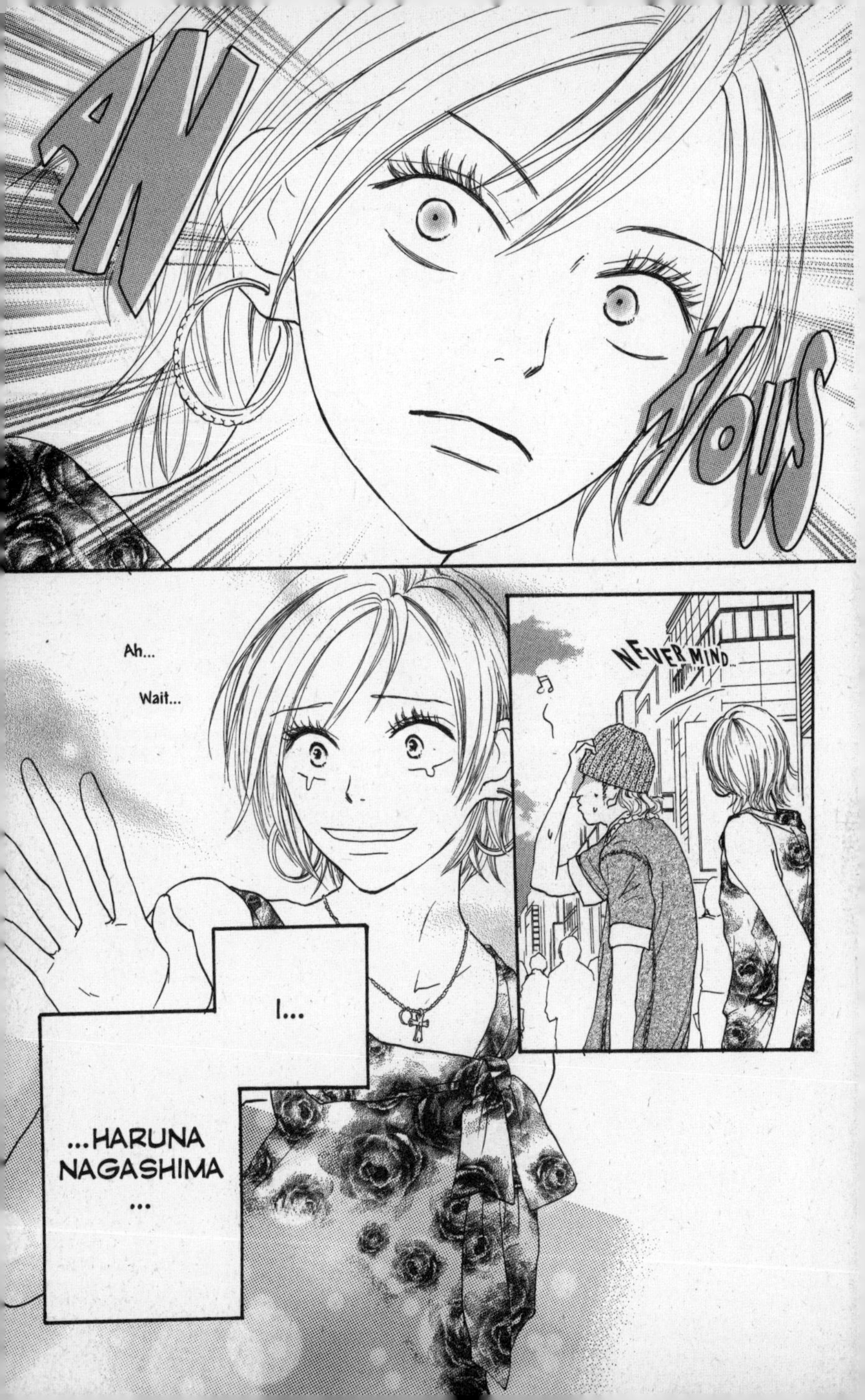
AH
NEVER MIND...
Ah...
Wait...
I...
...HARUNA NAGASHIMA ...

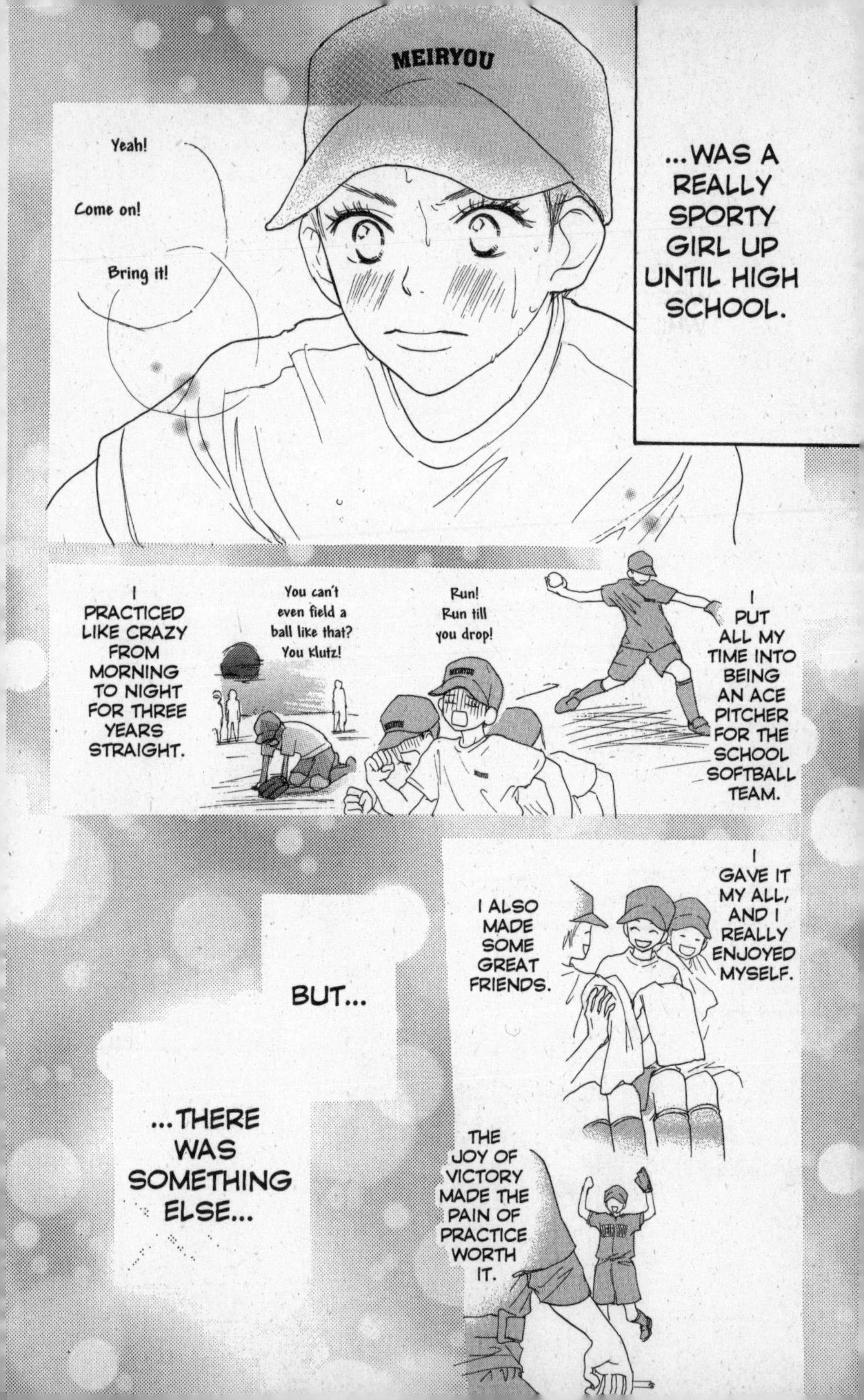
...WAS A REALLY SPORTY GIRL UP UNTIL HIGH SCHOOL.
MEIRYOU
Yeah!
Come on!
Bring it!
I PUT ALL MY TIME INTO BEING AN ACE PITCHER FOR THE SCHOOL SOFTBALL TEAM.
Run! Run till you drop!
You can't even field a ball like that? You klutz!
I PRACTICED LIKE CRAZY FROM MORNING TO NIGHT FOR THREE YEARS STRAIGHT.
I GAVE IT MY ALL, AND I REALLY ENJOYED MYSELF.
I ALSO MADE SOME GREAT FRIENDS.
THE JOY OF VICTORY MADE THE PAIN OF PRACTICE WORTH IT.
BUT...
...THERE WAS SOMETHING ELSE...

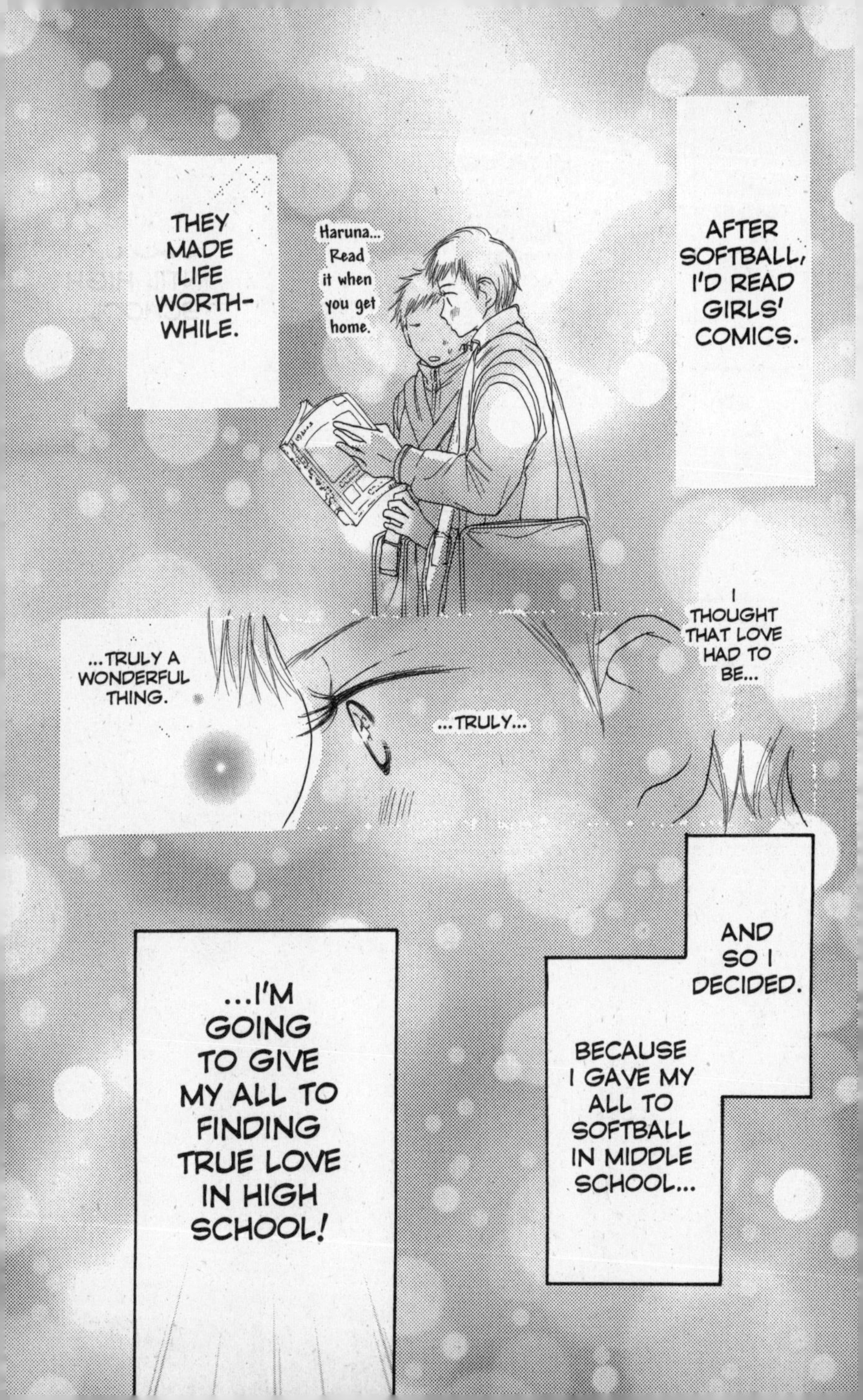
AFTER SOFTBALL, I'D READ GIRLS' COMICS.
Haruna... Read it when you get home.
THEY MADE LIFE WORTH-WHILE.
I THOUGHT THAT LOVE HAD TO BE...
...TRULY...
...TRULY A WONDERFUL THING.
AND SO I DECIDED.
BECAUSE I GAVE MY ALL TO SOFTBALL IN MIDDLE SCHOOL...
...I'M GOING TO GIVE MY ALL TO FINDING TRUE LOVE IN HIGH SCHOOL!

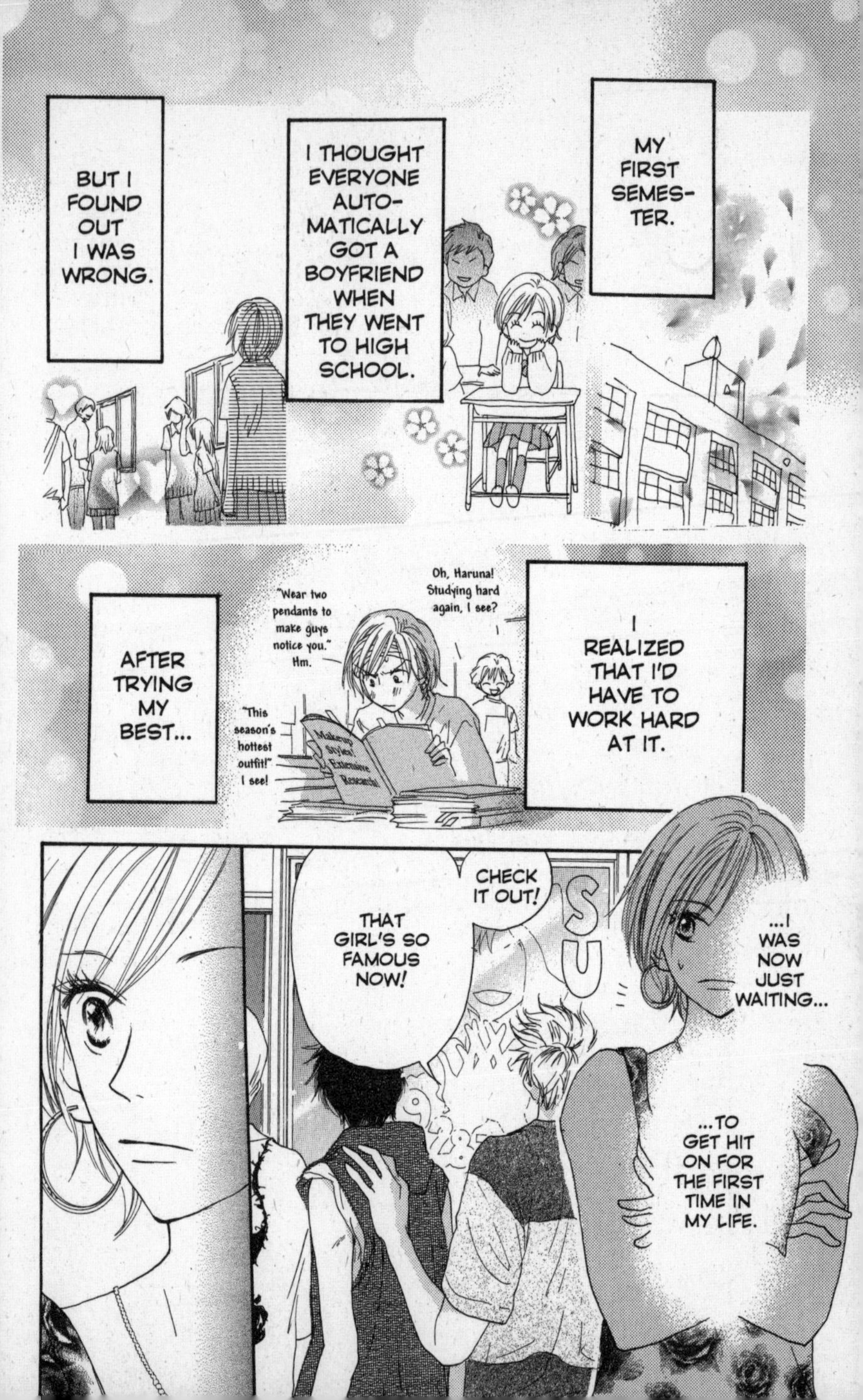
MY FIRST SEMES-TER.
I THOUGHT EVERYONE AUTO-MATICALLY GOT A BOYFRIEND WHEN THEY WENT TO HIGH SCHOOL.
BUT I FOUND OUT I WAS WRONG.
I REALIZED THAT I'D HAVE TO WORK HARD AT IT.
Oh, Haruna! Studying hard again, I see?
"Wear two pendants to make guys notice you." Hm.
"This season's hottest outfit!" I see!
AFTER TRYING MY BEST...
...I WAS NOW JUST WAITING...
...TO GET HIT ON FOR THE FIRST TIME IN MY LIFE.
SU
CHECK IT OUT!
THAT GIRL'S SO FAMOUS NOW!

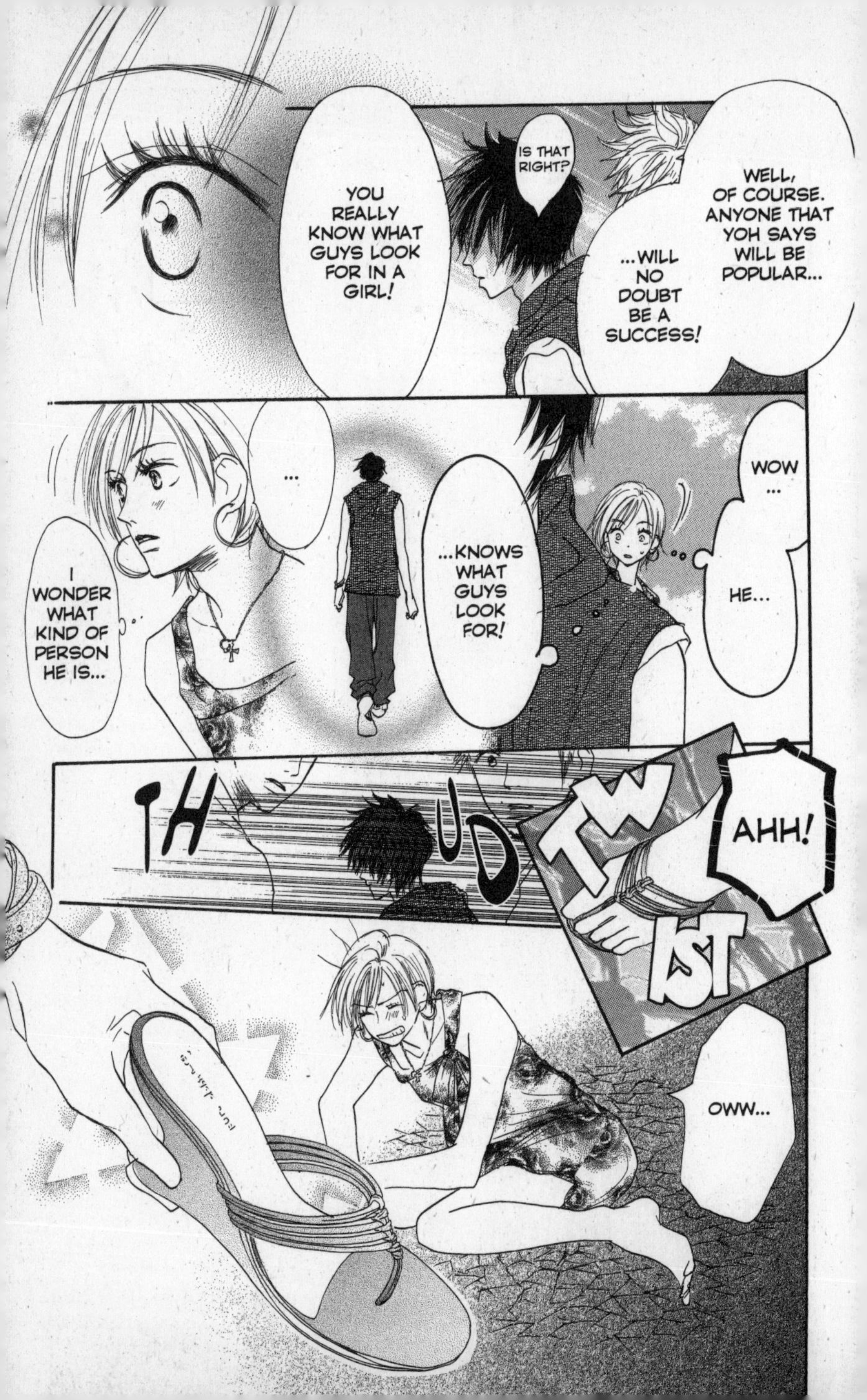
WELL, OF COURSE. ANYONE THAT YOH SAYS WILL BE POPULAR...
...WILL NO DOUBT BE A SUCCESS!
IS THAT RIGHT?
YOU REALLY KNOW WHAT GUYS LOOK FOR IN A GIRL!
WOW... HE...
...KNOWS WHAT GUYS LOOK FOR!
...
I WONDER WHAT KIND OF PERSON HE IS...
AHH!
TWIST
THUD
OWW...

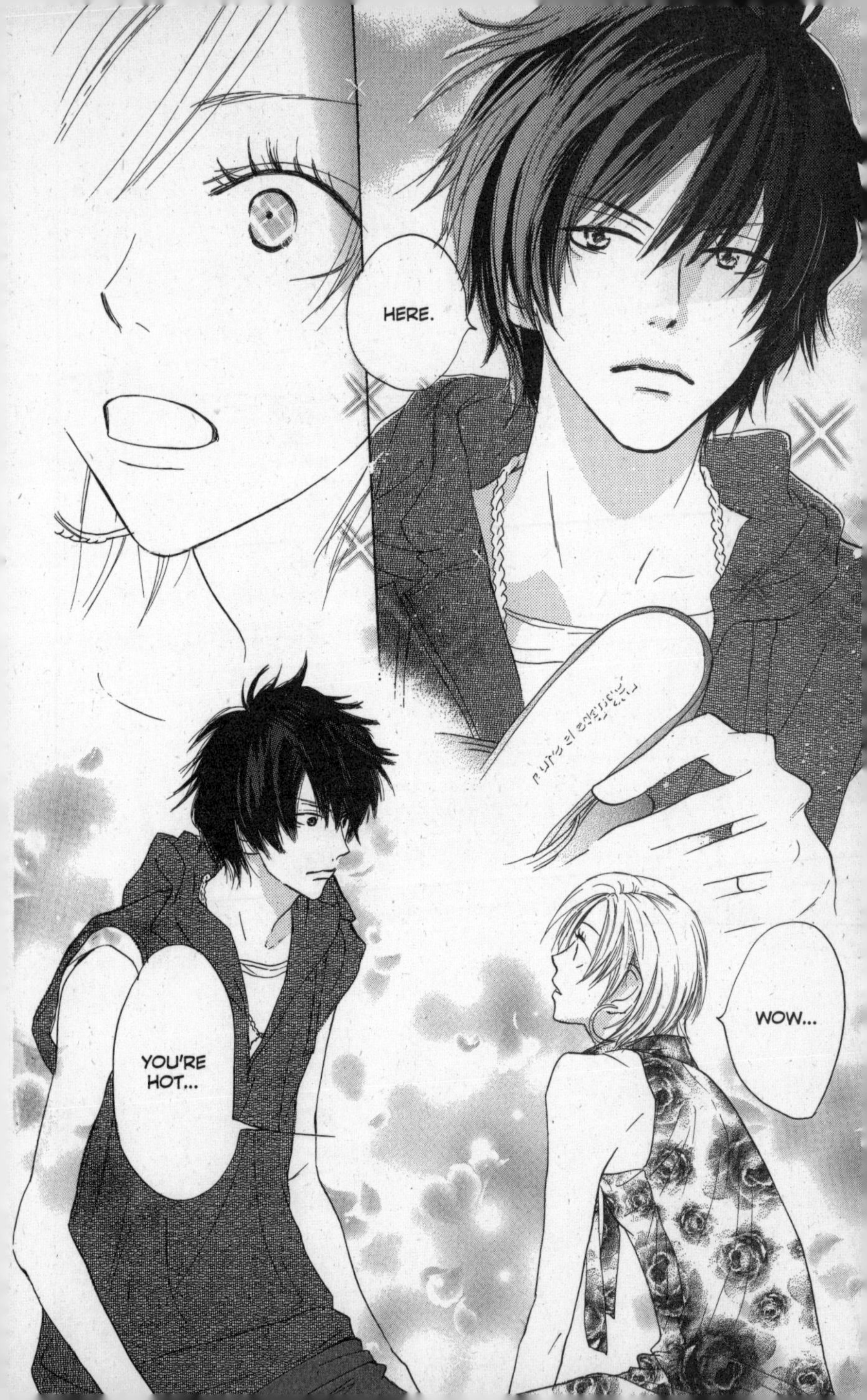
HERE.
WOW...
YOU'RE HOT...

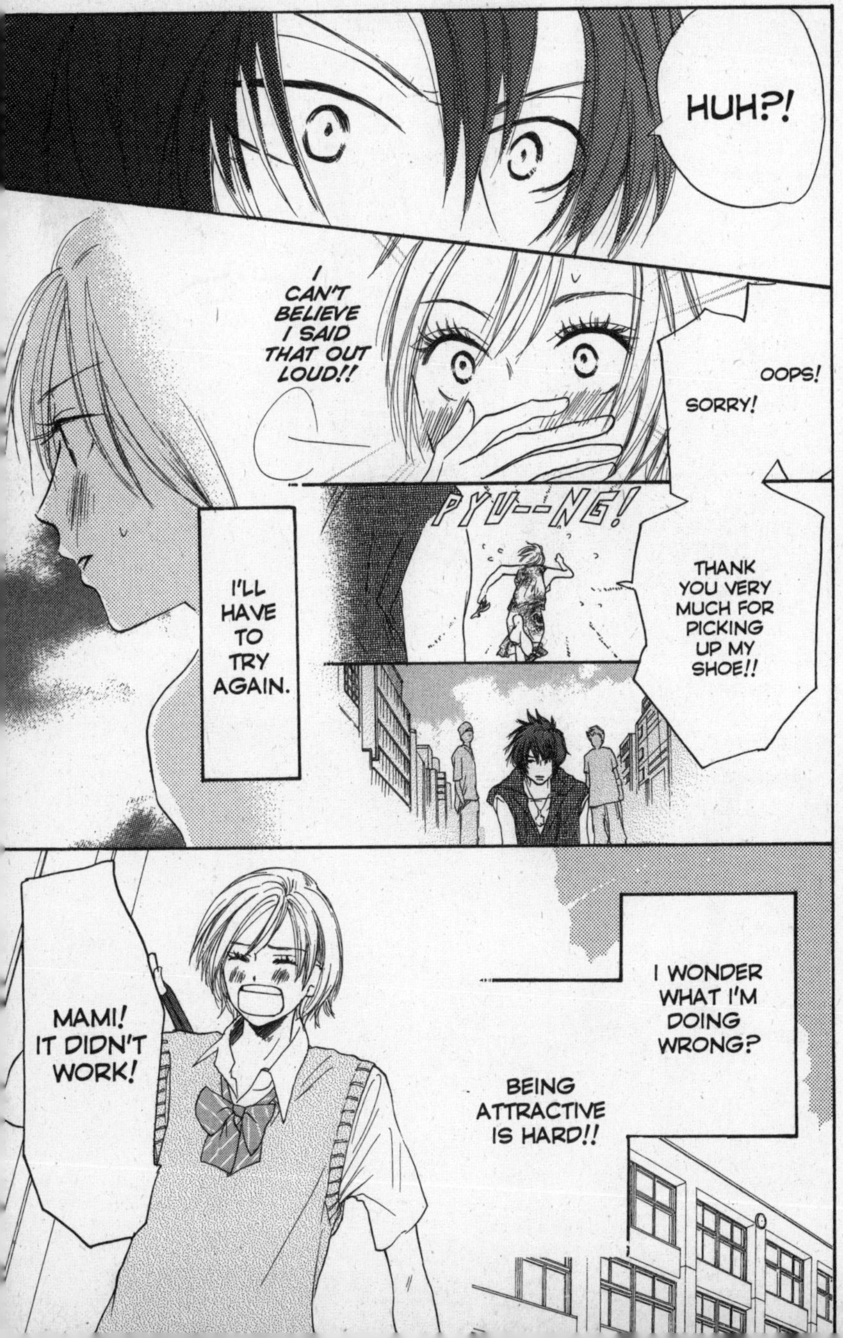
HUH?!
OOPS! SORRY!
I CAN'T BELIEVE I SAID THAT OUT LOUD!!
PYU--NG!
THANK YOU VERY MUCH FOR PICKING UP MY SHOE!!
I'LL HAVE TO TRY AGAIN.
I WONDER WHAT I'M DOING WRONG?
BEING ATTRACTIVE IS HARD!!
MAMI! IT DIDN'T WORK!

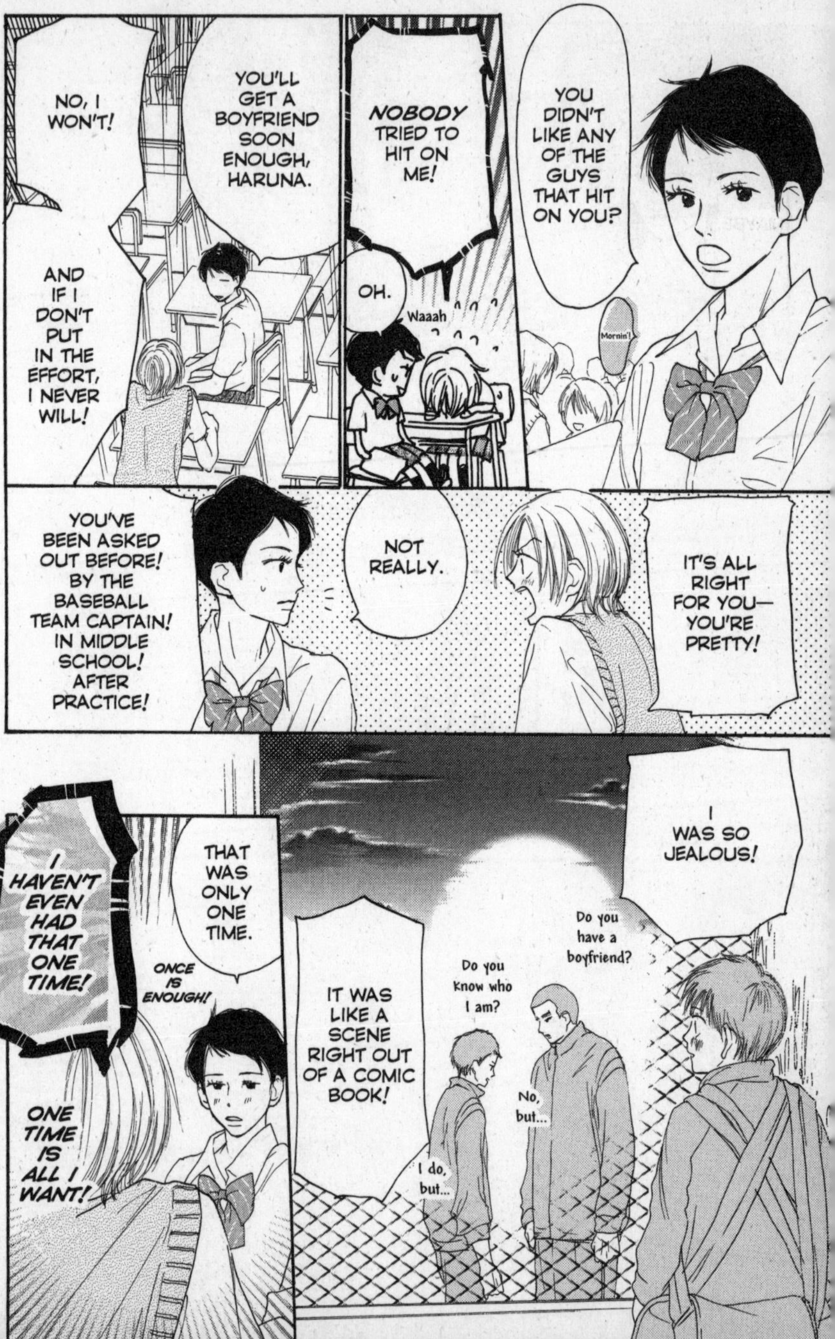
YOU DIDN'T LIKE ANY OF THE GUYS THAT HIT ON YOU?
Mornin'!
NOBODY TRIED TO HIT ON ME!
OH.
Waaah
YOU'LL GET A BOYFRIEND SOON ENOUGH, HARUNA.
NO, I WON'T!
AND IF I DON'T PUT IN THE EFFORT, I NEVER WILL!
IT'S ALL RIGHT FOR YOU—YOU'RE PRETTY!
NOT REALLY.
YOU'VE BEEN ASKED OUT BEFORE! BY THE BASEBALL TEAM CAPTAIN! IN MIDDLE SCHOOL! AFTER PRACTICE!
I WAS SO JEALOUS!
Do you have a boyfriend?
Do you know who I am?
No, but...
IT WAS LIKE A SCENE RIGHT OUT OF A COMIC BOOK!
I do, but...
THAT WAS ONLY ONE TIME.
ONCE IS ENOUGH!
I HAVEN'T EVEN HAD THAT ONE TIME!
ONE TIME IS ALL I WANT!

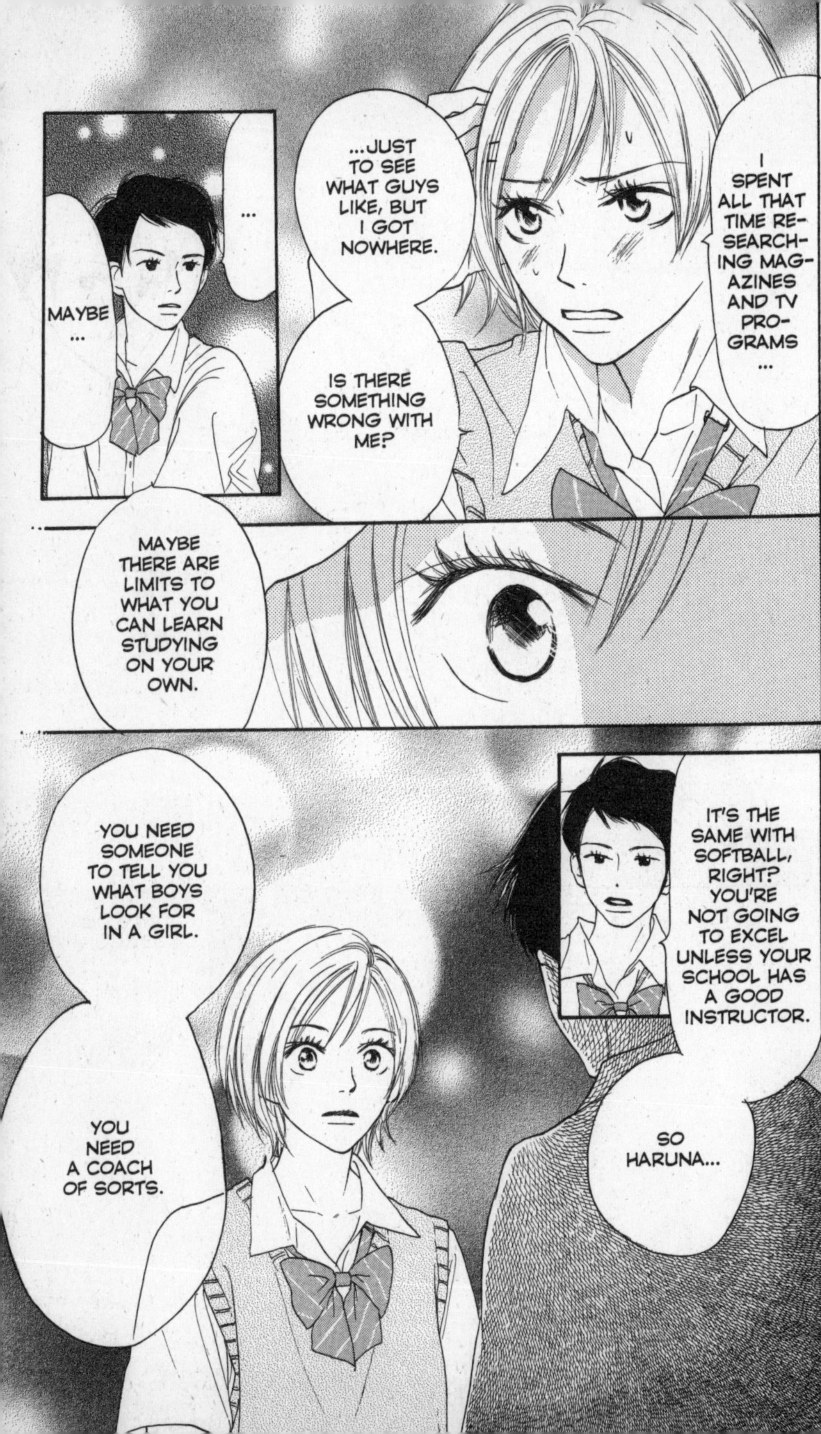
I SPENT ALL THAT TIME RE-SEARCHING MAGAZINES AND TV PROGRAMS...
...JUST TO SEE WHAT GUYS LIKE, BUT I GOT NOWHERE.
IS THERE SOMETHING WRONG WITH ME?
...
MAYBE...
MAYBE THERE ARE LIMITS TO WHAT YOU CAN LEARN STUDYING ON YOUR OWN.
IT'S THE SAME WITH SOFTBALL, RIGHT? YOU'RE NOT GOING TO EXCEL UNLESS YOUR SCHOOL HAS A GOOD INSTRUCTOR.
SO HARUNA...
YOU NEED SOMEONE TO TELL YOU WHAT BOYS LOOK FOR IN A GIRL.
YOU NEED A COACH OF SORTS.

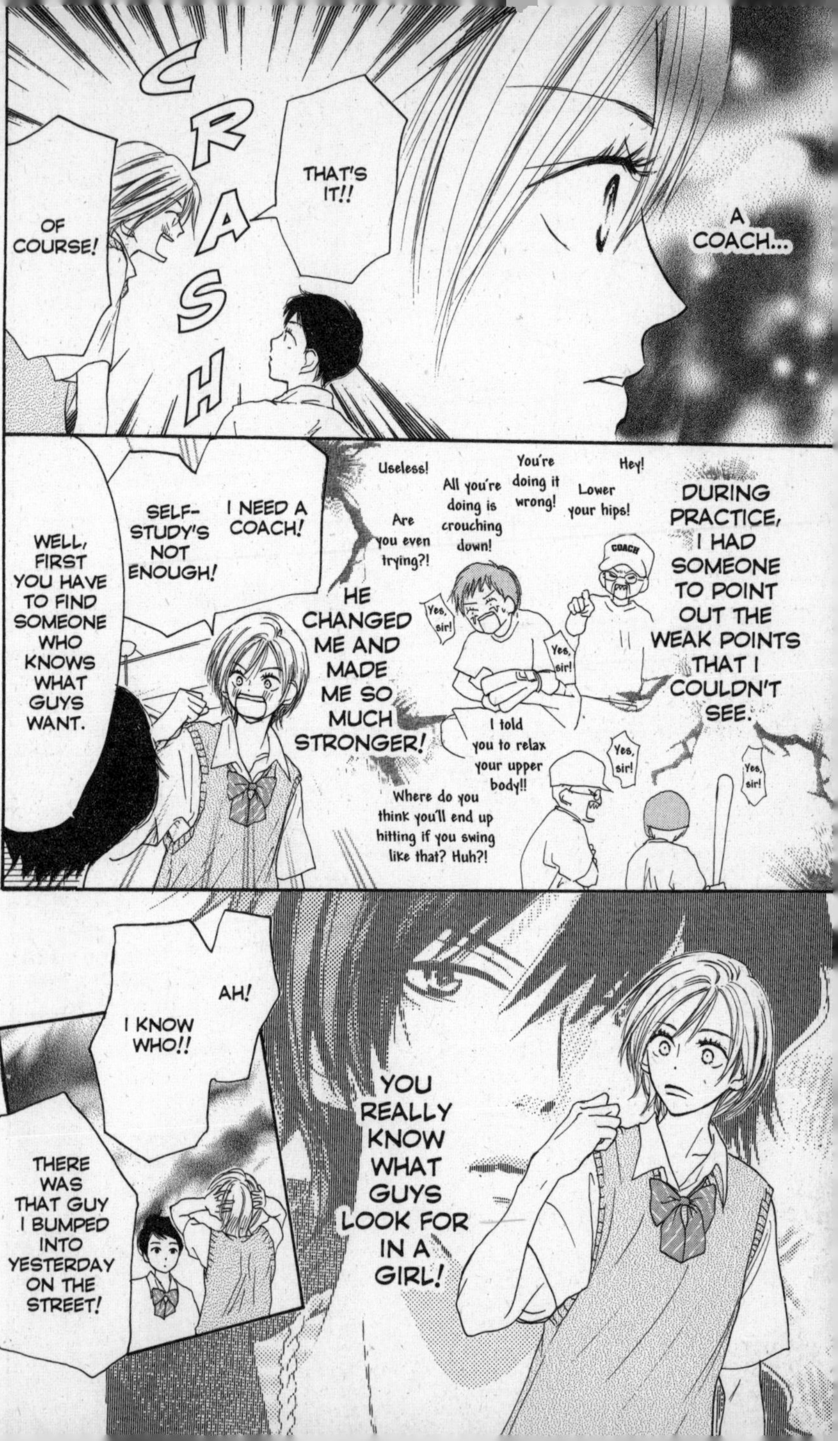
A COACH...
THAT'S IT!!
CRASH
OF COURSE!
DURING PRACTICE, I HAD SOMEONE TO POINT OUT THE WEAK POINTS THAT I COULDN'T SEE.
Hey!
Lower your hips!
You're doing it wrong!
All you're doing is crouching down!
Useless!
Are you even trying?!
Yes, sir!
Yes, sir!
Yes, sir!
Yes, sir!
I told you to relax your upper body!!
Where do you think you'll end up hitting if you swing like that? Huh?!
HE CHANGED ME AND MADE ME SO MUCH STRONGER!
I NEED A COACH!
SELF-STUDY'S NOT ENOUGH!
WELL, FIRST YOU HAVE TO FIND SOMEONE WHO KNOWS WHAT GUYS WANT.
YOU REALLY KNOW WHAT GUYS LOOK FOR IN A GIRL!
AH!
I KNOW WHO!!
THERE WAS THAT GUY I BUMPED INTO YESTERDAY ON THE STREET!

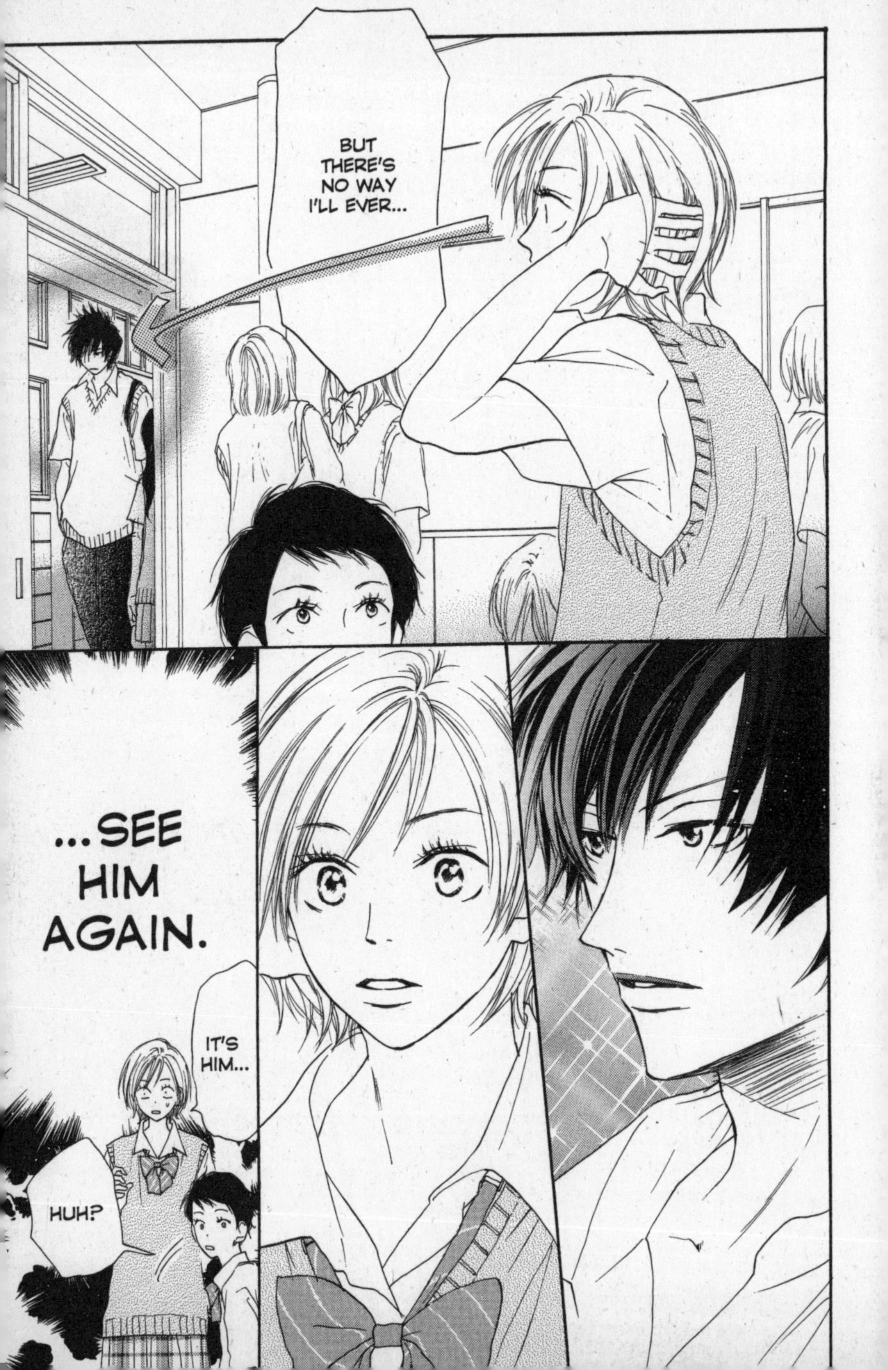
BUT THERE'S NO WAY I'LL EVER...
...SEE HIM AGAIN.
IT'S HIM...
HUH?

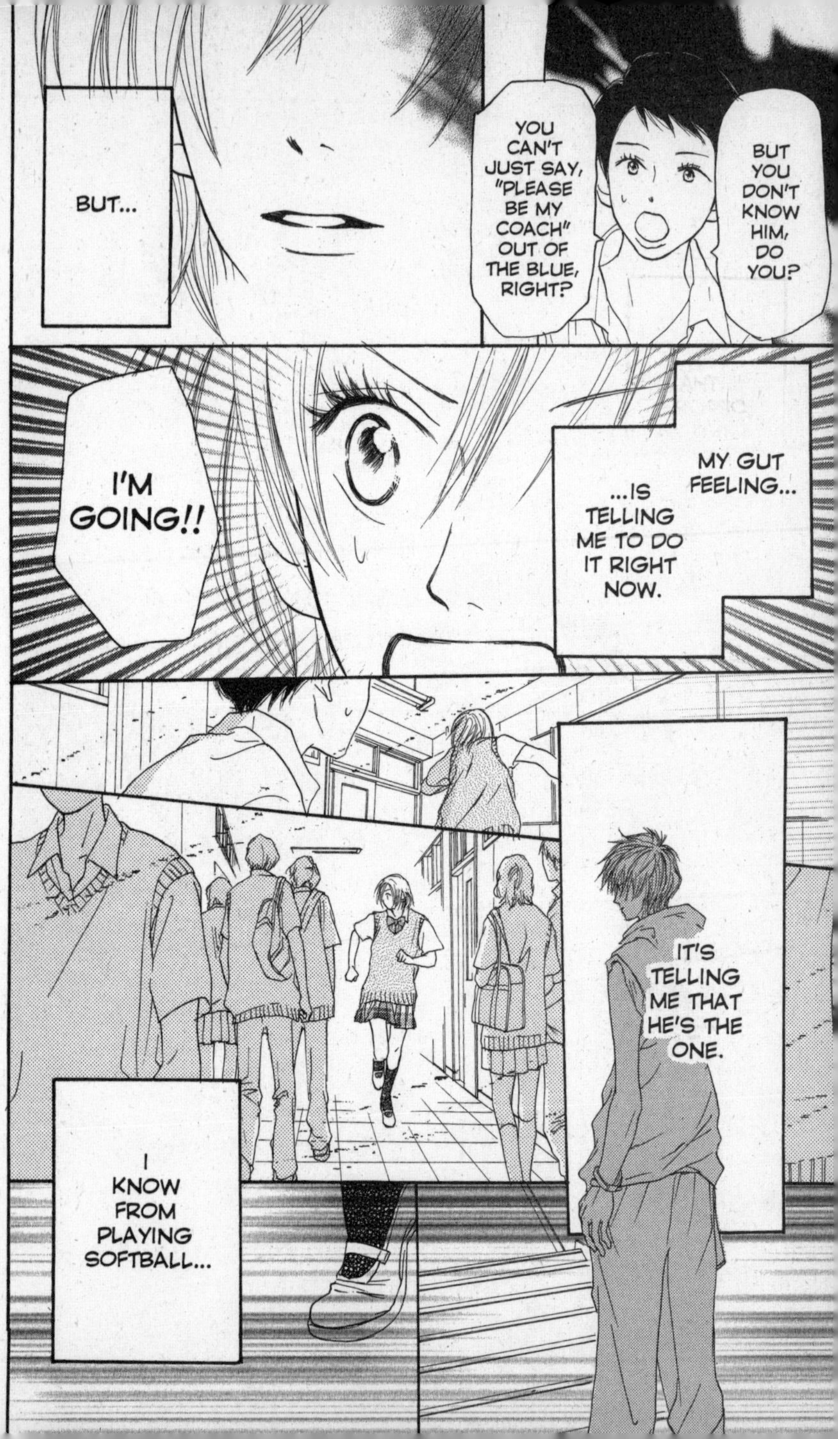
BUT YOU DON'T KNOW HIM, DO YOU?
YOU CAN'T JUST SAY, "PLEASE BE MY COACH" OUT OF THE BLUE, RIGHT?
BUT...
MY GUT FEELING...
...IS TELLING ME TO DO IT RIGHT NOW.
I'M GOING!!
IT'S TELLING ME THAT HE'S THE ONE.
I KNOW FROM PLAYING SOFTBALL...

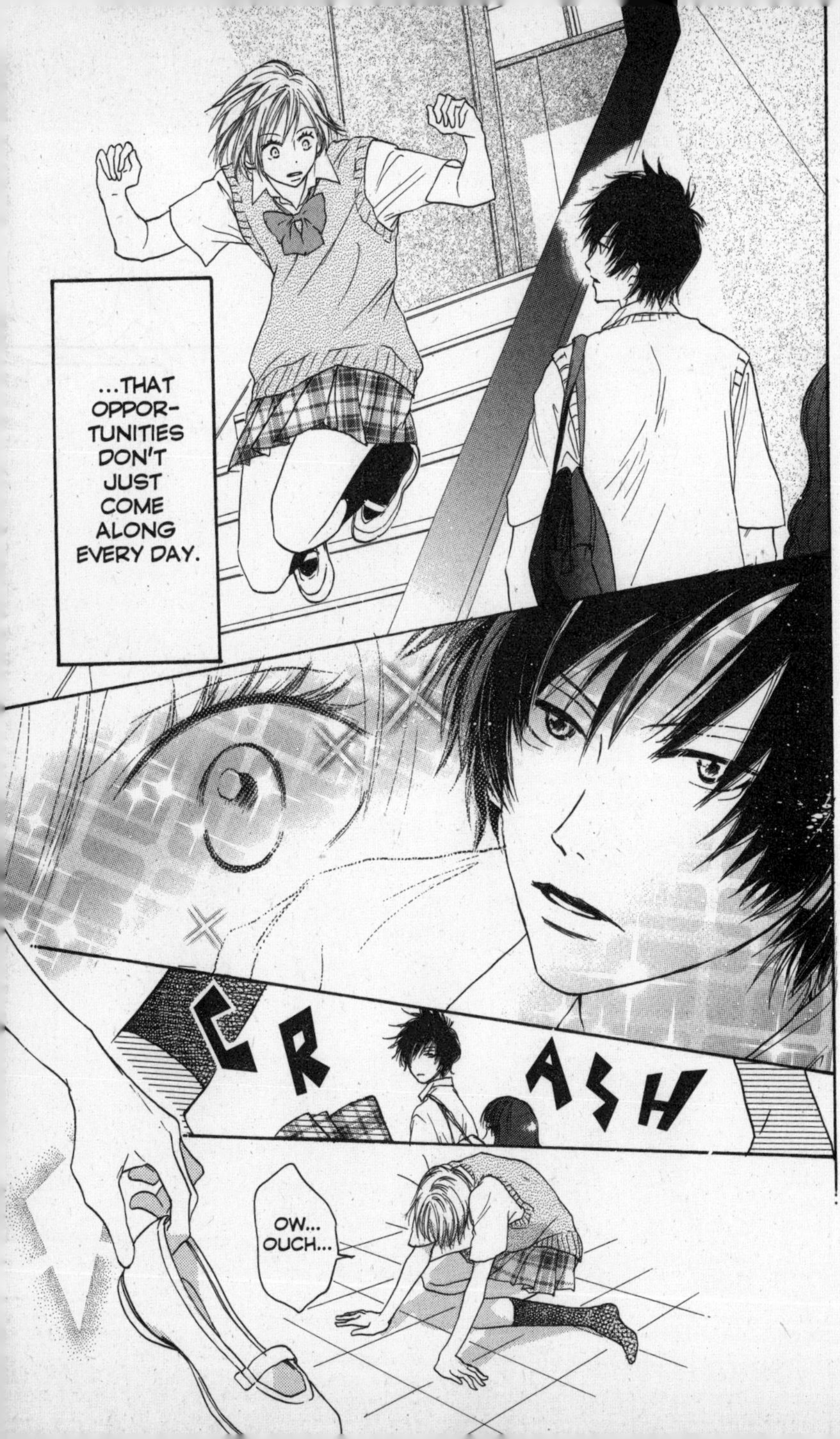
...THAT OPPOR-TUNITIES DON'T JUST COME ALONG EVERY DAY.
CRASH
OW... OUCH...

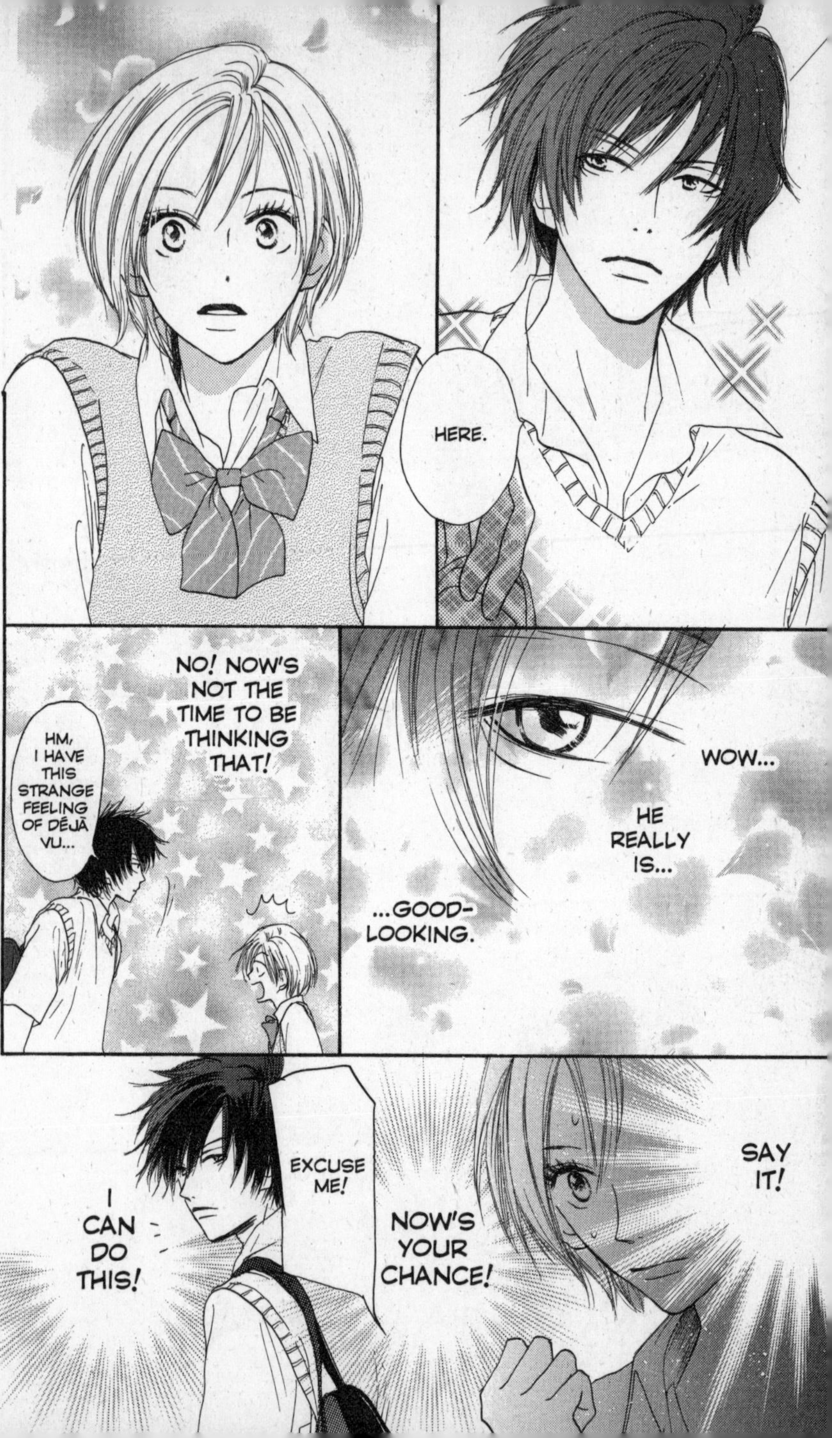
HERE.
WOW...
HE REALLY IS...
...GOOD-LOOKING.
NO! NOW'S NOT THE TIME TO BE THINKING THAT!
HM, I HAVE THIS STRANGE FEELING OF DÉJÀ VU...
SAY IT!
NOW'S YOUR CHANCE!
EXCUSE ME!
I CAN DO THIS!

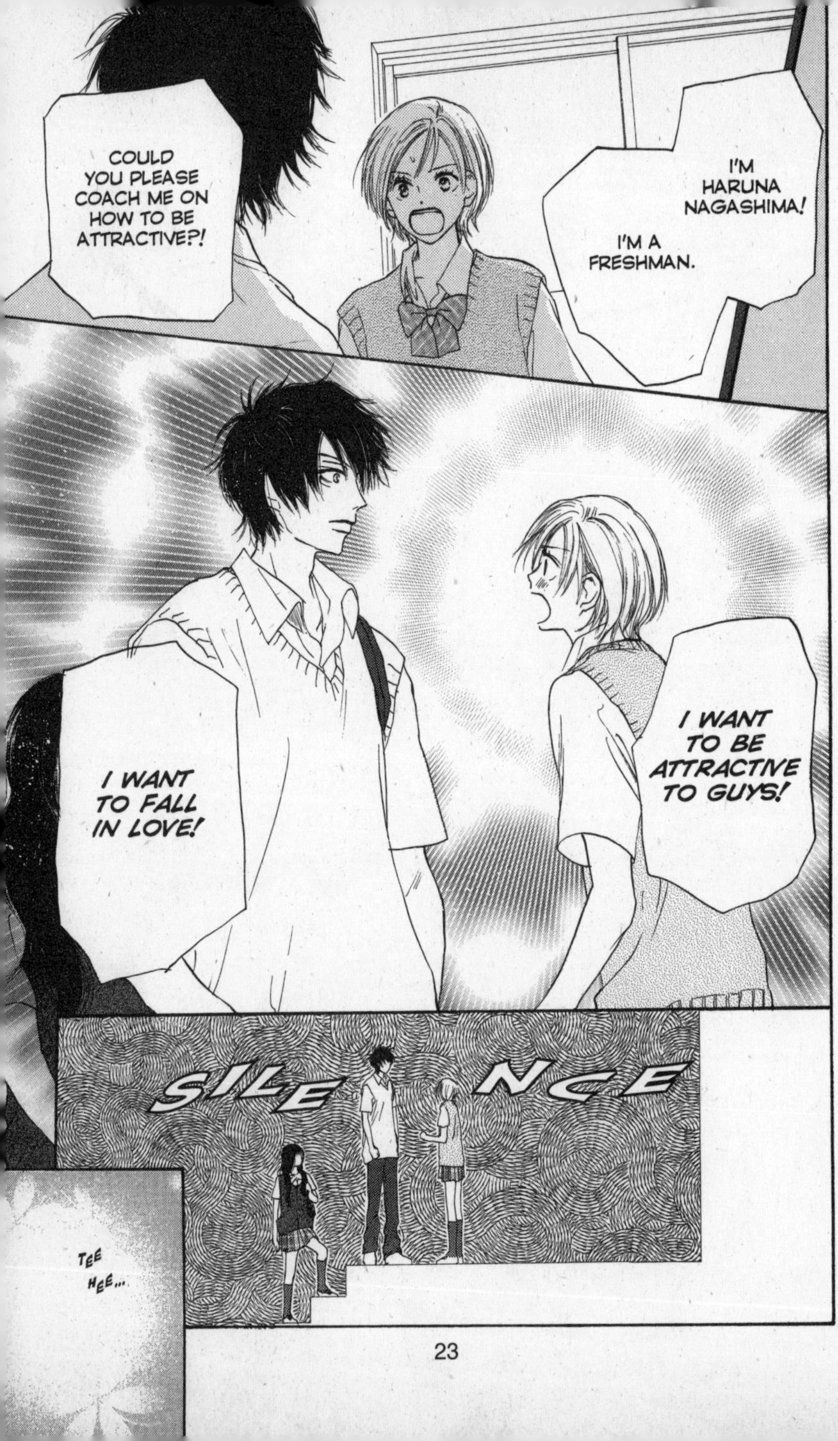
I'M HARUNA NAGASHIMA!
I'M A FRESHMAN.
COULD YOU PLEASE COACH ME ON HOW TO BE ATTRACTIVE?!
I WANT TO BE ATTRACTIVE TO GUYS!
I WANT TO FALL IN LOVE!
SILENCE
TEE HEE...

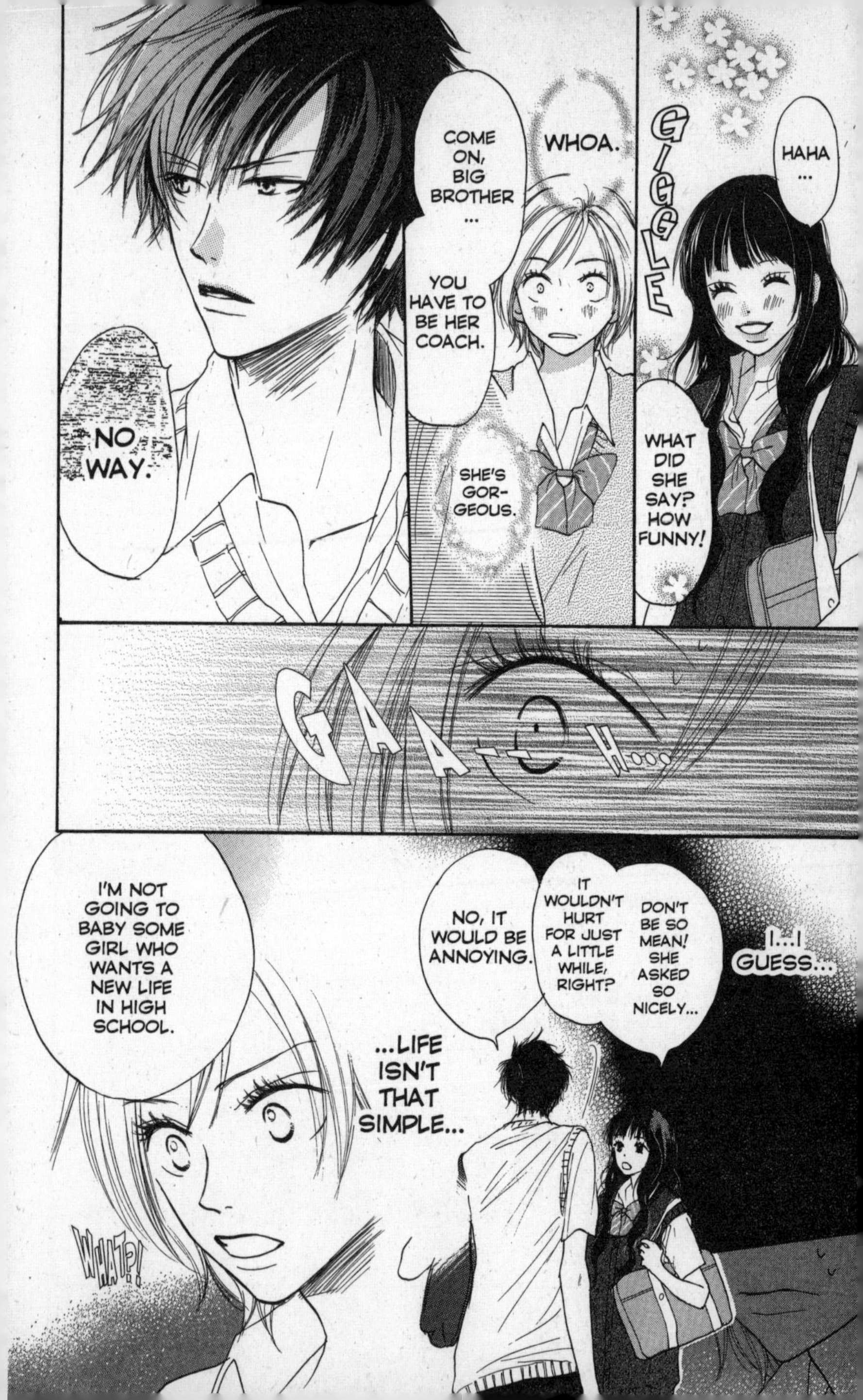
GIGGLE
HAHA...
WHAT DID SHE SAY? HOW FUNNY!
WHOA.
COME ON, BIG BROTHER...
YOU HAVE TO BE HER COACH.
SHE'S GORGEOUS.
NO WAY.
GAA-O-H...
I...I GUESS...
DON'T BE SO MEAN! SHE ASKED SO NICELY...
IT WOULDN'T HURT FOR JUST A LITTLE WHILE, RIGHT?
NO, IT WOULD BE ANNOYING.
I'M NOT GOING TO BABY SOME GIRL WHO WANTS A NEW LIFE IN HIGH SCHOOL.
...LIFE ISN'T THAT SIMPLE...
WHAT?!

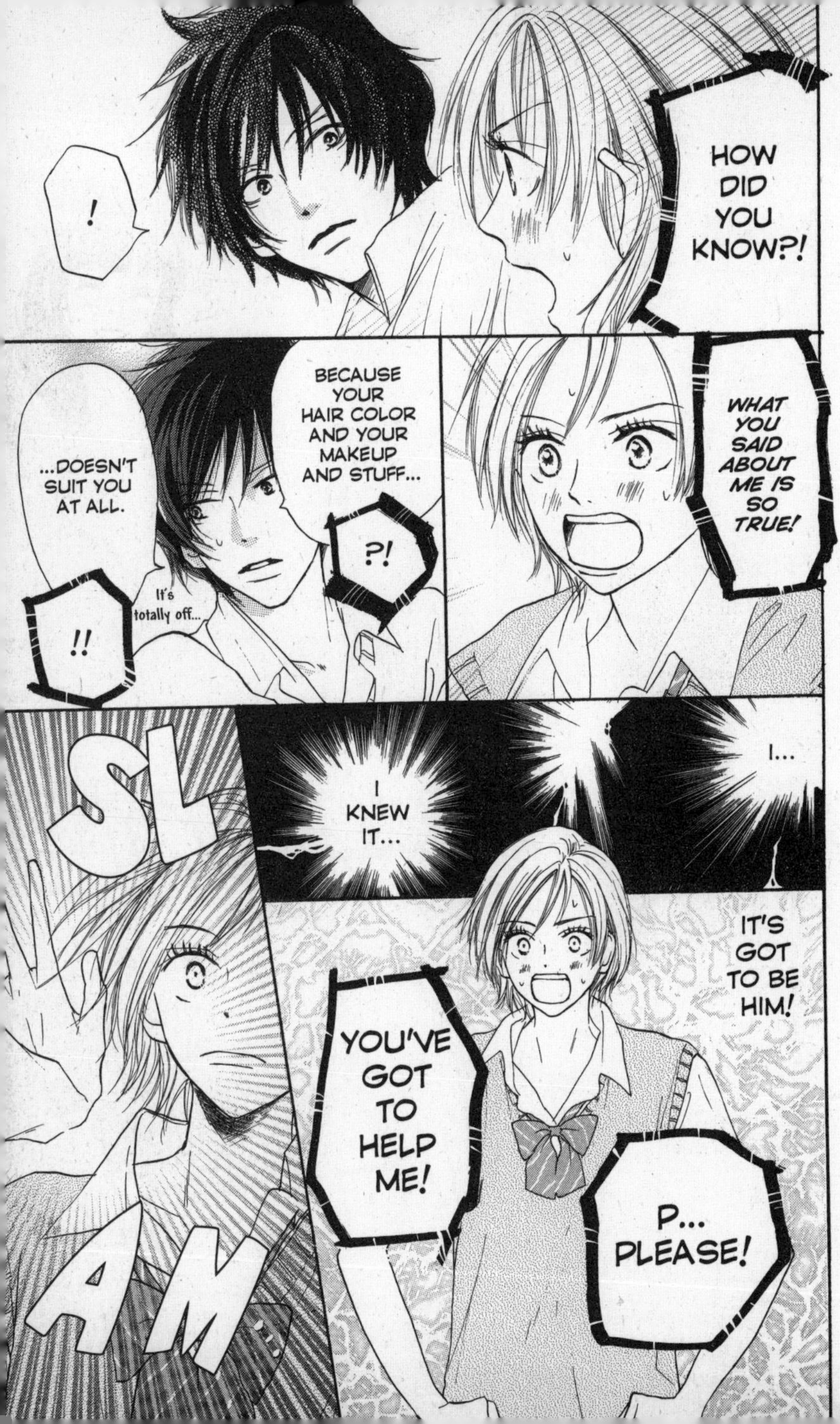
HOW DID YOU KNOW?!
!
WHAT YOU SAID ABOUT ME IS SO TRUE!
BECAUSE YOUR HAIR COLOR AND YOUR MAKEUP AND STUFF...
?!
...DOESN'T SUIT YOU AT ALL.
It's totally off...
!!
I...
I KNEW IT...
IT'S GOT TO BE HIM!
YOU'VE GOT TO HELP ME!
P... PLEASE!
SLAM

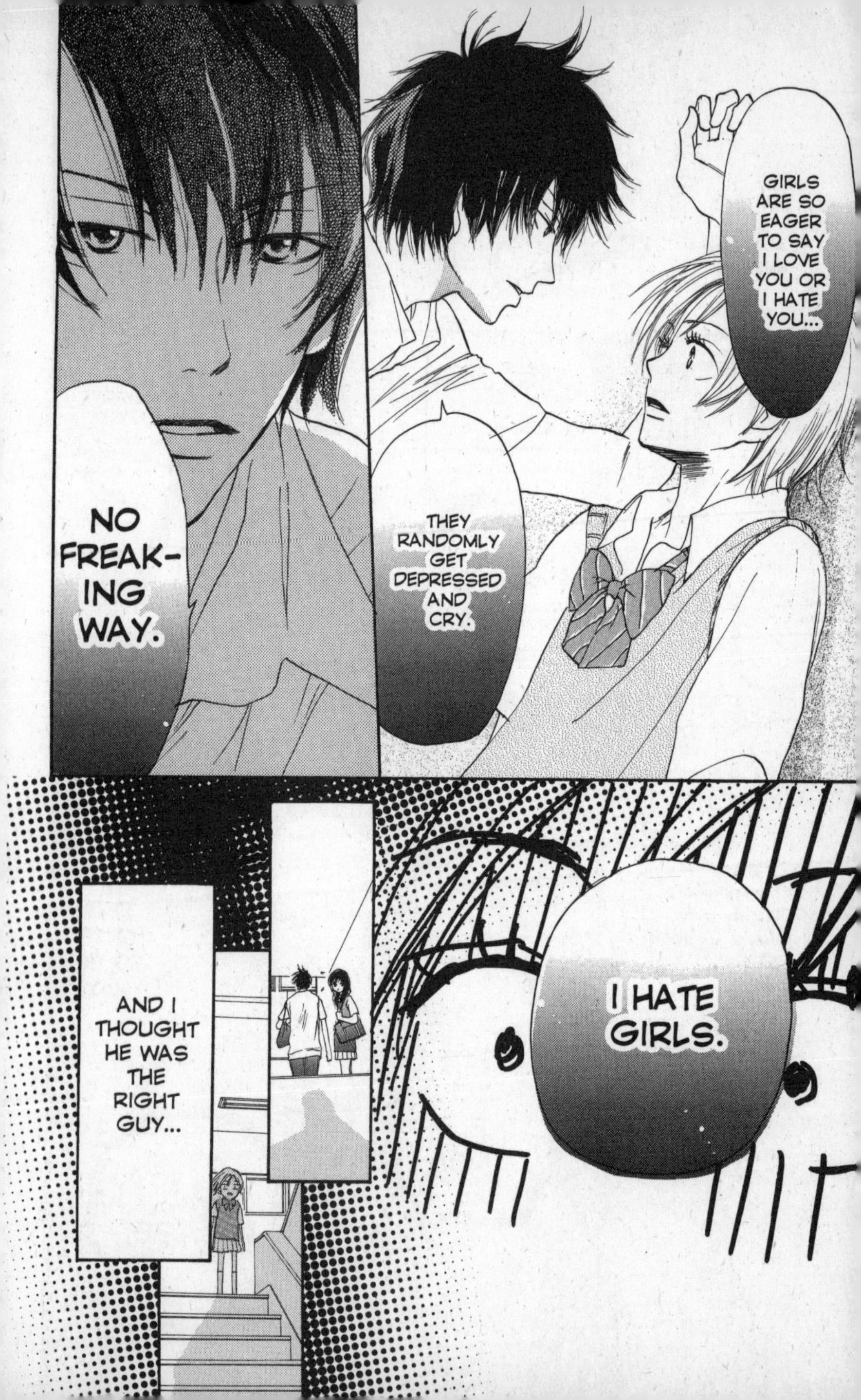
GIRLS ARE SO EAGER TO SAY I LOVE YOU OR I HATE YOU...
THEY RANDOMLY GET DEPRESSED AND CRY.
NO FREAKING-ING WAY.
I HATE GIRLS.
AND I THOUGHT HE WAS THE RIGHT GUY...

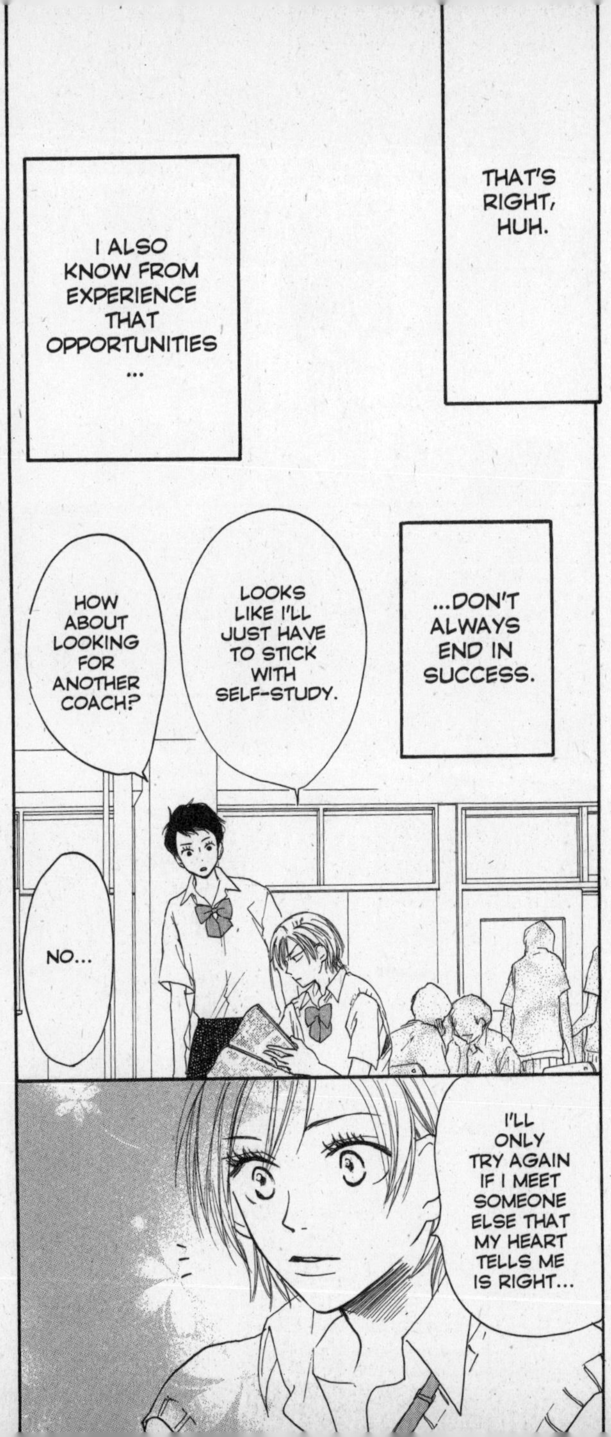
THAT'S RIGHT, HUH.
I ALSO KNOW FROM EXPERIENCE THAT OPPORTUNITIES ...
...DON'T ALWAYS END IN SUCCESS.
LOOKS LIKE I'LL JUST HAVE TO STICK WITH SELF-STUDY.
HOW ABOUT LOOKING FOR ANOTHER COACH?
NO...
I'LL ONLY TRY AGAIN IF I MEET SOMEONE ELSE THAT MY HEART TELLS ME IS RIGHT...

1

Hello! Kawahara here.

Thank you for picking up my comic!

I'd be delighted if you enjoy it a little. If you enjoy it lots, then I'd be even more delighted.

Thanks to so many people, I've been able to release another title of my own. At any rate, the people who've helped me out have grown in number over the years. I wonder why that is? Tee hee.

↑ Can't take for granted!

↑ Can't act cutesy!

I've caught a cold.

My throat hurts.

2004.
Kazune Kawahara.

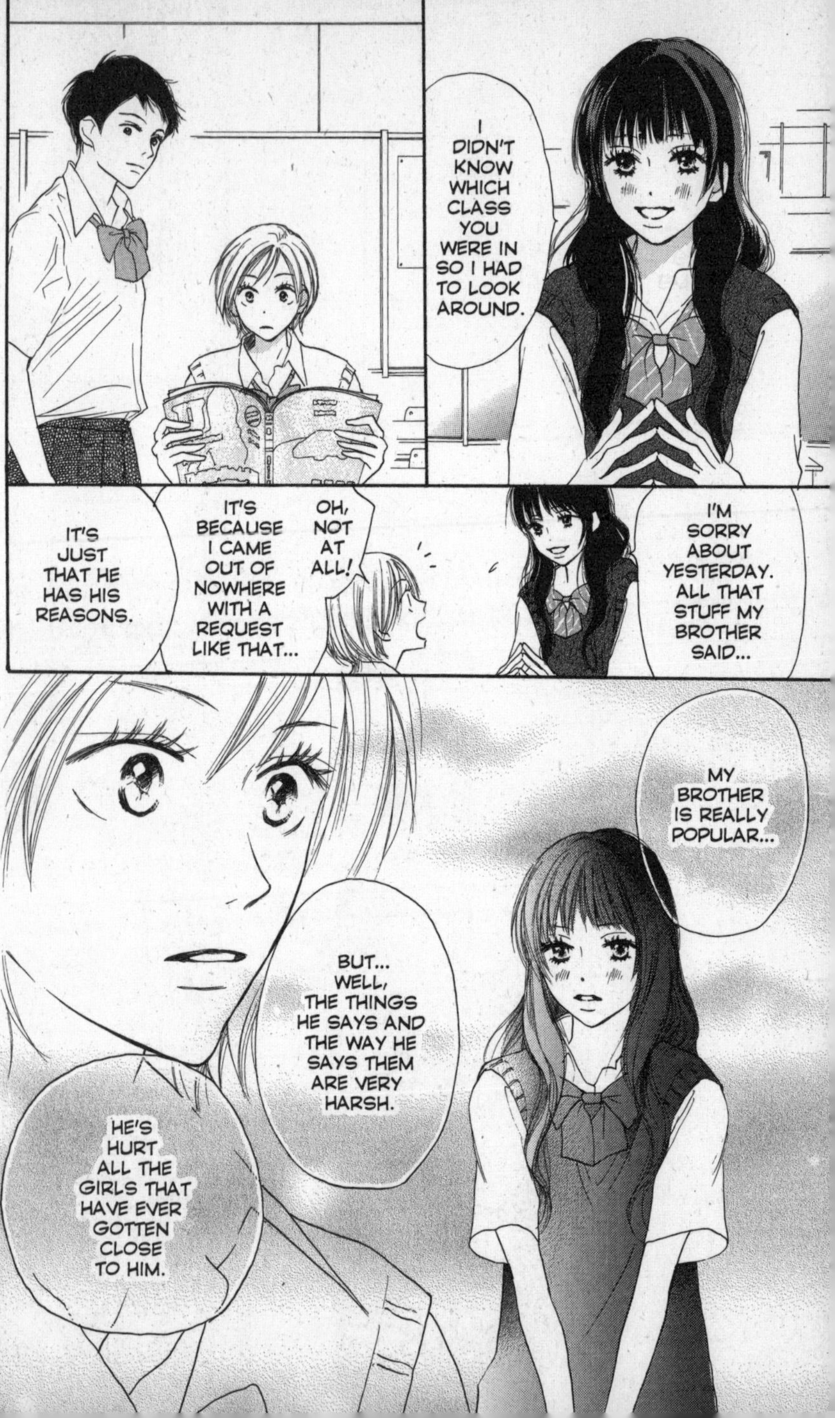
I DIDN'T KNOW WHICH CLASS YOU WERE IN SO I HAD TO LOOK AROUND.
I'M SORRY ABOUT YESTERDAY. ALL THAT STUFF MY BROTHER SAID...
OH, NOT AT ALL!
IT'S BECAUSE I CAME OUT OF NOWHERE WITH A REQUEST LIKE THAT...
IT'S JUST THAT HE HAS HIS REASONS.
MY BROTHER IS REALLY POPULAR...
BUT... WELL, THE THINGS HE SAYS AND THE WAY HE SAYS THEM ARE VERY HARSH.
HE'S HURT ALL THE GIRLS THAT HAVE EVER GOTTEN CLOSE TO HIM.

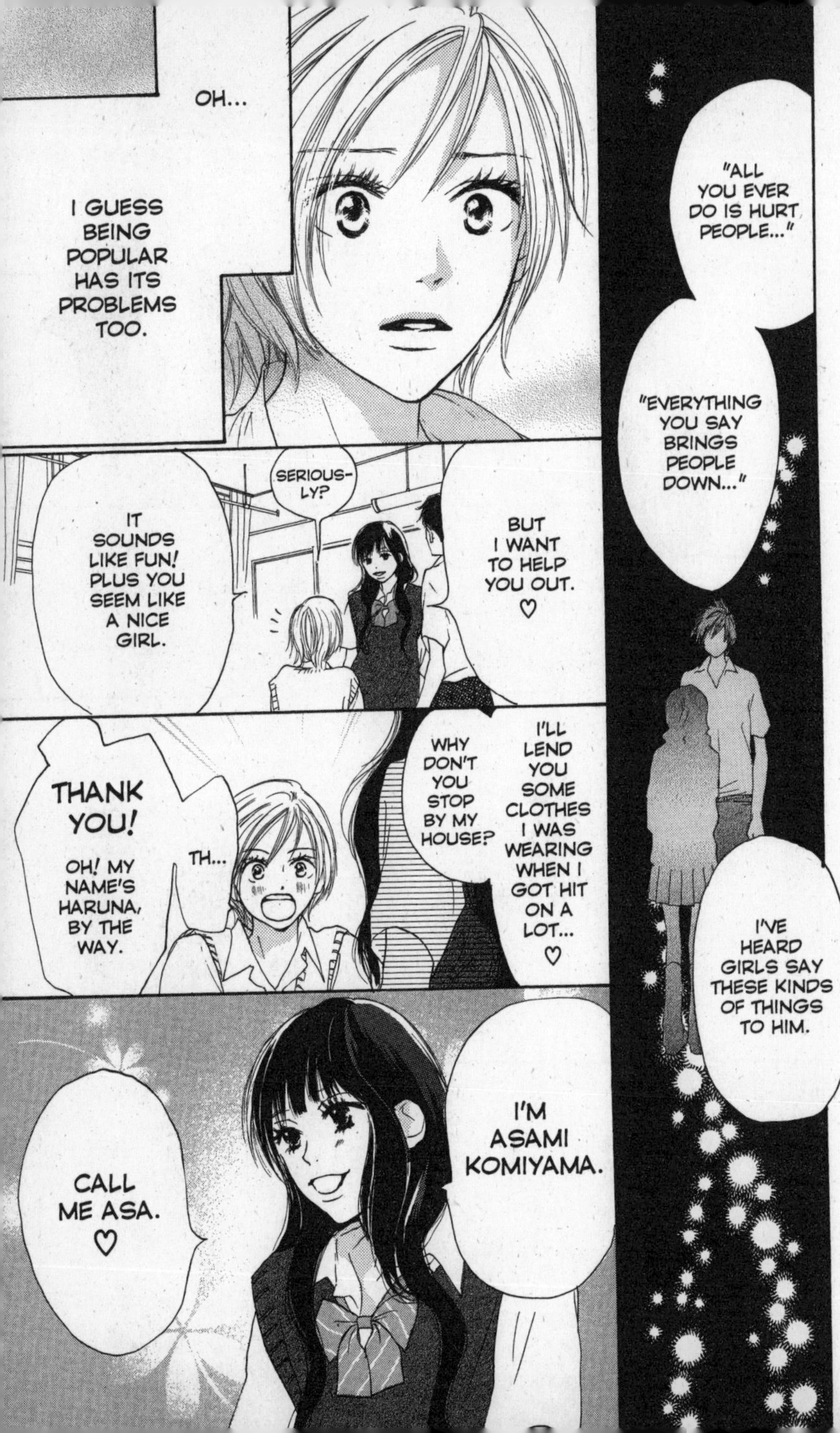
"ALL YOU EVER DO IS HURT PEOPLE..."
"EVERYTHING YOU SAY BRINGS PEOPLE DOWN..."
I'VE HEARD GIRLS SAY THESE KINDS OF THINGS TO HIM.
OH...
I GUESS BEING POPULAR HAS ITS PROBLEMS TOO.
BUT I WANT TO HELP YOU OUT. ♡
SERIOUSLY?
IT SOUNDS LIKE FUN! PLUS YOU SEEM LIKE A NICE GIRL.
I'LL LEND YOU SOME CLOTHES I WAS WEARING WHEN I GOT HIT ON A LOT... ♡
WHY DON'T YOU STOP BY MY HOUSE?
TH...
THANK YOU!
OH! MY NAME'S HARUNA, BY THE WAY.
I'M ASAMI KOMIYAMA.
CALL ME ASA. ♡

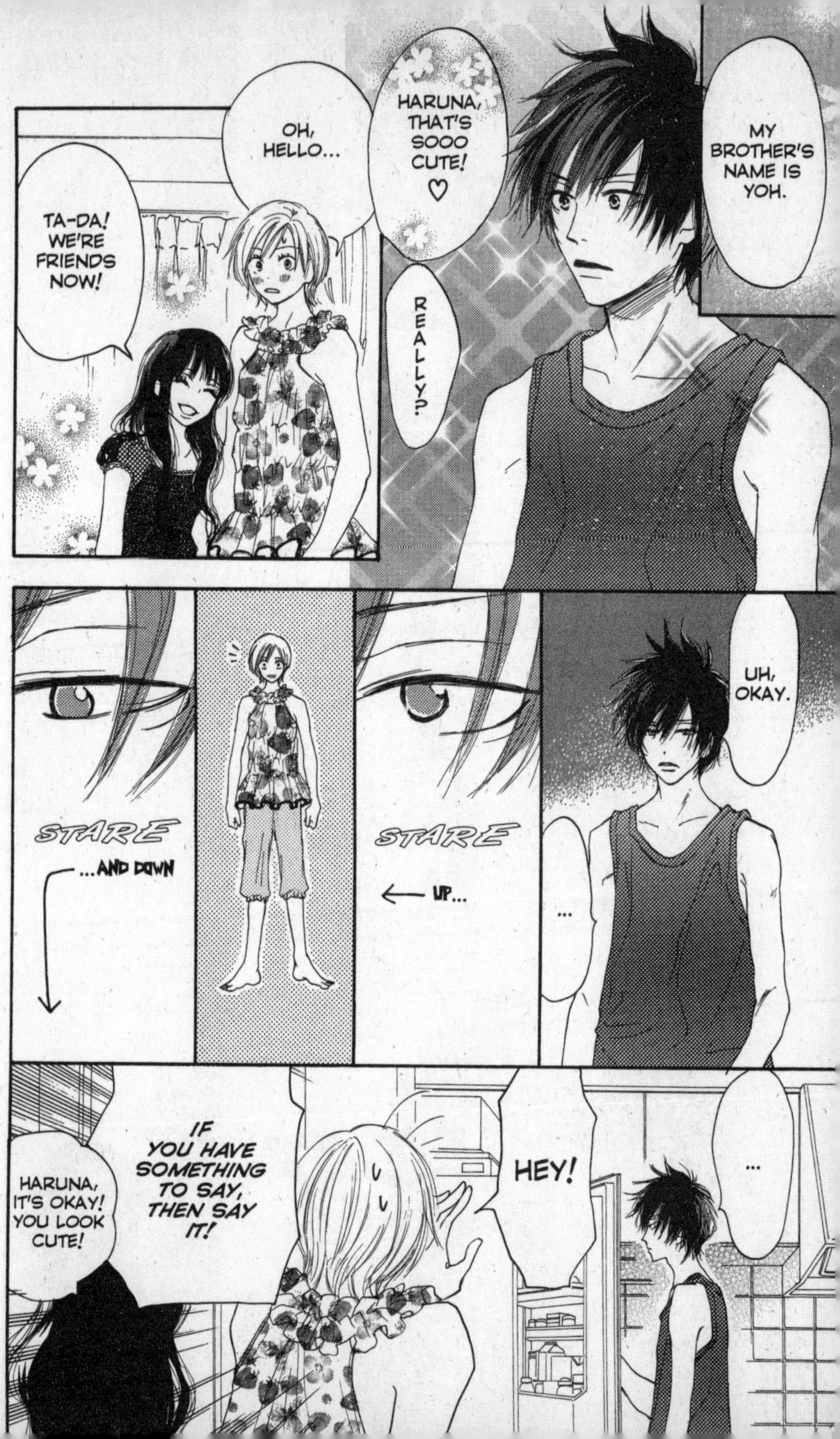
MY BROTHER'S NAME IS YOH.
HARUNA, THAT'S SOOO CUTE! ♡
REALLY?
OH, HELLO...
TA-DA! WE'RE FRIENDS NOW!
UH, OKAY.
...
STARE
UP...
STARE
...AND DOWN
...
HEY!
IF YOU HAVE SOMETHING TO SAY, THEN SAY IT!
HARUNA, IT'S OKAY! YOU LOOK CUTE!

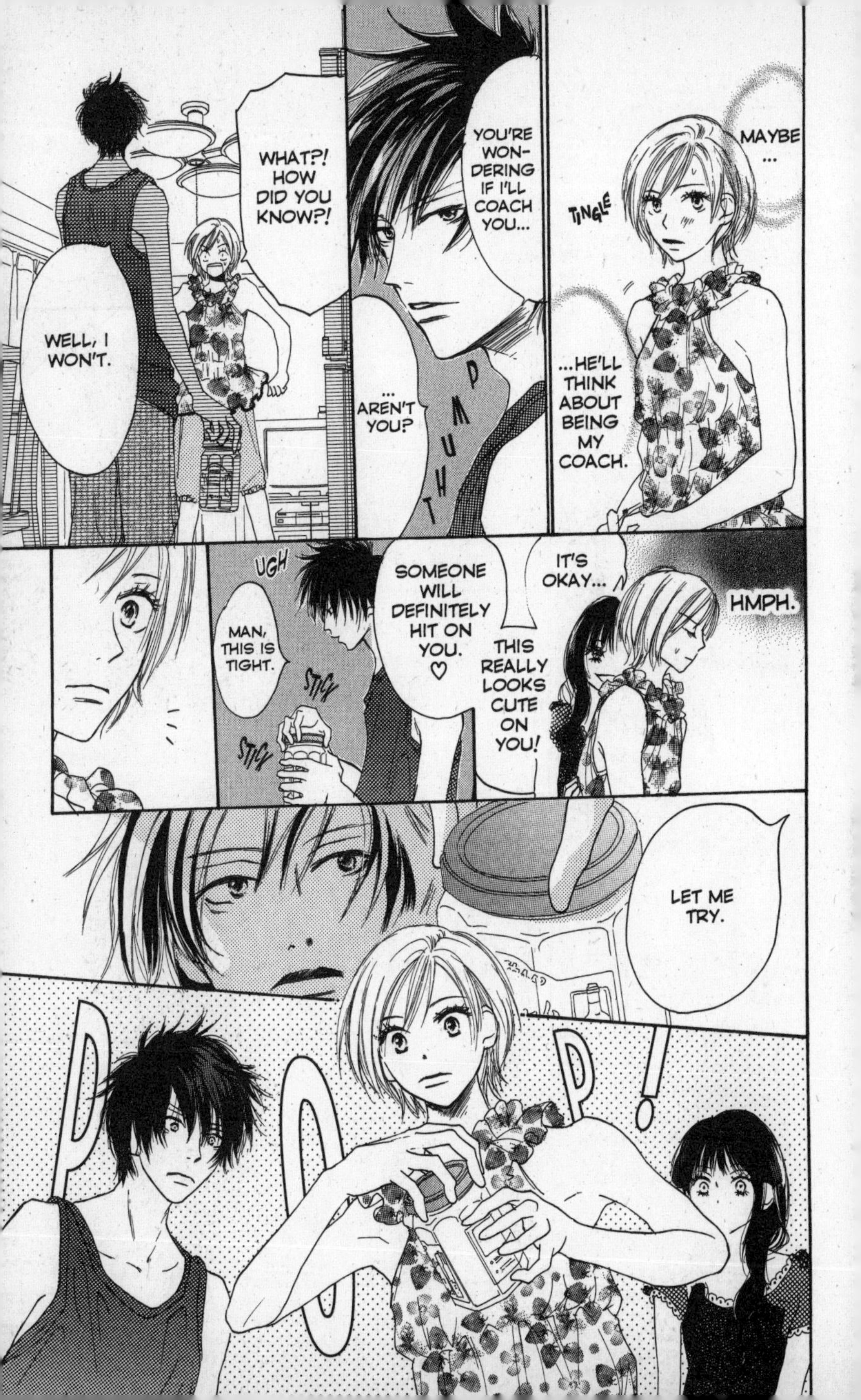
MAYBE ...
TINGLE
...HE'LL THINK ABOUT BEING MY COACH.
YOU'RE WON-DERING IF I'LL COACH YOU...
... AREN'T YOU?
THUMP
WHAT?! HOW DID YOU KNOW?!
WELL, I WON'T.
HMPH.
IT'S OKAY...
THIS REALLY LOOKS CUTE ON YOU!
SOMEONE WILL DEFINITELY HIT ON YOU. ♡
UGH
MAN, THIS IS TIGHT.
STICK
STICK
LET ME TRY.
POP
!

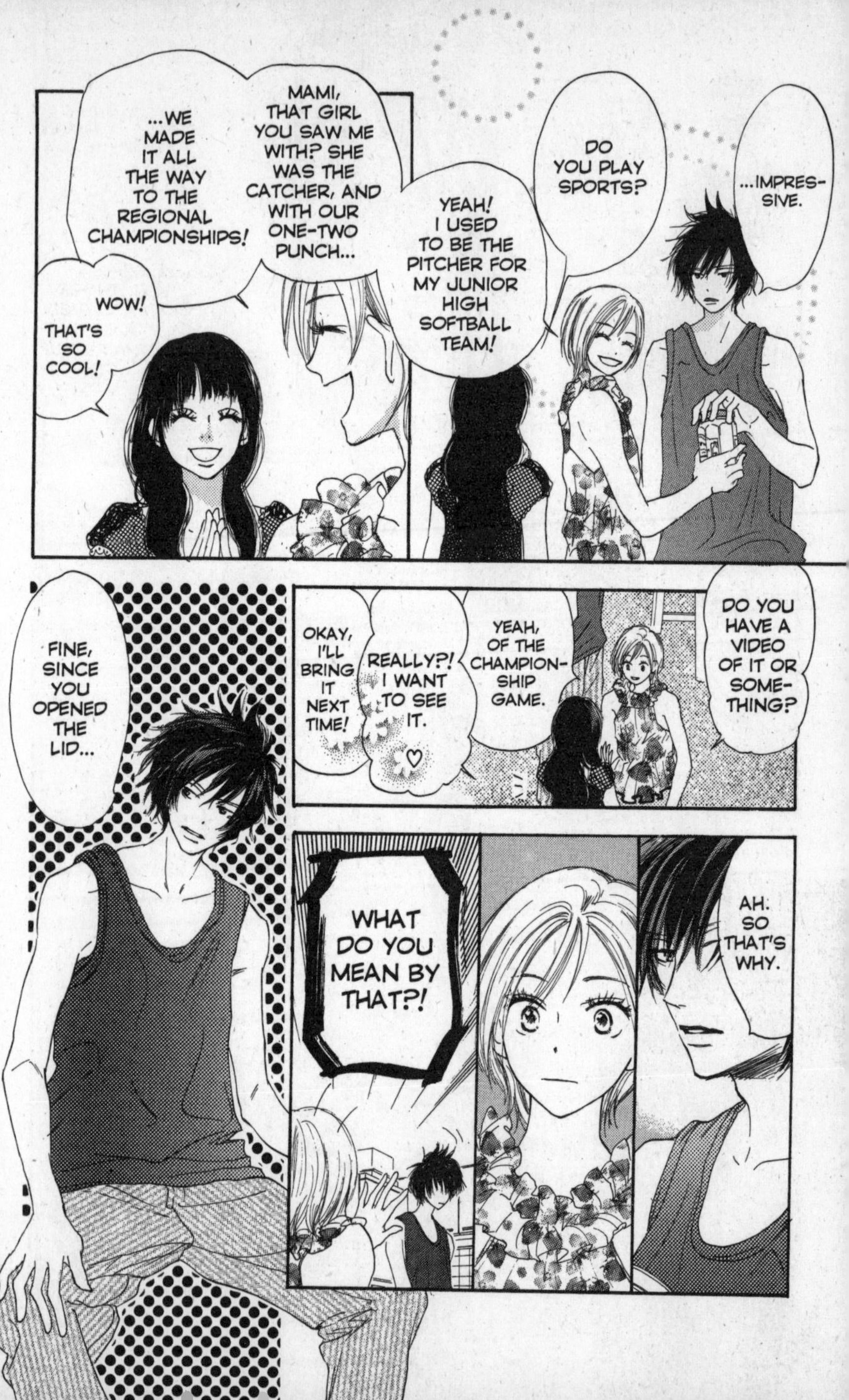
...IMPRESSIVE.
DO YOU PLAY SPORTS?
YEAH! I USED TO BE THE PITCHER FOR MY JUNIOR HIGH SOFTBALL TEAM!
MAMI, THAT GIRL YOU SAW ME WITH? SHE WAS THE CATCHER, AND WITH OUR ONE-TWO PUNCH...
...WE MADE IT ALL THE WAY TO THE REGIONAL CHAMPIONSHIPS!
WOW! THAT'S SO COOL!
DO YOU HAVE A VIDEO OF IT OR SOMETHING?
YEAH, OF THE CHAMPIONSHIP GAME.
REALLY?! I WANT TO SEE IT. ♡
OKAY, I'LL BRING IT NEXT TIME!
AH: SO THAT'S WHY.
WHAT DO YOU MEAN BY THAT?!
FINE, SINCE YOU OPENED THE LID...

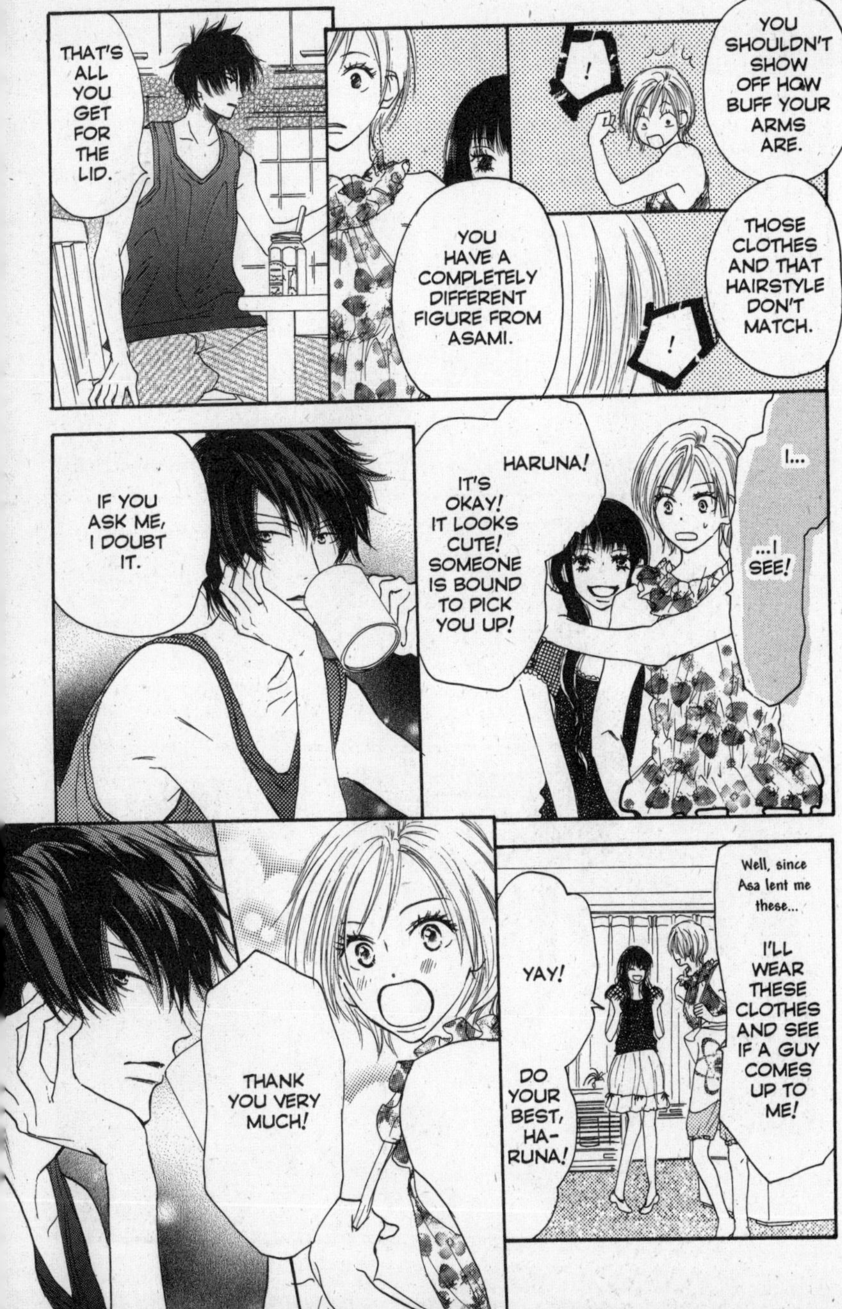
!
YOU SHOULDN'T SHOW OFF HOW BUFF YOUR ARMS ARE.
THOSE CLOTHES AND THAT HAIRSTYLE DON'T MATCH.
!
YOU HAVE A COMPLETELY DIFFERENT FIGURE FROM ASAMI.
THAT'S ALL YOU GET FOR THE LID.
I...
...I SEE!
HARUNA! IT'S OKAY! IT LOOKS CUTE! SOMEONE IS BOUND TO PICK YOU UP!
IF YOU ASK ME, I DOUBT IT.
Well, since Asa lent me these...
I'LL WEAR THESE CLOTHES AND SEE IF A GUY COMES UP TO ME!
YAY!
DO YOUR BEST, HA-RUNA!
THANK YOU VERY MUCH!

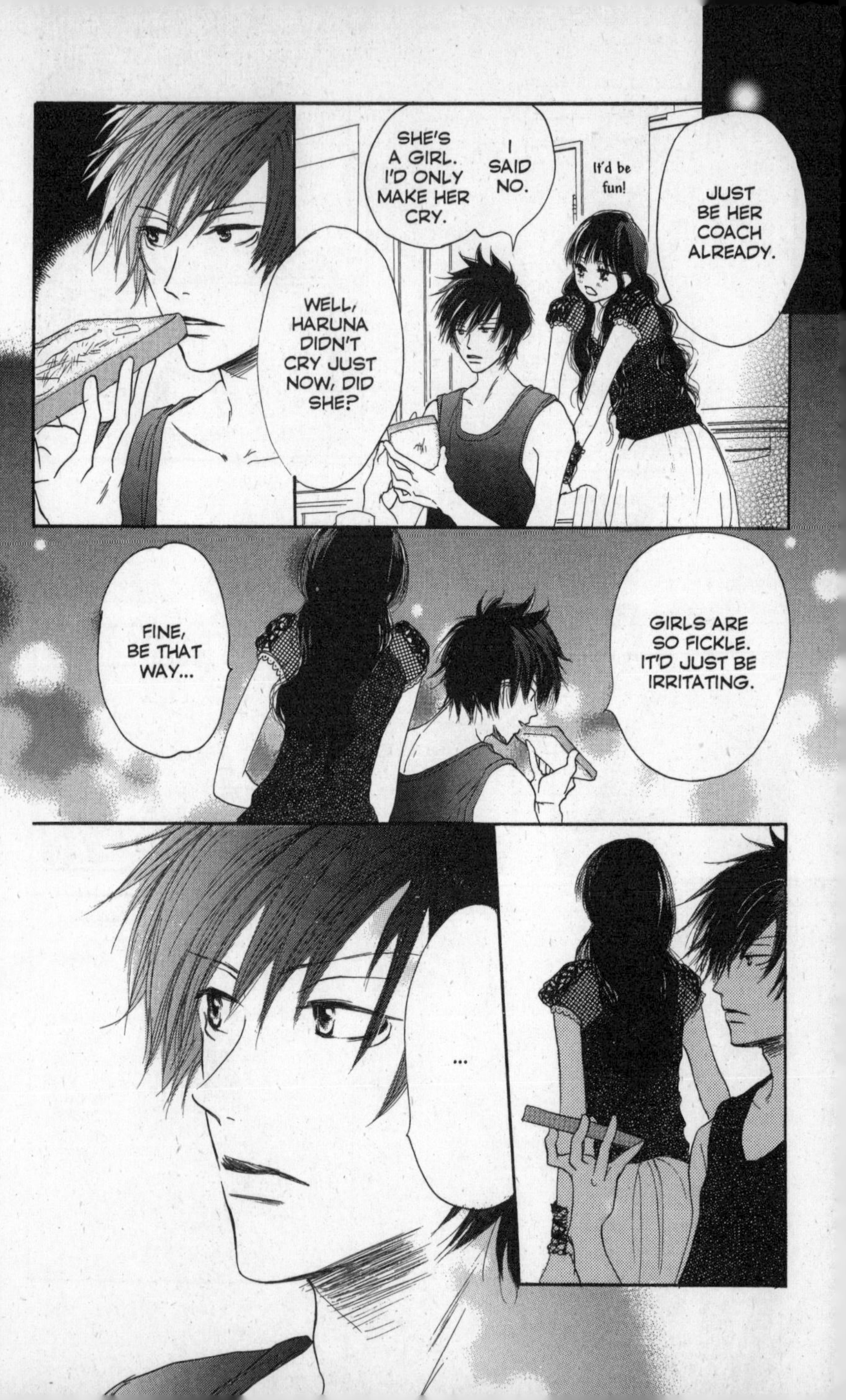
JUST BE HER COACH ALREADY.
It'd be fun!
I SAID NO.
SHE'S A GIRL. I'D ONLY MAKE HER CRY.
WELL, HARUNA DIDN'T CRY JUST NOW, DID SHE?
GIRLS ARE SO FICKLE. IT'D JUST BE IRRITATING.
FINE, BE THAT WAY...
...

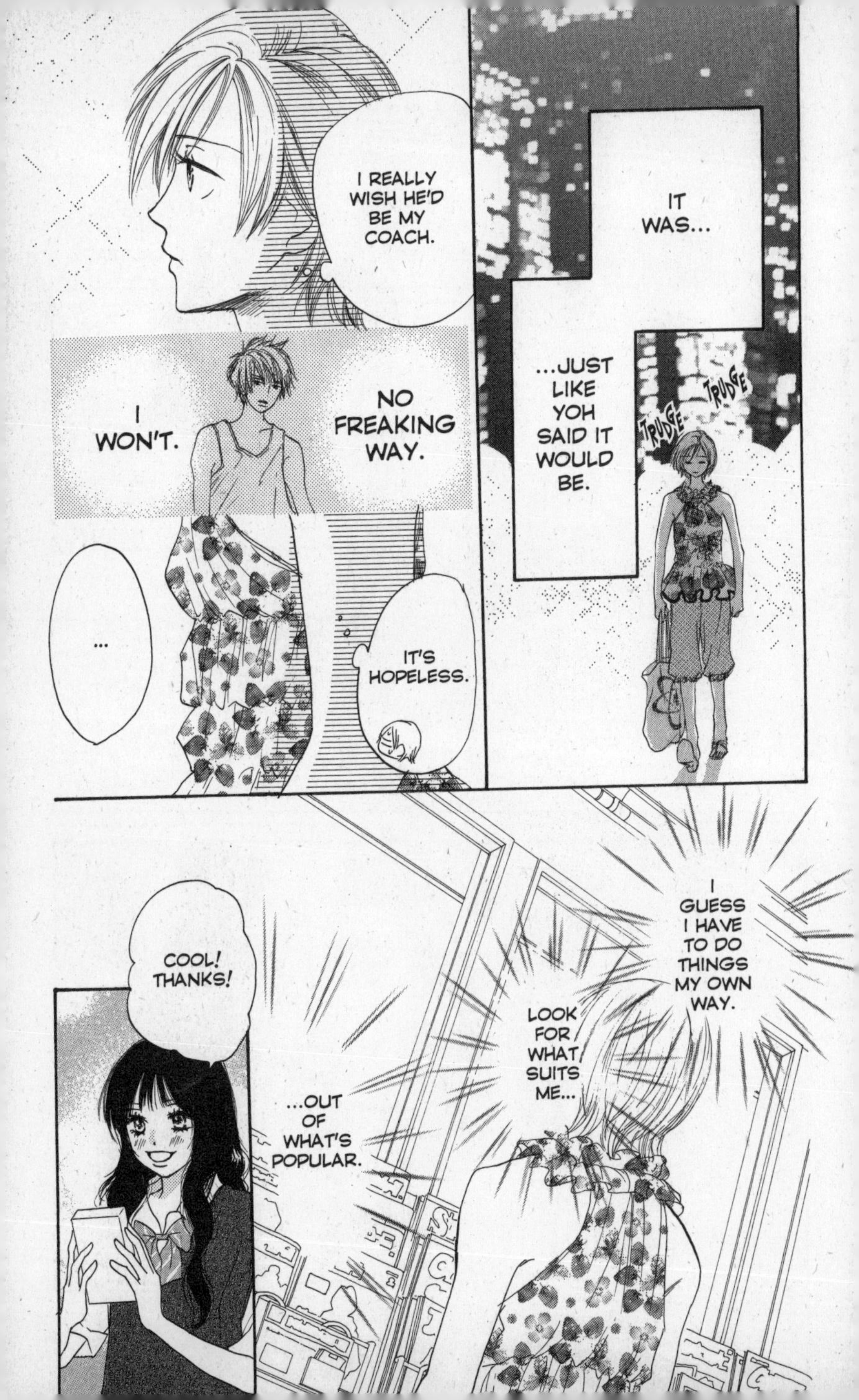

IT WAS...
...JUST LIKE YOH SAID IT WOULD BE.
TRUDGE TRUDGE
I REALLY WISH HE'D BE MY COACH.
NO FREAKING WAY.
I WON'T.
IT'S HOPELESS.
...
I GUESS I HAVE TO DO THINGS MY OWN WAY.
LOOK FOR WHAT SUITS ME...
...OUT OF WHAT'S POPULAR.
COOL! THANKS!

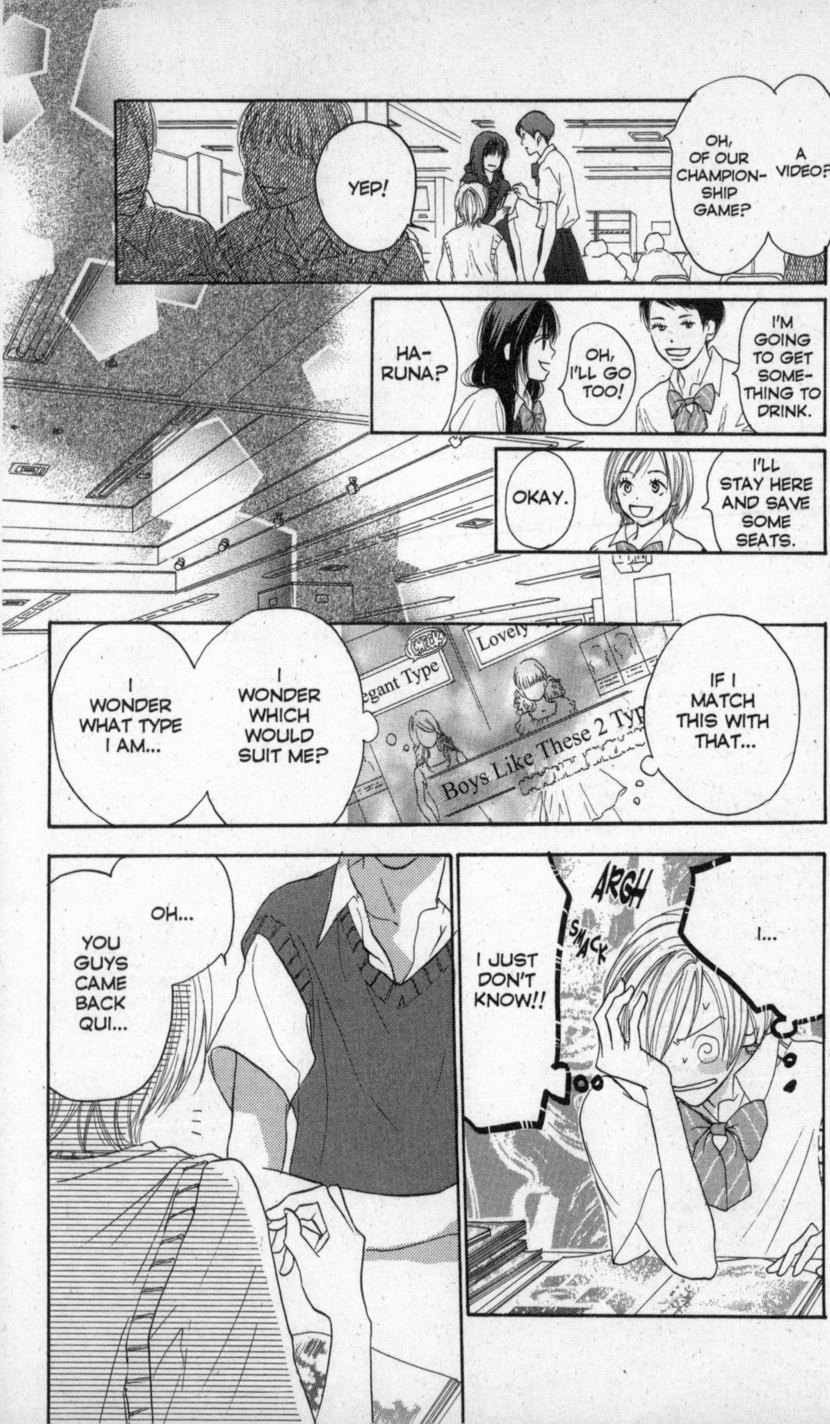
A VIDEO?
OH, OF OUR CHAMPION-SHIP GAME?
YEP!
I'M GOING TO GET SOME-THING TO DRINK.
OH, I'LL GO TOO!
HA-RUNA?
I'LL STAY HERE AND SAVE SOME SEATS.
OKAY.
IF I MATCH THIS WITH THAT...
Lovely
CHECK
egant Type
Boys Like These 2 Typ
I WONDER WHICH WOULD SUIT ME?
I WONDER WHAT TYPE I AM...
I...
ARGH
SMACK
I JUST DON'T KNOW!!
OH...
YOU GUYS CAME BACK QUI...

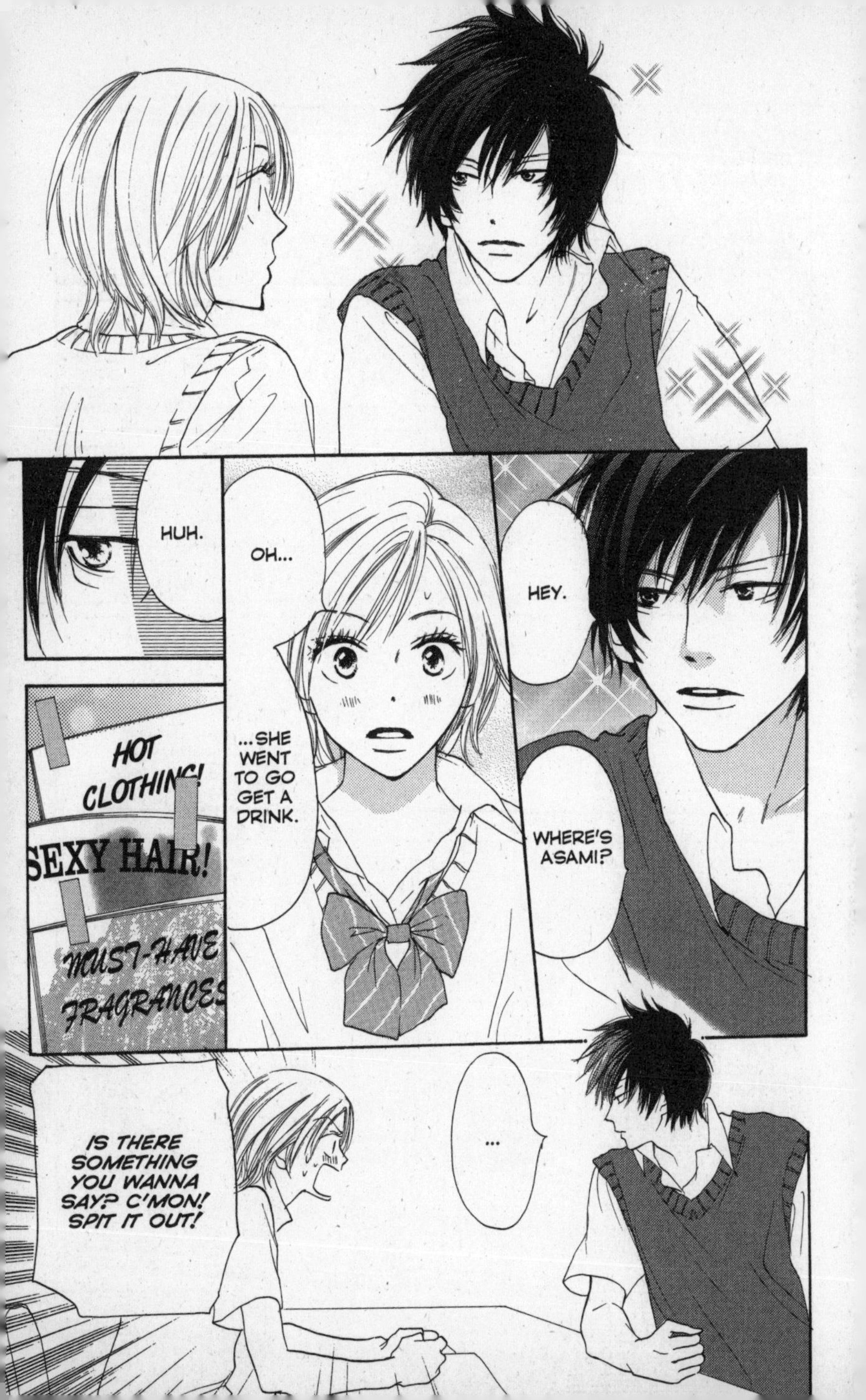
HEY.
WHERE'S ASAMI?
OH...
...SHE WENT TO GO GET A DRINK.
HUH.
HOT CLOTHIN
SEXY HAIR!
MUST-HAVE FRAGRANCES
...
IS THERE SOMETHING YOU WANNA SAY? C'MON! SPIT IT OUT!

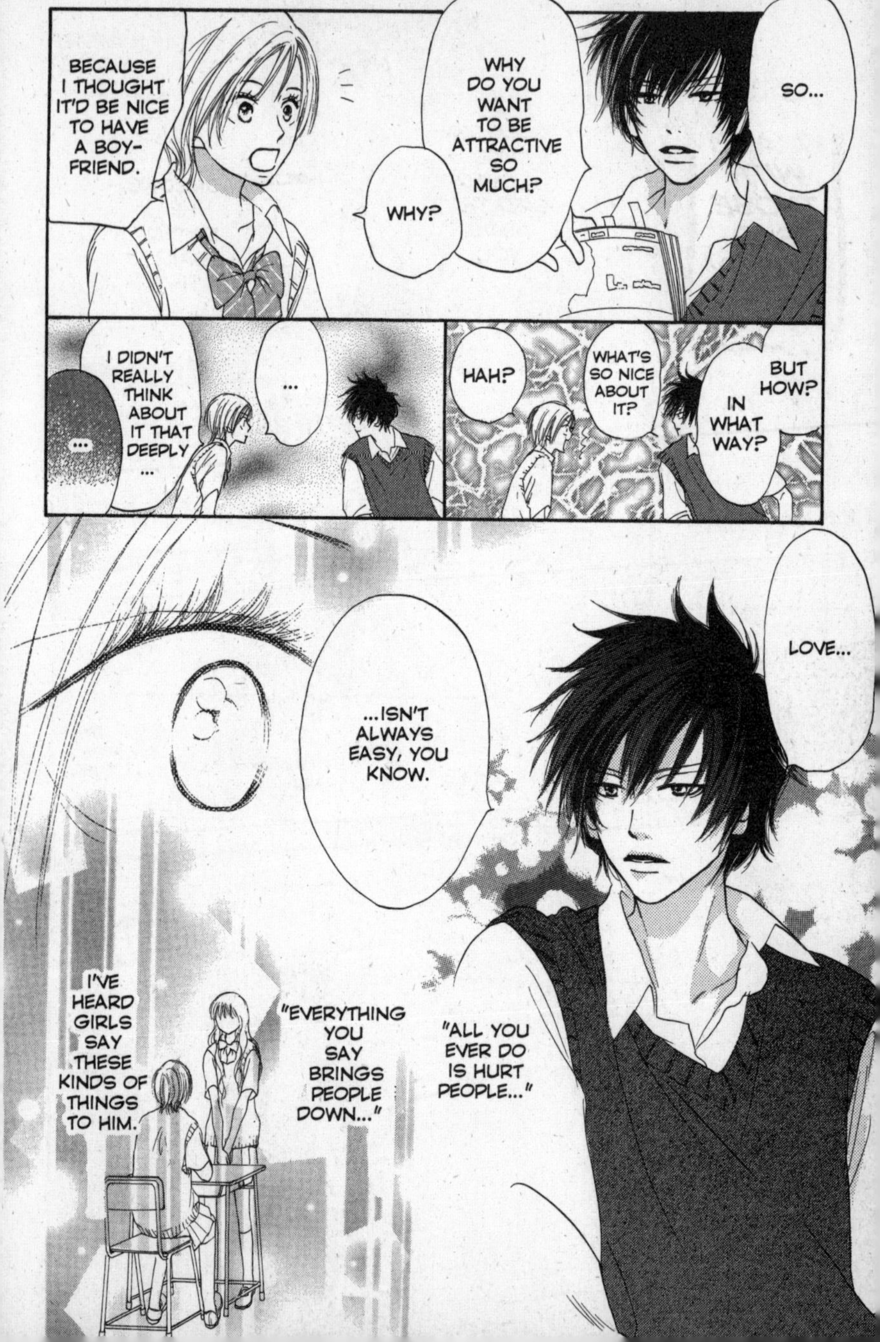
SO...
WHY DO YOU WANT TO BE ATTRACTIVE SO MUCH?
WHY?
BECAUSE I THOUGHT IT'D BE NICE TO HAVE A BOY-FRIEND.
BUT HOW?
IN WHAT WAY?
WHAT'S SO NICE ABOUT IT?
HAH?
...
I DIDN'T REALLY THINK ABOUT IT THAT DEEPLY ...
...
LOVE...
...ISN'T ALWAYS EASY, YOU KNOW.
"ALL YOU EVER DO IS HURT PEOPLE..."
"EVERYTHING YOU SAY BRINGS PEOPLE DOWN..."
I'VE HEARD GIRLS SAY THESE KINDS OF THINGS TO HIM.

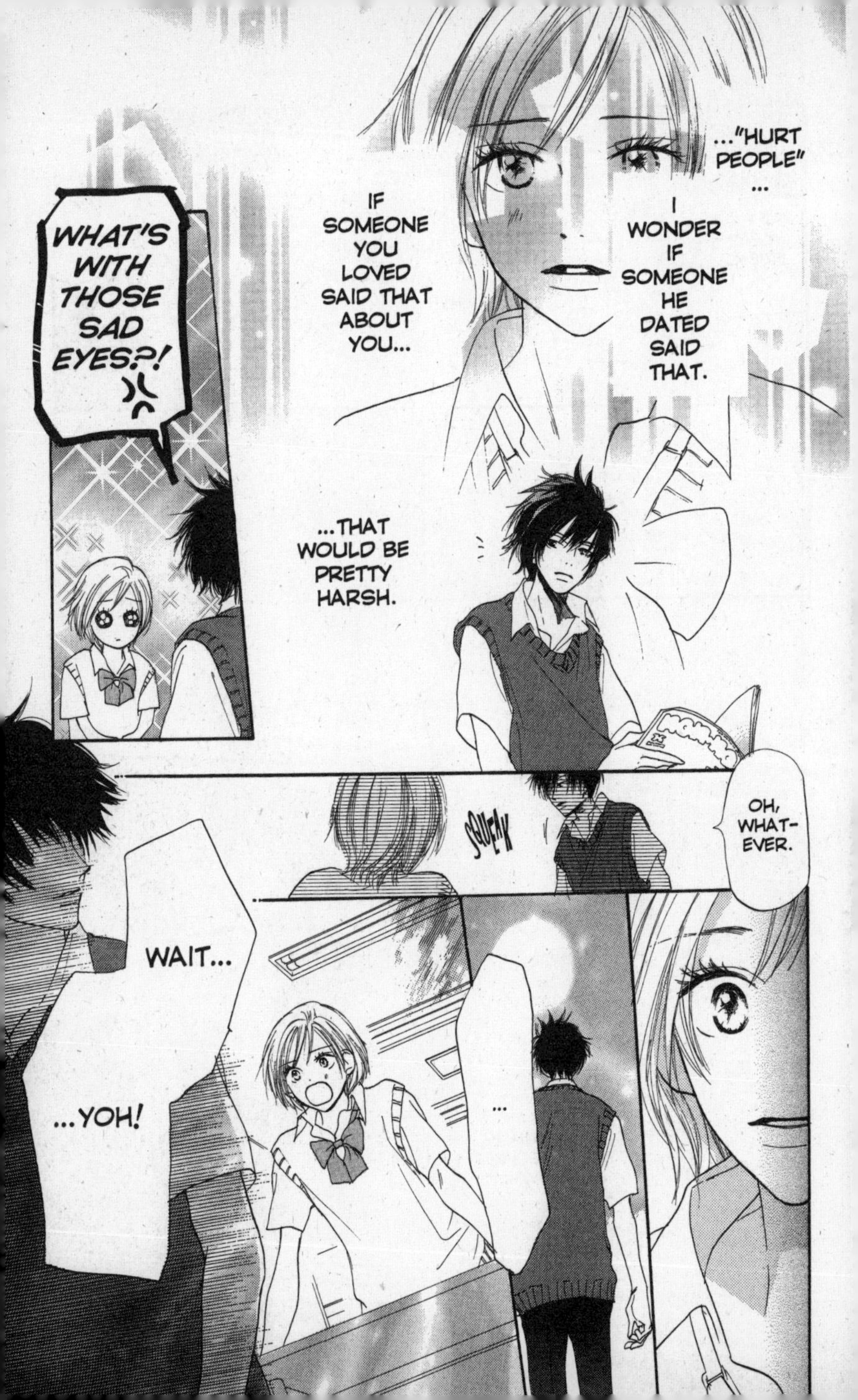
..."HURT PEOPLE"...
I WONDER IF SOMEONE HE DATED SAID THAT.
IF SOMEONE YOU LOVED SAID THAT ABOUT YOU...
...THAT WOULD BE PRETTY HARSH.
WHAT'S WITH THOSE SAD EYES?!
OH, WHAT-EVER.
SQUEAK
...
WAIT...
...YOH!

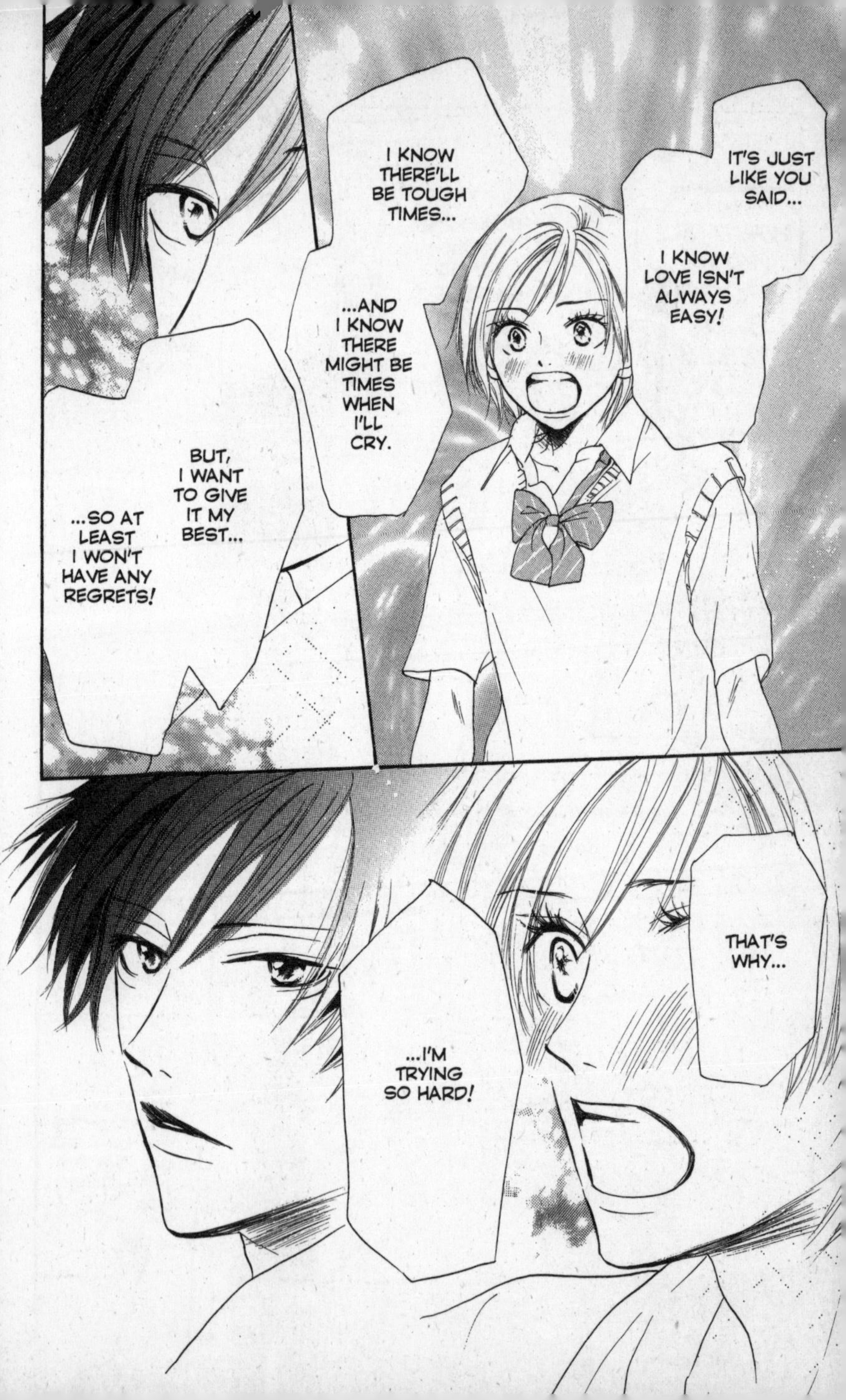
IT'S JUST LIKE YOU SAID...
I KNOW LOVE ISN'T ALWAYS EASY!
I KNOW THERE'LL BE TOUGH TIMES...
...AND I KNOW THERE MIGHT BE TIMES WHEN I'LL CRY.
BUT, I WANT TO GIVE IT MY BEST...
...SO AT LEAST I WON'T HAVE ANY REGRETS!
THAT'S WHY...
...I'M TRYING SO HARD!

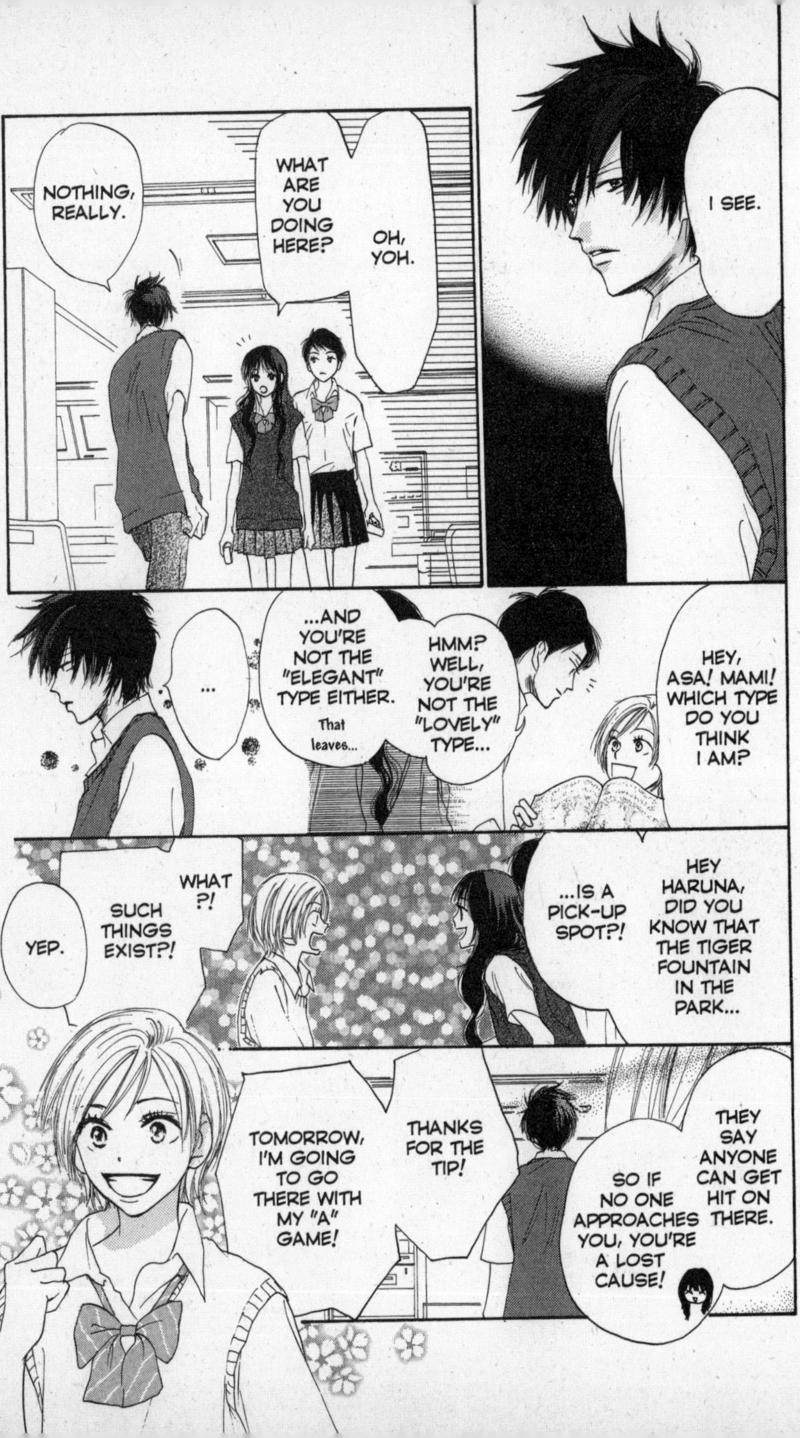
I SEE.
OH, YOH.
WHAT ARE YOU DOING HERE?
NOTHING, REALLY.
HEY, ASA! MAMI! WHICH TYPE DO YOU THINK I AM?
HMM? WELL, YOU'RE NOT THE "LOVELY" TYPE...
...AND YOU'RE NOT THE "ELEGANT" TYPE EITHER.
That leaves...
...
HEY HARUNA, DID YOU KNOW THAT THE TIGER FOUNTAIN IN THE PARK...
...IS A PICK-UP SPOT?!
WHAT?!
SUCH THINGS EXIST?!
YEP.
THEY SAY ANYONE CAN GET HIT ON THERE.
SO IF NO ONE APPROACHES YOU, YOU'RE A LOST CAUSE!
THANKS FOR THE TIP!
TOMORROW, I'M GOING TO GO THERE WITH MY "A" GAME!

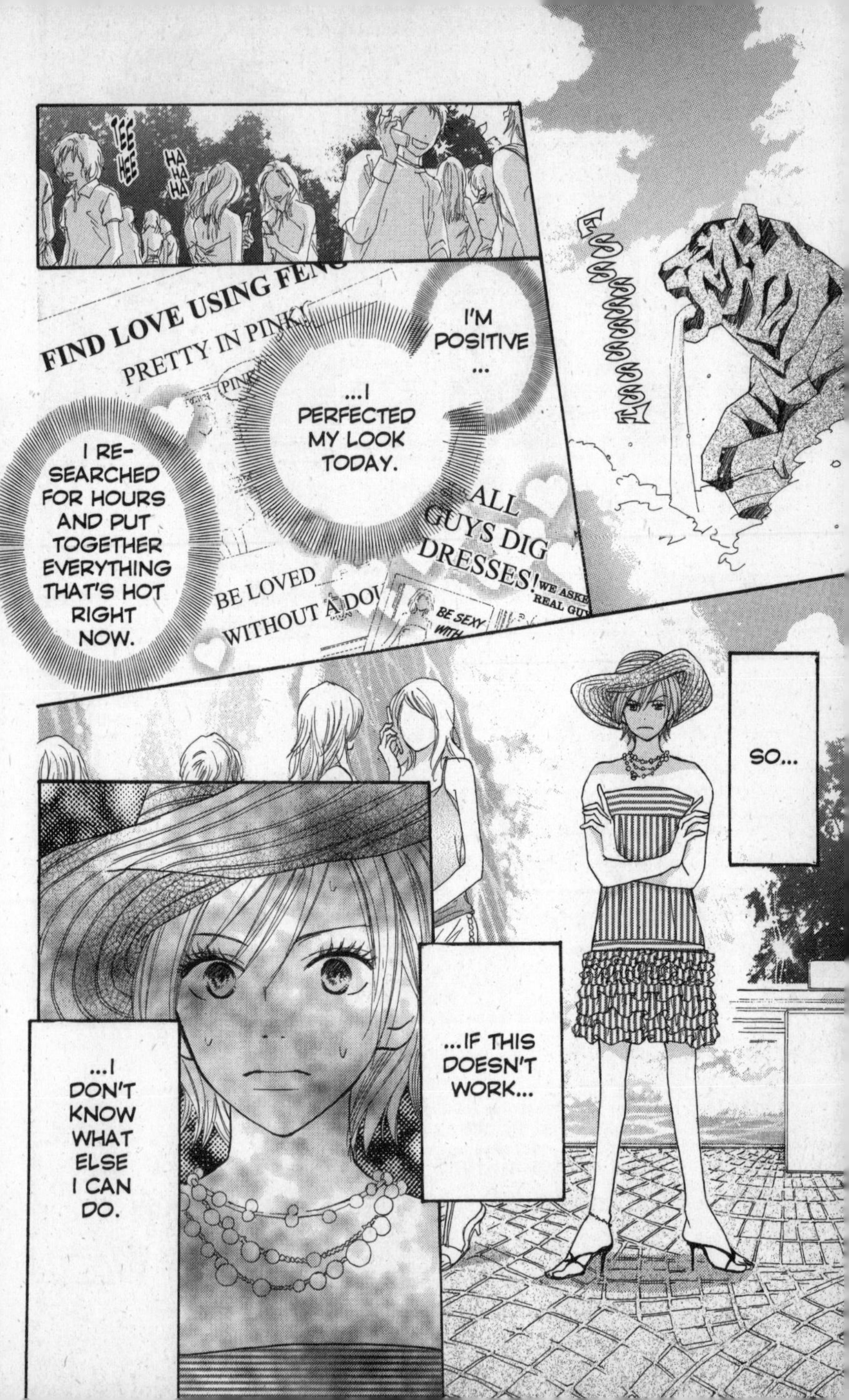
TEE HEE
HA HA HA
FIND LOVE USING FENG
PRETTY IN PINK!
PINK
I'M POSITIVE ...
...I PERFECTED MY LOOK TODAY.
I RE-SEARCHED FOR HOURS AND PUT TOGETHER EVERYTHING THAT'S HOT RIGHT NOW.
ALL GUYS DIG DRESSES!
BE LOVED
BE SEXY WITH
SO...
...IF THIS DOESN'T WORK...
...I DON'T KNOW WHAT ELSE I CAN DO.

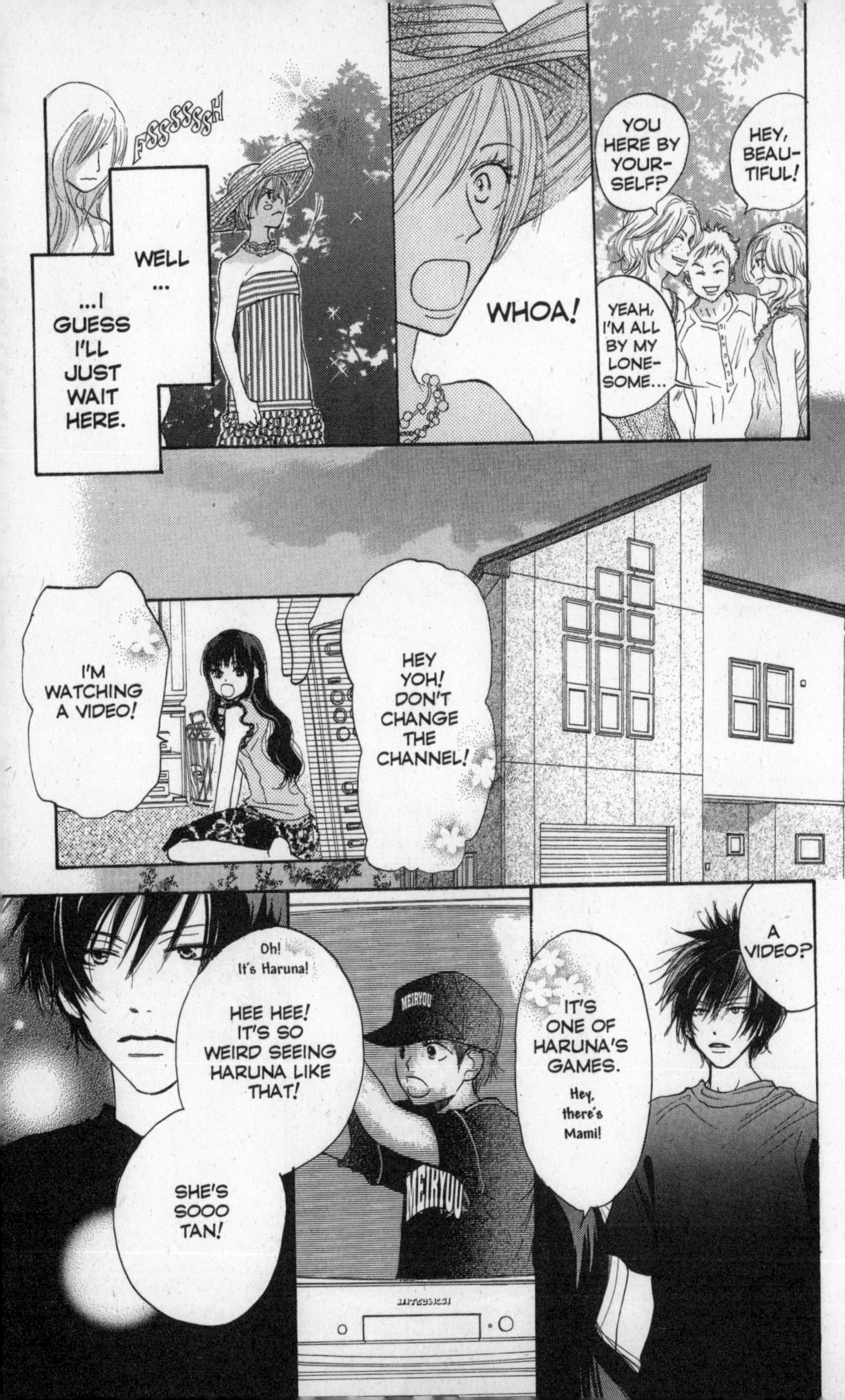
HEY, BEAUTIFUL!
YOU HERE BY YOURSELF?
YEAH, I'M ALL BY MY LONESOME...
WHOA!
FSSSSSSH
WELL ...
...I GUESS I'LL JUST WAIT HERE.
HEY YOH! DON'T CHANGE THE CHANNEL!
I'M WATCHING A VIDEO!
A VIDEO?
IT'S ONE OF HARUNA'S GAMES.
Hey, there's Mami!
Oh! It's Haruna!
HEE HEE! IT'S SO WEIRD SEEING HARUNA LIKE THAT!
SHE'S SOOO TAN!

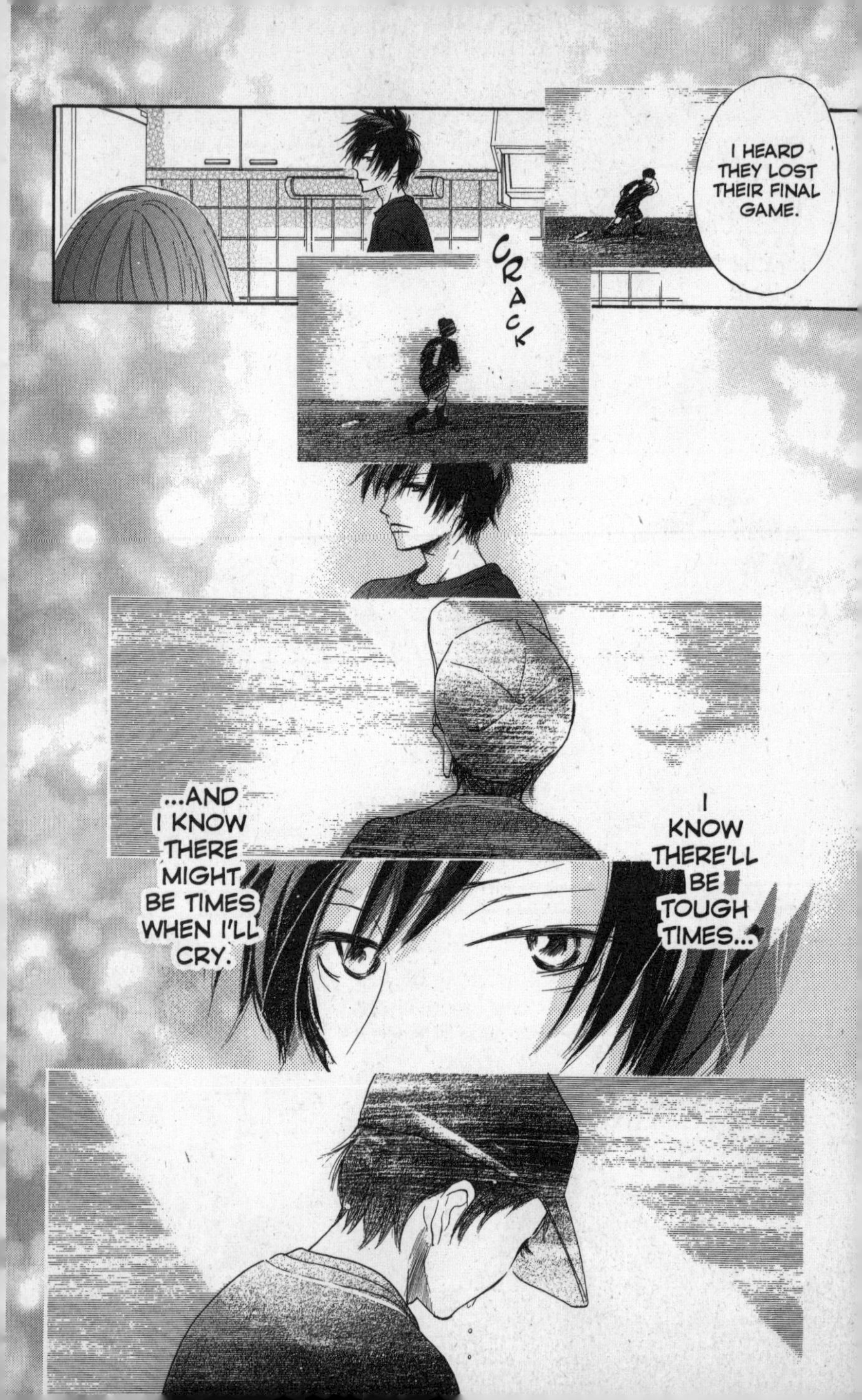
I HEARD THEY LOST THEIR FINAL GAME.
CRACK
I KNOW THERE'LL BE TOUGH TIMES...
...AND I KNOW THERE MIGHT BE TIMES WHEN I'LL CRY.

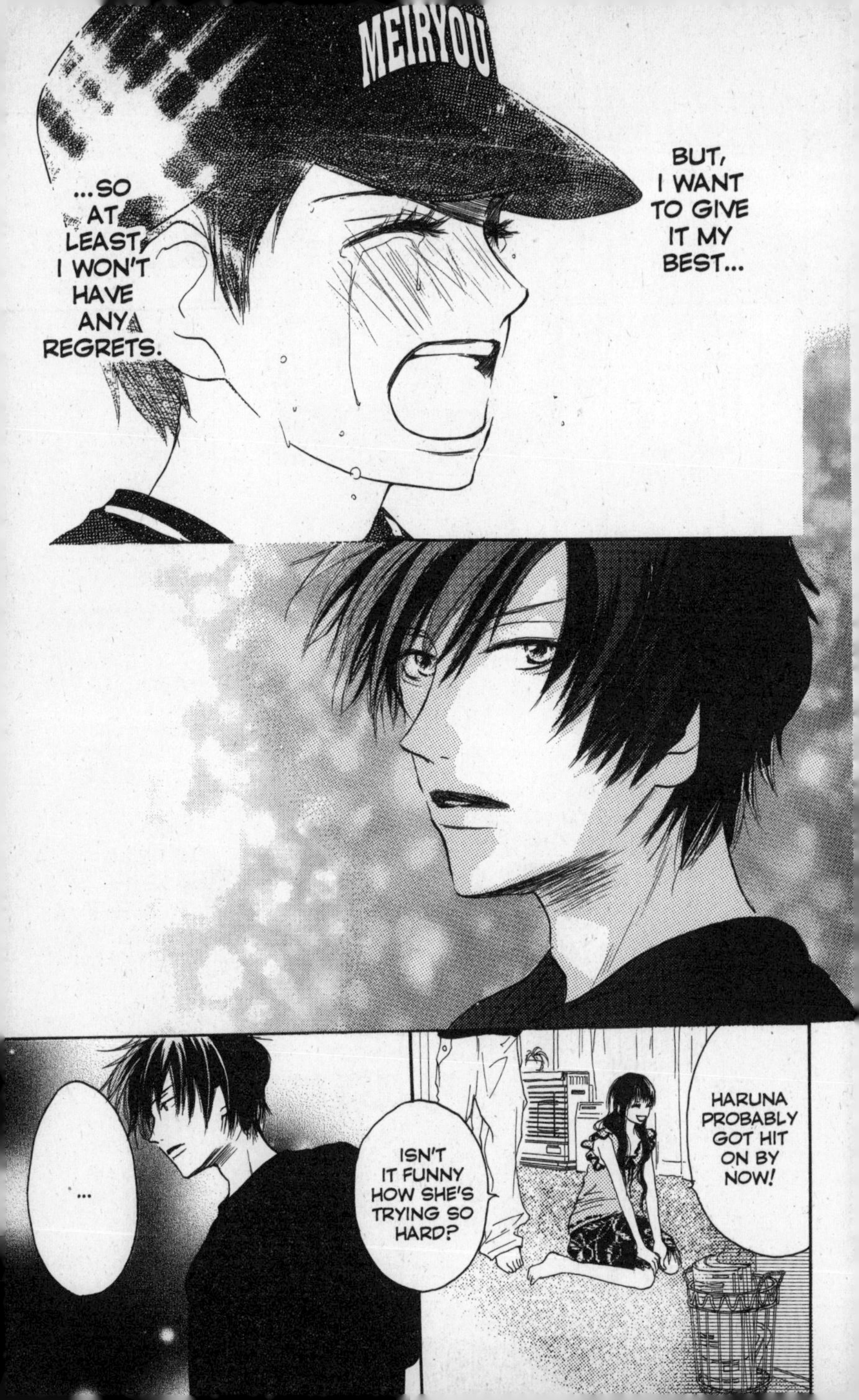
BUT, I WANT TO GIVE IT MY BEST...
...SO AT LEAST I WON'T HAVE ANY REGRETS.
HARUNA PROBABLY GOT HIT ON BY NOW!
ISN'T IT FUNNY HOW SHE'S TRYING SO HARD?
...

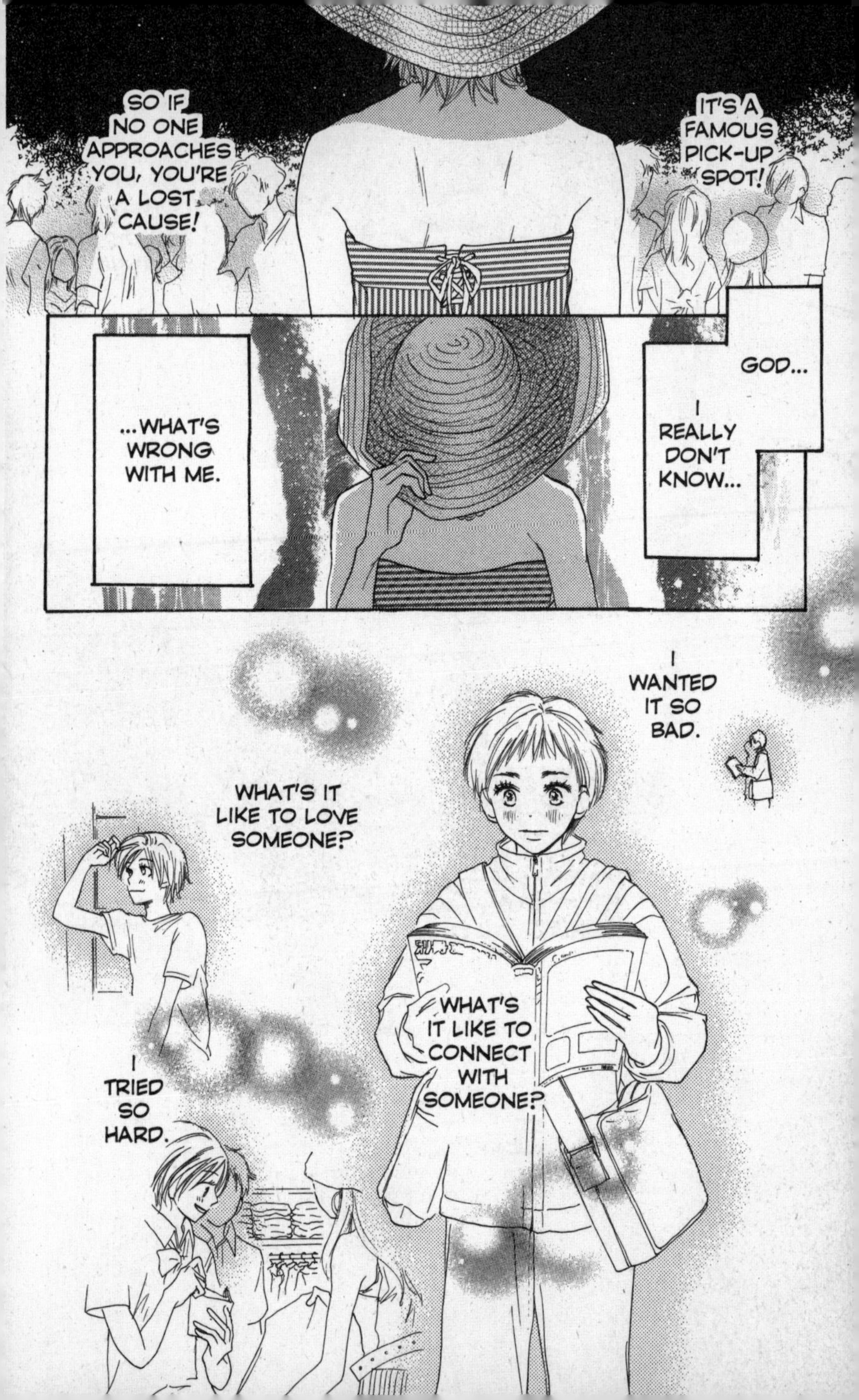
IT'S A FAMOUS PICK-UP SPOT!
SO IF NO ONE APPROACHES YOU, YOU'RE A LOST CAUSE!
GOD... I REALLY DON'T KNOW...
...WHAT'S WRONG WITH ME.
I WANTED IT SO BAD.
WHAT'S IT LIKE TO LOVE SOMEONE?
WHAT'S IT LIKE TO CONNECT WITH SOMEONE?
I TRIED SO HARD.

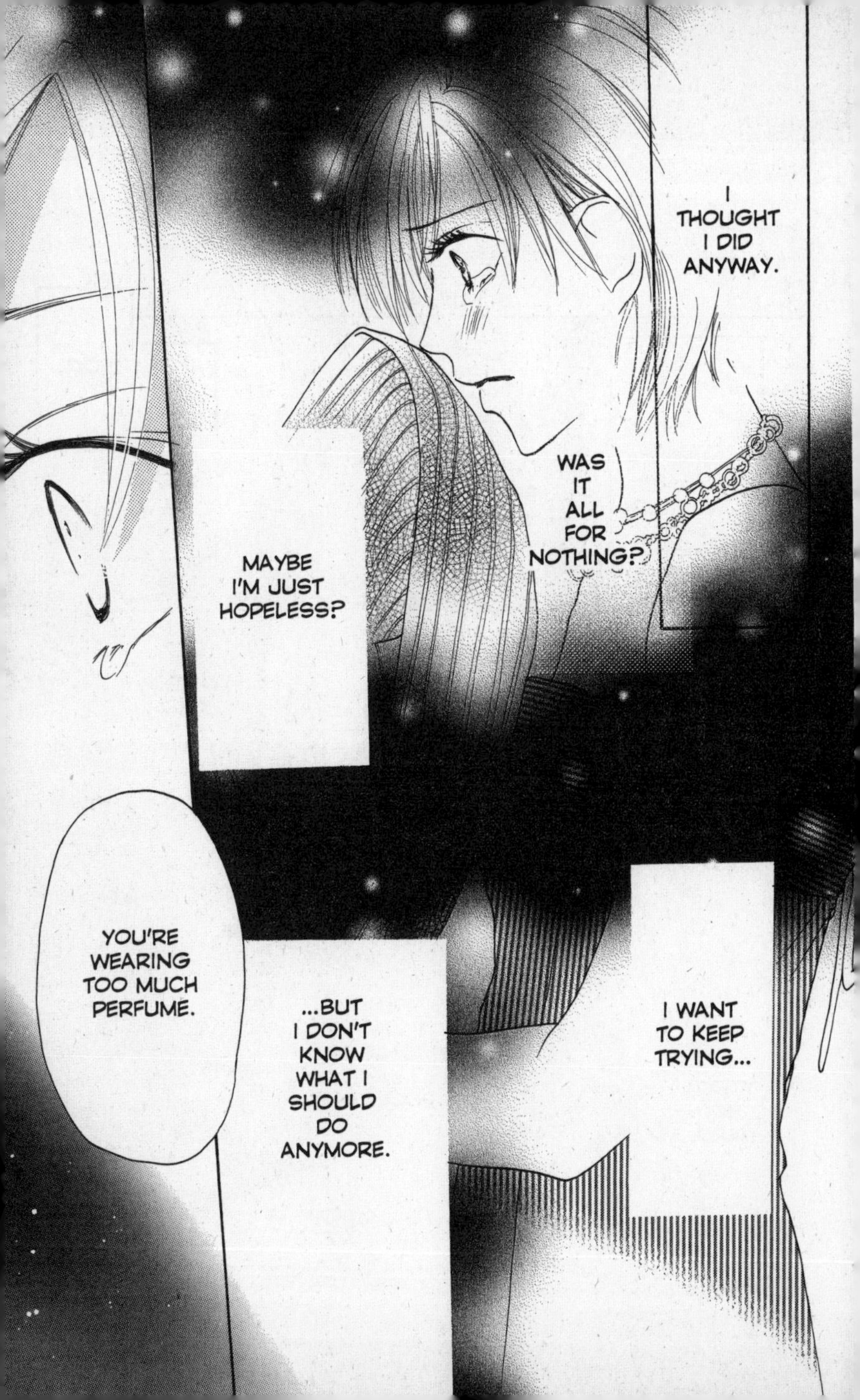
I THOUGHT I DID ANYWAY.
WAS IT ALL FOR NOTHING?
MAYBE I'M JUST HOPELESS?
I WANT TO KEEP TRYING...
...BUT I DON'T KNOW WHAT I SHOULD DO ANYMORE.
YOU'RE WEARING TOO MUCH PERFUME.

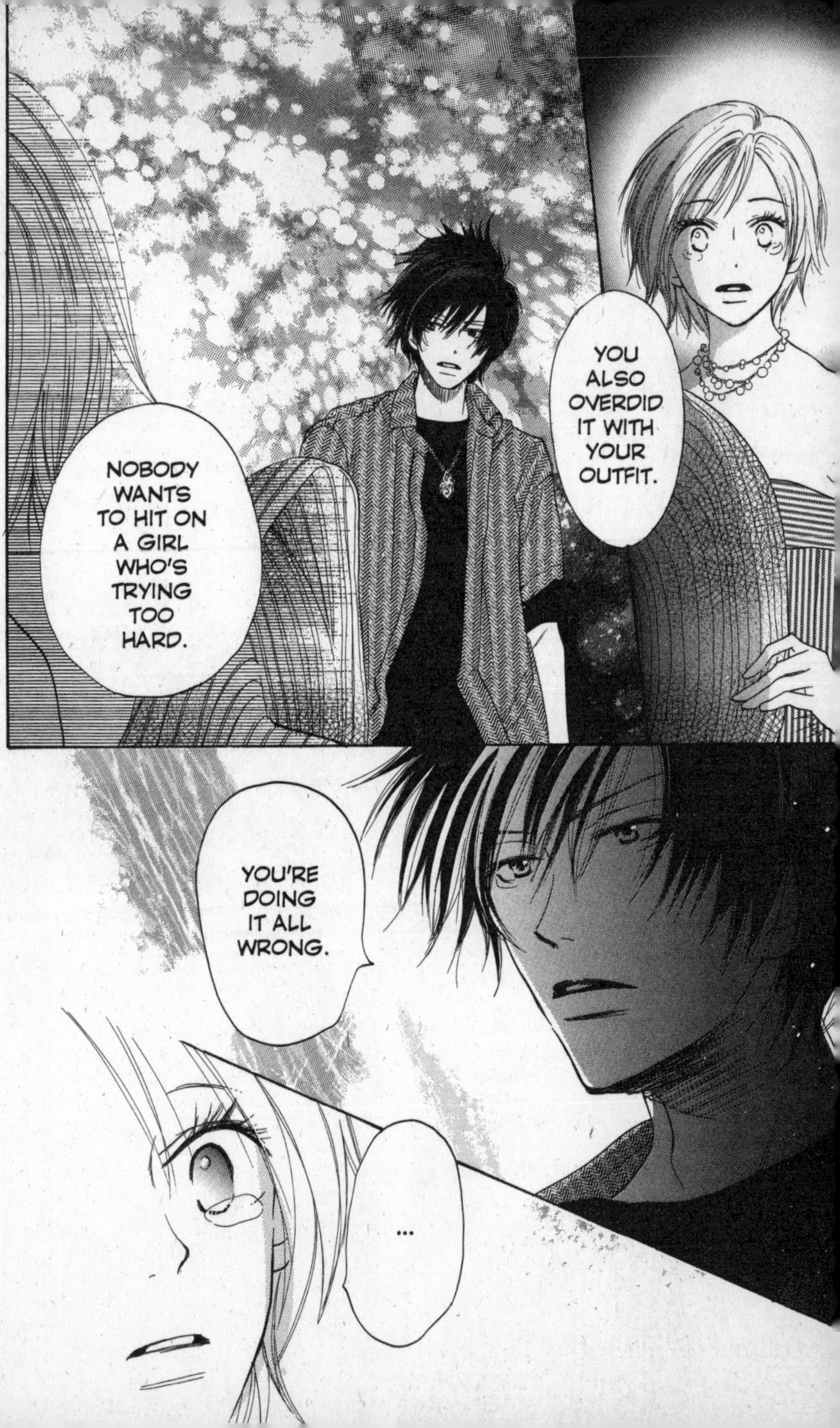
YOU ALSO OVERDID IT WITH YOUR OUTFIT.
NOBODY WANTS TO HIT ON A GIRL WHO'S TRYING TOO HARD.
YOU'RE DOING IT ALL WRONG.
...

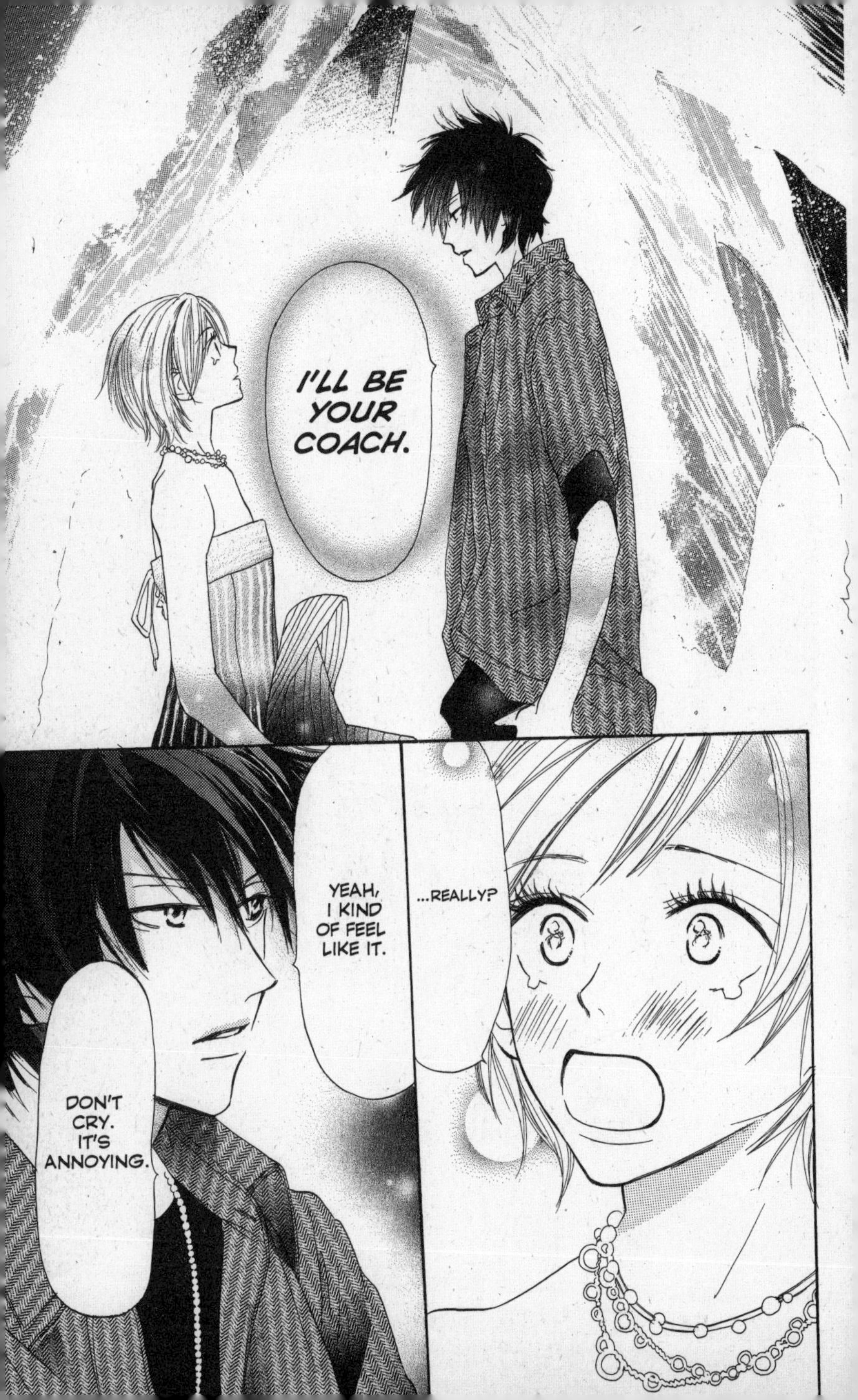
I'LL BE YOUR COACH.
...REALLY?
YEAH, I KIND OF FEEL LIKE IT.
DON'T CRY. IT'S ANNOYING.

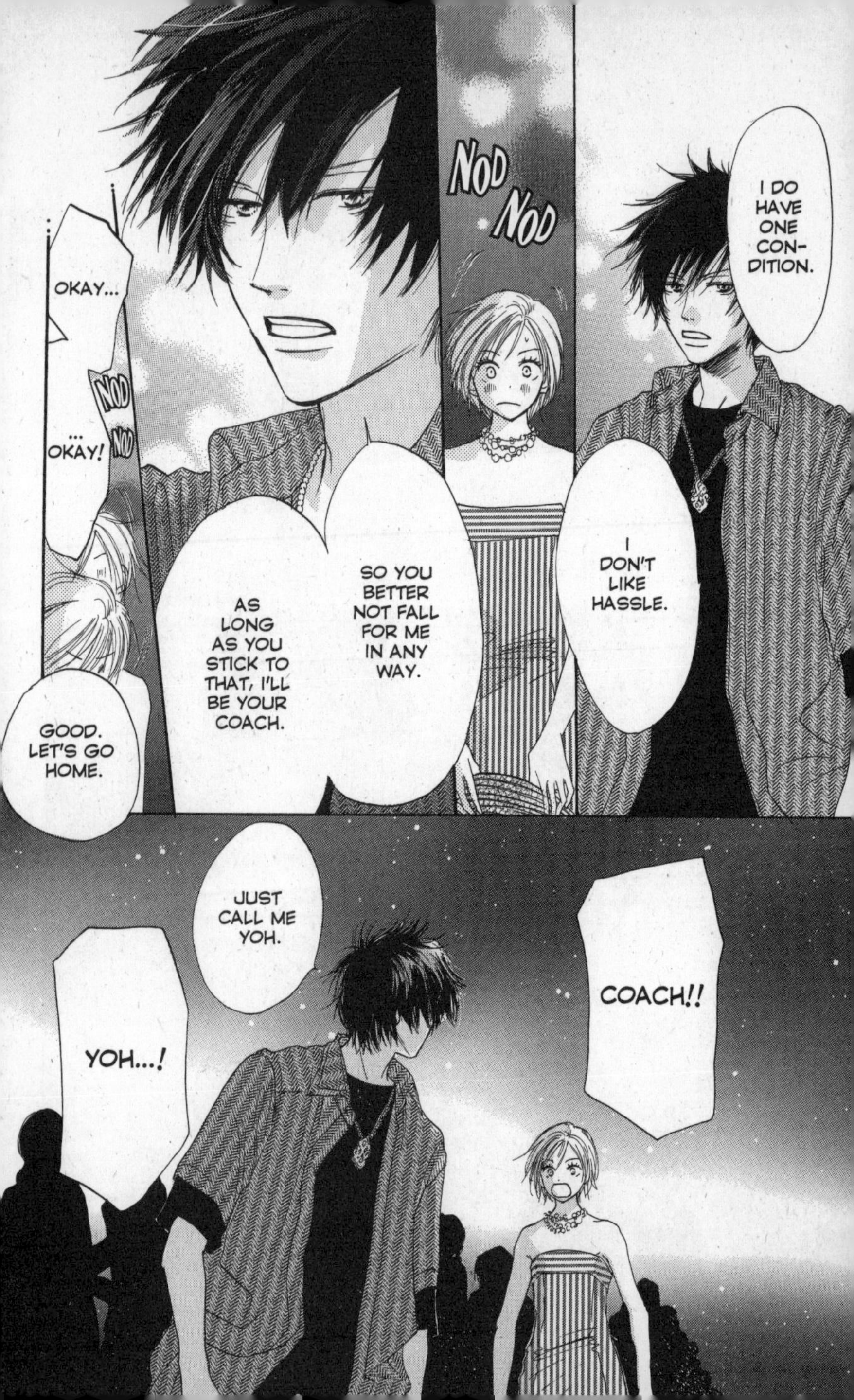
I DO HAVE ONE CON-DITION.
I DON'T LIKE HASSLE.
NOD NOD
SO YOU BETTER NOT FALL FOR ME IN ANY WAY.
AS LONG AS YOU STICK TO THAT, I'LL BE YOUR COACH.
OKAY...
NOD
...OKAY!
NOD
GOOD. LET'S GO HOME.
COACH!!
JUST CALL ME YOH.
YOH...!

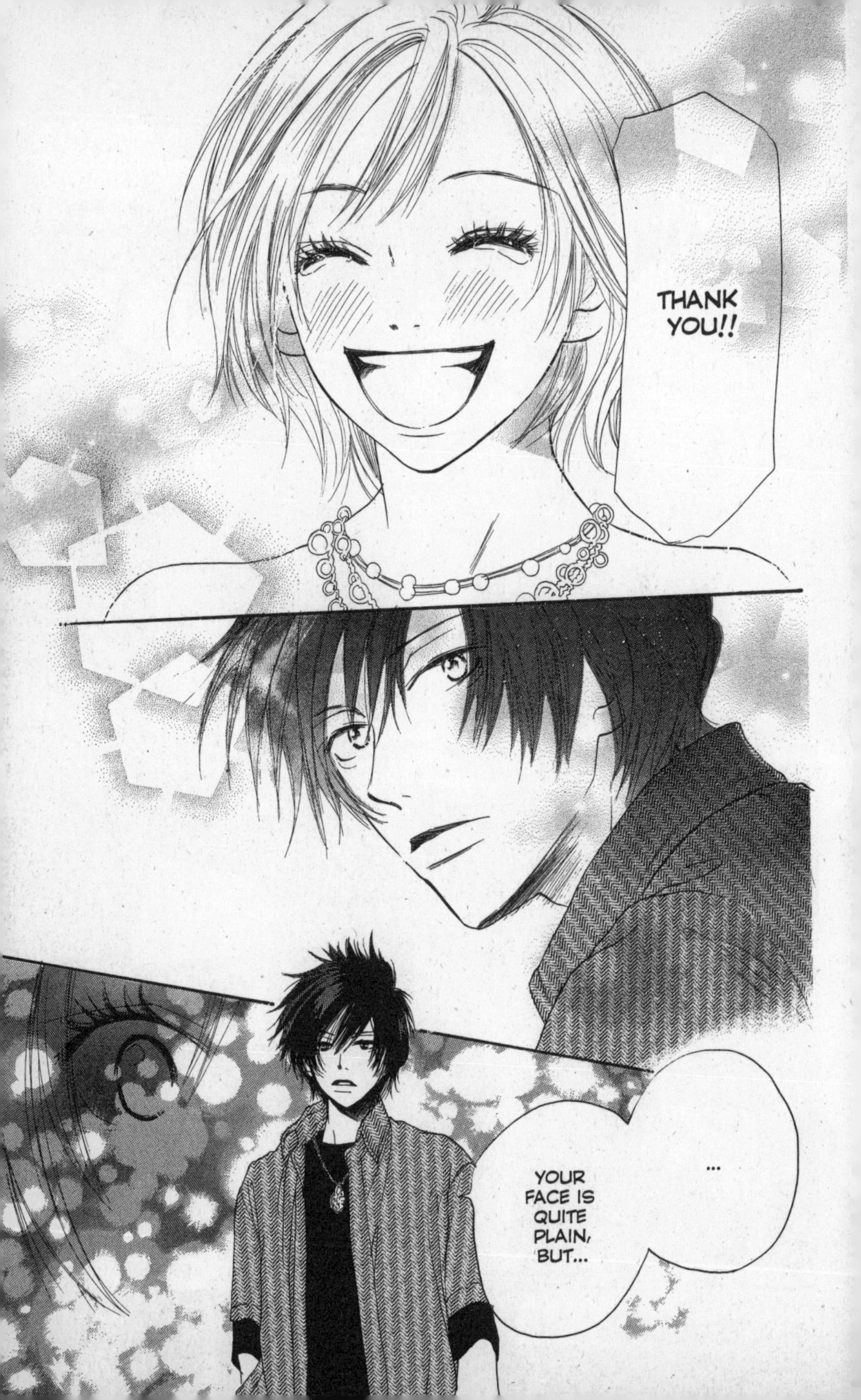
THANK YOU!!
...
YOUR FACE IS QUITE PLAIN, BUT...

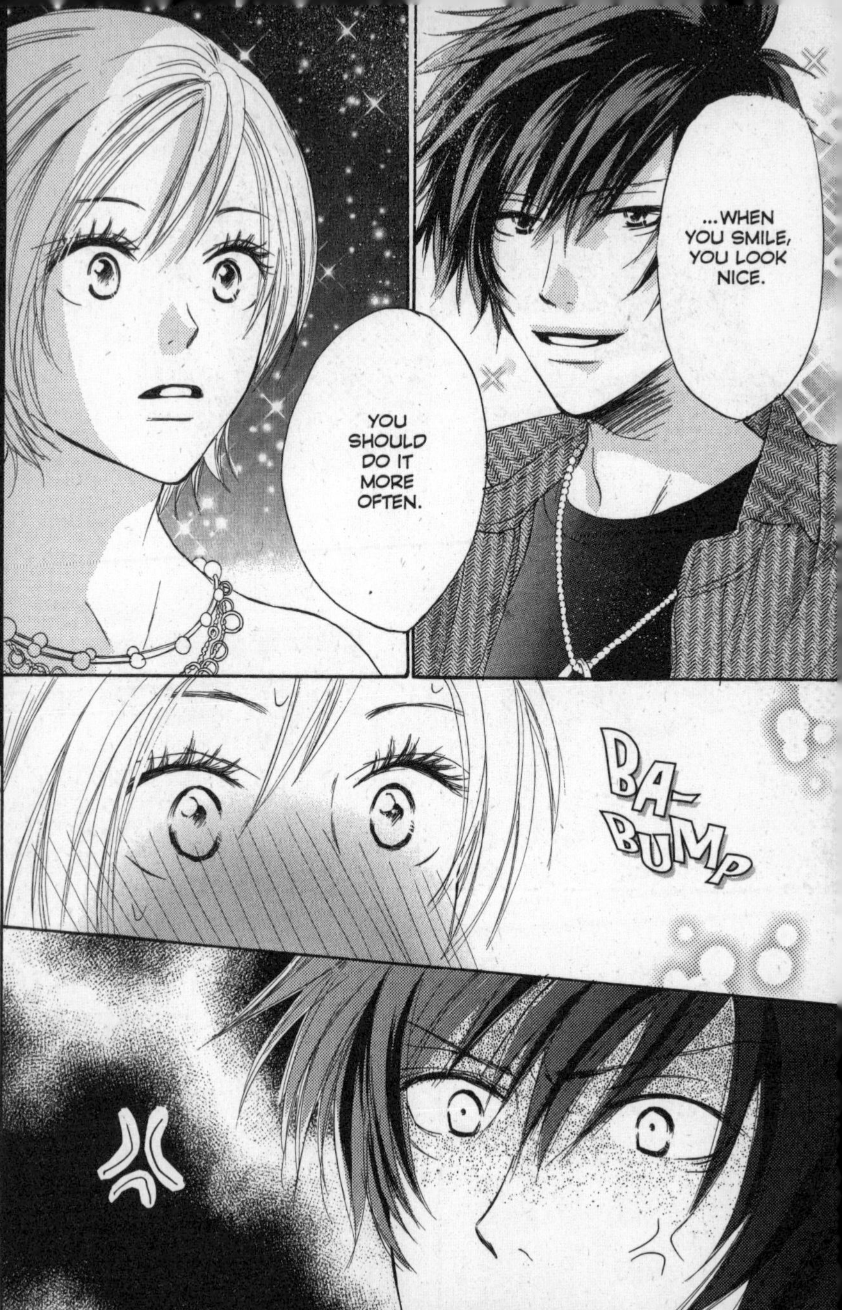
...WHEN YOU SMILE, YOU LOOK NICE.
YOU SHOULD DO IT MORE OFTEN.
BA-BUMP

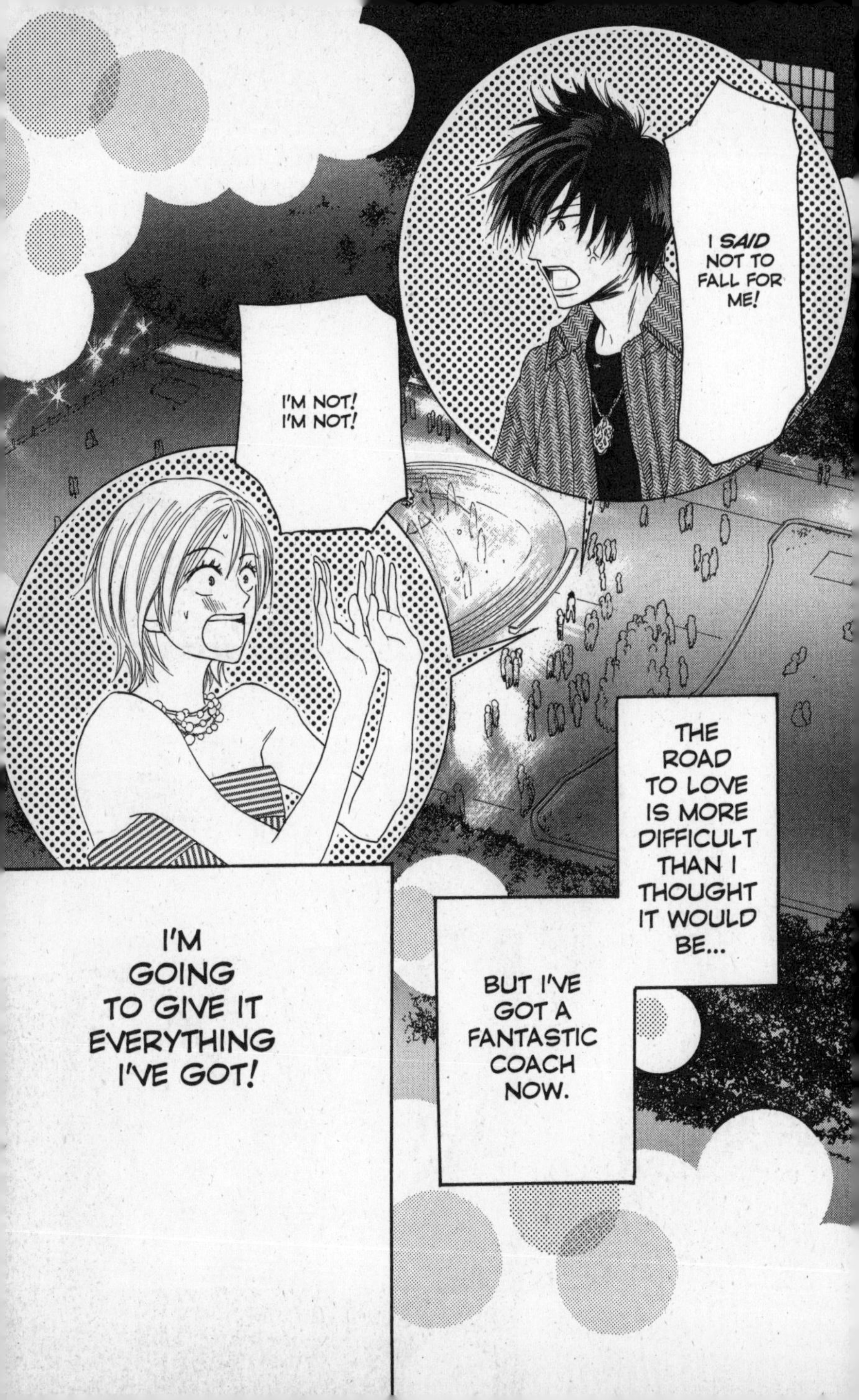
I *SAID* NOT TO FALL FOR ME!
I'M NOT! I'M NOT!
THE ROAD TO LOVE IS MORE DIFFICULT THAN I THOUGHT IT WOULD BE...
BUT I'VE GOT A FANTASTIC COACH NOW.
I'M GOING TO GIVE IT EVERYTHING I'VE GOT!

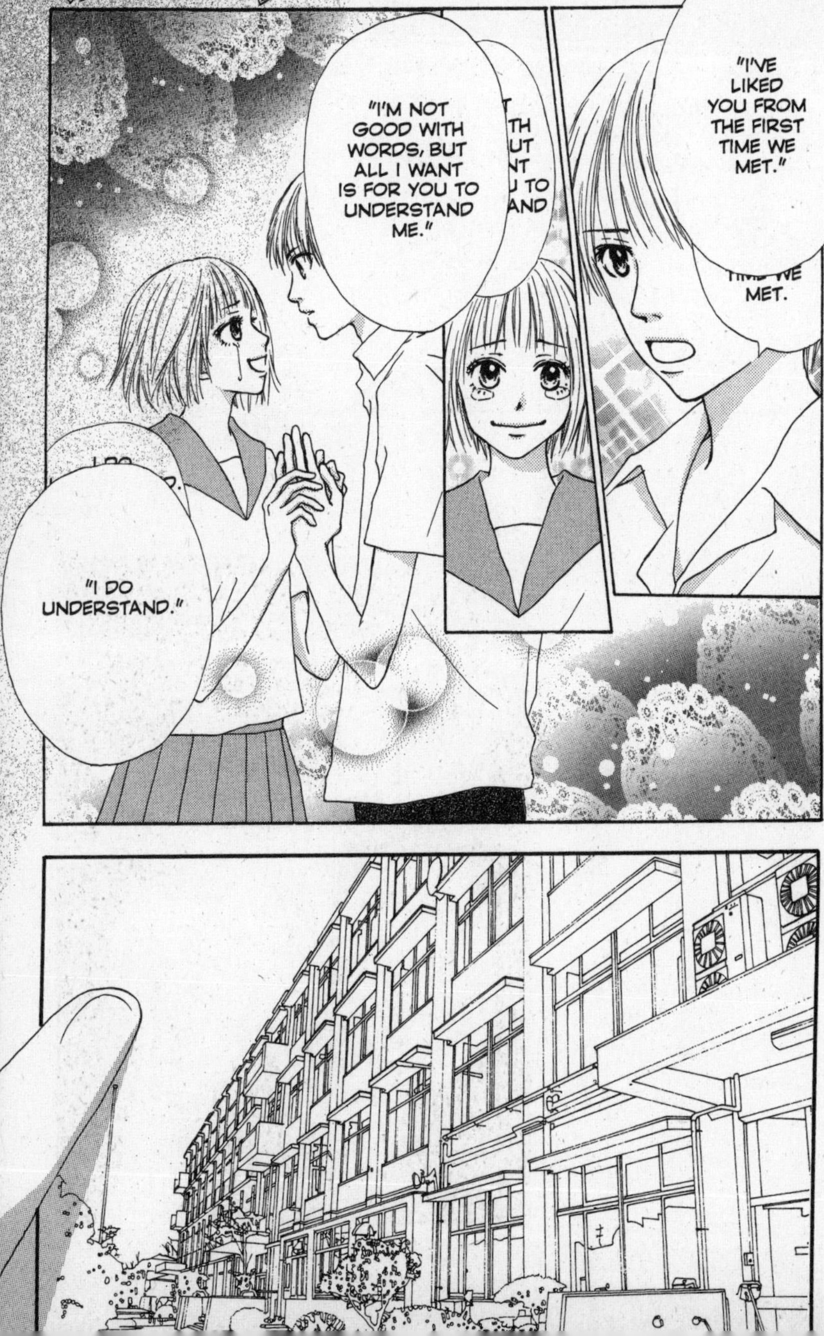
"I'VE LIKED YOU FROM THE FIRST TIME WE MET."
"I'M NOT GOOD WITH WORDS, BUT ALL I WANT IS FOR YOU TO UNDERSTAND ME."
"I DO UNDERSTAND."

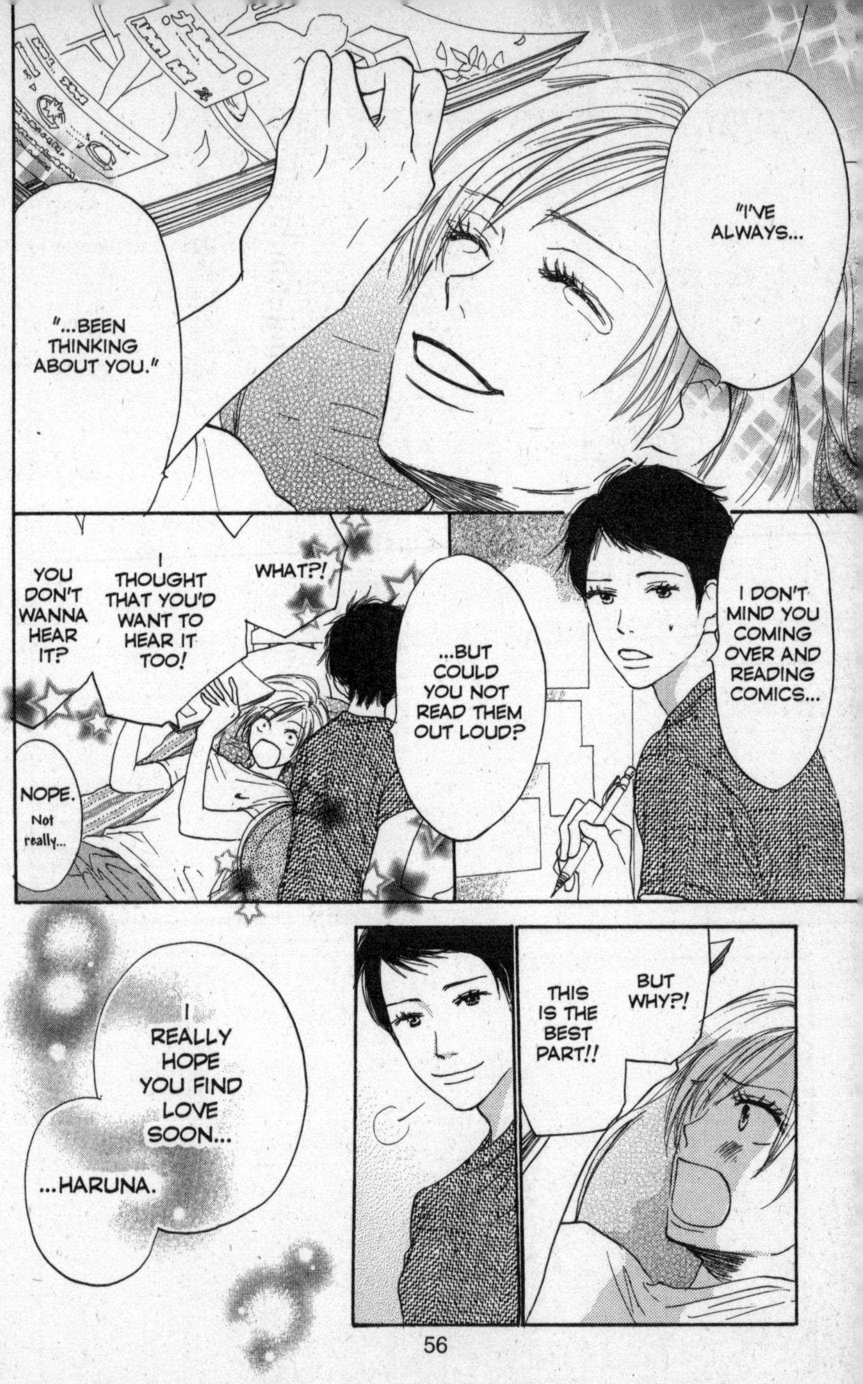
"I'VE ALWAYS...
"...BEEN THINKING ABOUT YOU."
I DON'T MIND YOU COMING OVER AND READING COMICS...
...BUT COULD YOU NOT READ THEM OUT LOUD?
WHAT?!
I THOUGHT THAT YOU'D WANT TO HEAR IT TOO!
YOU DON'T WANNA HEAR IT?
NOPE.
Not really...
BUT WHY?!
THIS IS THE BEST PART!!
I REALLY HOPE YOU FIND LOVE SOON...
...HARUNA.

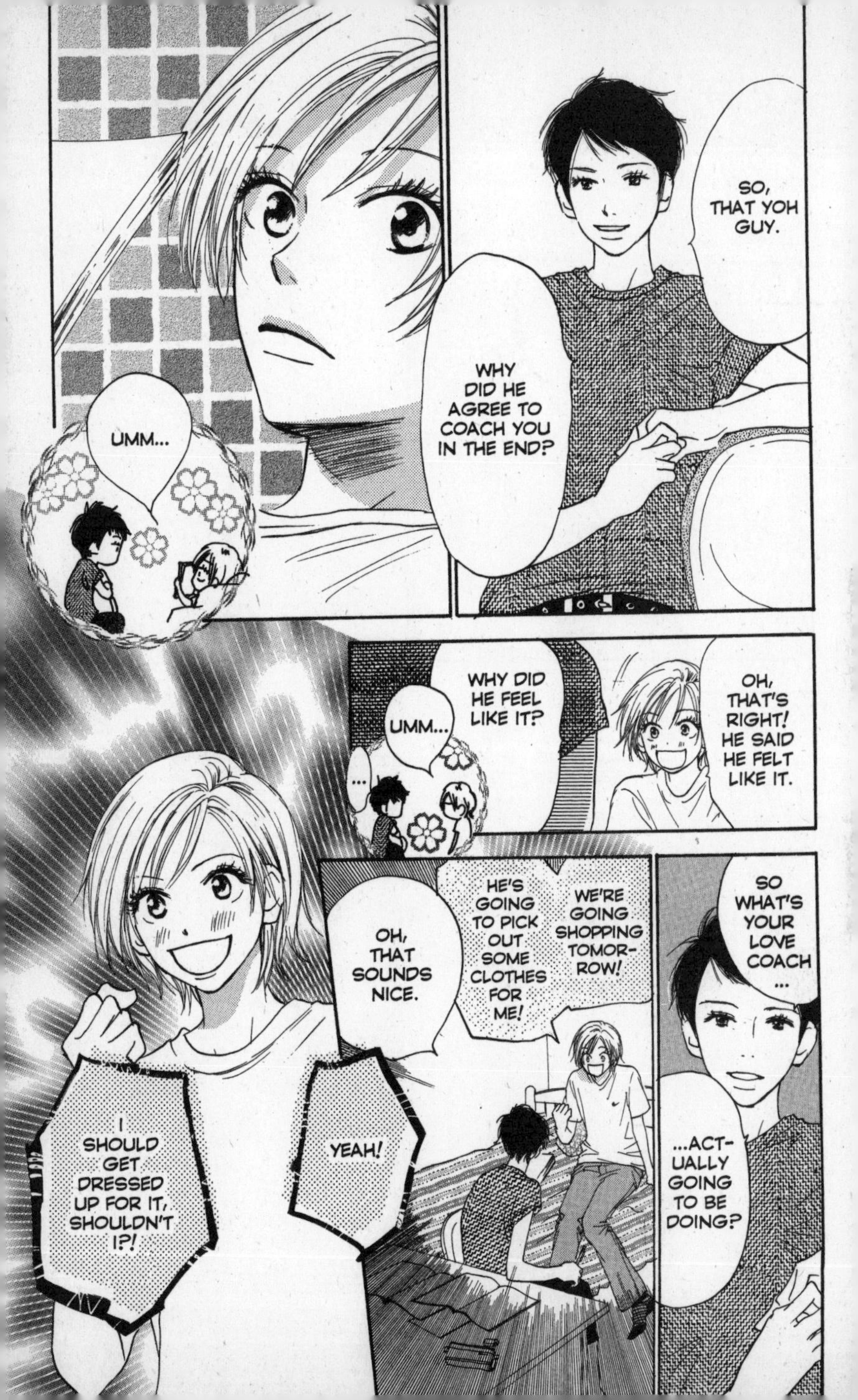
SO, THAT YOH GUY.
WHY DID HE AGREE TO COACH YOU IN THE END?
UMM...
OH, THAT'S RIGHT! HE SAID HE FELT LIKE IT.
WHY DID HE FEEL LIKE IT?
UMM...
...
SO WHAT'S YOUR LOVE COACH ...
...ACT-UALLY GOING TO BE DOING?
WE'RE GOING SHOPPING TOMOR-ROW!
HE'S GOING TO PICK OUT SOME CLOTHES FOR ME!
OH, THAT SOUNDS NICE.
YEAH!
I SHOULD GET DRESSED UP FOR IT, SHOULDN'T I?!

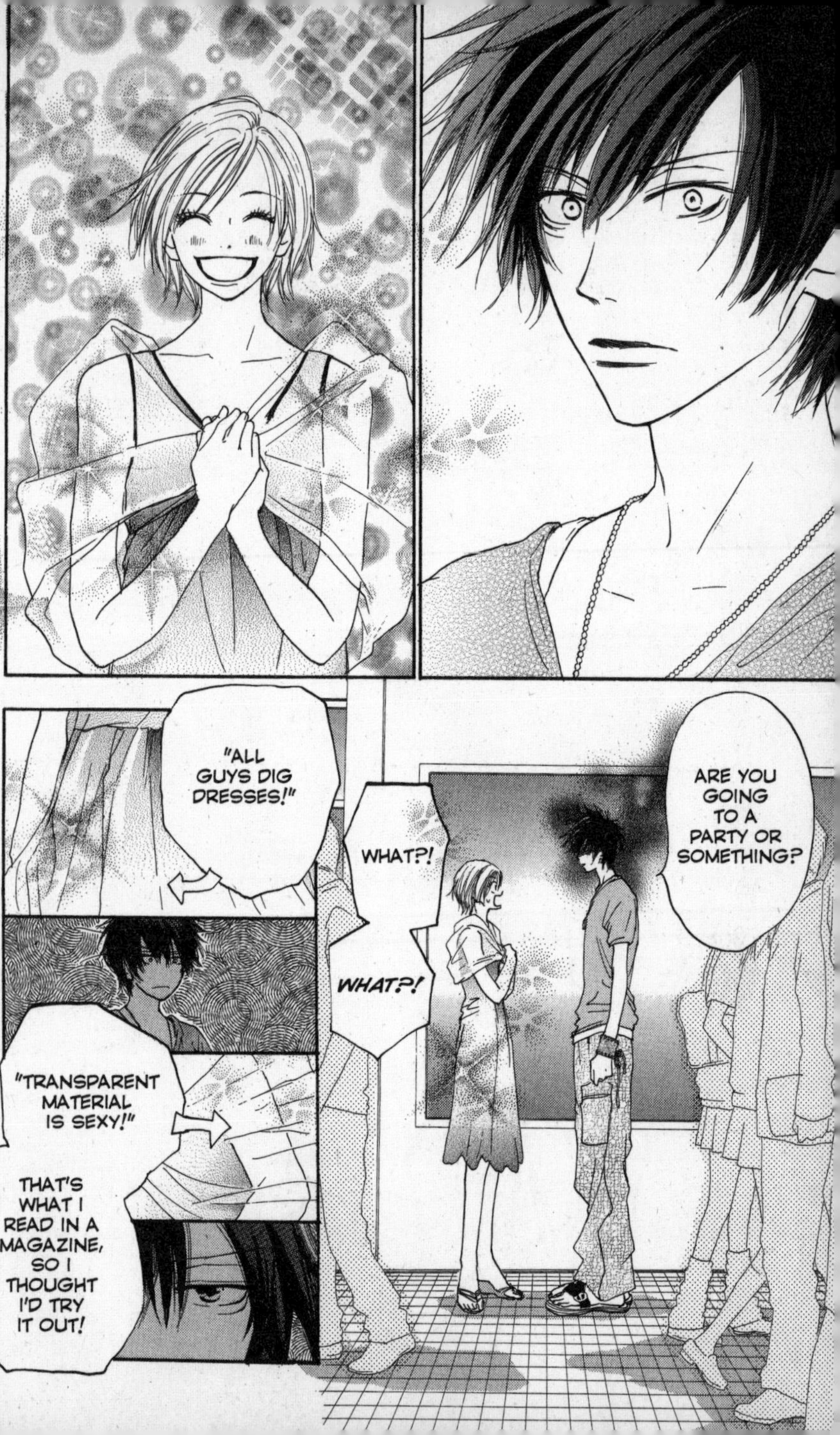
ARE YOU GOING TO A PARTY OR SOMETHING?
WHAT?!
WHAT?!
"ALL GUYS DIG DRESSES!"
"TRANSPARENT MATERIAL IS SEXY!"
THAT'S WHAT I READ IN A MAGAZINE, SO I THOUGHT I'D TRY IT OUT!

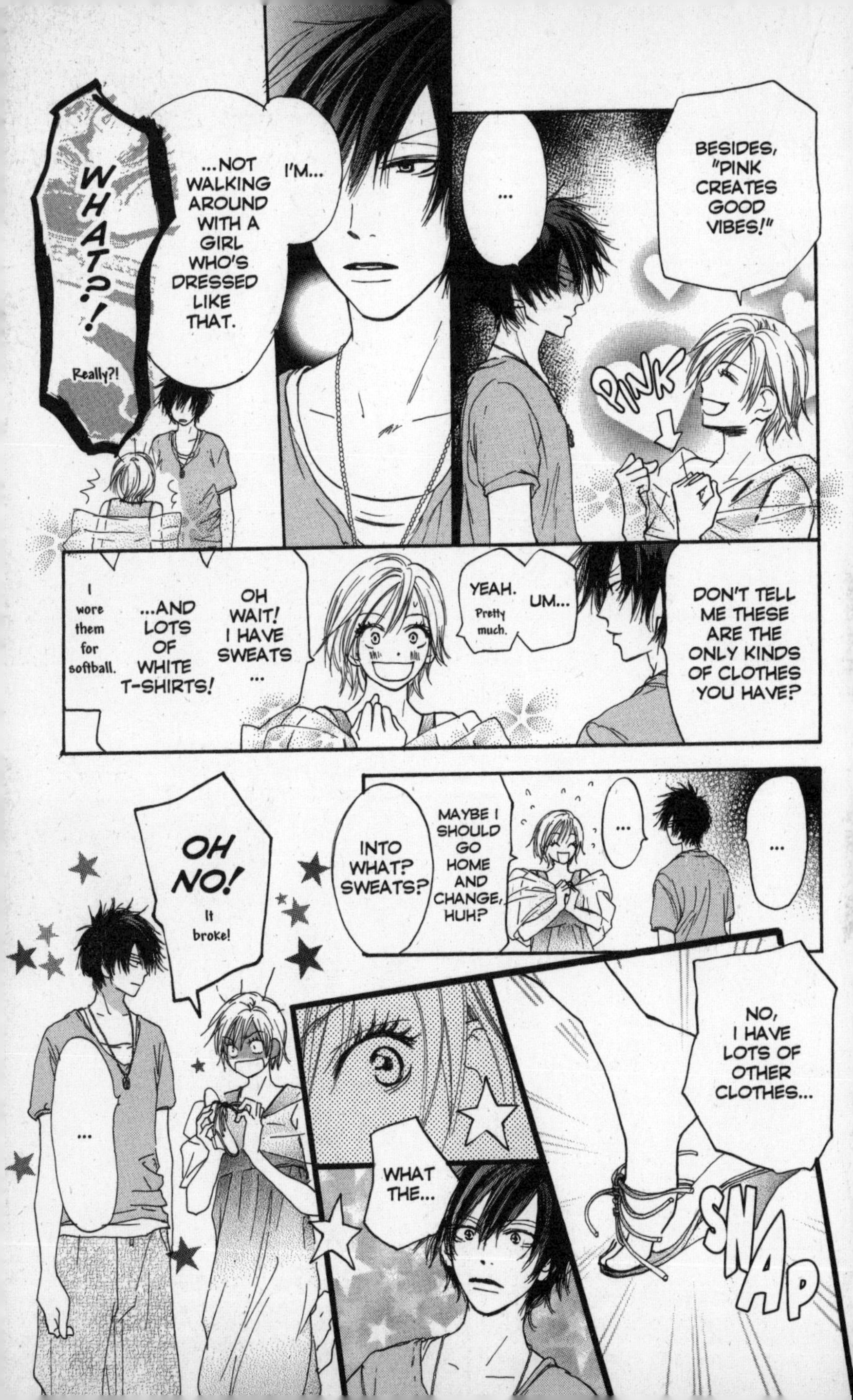
BESIDES, "PINK CREATES GOOD VIBES!"
PINK
...
I'M...
...NOT WALKING AROUND WITH A GIRL WHO'S DRESSED LIKE THAT.
WHAT?!
Really?!
DON'T TELL ME THESE ARE THE ONLY KINDS OF CLOTHES YOU HAVE?
UM...
YEAH.
Pretty much.
OH WAIT! I HAVE SWEATS...
...AND LOTS OF WHITE T-SHIRTS!
I wore them for softball.
...
...
MAYBE I SHOULD GO HOME AND CHANGE, HUH?
INTO WHAT? SWEATS?
NO, I HAVE LOTS OF OTHER CLOTHES...
SNAP
WHAT THE...
OH NO!
It broke!
...

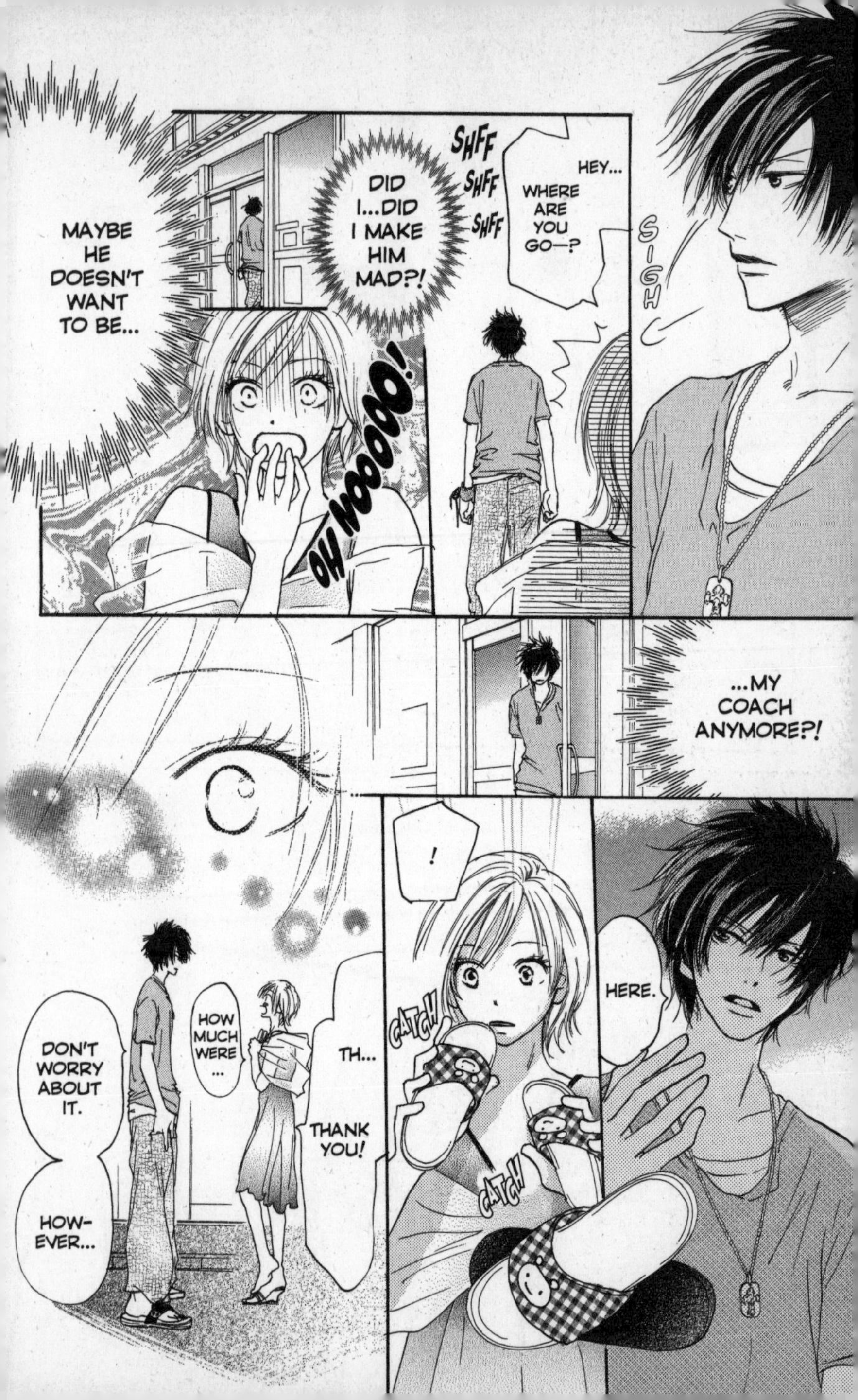
SIGH
HEY...
WHERE ARE YOU GO—?
SHFF
SHFF
SHFF
DID I...DID I MAKE HIM MAD?!
OH NOOOOO!
MAYBE HE DOESN'T WANT TO BE...
...MY COACH ANYMORE?!
HERE.
!
CATCH
CATCH
TH...
THANK YOU!
HOW MUCH WERE ...
DON'T WORRY ABOUT IT.
HOW-EVER...

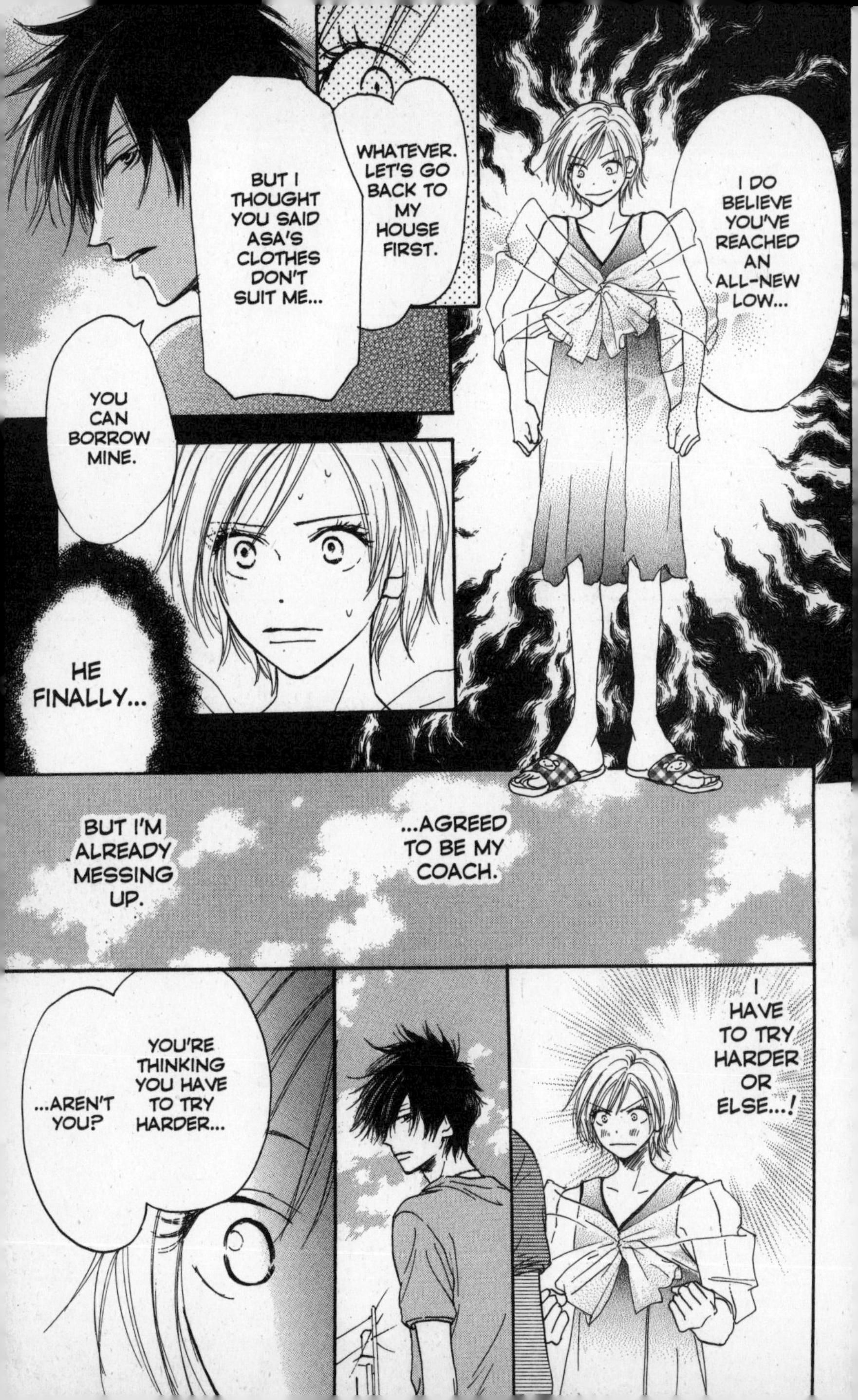
I DO BELIEVE YOU'VE REACHED AN ALL-NEW LOW...
WHATEVER. LET'S GO BACK TO MY HOUSE FIRST.
BUT I THOUGHT YOU SAID ASA'S CLOTHES DON'T SUIT ME...
YOU CAN BORROW MINE.
HE FINALLY...
...AGREED TO BE MY COACH.
BUT I'M ALREADY MESSING UP.
I HAVE TO TRY HARDER OR ELSE...!
YOU'RE THINKING YOU HAVE TO TRY HARDER...
...AREN'T YOU?

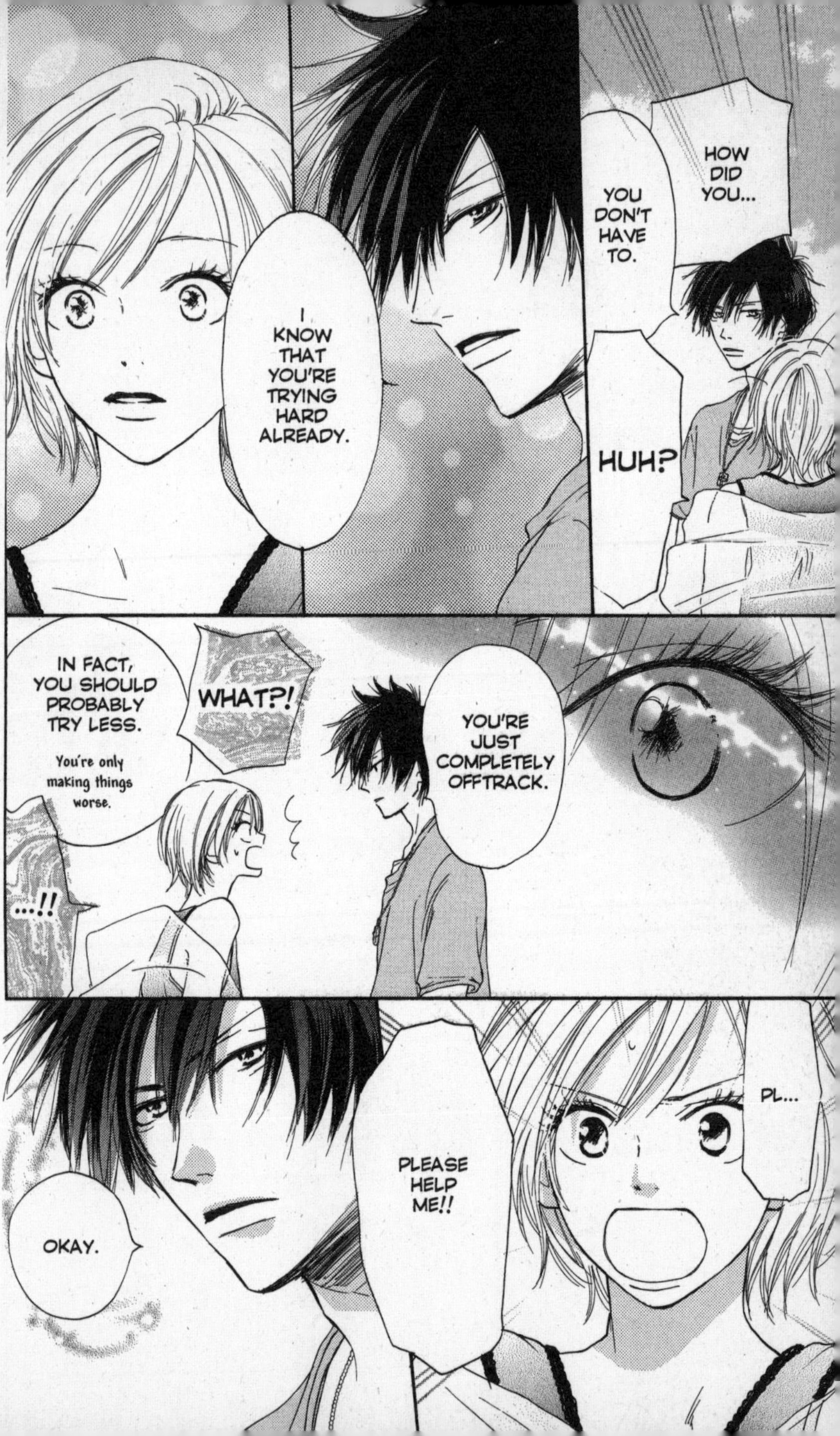
HOW DID YOU...
YOU DON'T HAVE TO.
HUH?
I KNOW THAT YOU'RE TRYING HARD ALREADY.
YOU'RE JUST COMPLETELY OFFTRACK.
WHAT?!
IN FACT, YOU SHOULD PROBABLY TRY LESS.
You're only making things worse.
...!!
PL...
PLEASE HELP ME!!
OKAY.

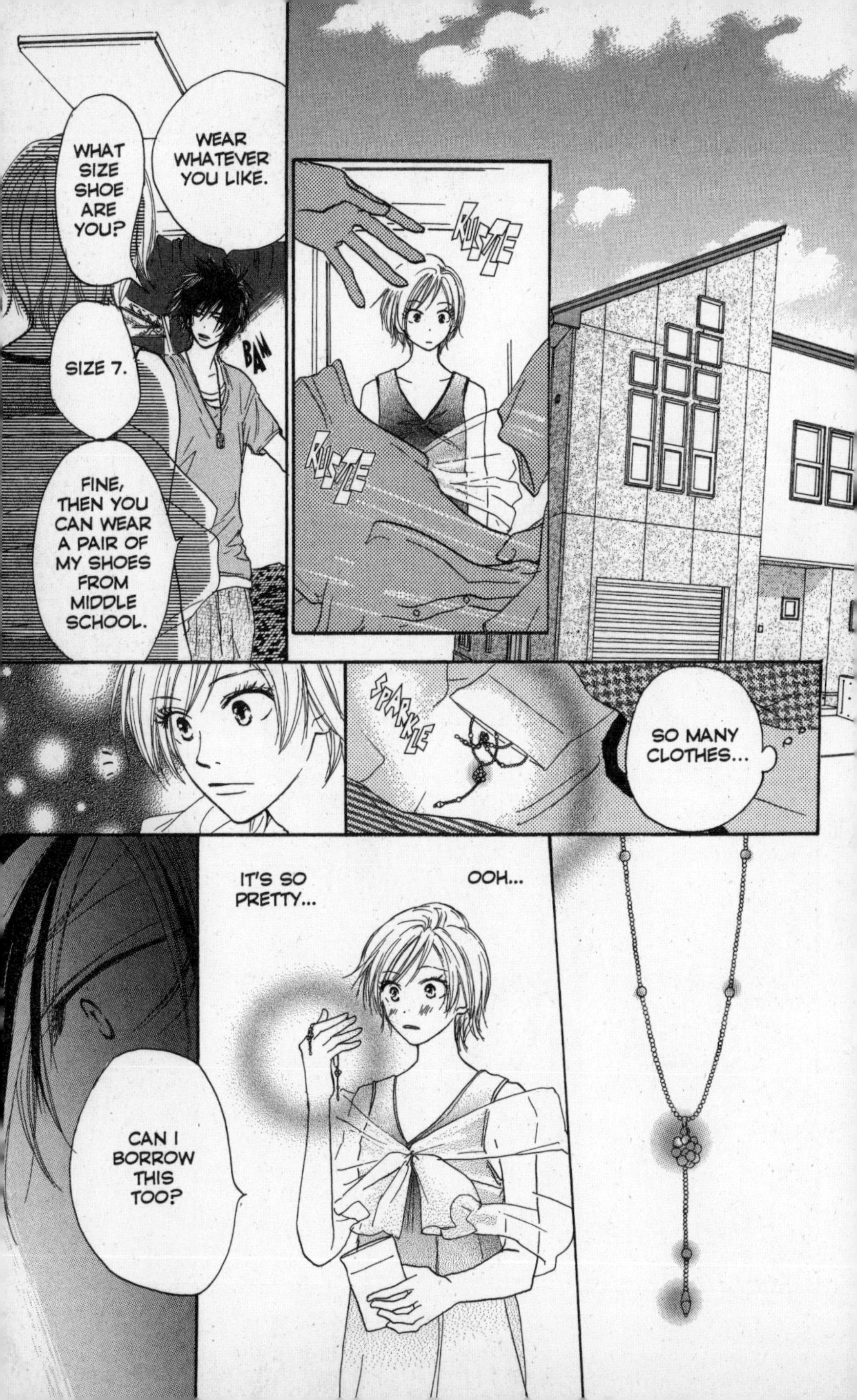
RUSTLE
RUSTLE
WEAR WHATEVER YOU LIKE.
WHAT SIZE SHOE ARE YOU?
BAM
SIZE 7.
FINE, THEN YOU CAN WEAR A PAIR OF MY SHOES FROM MIDDLE SCHOOL.
SO MANY CLOTHES...
SPARKLE
OOH...
IT'S SO PRETTY...
CAN I BORROW THIS TOO?

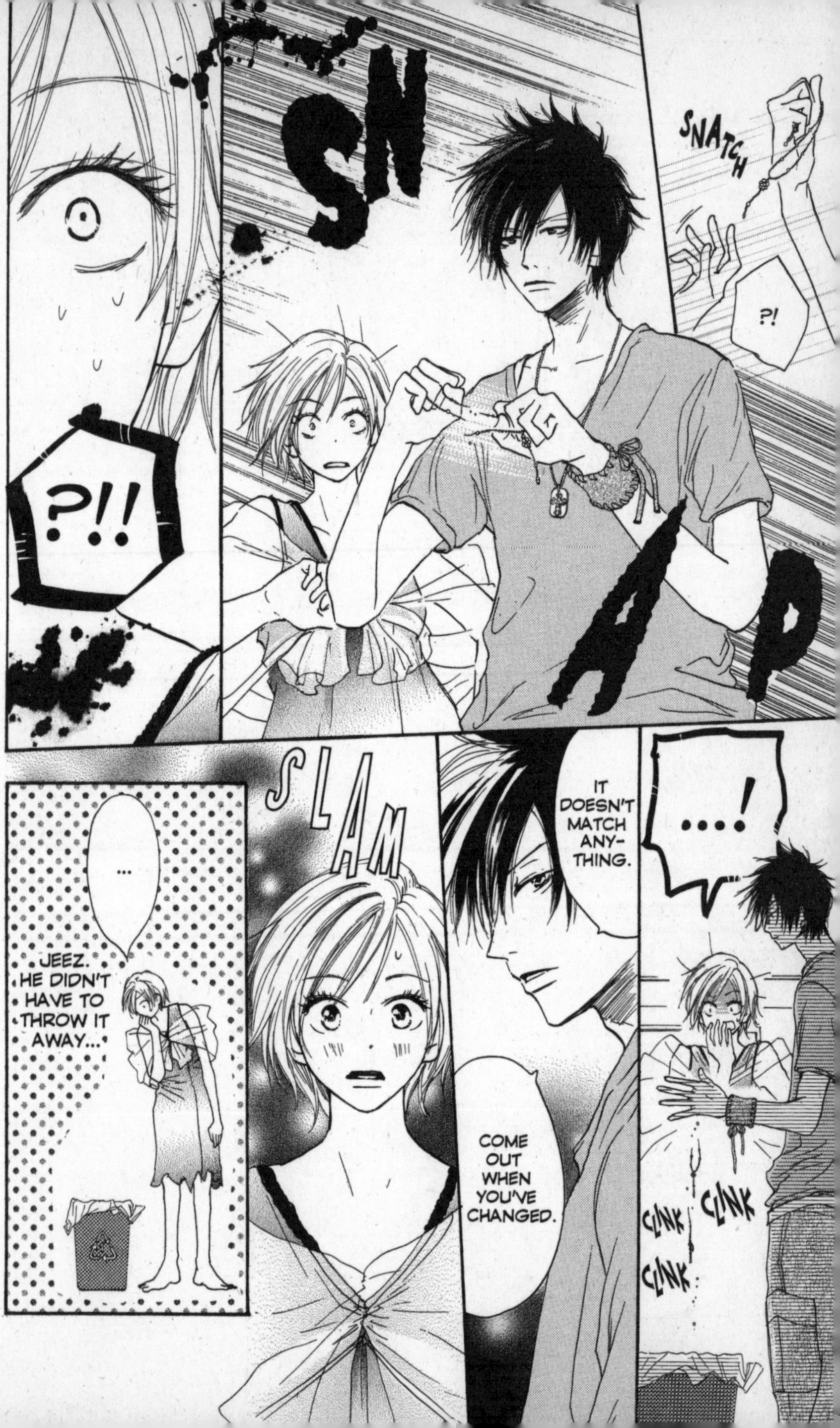
SNATCH
?!
SNAP
?!!
...!
CLINK
CLINK
CLINK
IT DOESN'T MATCH ANYTHING.
COME OUT WHEN YOU'VE CHANGED.
SLAM
...
JEEZ. HE DIDN'T HAVE TO THROW IT AWAY...

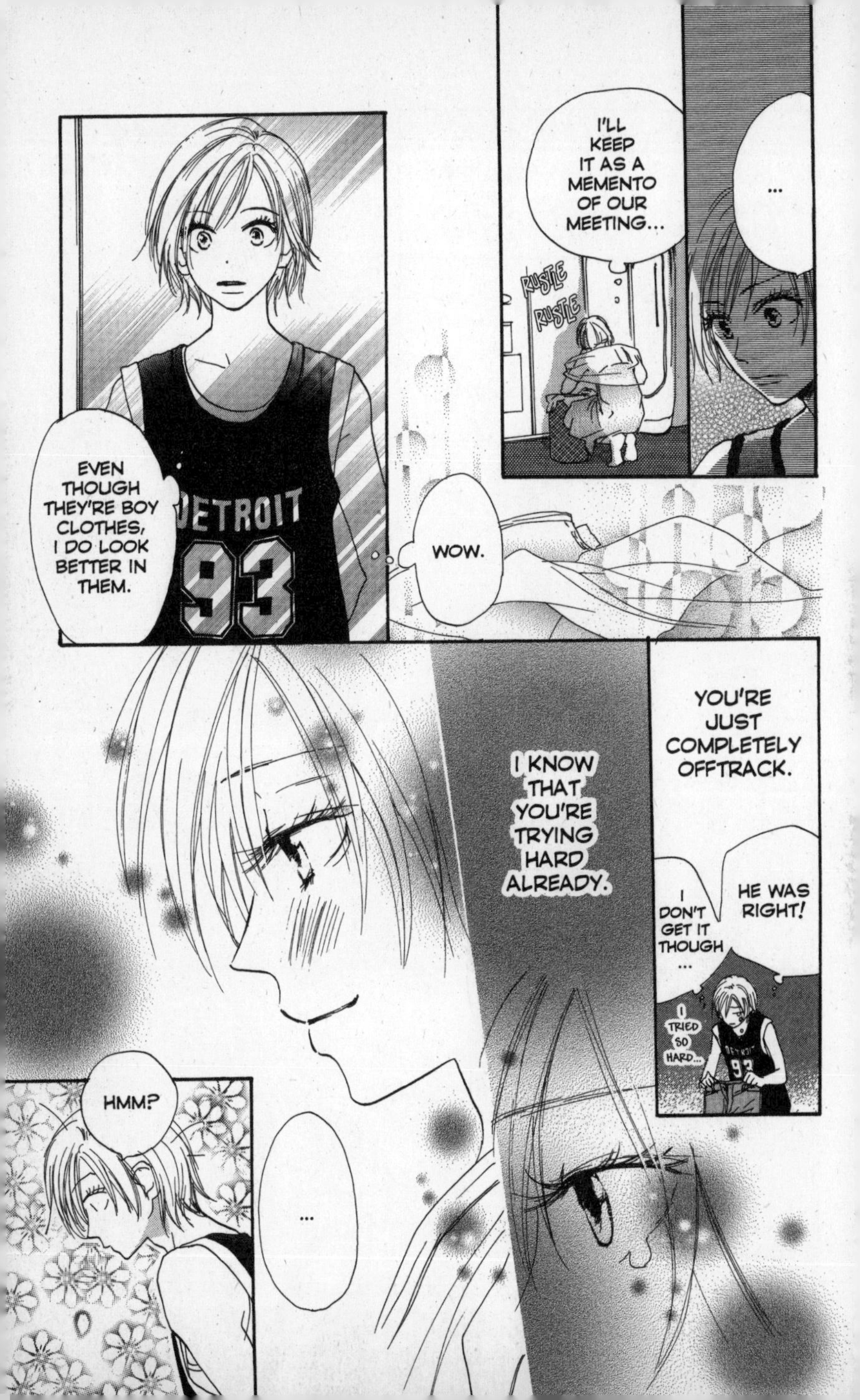
...
I'LL KEEP IT AS A MEMENTO OF OUR MEETING...
RUSTLE
RUSTLE
WOW.
EVEN THOUGH THEY'RE BOY CLOTHES, I DO LOOK BETTER IN THEM.
YOU'RE JUST COMPLETELY OFFTRACK.
HE WAS RIGHT!
I DON'T GET IT THOUGH...
I TRIED SO HARD...
I KNOW THAT YOU'RE TRYING HARD ALREADY.
...
HMM?

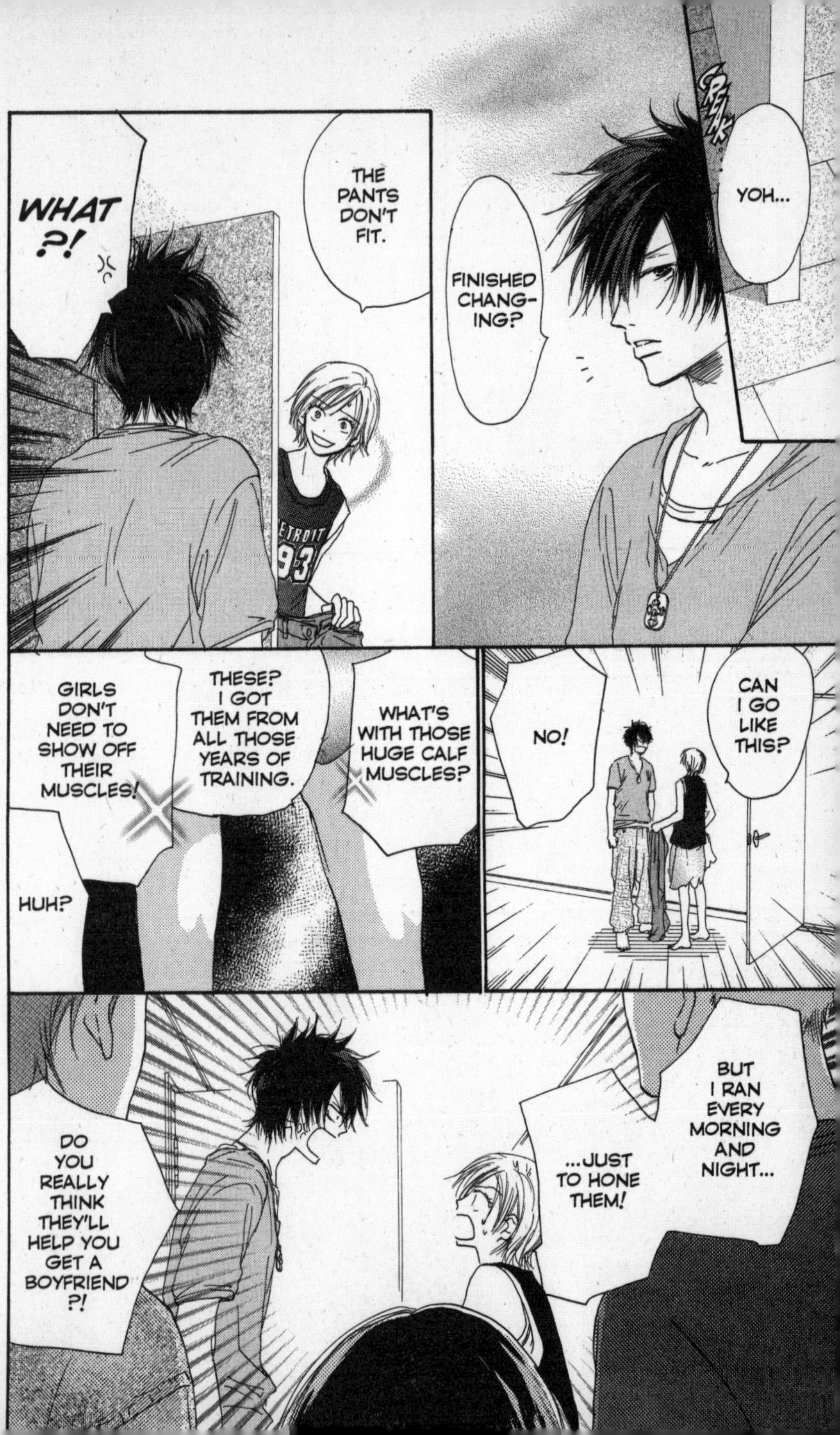
CREAK
YOH...
FINISHED CHANGING?
THE PANTS DON'T FIT.
WHAT?!
CAN I GO LIKE THIS?
NO!
WHAT'S WITH THOSE HUGE CALF MUSCLES?
THESE? I GOT THEM FROM ALL THOSE YEARS OF TRAINING.
GIRLS DON'T NEED TO SHOW OFF THEIR MUSCLES!
HUH?
BUT I RAN EVERY MORNING AND NIGHT...
...JUST TO HONE THEM!
DO YOU REALLY THINK THEY'LL HELP YOU GET A BOYFRIEND?!

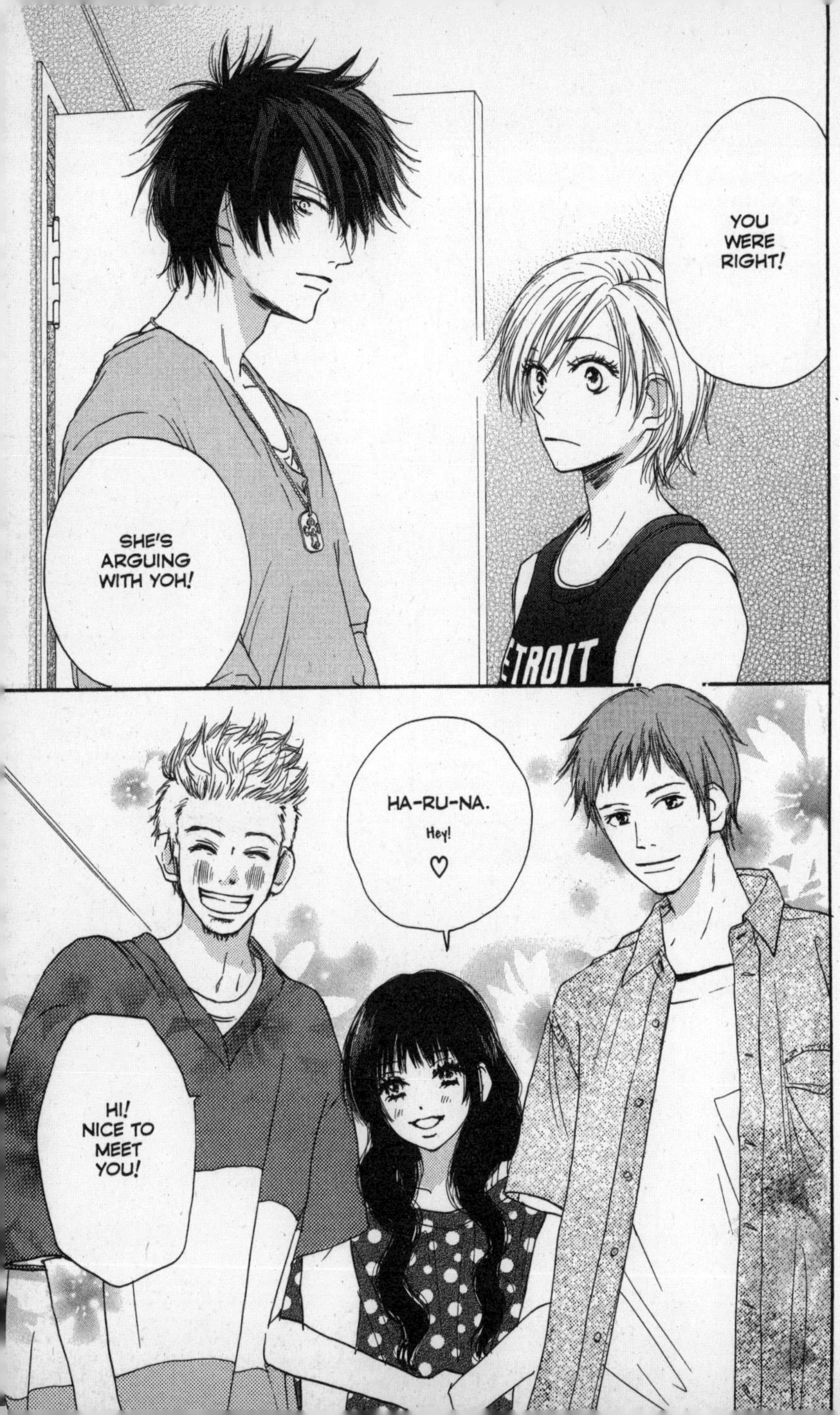
YOU WERE RIGHT!
SHE'S ARGUING WITH YOH!
HA-RU-NA.
Hey! ♡
HI! NICE TO MEET YOU!
ETROIT

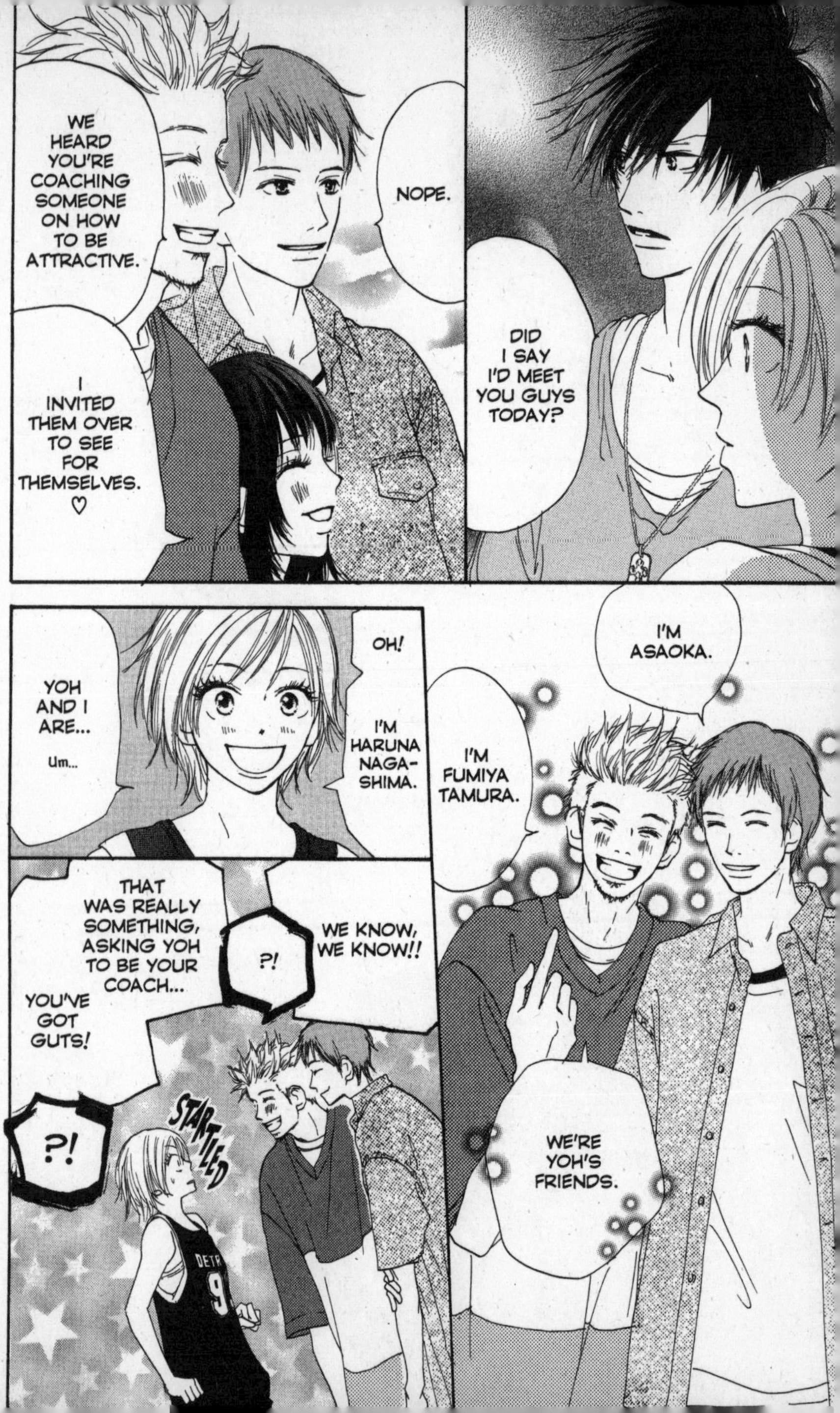
DID I SAY I'D MEET YOU GUYS TODAY?
NOPE.
WE HEARD YOU'RE COACHING SOMEONE ON HOW TO BE ATTRACTIVE.
I INVITED THEM OVER TO SEE FOR THEMSELVES. ♡
I'M ASAOKA.
I'M FUMIYA TAMURA.
WE'RE YOH'S FRIENDS.
OH!
I'M HARUNA NAGA-SHIMA.
YOH AND I ARE...
Um...
WE KNOW, WE KNOW!!
?!
THAT WAS REALLY SOMETHING, ASKING YOH TO BE YOUR COACH...
YOU'VE GOT GUTS!
STARTLED
?!

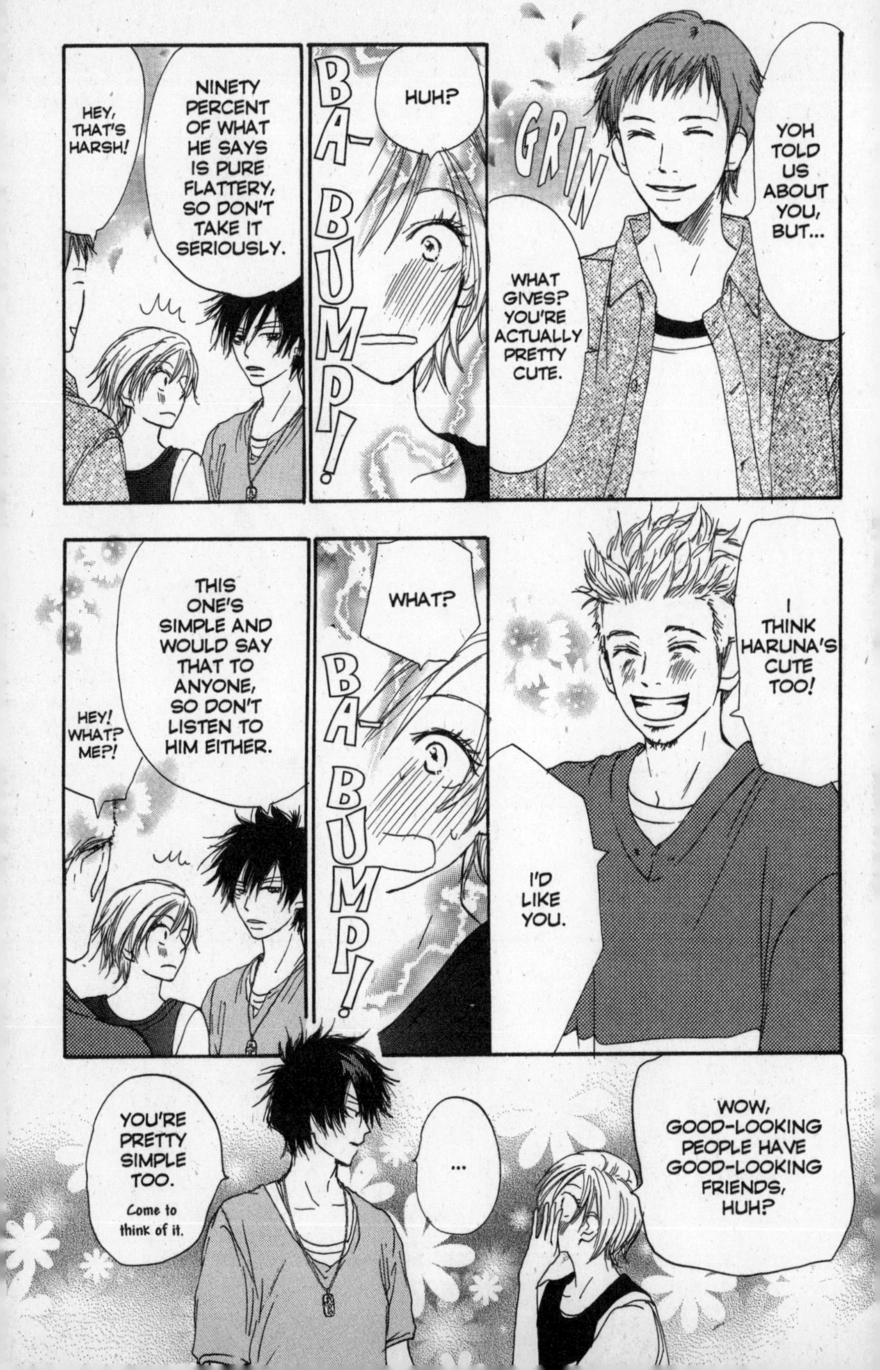
YOH TOLD US ABOUT YOU, BUT...
GRIN
WHAT GIVES? YOU'RE ACTUALLY PRETTY CUTE.
HUH?
BA-BUMP!
NINETY PERCENT OF WHAT HE SAYS IS PURE FLATTERY, SO DON'T TAKE IT SERIOUSLY.
HEY, THAT'S HARSH!
I THINK HARUNA'S CUTE TOO!
I'D LIKE YOU.
WHAT?
BA-BUMP!
THIS ONE'S SIMPLE AND WOULD SAY THAT TO ANYONE, SO DON'T LISTEN TO HIM EITHER.
HEY! WHAT? ME?!
WOW, GOOD-LOOKING PEOPLE HAVE GOOD-LOOKING FRIENDS, HUH?
...
YOU'RE PRETTY SIMPLE TOO.
Come to think of it.

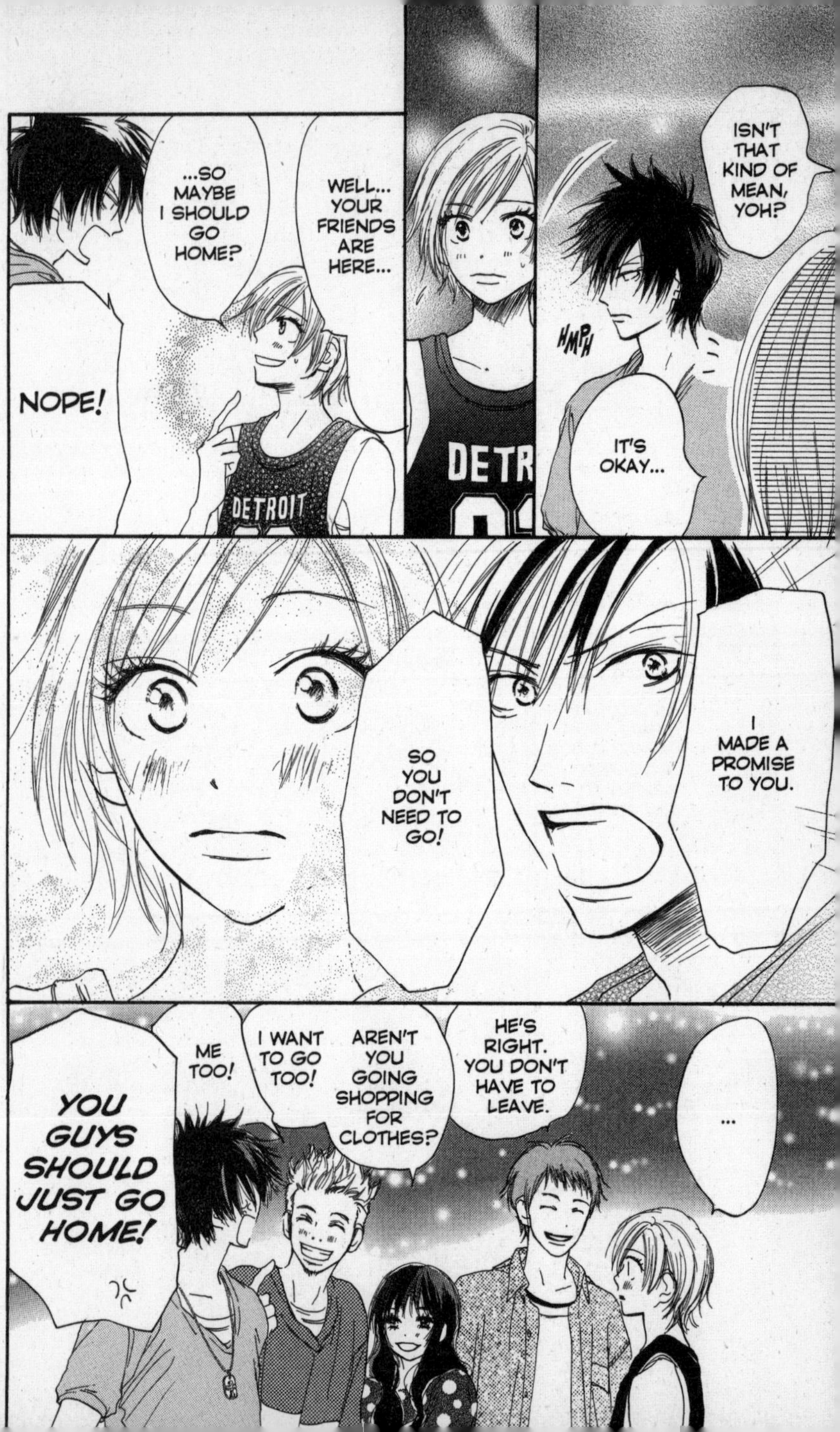
ISN'T THAT KIND OF MEAN, YOH?
HMPH
IT'S OKAY...
WELL... YOUR FRIENDS ARE HERE...
...SO MAYBE I SHOULD GO HOME?
NOPE!
DETROIT
I MADE A PROMISE TO YOU.
SO YOU DON'T NEED TO GO!
...
HE'S RIGHT. YOU DON'T HAVE TO LEAVE.
AREN'T YOU GOING SHOPPING FOR CLOTHES?
I WANT TO GO TOO!
ME TOO!
YOU GUYS SHOULD JUST GO HOME!

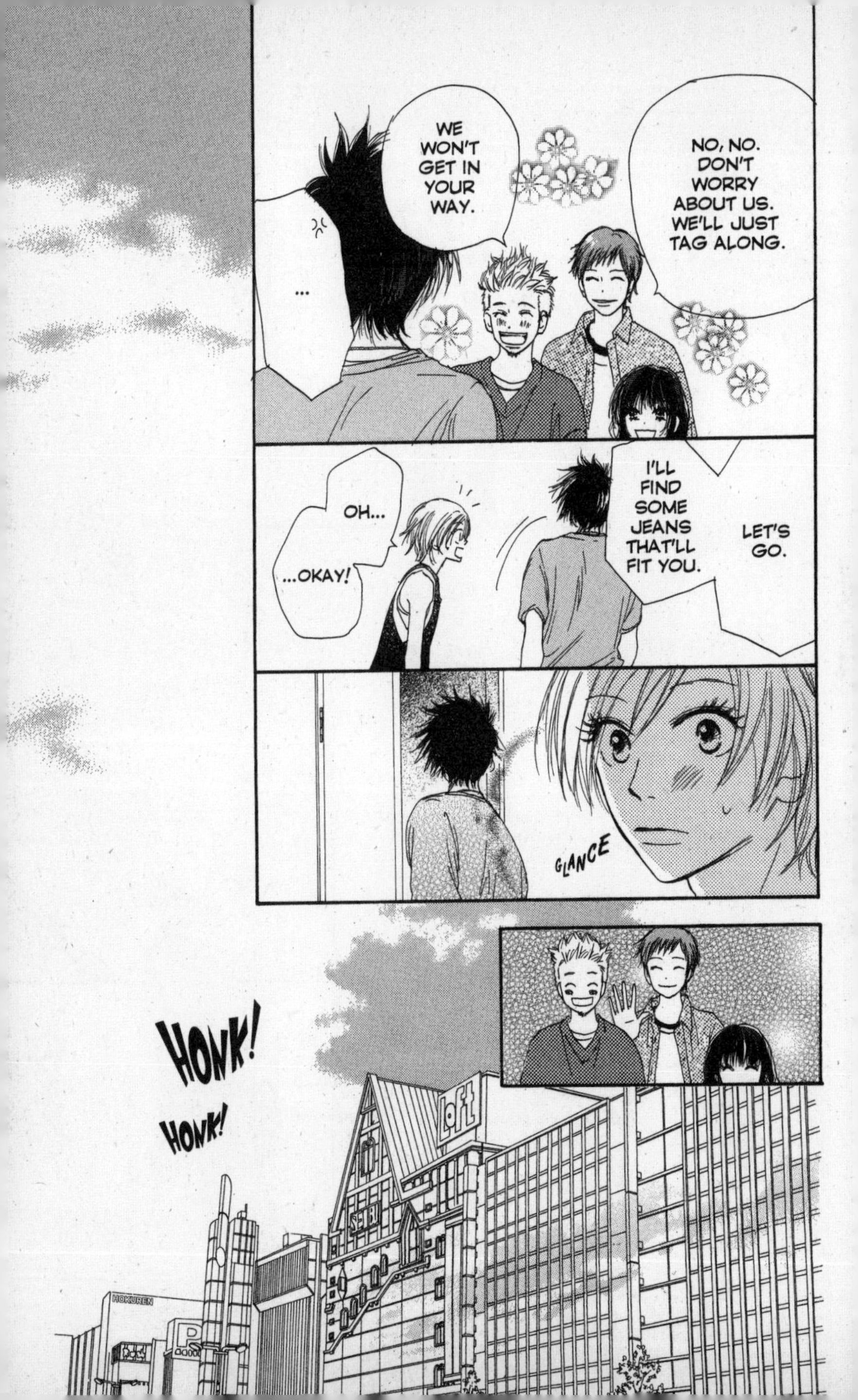
NO, NO. DON'T WORRY ABOUT US. WE'LL JUST TAG ALONG.
WE WON'T GET IN YOUR WAY.
...
I'LL FIND SOME JEANS THAT'LL FIT YOU.
LET'S GO.
OH...
...OKAY!
GLANCE
HONK!
HONK!
Loft
SEIBU
HOKUREN

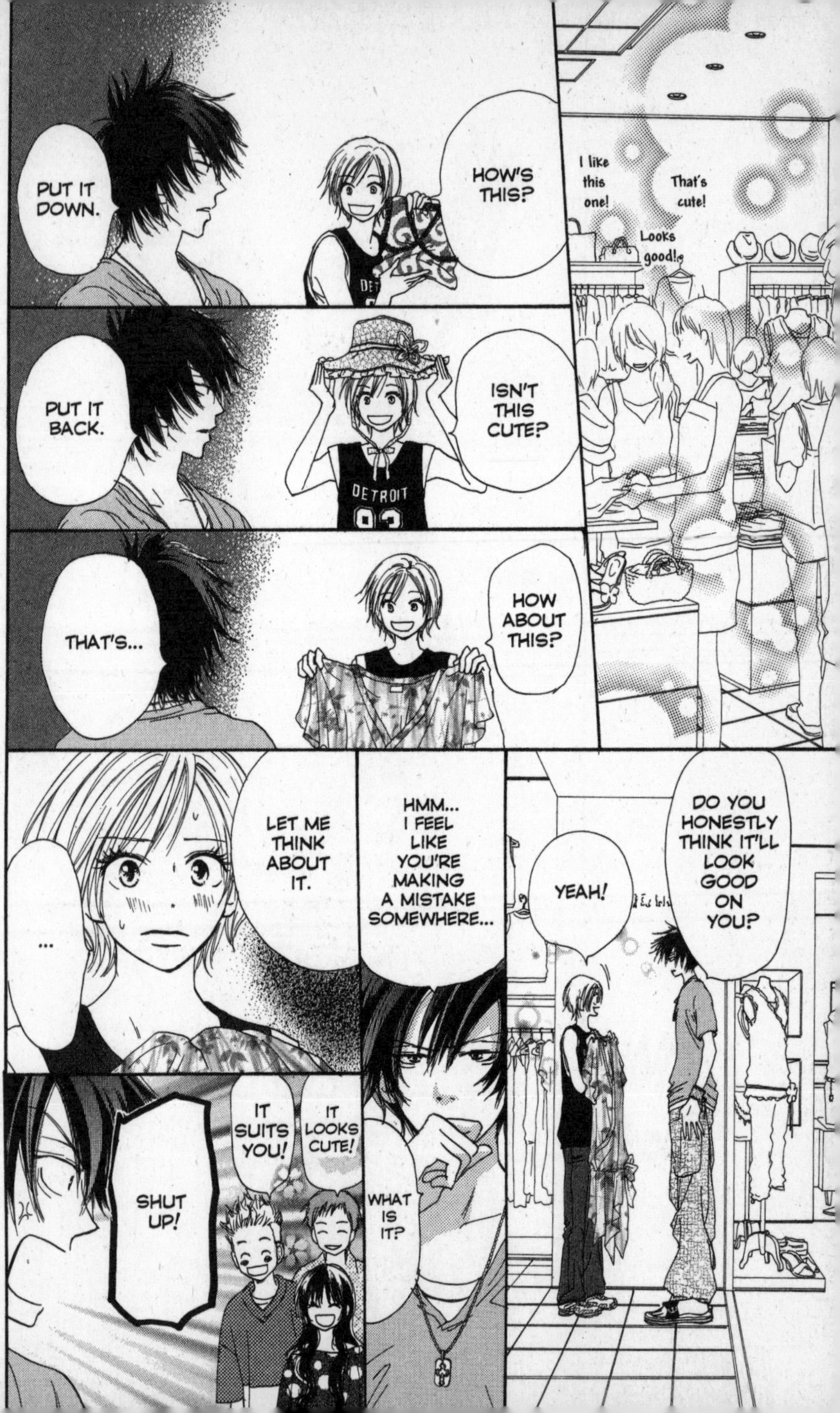

That's cute!
I like this one!
Looks good!
HOW'S THIS?
PUT IT DOWN.
ISN'T THIS CUTE?
PUT IT BACK.
HOW ABOUT THIS?
THAT'S...
DO YOU HONESTLY THINK IT'LL LOOK GOOD ON YOU?
YEAH!
HMM... I FEEL LIKE YOU'RE MAKING A MISTAKE SOMEWHERE...
WHAT IS IT?
LET ME THINK ABOUT IT.
...
IT LOOKS CUTE!
IT SUITS YOU!
SHUT UP!

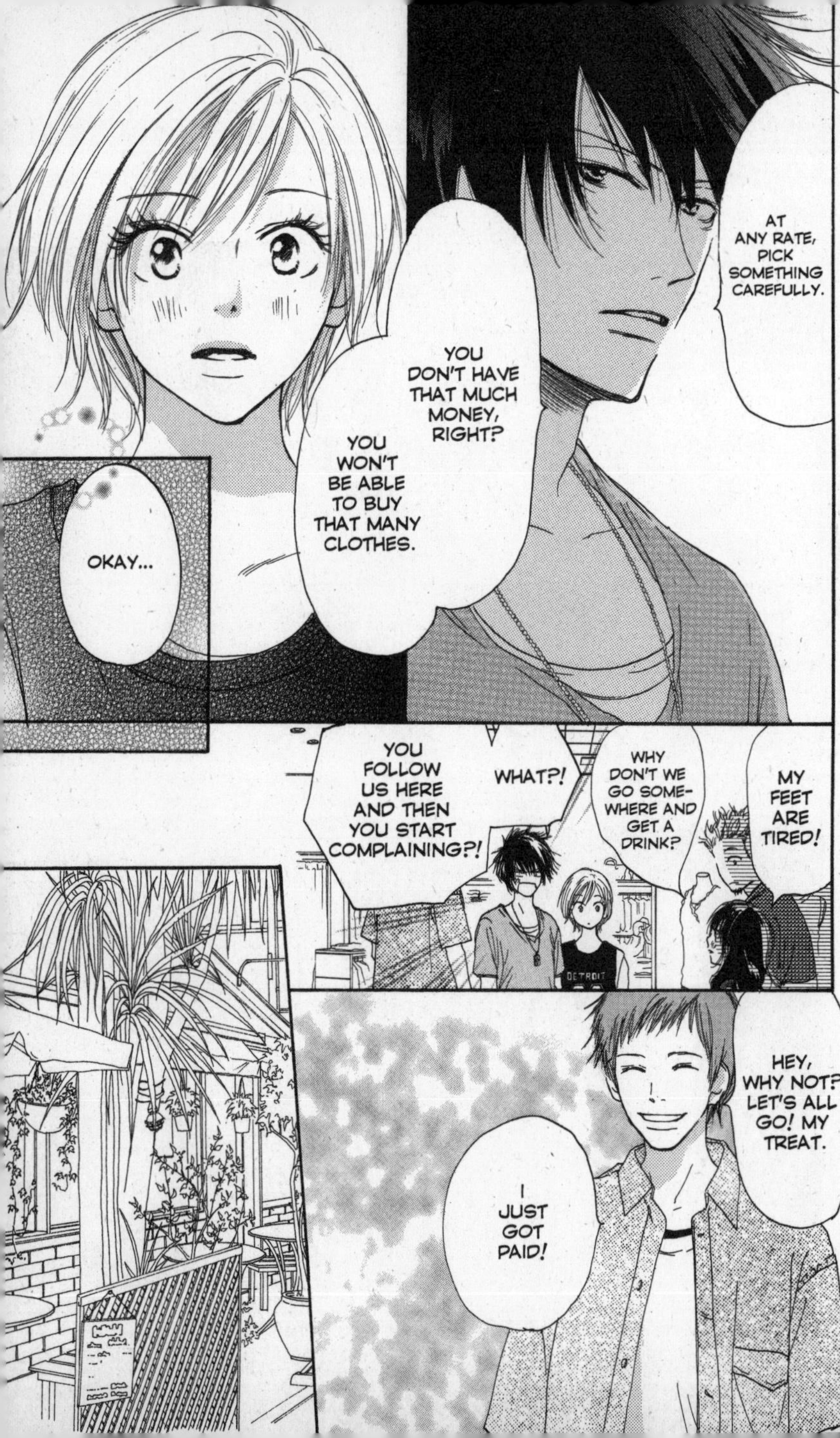
AT ANY RATE, PICK SOMETHING CAREFULLY.
YOU DON'T HAVE THAT MUCH MONEY, RIGHT?
YOU WON'T BE ABLE TO BUY THAT MANY CLOTHES.
OKAY...
MY FEET ARE TIRED!
WHY DON'T WE GO SOME-WHERE AND GET A DRINK?
WHAT?!
YOU FOLLOW US HERE AND THEN YOU START COMPLAINING?!
DETROIT
HEY, WHY NOT? LET'S ALL GO! MY TREAT.
I JUST GOT PAID!

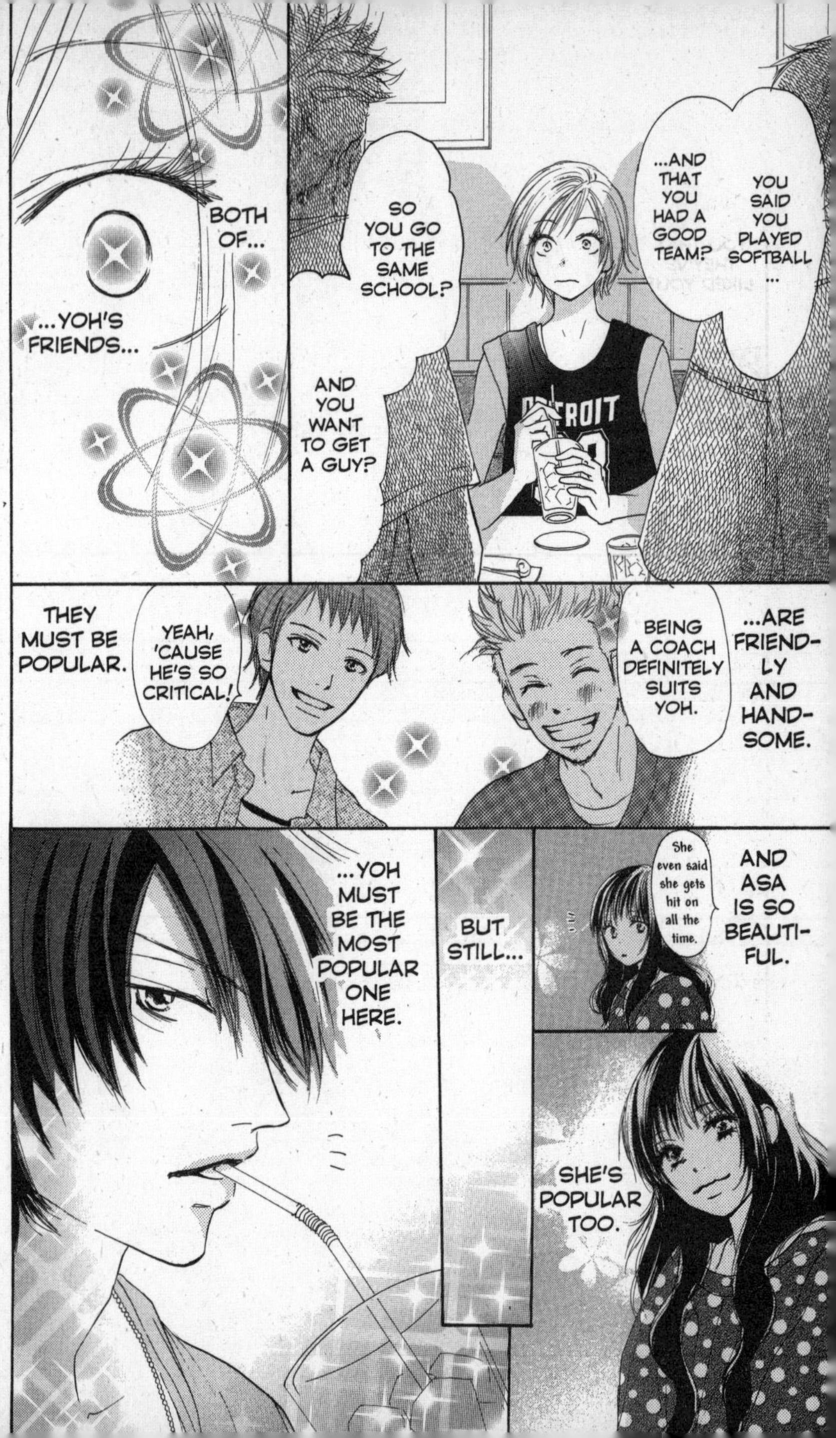
YOU SAID YOU PLAYED SOFTBALL ...
...AND THAT YOU HAD A GOOD TEAM?
SO YOU GO TO THE SAME SCHOOL?
AND YOU WANT TO GET A GUY?
BOTH OF...
...YOH'S FRIENDS...
...ARE FRIENDLY AND HANDSOME.
BEING A COACH DEFINITELY SUITS YOH.
YEAH, 'CAUSE HE'S SO CRITICAL!
THEY MUST BE POPULAR.
AND ASA IS SO BEAUTIFUL.
She even said she gets hit on all the time.
SHE'S POPULAR TOO.
BUT STILL...
...YOH MUST BE THE MOST POPULAR ONE HERE.

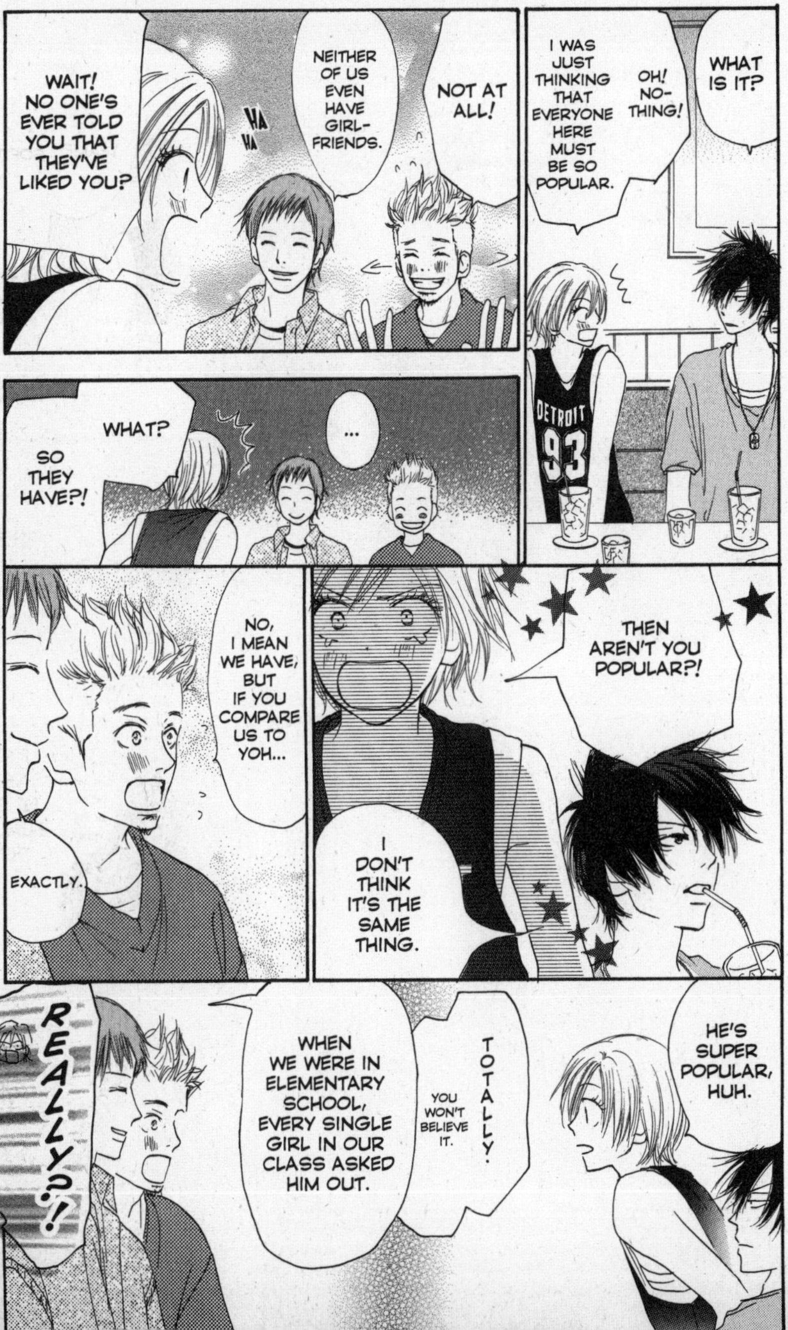
WHAT IS IT?
OH! NO-THING!
I WAS JUST THINKING THAT EVERYONE HERE MUST BE SO POPULAR.
NOT AT ALL!
NEITHER OF US EVEN HAVE GIRL-FRIENDS.
HA HA
WAIT! NO ONE'S EVER TOLD YOU THAT THEY'VE LIKED YOU?
...
WHAT?
SO THEY HAVE?!
THEN AREN'T YOU POPULAR?!
I DON'T THINK IT'S THE SAME THING.
NO, I MEAN WE HAVE, BUT IF YOU COMPARE US TO YOH...
EXACTLY.
HE'S SUPER POPULAR, HUH.
TOTALLY.
YOU WON'T BELIEVE IT.
WHEN WE WERE IN ELEMENTARY SCHOOL, EVERY SINGLE GIRL IN OUR CLASS ASKED HIM OUT.
REALLY?!

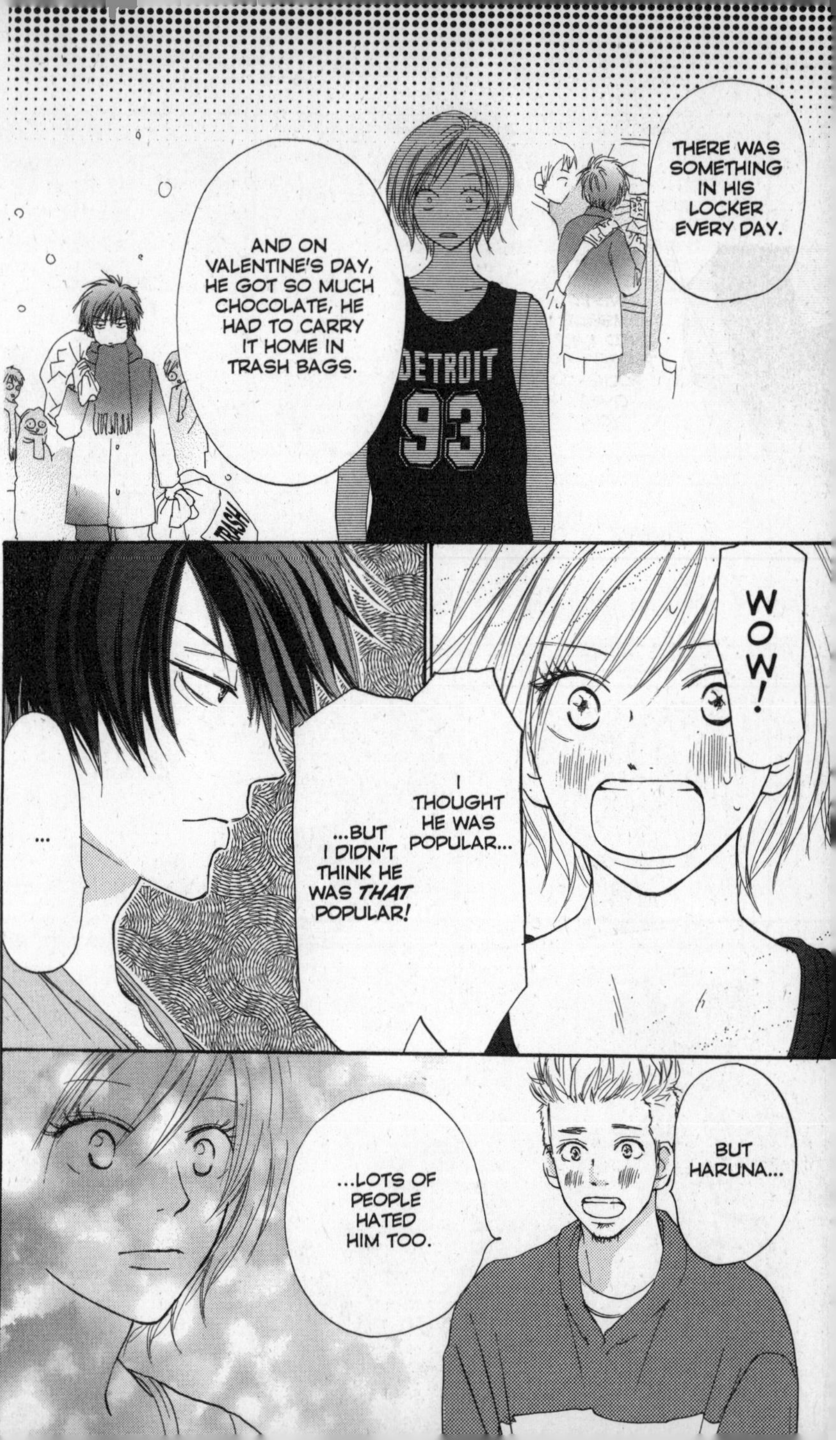
THERE WAS SOMETHING IN HIS LOCKER EVERY DAY.
AND ON VALENTINE'S DAY, HE GOT SO MUCH CHOCOLATE, HE HAD TO CARRY IT HOME IN TRASH BAGS.
DETROIT 93
TRASH
WOW!
I THOUGHT HE WAS POPULAR...
...BUT I DIDN'T THINK HE WAS *THAT* POPULAR!
...
BUT HARUNA...
...LOTS OF PEOPLE HATED HIM TOO.

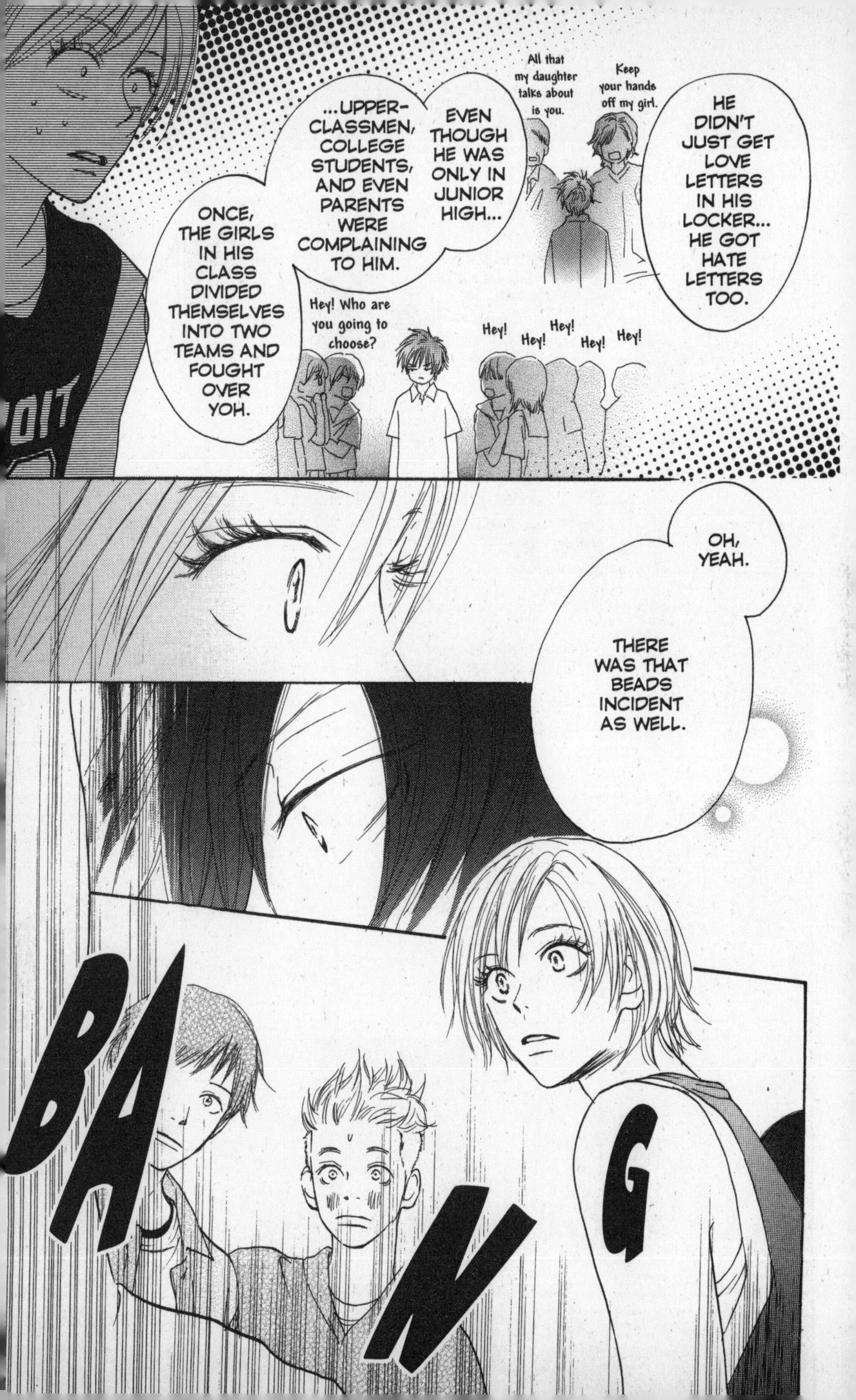
HE DIDN'T JUST GET LOVE LETTERS IN HIS LOCKER... HE GOT HATE LETTERS TOO.
Keep your hands off my girl.
All that my daughter talks about is you.
EVEN THOUGH HE WAS ONLY IN JUNIOR HIGH...
...UPPER-CLASSMEN, COLLEGE STUDENTS, AND EVEN PARENTS WERE COMPLAINING TO HIM.
Hey!
Hey!
Hey!
Hey!
Hey!
Hey! Who are you going to choose?
ONCE, THE GIRLS IN HIS CLASS DIVIDED THEMSELVES INTO TWO TEAMS AND FOUGHT OVER YOH.
OH, YEAH.
THERE WAS THAT BEADS INCIDENT AS WELL.
BANG

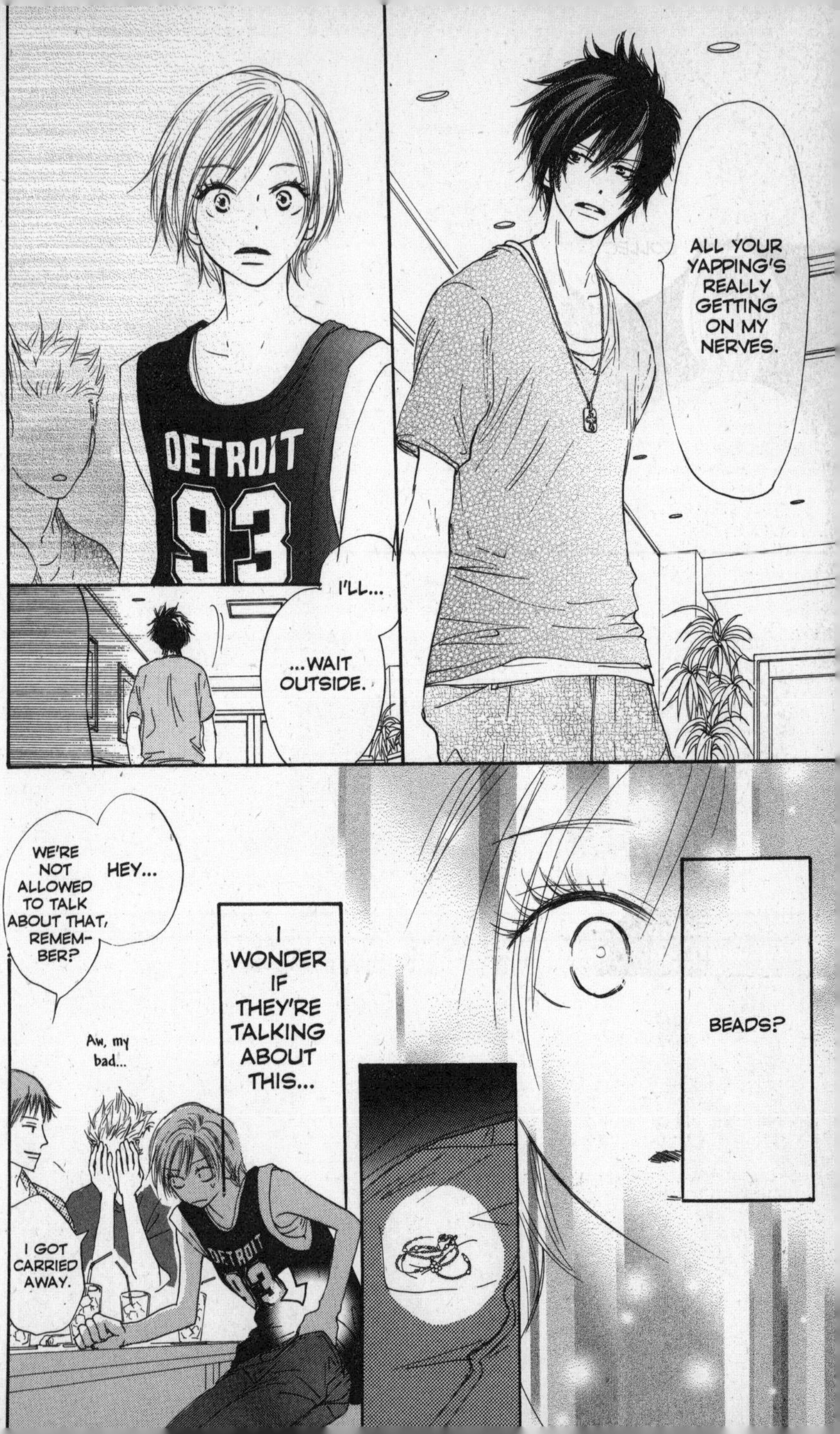
ALL YOUR YAPPING'S REALLY GETTING ON MY NERVES.
I'LL...
...WAIT OUTSIDE.
BEADS?
I WONDER IF THEY'RE TALKING ABOUT THIS...
HEY...
WE'RE NOT ALLOWED TO TALK ABOUT THAT, REMEMBER?
Aw, my bad...
I GOT CARRIED AWAY.

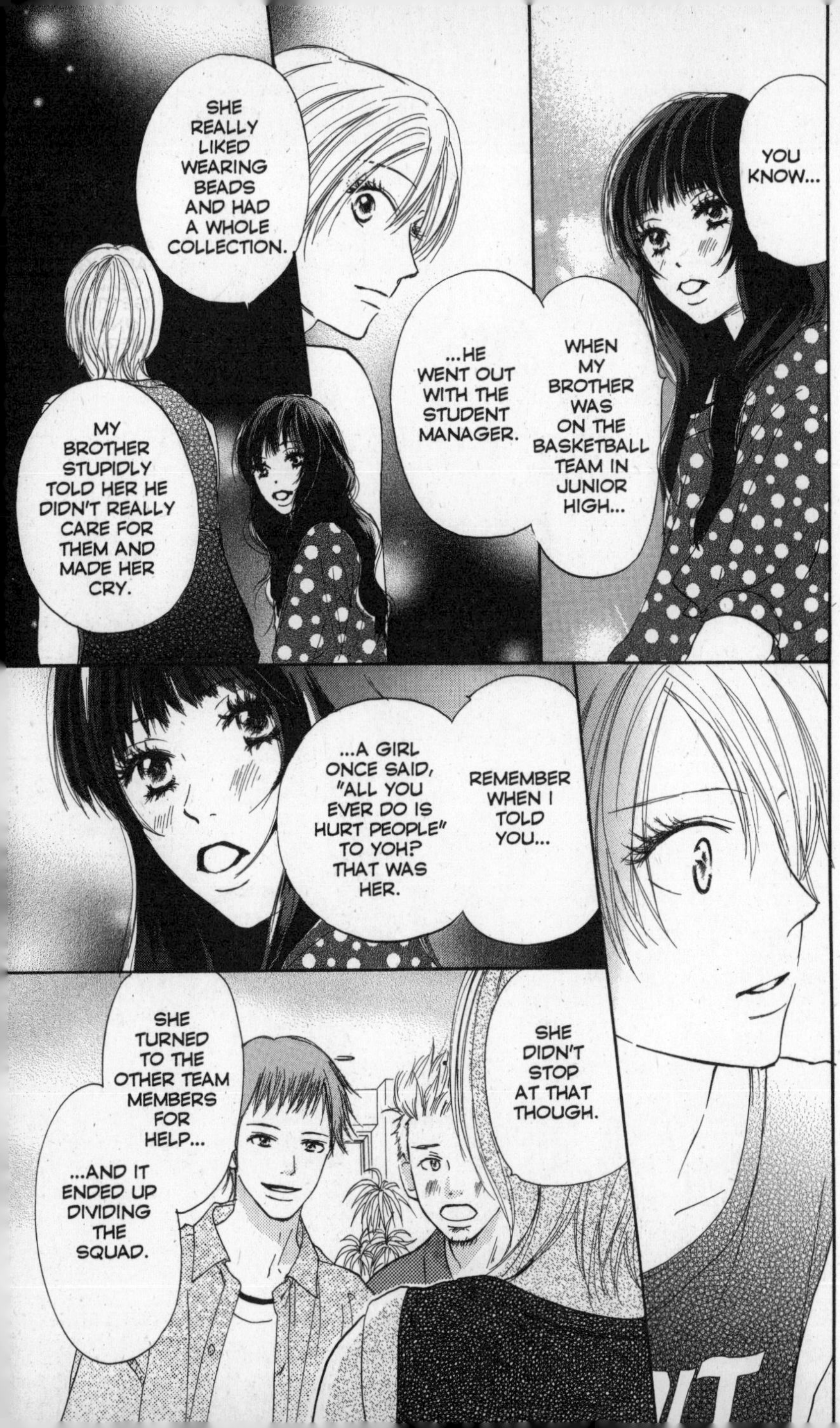

YOU KNOW...
WHEN MY BROTHER WAS ON THE BASKETBALL TEAM IN JUNIOR HIGH...
...HE WENT OUT WITH THE STUDENT MANAGER.
SHE REALLY LIKED WEARING BEADS AND HAD A WHOLE COLLECTION.
MY BROTHER STUPIDLY TOLD HER HE DIDN'T REALLY CARE FOR THEM AND MADE HER CRY.
REMEMBER WHEN I TOLD YOU...
...A GIRL ONCE SAID, "ALL YOU EVER DO IS HURT PEOPLE" TO YOH? THAT WAS HER.
SHE DIDN'T STOP AT THAT THOUGH.
SHE TURNED TO THE OTHER TEAM MEMBERS FOR HELP...
...AND IT ENDED UP DIVIDING THE SQUAD.

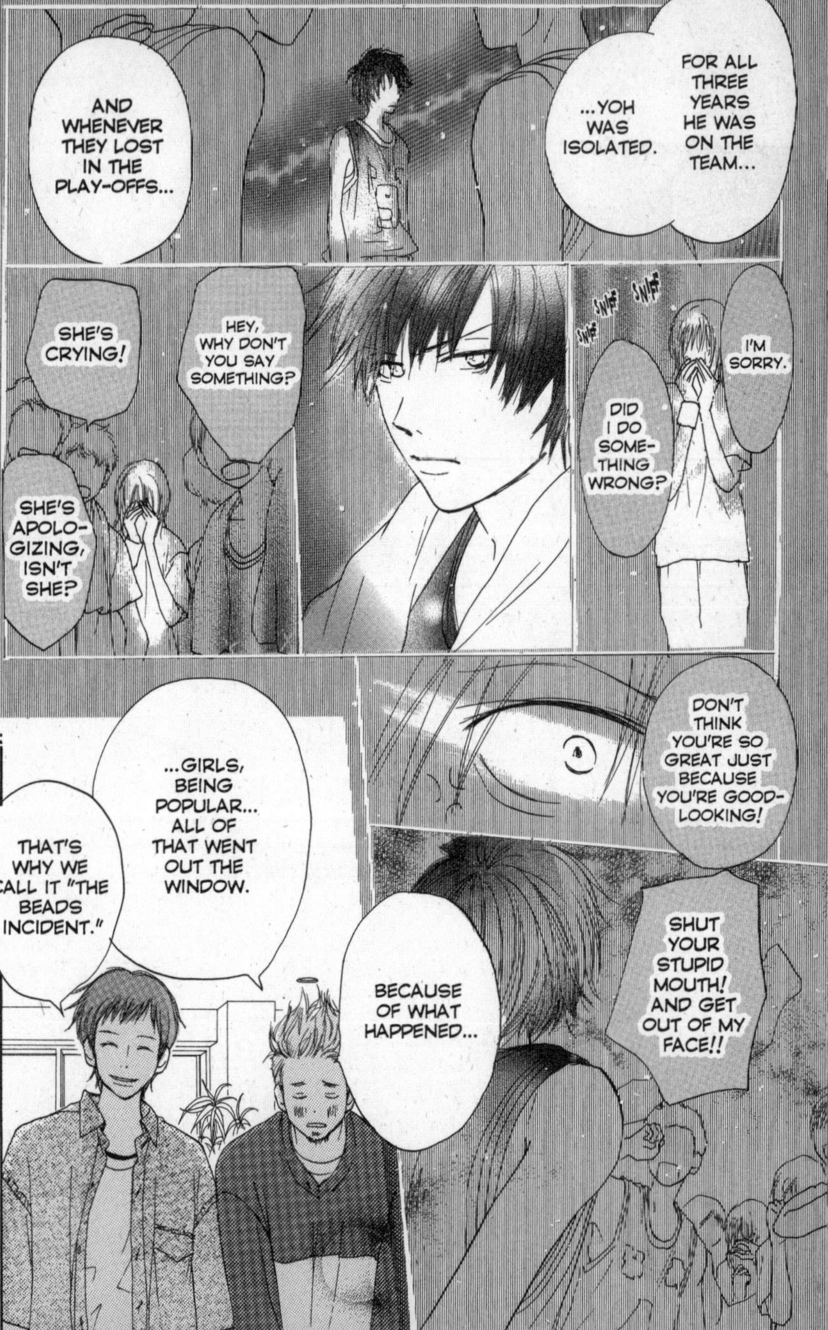
FOR ALL THREE YEARS HE WAS ON THE TEAM...
...YOH WAS ISOLATED.
AND WHENEVER THEY LOST IN THE PLAY-OFFS...
SNIFF SNIFF SNIFF
I'M SORRY.
DID I DO SOME-THING WRONG?
HEY, WHY DON'T YOU SAY SOMETHING?
SHE'S CRYING!
SHE'S APOLO-GIZING, ISN'T SHE?
DON'T THINK YOU'RE SO GREAT JUST BECAUSE YOU'RE GOOD-LOOKING!
SHUT YOUR STUPID MOUTH! AND GET OUT OF MY FACE!!
BECAUSE OF WHAT HAPPENED...
...GIRLS, BEING POPULAR... ALL OF THAT WENT OUT THE WINDOW.
THAT'S WHY WE CALL IT "THE BEADS INCIDENT."

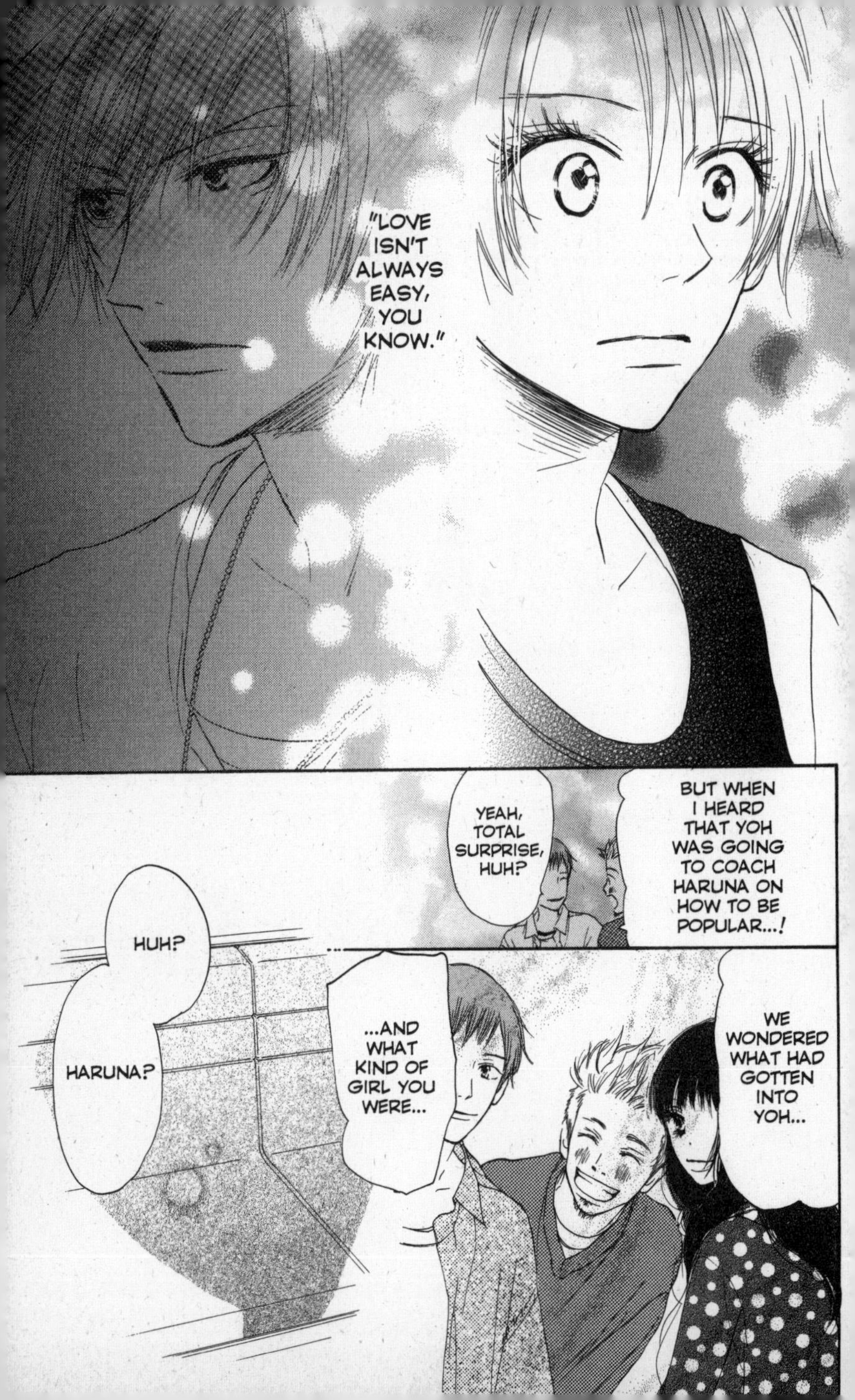
"LOVE ISN'T ALWAYS EASY, YOU KNOW."
BUT WHEN I HEARD THAT YOH WAS GOING TO COACH HARUNA ON HOW TO BE POPULAR...!
YEAH, TOTAL SURPRISE, HUH?
WE WONDERED WHAT HAD GOTTEN INTO YOH...
...AND WHAT KIND OF GIRL YOU WERE...
HUH?
HARUNA?

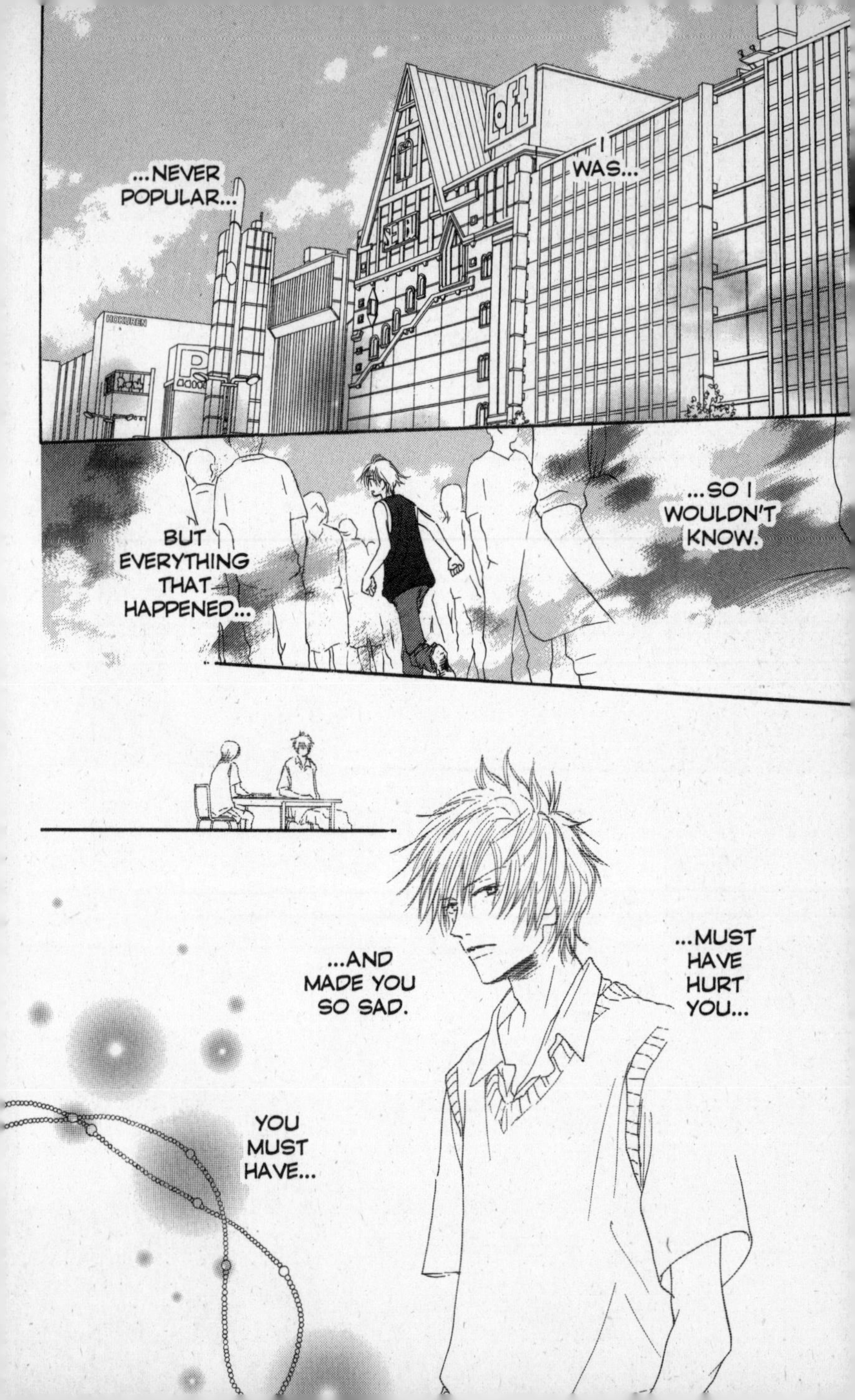
I WAS...
...NEVER POPULAR...
...SO I WOULDN'T KNOW.
BUT EVERYTHING THAT HAPPENED...
...MUST HAVE HURT YOU...
...AND MADE YOU SO SAD.
YOU MUST HAVE...

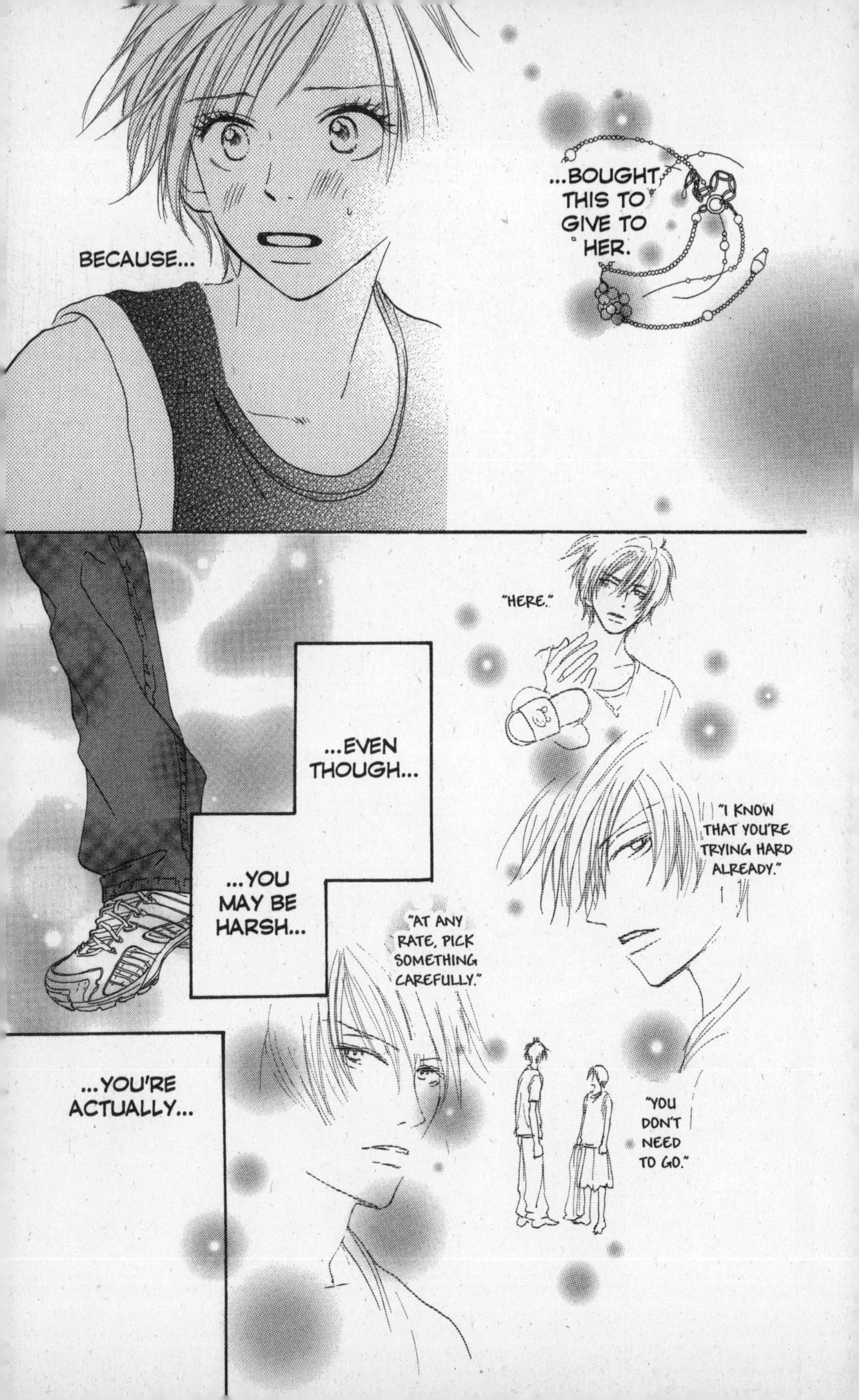
...BOUGHT THIS TO GIVE TO HER.
BECAUSE...
"HERE."
...EVEN THOUGH...
"I KNOW THAT YOU'RE TRYING HARD ALREADY."
...YOU MAY BE HARSH...
"AT ANY RATE, PICK SOMETHING CAREFULLY."
"YOU DON'T NEED TO GO."
...YOU'RE ACTUALLY...

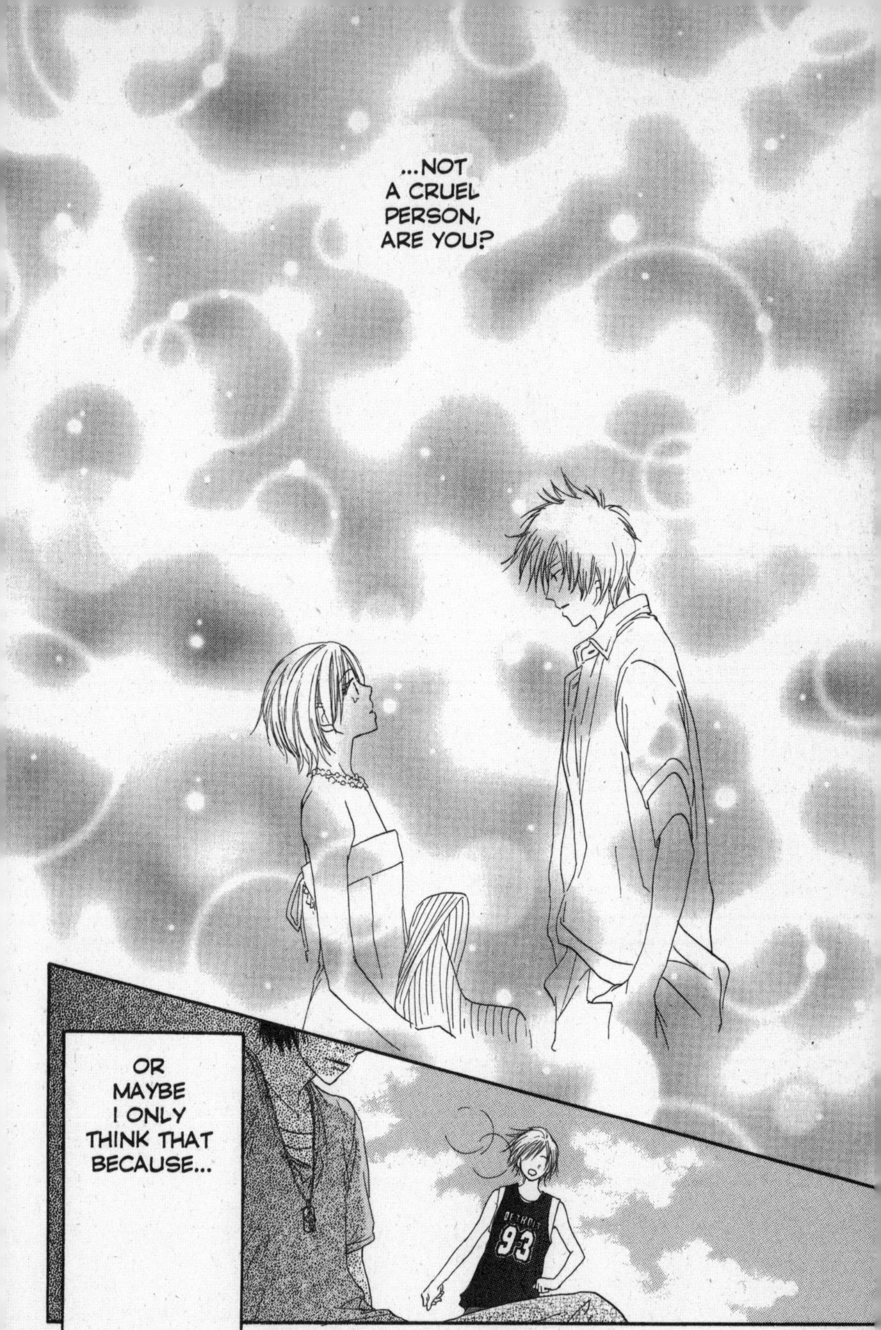
...NOT A CRUEL PERSON, ARE YOU?
OR MAYBE I ONLY THINK THAT BECAUSE...
DETROIT 93

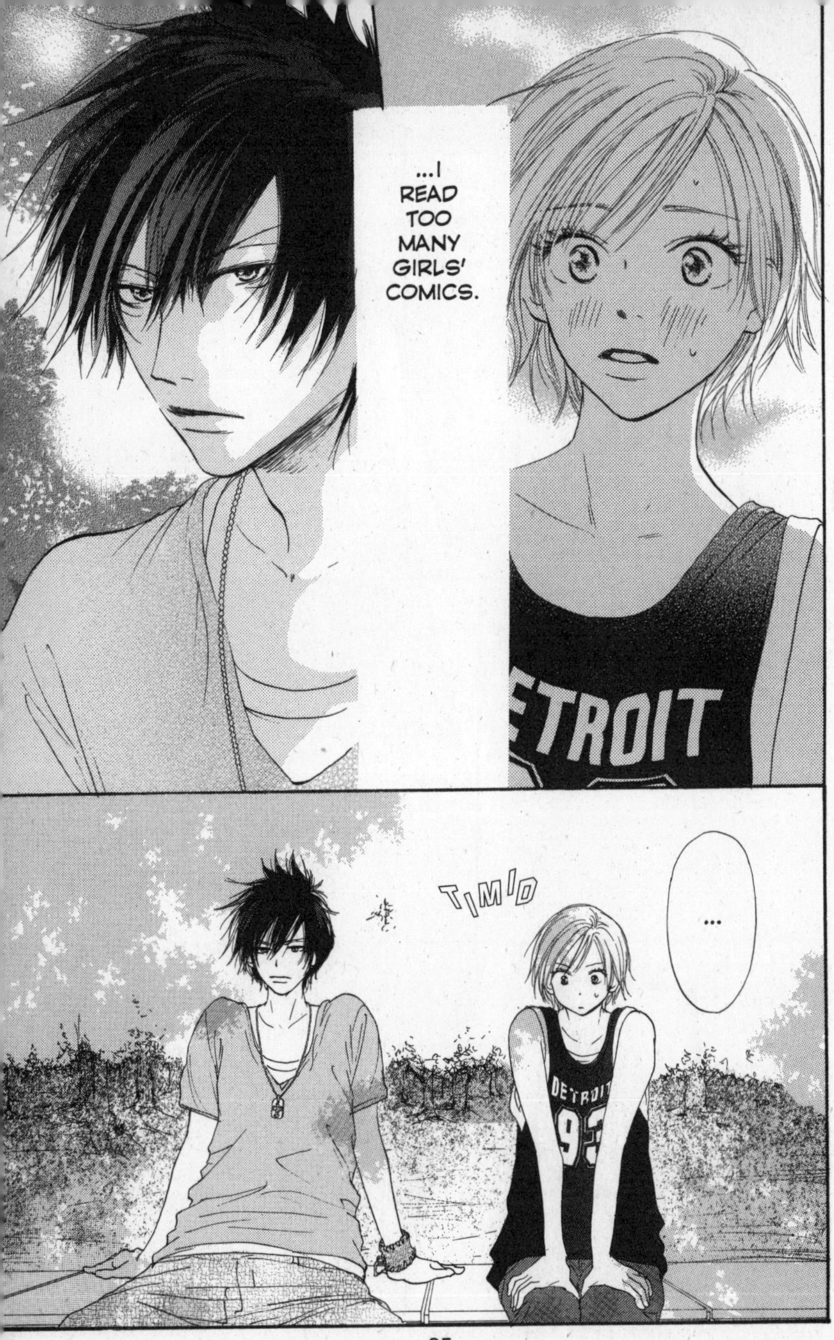
...I READ TOO MANY GIRLS' COMICS.
DETROIT
...
TIMID
DETROIT

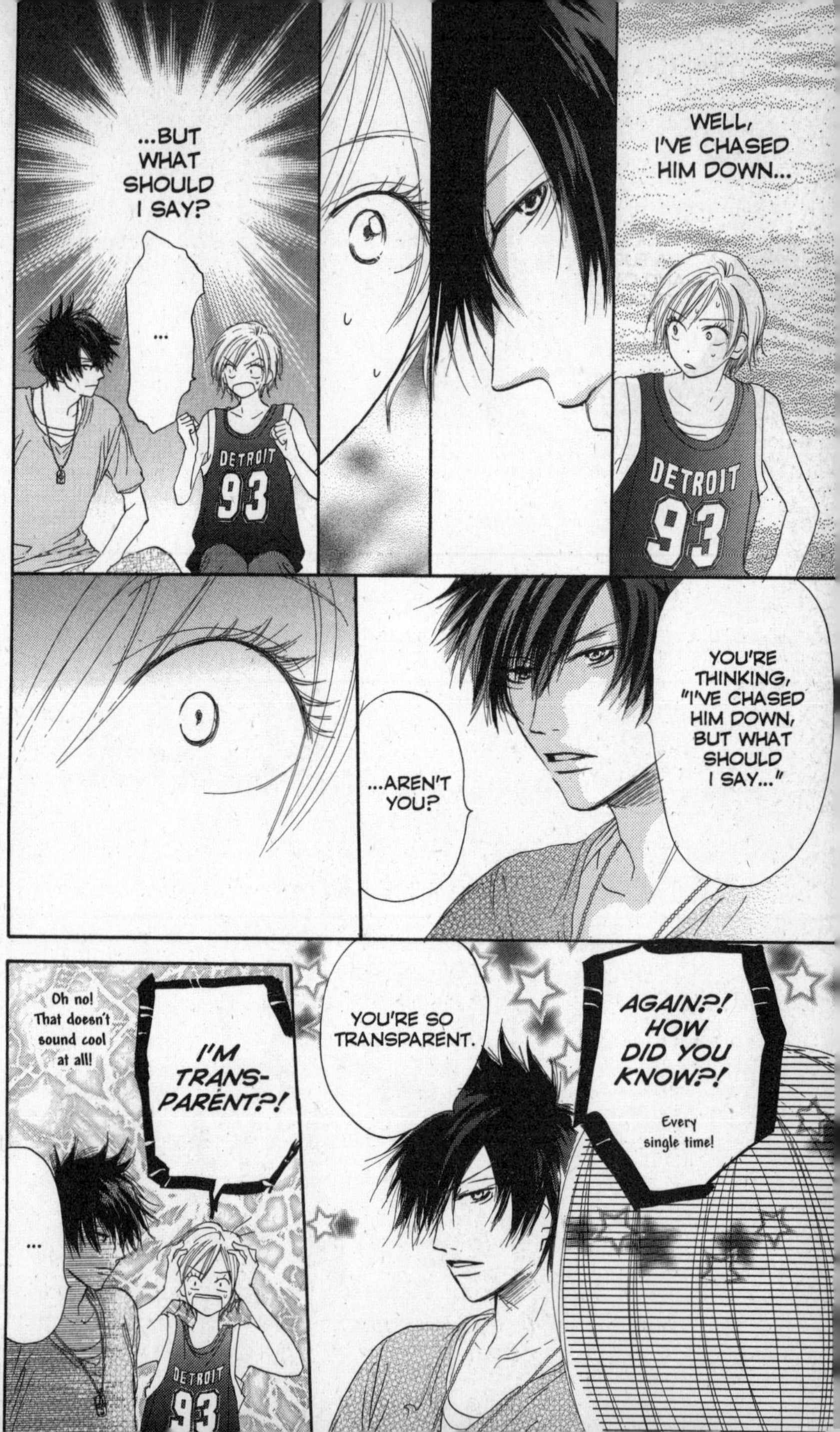
WELL, I'VE CHASED HIM DOWN...
...BUT WHAT SHOULD I SAY?
...
YOU'RE THINKING, "I'VE CHASED HIM DOWN, BUT WHAT SHOULD I SAY..."
...AREN'T YOU?
AGAIN?! HOW DID YOU KNOW?!
Every single time!
YOU'RE SO TRANSPARENT.
I'M TRANS-PARENT?!
Oh no! That doesn't sound cool at all!
...

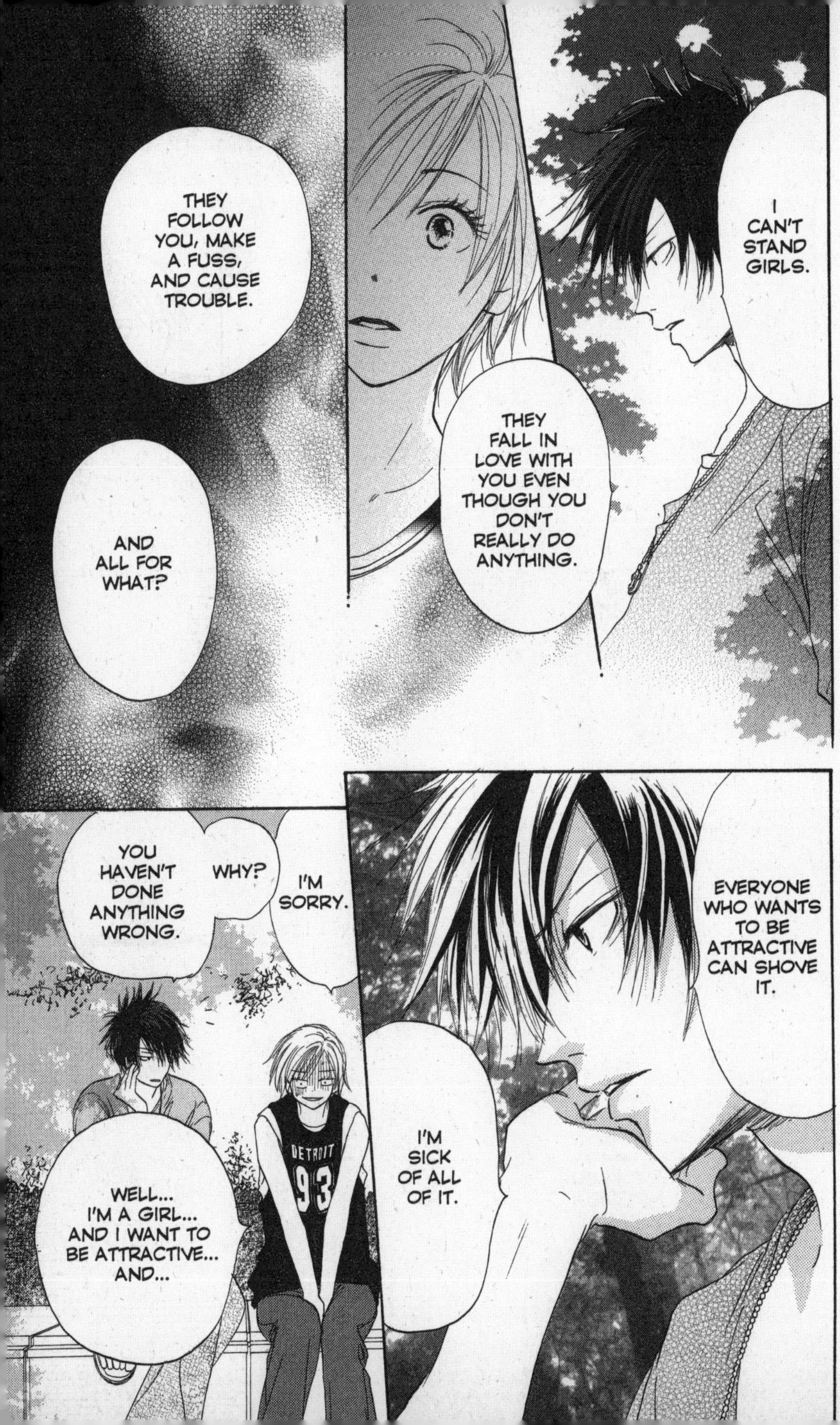
I CAN'T STAND GIRLS.
THEY FALL IN LOVE WITH YOU EVEN THOUGH YOU DON'T REALLY DO ANYTHING.
THEY FOLLOW YOU, MAKE A FUSS, AND CAUSE TROUBLE.
AND ALL FOR WHAT?
EVERYONE WHO WANTS TO BE ATTRACTIVE CAN SHOVE IT.
I'M SICK OF ALL OF IT.
I'M SORRY.
WHY?
YOU HAVEN'T DONE ANYTHING WRONG.
DETROIT 93
WELL... I'M A GIRL... AND I WANT TO BE ATTRACTIVE... AND...

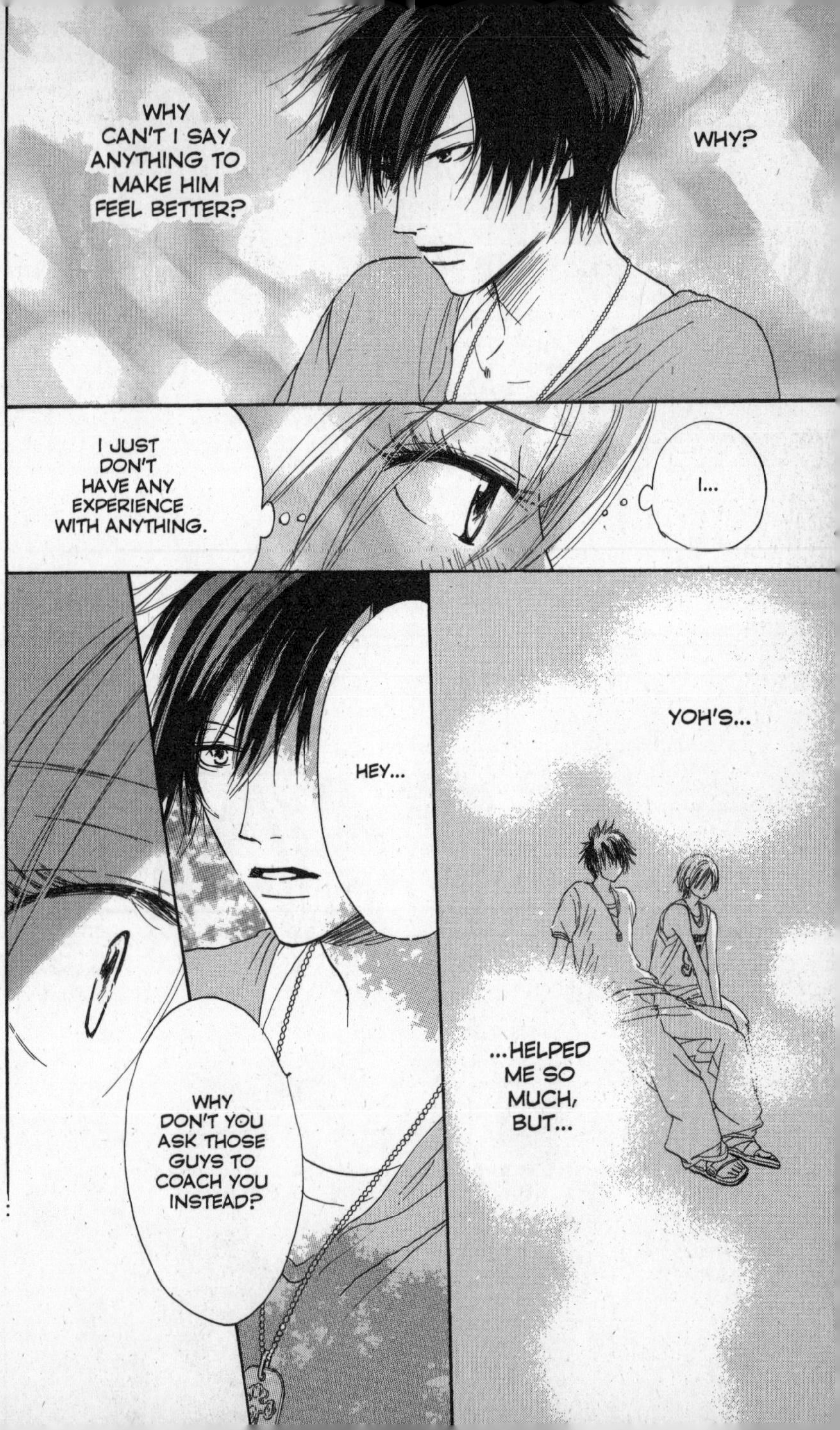
WHY?
WHY CAN'T I SAY ANYTHING TO MAKE HIM FEEL BETTER?
I...
I JUST DON'T HAVE ANY EXPERIENCE WITH ANYTHING.
YOH'S...
...HELPED ME SO MUCH, BUT...
HEY...
WHY DON'T YOU ASK THOSE GUYS TO COACH YOU INSTEAD?

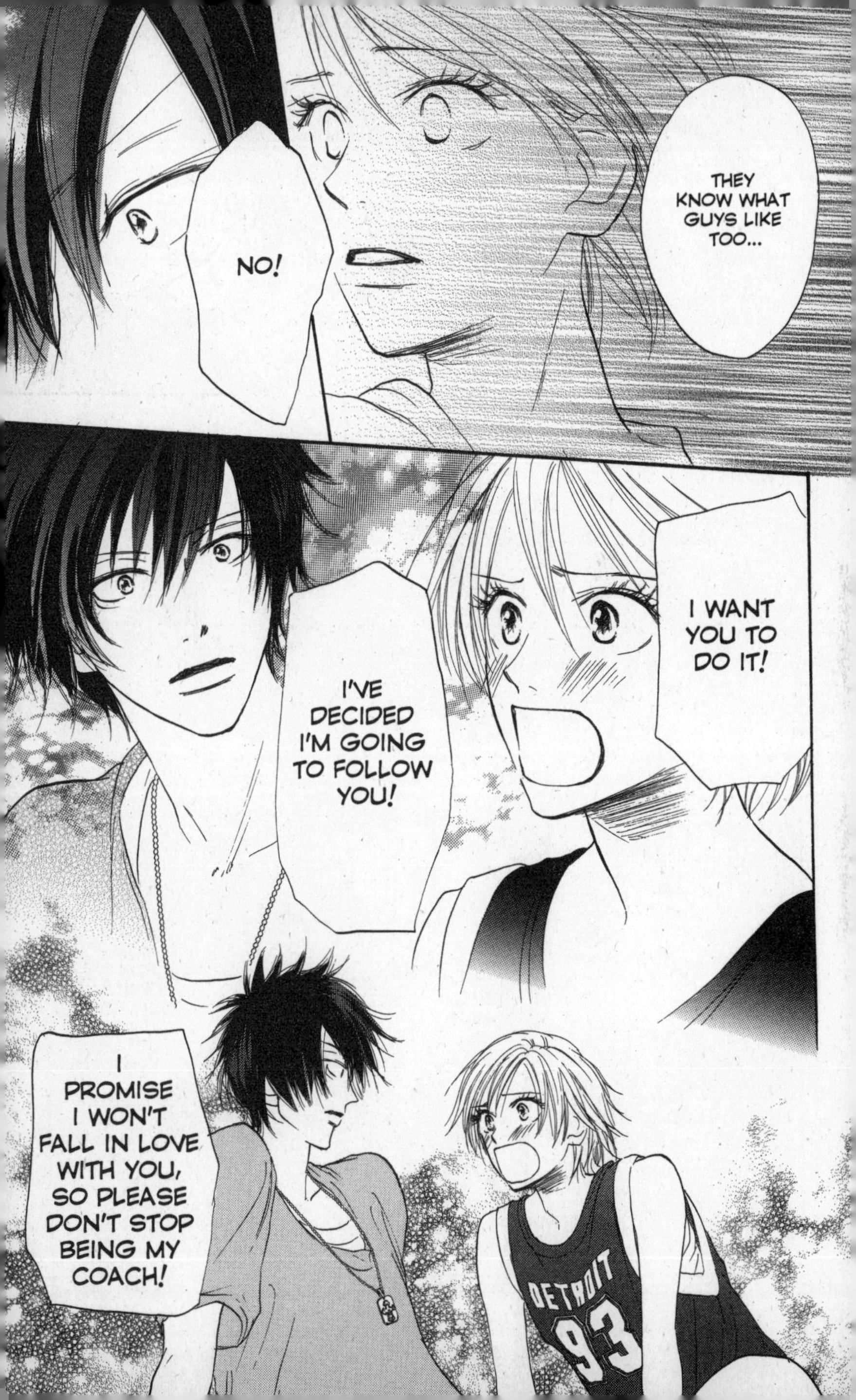
THEY KNOW WHAT GUYS LIKE TOO...
NO!
I WANT YOU TO DO IT!
I'VE DECIDED I'M GOING TO FOLLOW YOU!
I PROMISE I WON'T FALL IN LOVE WITH YOU, SO PLEASE DON'T STOP BEING MY COACH!

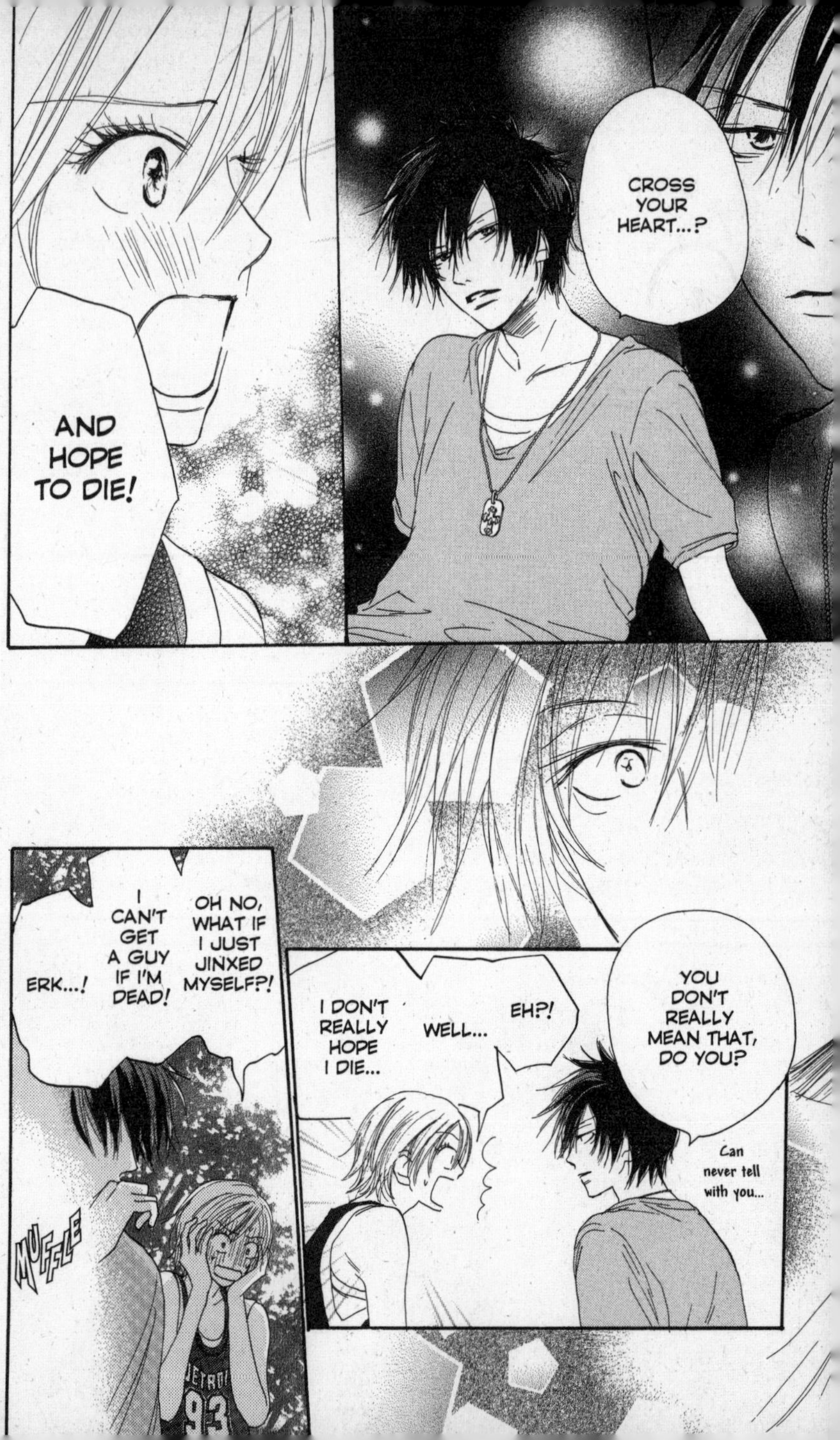
CROSS YOUR HEART...?
AND HOPE TO DIE!
YOU DON'T REALLY MEAN THAT, DO YOU?
Can never tell with you...
EH?!
WELL...
I DON'T REALLY HOPE I DIE...
OH NO, WHAT IF I JUST JINXED MYSELF?!
I CAN'T GET A GUY IF I'M DEAD!
ERK...!
MUFFLE

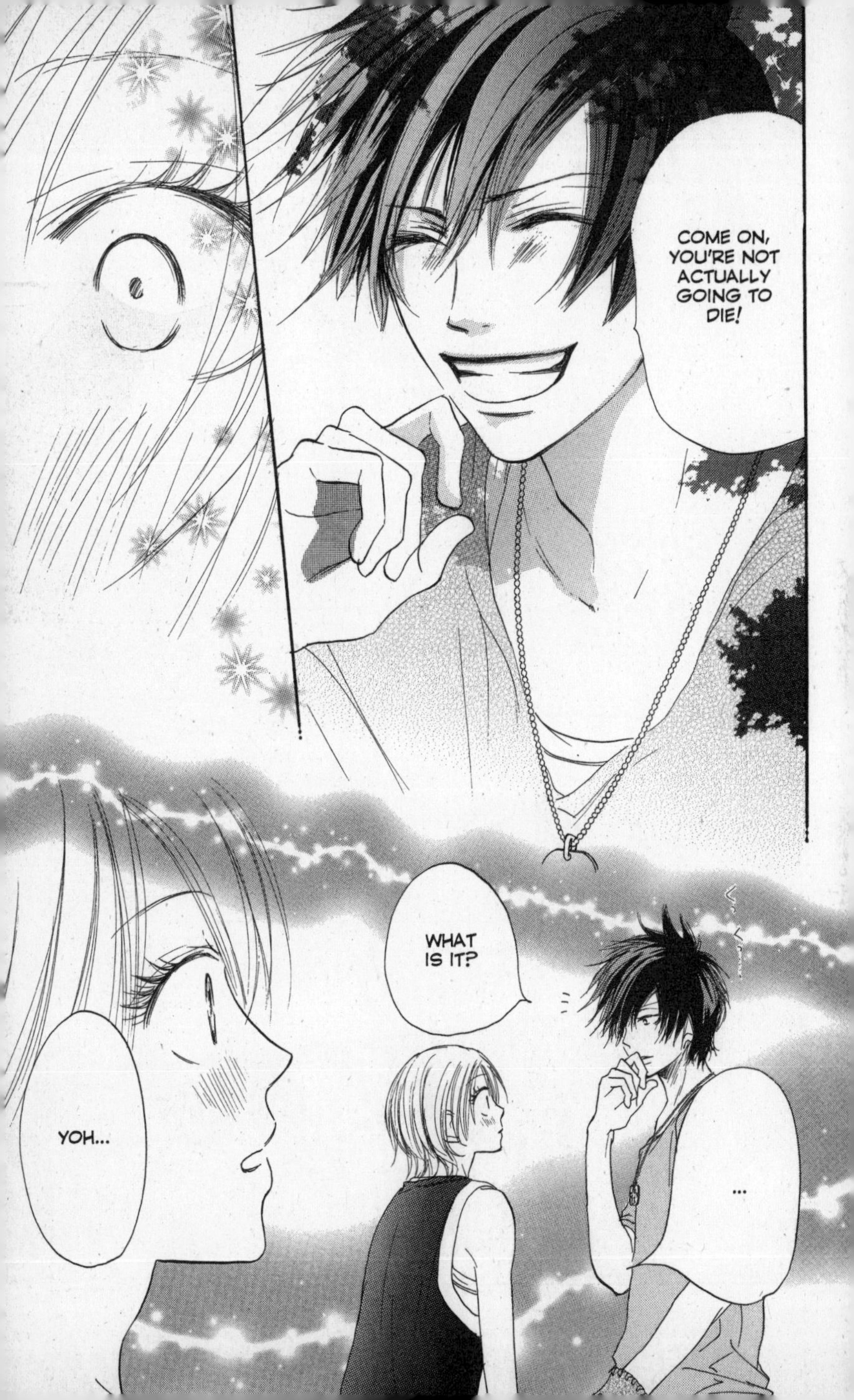
COME ON, YOU'RE NOT ACTUALLY GOING TO DIE!
YOH...
WHAT IS IT?
...

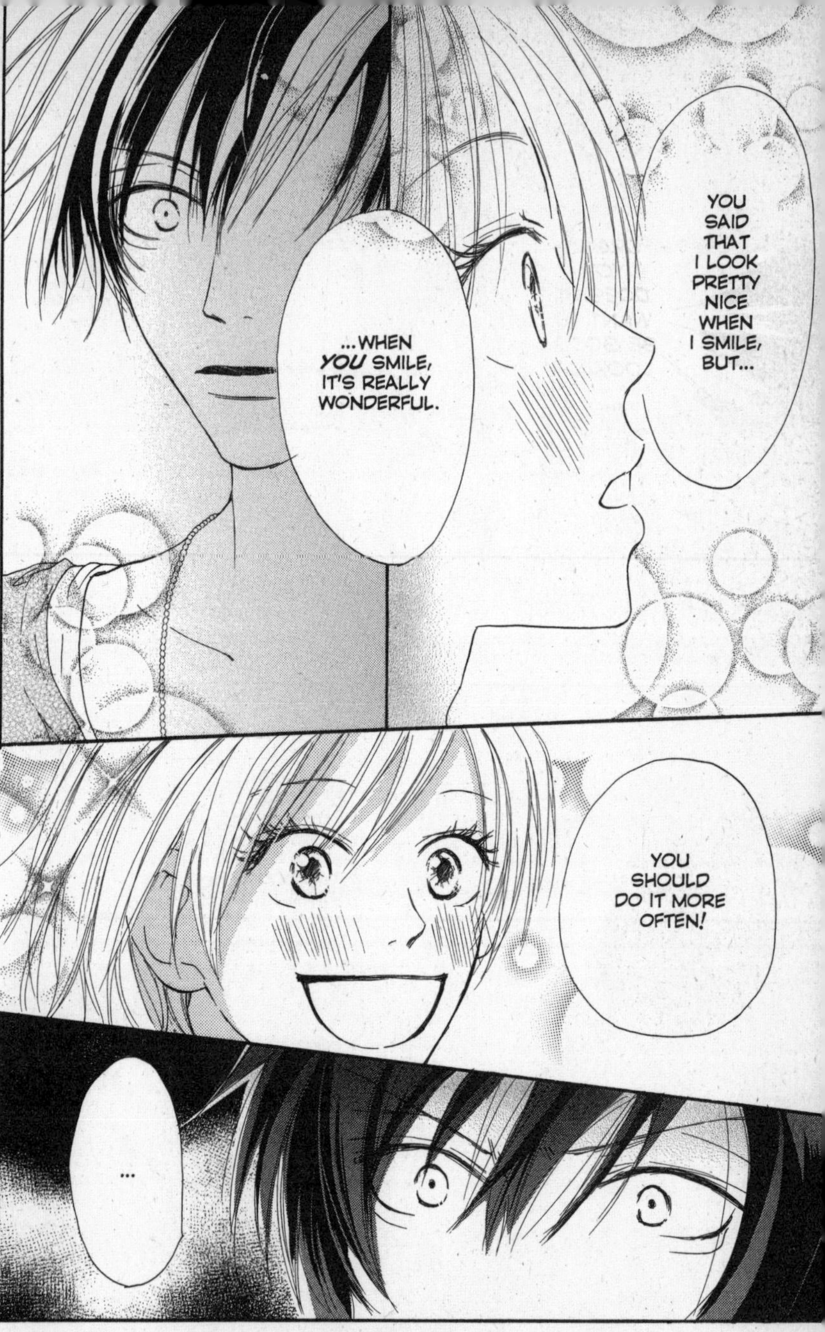
YOU SAID THAT I LOOK PRETTY NICE WHEN I SMILE, BUT...
...WHEN *YOU* SMILE, IT'S REALLY WONDERFUL.
YOU SHOULD DO IT MORE OFTEN!
...

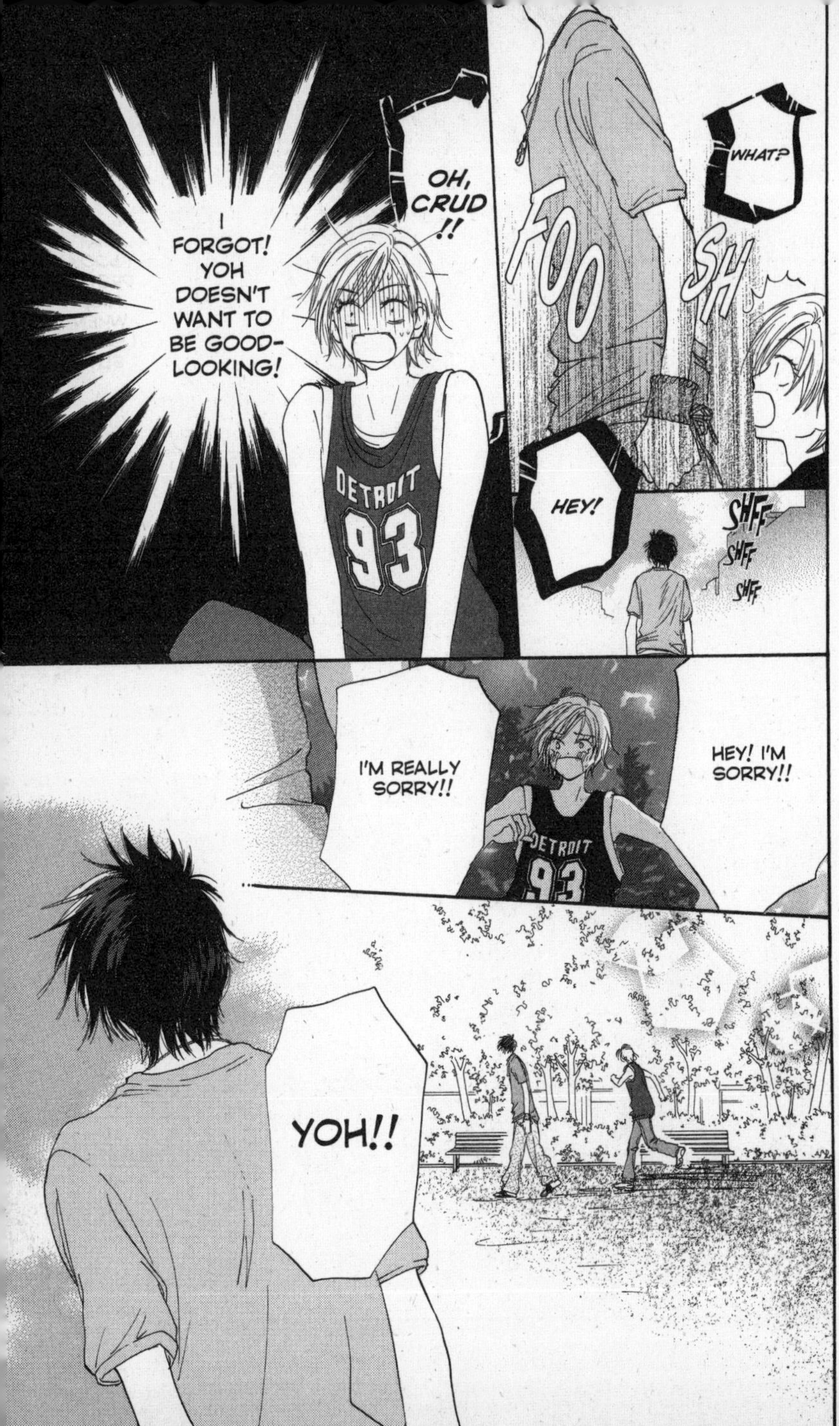
WHAT?
FOOSH
HEY!
SHFF
SHFF
SHFF
OH, CRUD!!
I FORGOT! YOH DOESN'T WANT TO BE GOOD-LOOKING!
HEY! I'M SORRY!!
I'M REALLY SORRY!!
YOH!!

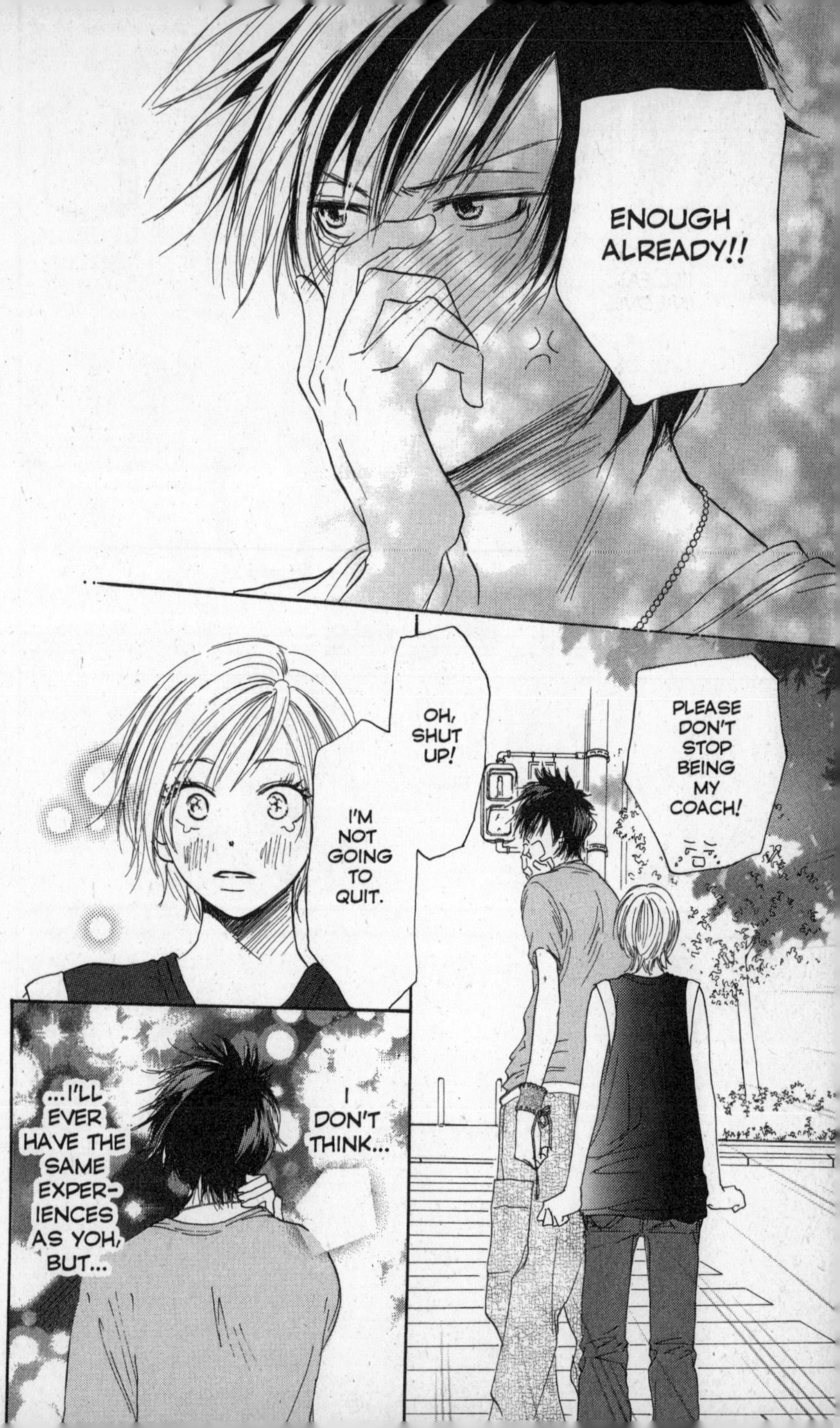
ENOUGH ALREADY!!
PLEASE DON'T STOP BEING MY COACH!
OH, SHUT UP!
I'M NOT GOING TO QUIT.
I DON'T THINK...
...I'LL EVER HAVE THE SAME EXPERIENCES AS YOH, BUT...

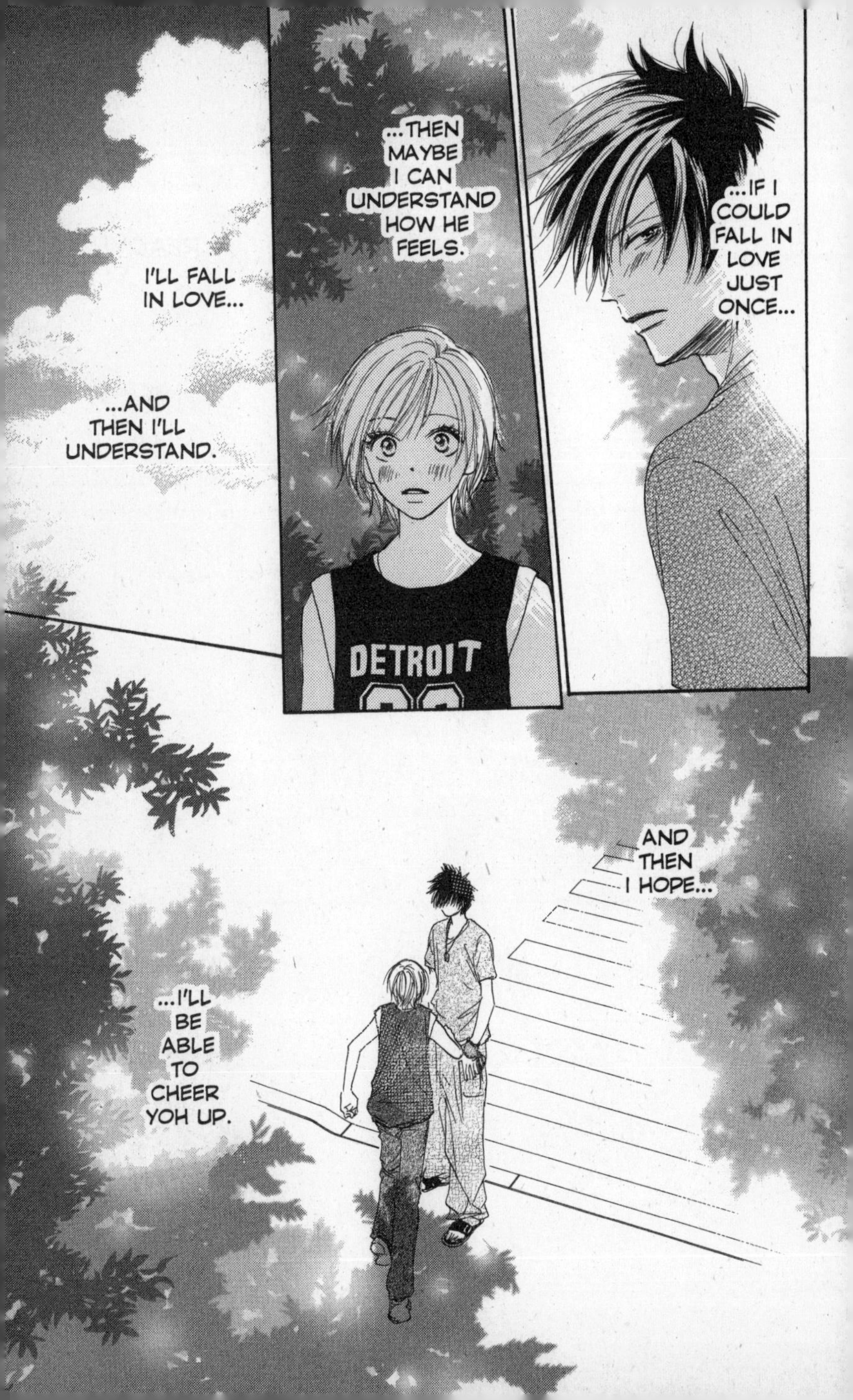
...IF I COULD FALL IN LOVE JUST ONCE...
...THEN MAYBE I CAN UNDERSTAND HOW HE FEELS.
DETROIT
I'LL FALL IN LOVE...
...AND THEN I'LL UNDERSTAND.
AND THEN I HOPE...
...I'LL BE ABLE TO CHEER YOH UP.

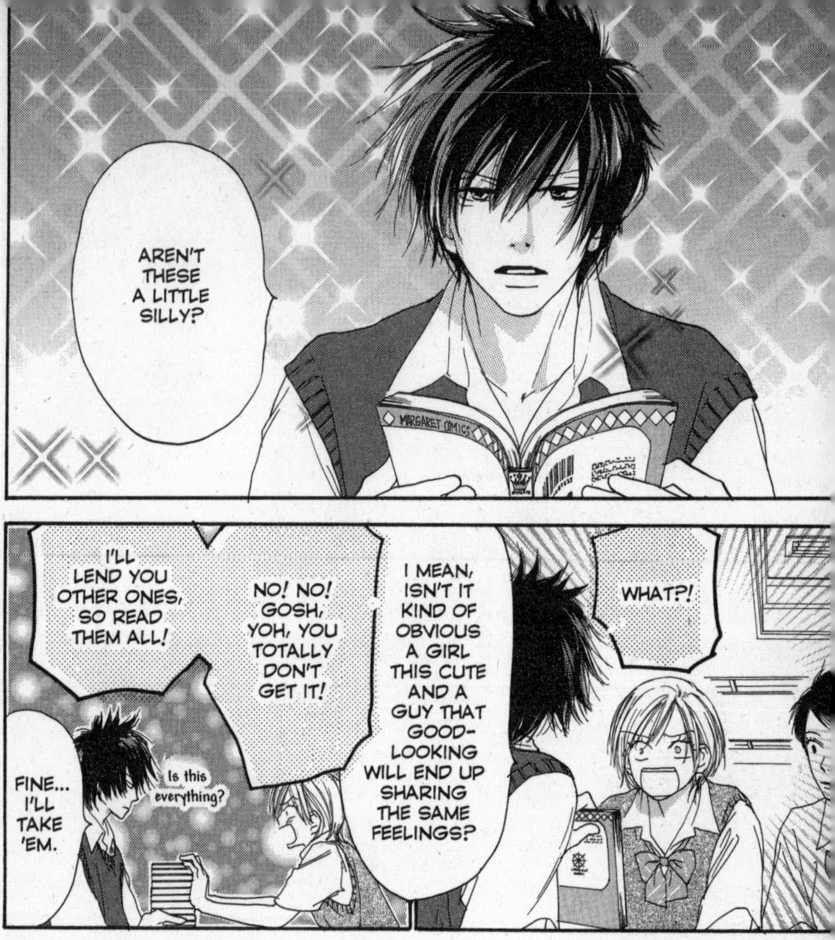
AREN'T THESE A LITTLE SILLY?
MARGARET COMICS
WHAT?!
I MEAN, ISN'T IT KIND OF OBVIOUS A GIRL THIS CUTE AND A GUY THAT GOOD-LOOKING WILL END UP SHARING THE SAME FEELINGS?
NO! NO! GOSH, YOH, YOU TOTALLY DON'T GET IT!
I'LL LEND YOU OTHER ONES, SO READ THEM ALL!
Is this everything?
FINE... I'LL TAKE 'EM.

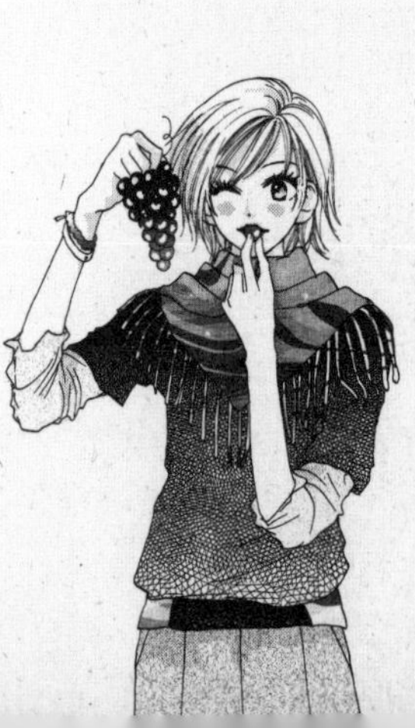

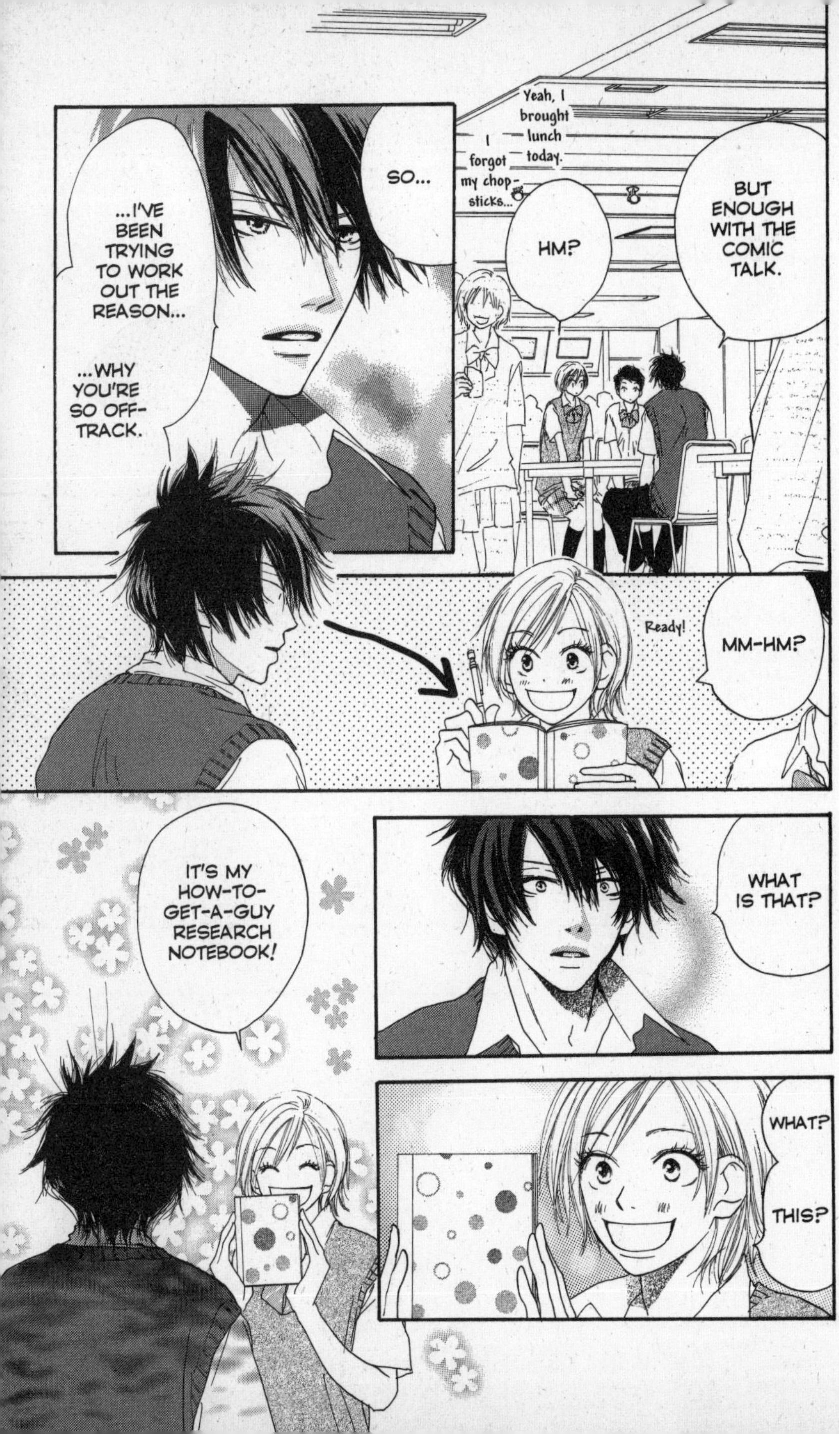
BUT ENOUGH WITH THE COMIC TALK.
HM?
Yeah, I brought lunch today.
I forgot my chop-sticks...
SO...
...I'VE BEEN TRYING TO WORK OUT THE REASON...
...WHY YOU'RE SO OFF-TRACK.
MM-HM?
Ready!
WHAT IS THAT?
WHAT?
THIS?
IT'S MY HOW-TO-GET-A-GUY RESEARCH NOTEBOOK!

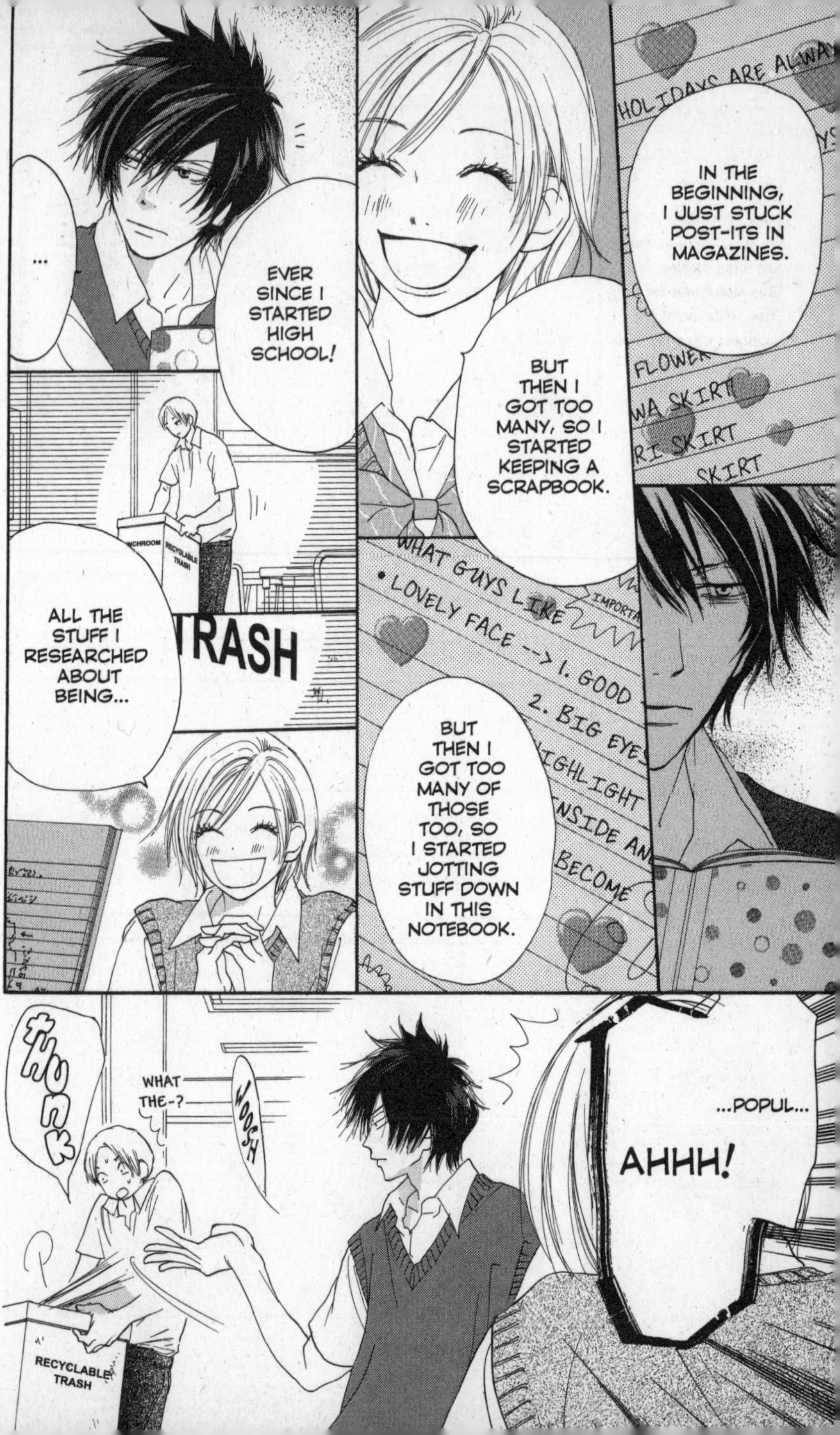
HOLIDAYS ARE ALWA
IN THE BEGINNING, I JUST STUCK POST-ITS IN MAGAZINES.
FLOWER
WA SKIRT
RI SKIRT
SKIRT
EVER SINCE I STARTED HIGH SCHOOL!
BUT THEN I GOT TOO MANY, SO I STARTED KEEPING A SCRAPBOOK.
...
WHAT GUYS LIKE
• LOVELY FACE --> 1. GOOD
2. BIG EYES
HIGHLIGHT
INSIDE AN
BECOME
IMPORTA
BUT THEN I GOT TOO MANY OF THOSE TOO, SO I STARTED JOTTING STUFF DOWN IN THIS NOTEBOOK.
RECYCLABLE TRASH
TRASH
ALL THE STUFF I RESEARCHED ABOUT BEING...
...POPUL...
AHHH!
WHAT THE-?
WOOSH
thunk
RECYCLABLE TRASH

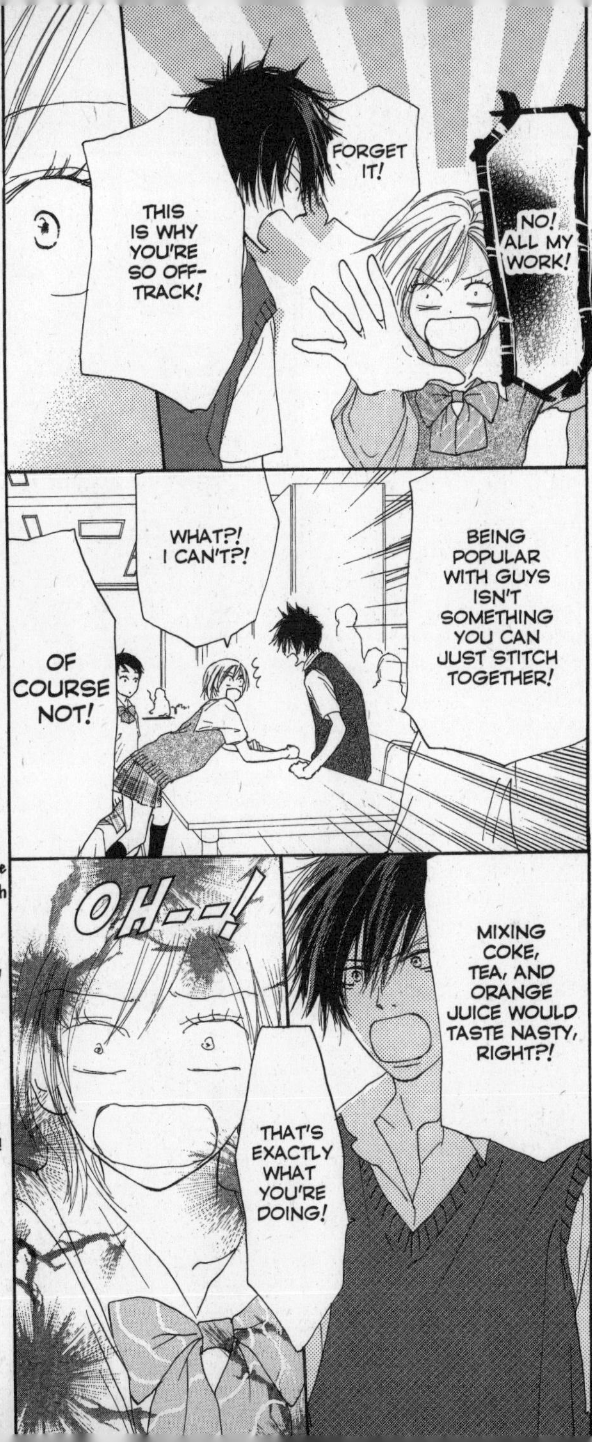
NO! ALL MY WORK!
FORGET IT!
THIS IS WHY YOU'RE SO OFF-TRACK!
BEING POPULAR WITH GUYS ISN'T SOMETHING YOU CAN JUST STITCH TOGETHER!
WHAT?! I CAN'T?!
OF COURSE NOT!
MIXING COKE, TEA, AND ORANGE JUICE WOULD TASTE NASTY, RIGHT?!
OH...!
THAT'S EXACTLY WHAT YOU'RE DOING!

2

Because I wrote about my older niece in the one-shot stories, my little sister told me, "Hey, write about the youngest niece too!" So that's what I'm doing. Sorry I keep talking about my family...

My youngest niece isn't even one yet, but she doesn't get anywhere near the kind of attention her sister got at that age.

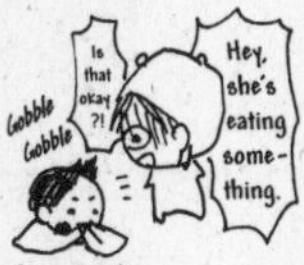
Hey, she's eating something.
Is that okay?!
Gobble Gobble

People aren't overprotective of her. In fact, I think it's quite the opposite.

When the older sister was her age, I'd be told to wash my hands before playing with her, but with this little one, no one even bothers.

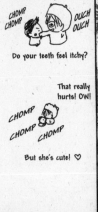

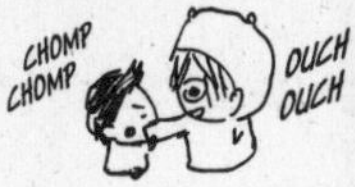
OUCH OUCH
CHOMP CHOMP

Do your teeth feel itchy?

That really hurts! OW!

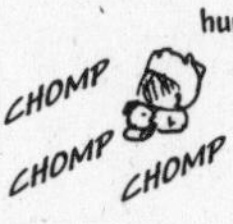
CHOMP CHOMP CHOMP

But she's cute! ♡

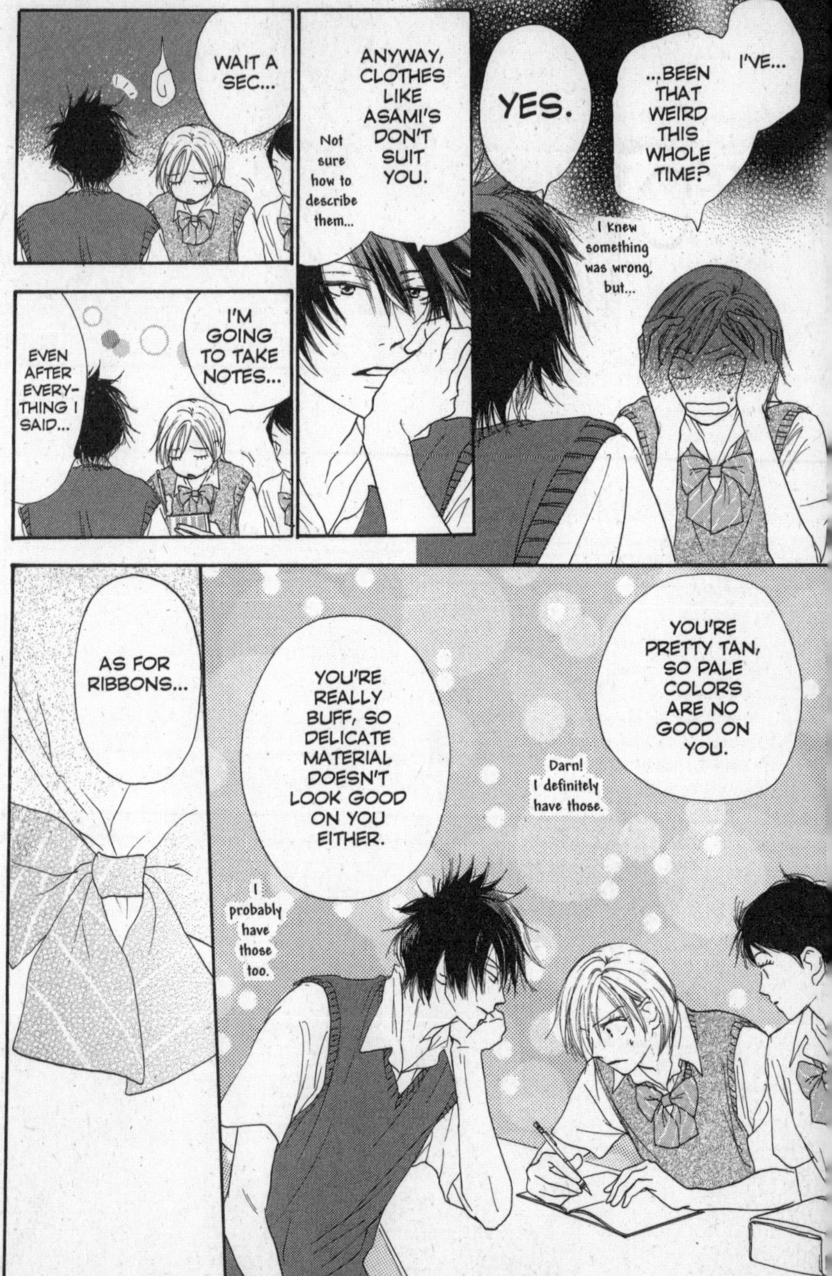
I'VE...
...BEEN THAT WEIRD THIS WHOLE TIME?
YES.
I knew something was wrong, but...
ANYWAY, CLOTHES LIKE ASAMI'S DON'T SUIT YOU.
Not sure how to describe them...
WAIT A SEC...
I'M GOING TO TAKE NOTES...
EVEN AFTER EVERYTHING I SAID...
YOU'RE PRETTY TAN, SO PALE COLORS ARE NO GOOD ON YOU.
Darn! I definitely have those.
YOU'RE REALLY BUFF, SO DELICATE MATERIAL DOESN'T LOOK GOOD ON YOU EITHER.
I probably have those too.
AS FOR RIBBONS...

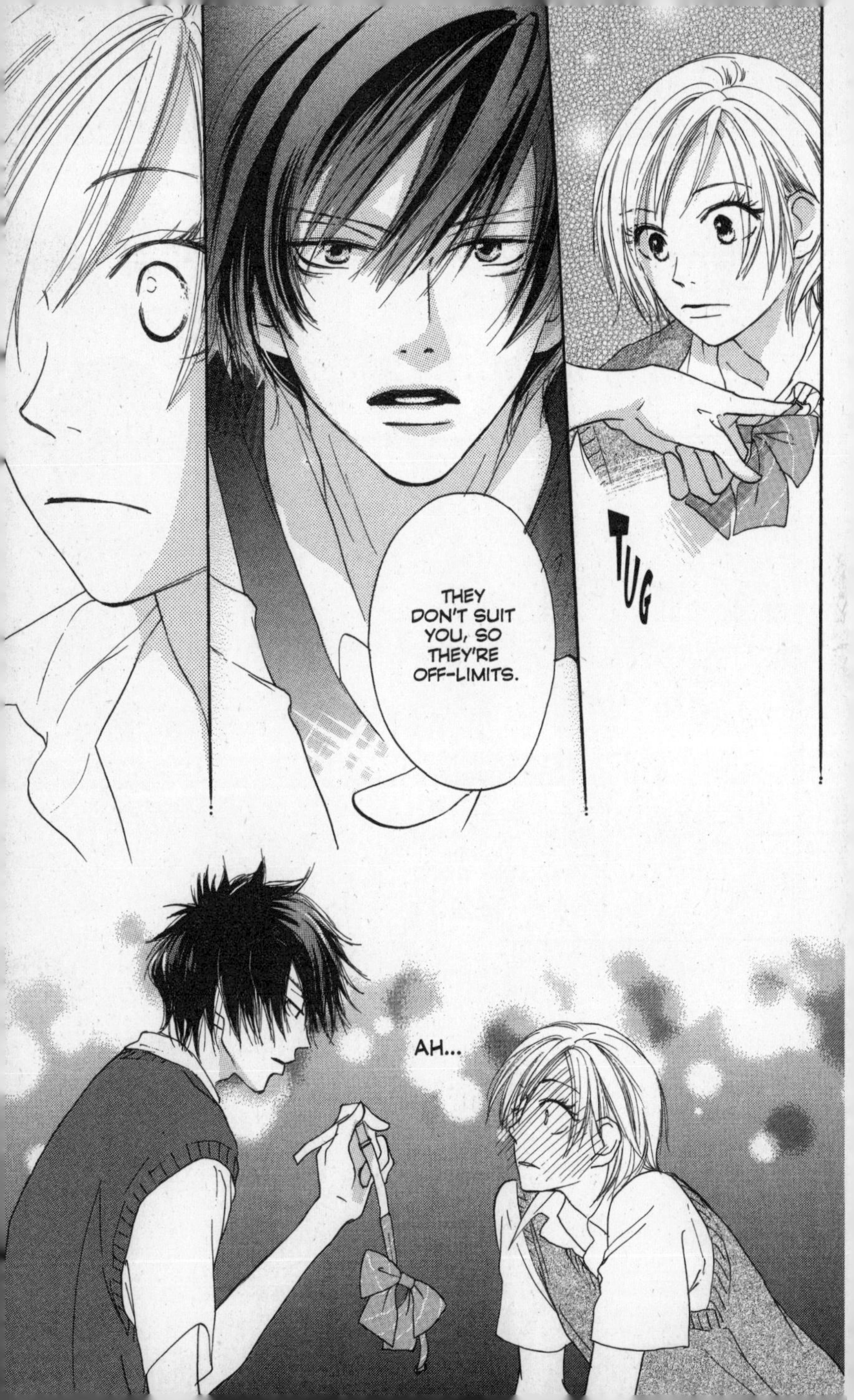
TUG
THEY DON'T SUIT YOU, SO THEY'RE OFF-LIMITS.
AH...

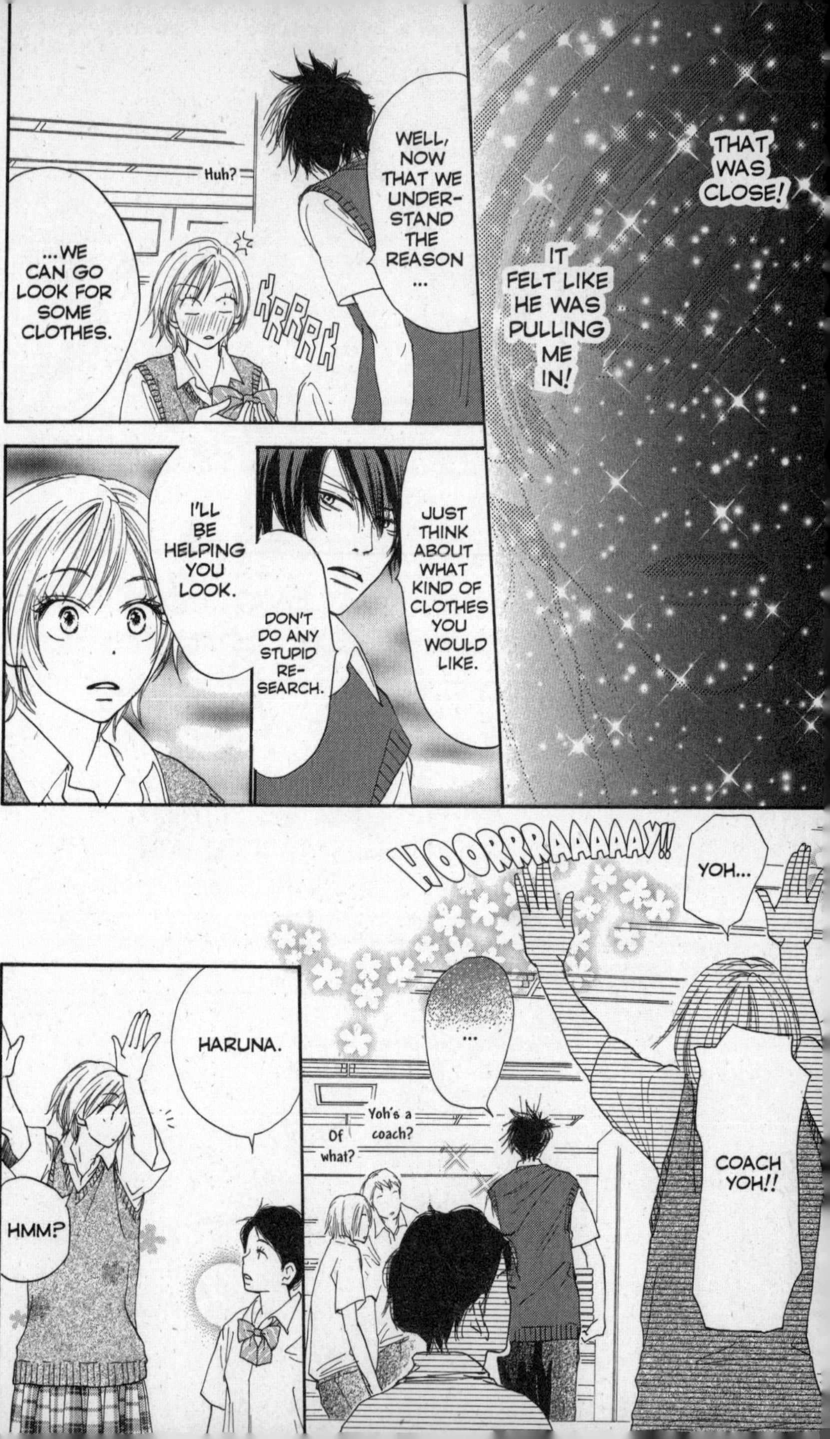
THAT WAS CLOSE!
IT FELT LIKE HE WAS PULLING ME IN!
WELL, NOW THAT WE UNDER-STAND THE REASON...
Huh?
KRRRK
...WE CAN GO LOOK FOR SOME CLOTHES.
JUST THINK ABOUT WHAT KIND OF CLOTHES YOU WOULD LIKE.
DON'T DO ANY STUPID RE-SEARCH.
I'LL BE HELPING YOU LOOK.
HOORRRAAAAAY!!
YOH...
COACH YOH!!
...
Yoh's a coach?
Of what?
HARUNA.
HMM?

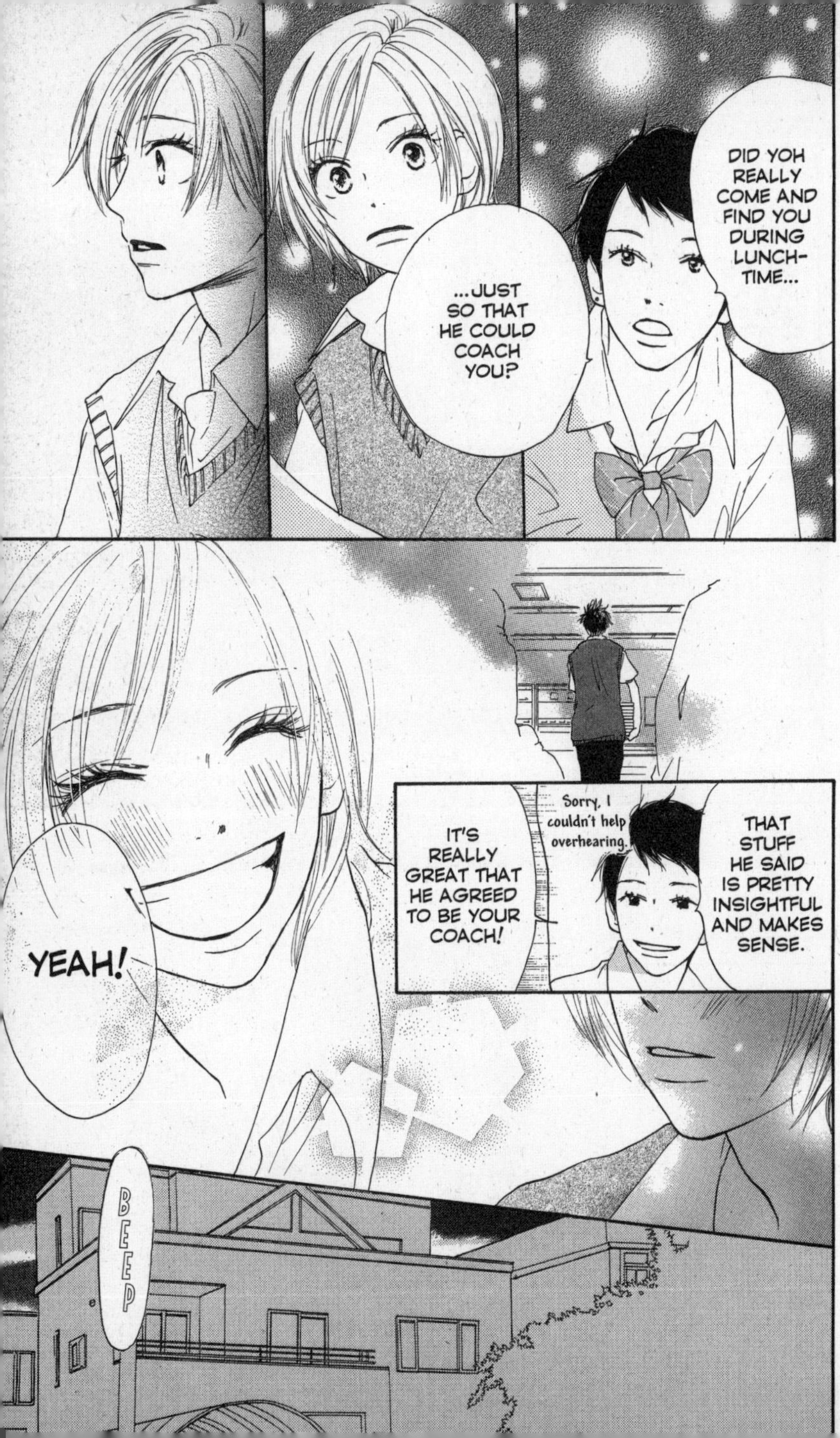
DID YOH REALLY COME AND FIND YOU DURING LUNCH-TIME...
...JUST SO THAT HE COULD COACH YOU?
THAT STUFF HE SAID IS PRETTY INSIGHTFUL AND MAKES SENSE.
Sorry, I couldn't help overhearing.
IT'S REALLY GREAT THAT HE AGREED TO BE YOUR COACH!
YEAH!
BEEP

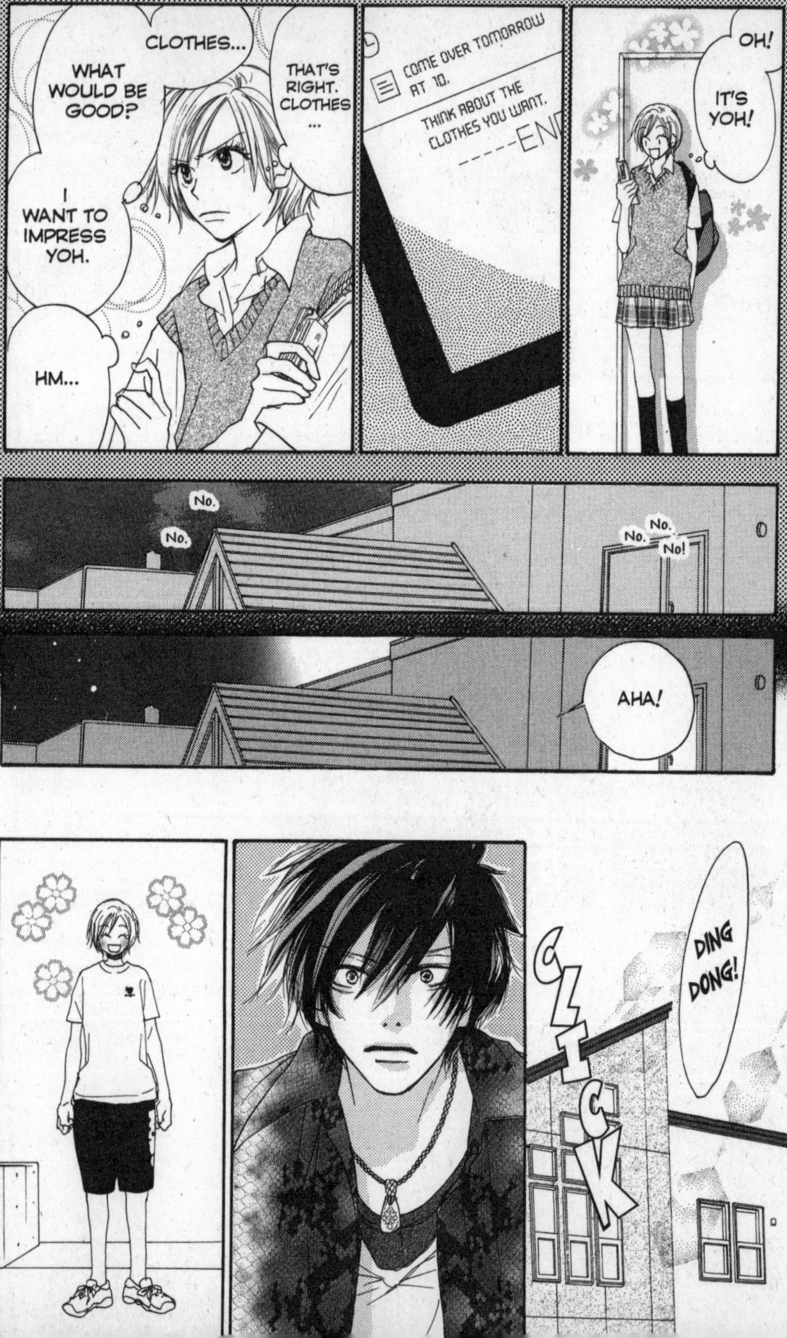
OH!
IT'S YOH!
COME OVER TOMORROW AT 10.
THINK ABOUT THE CLOTHES YOU WANT.
-----END
THAT'S RIGHT. CLOTHES ...
CLOTHES...
WHAT WOULD BE GOOD?
I WANT TO IMPRESS YOH.
HM...
No.
No.
No!
No.
No.
AHA!
DING DONG!
CLICK

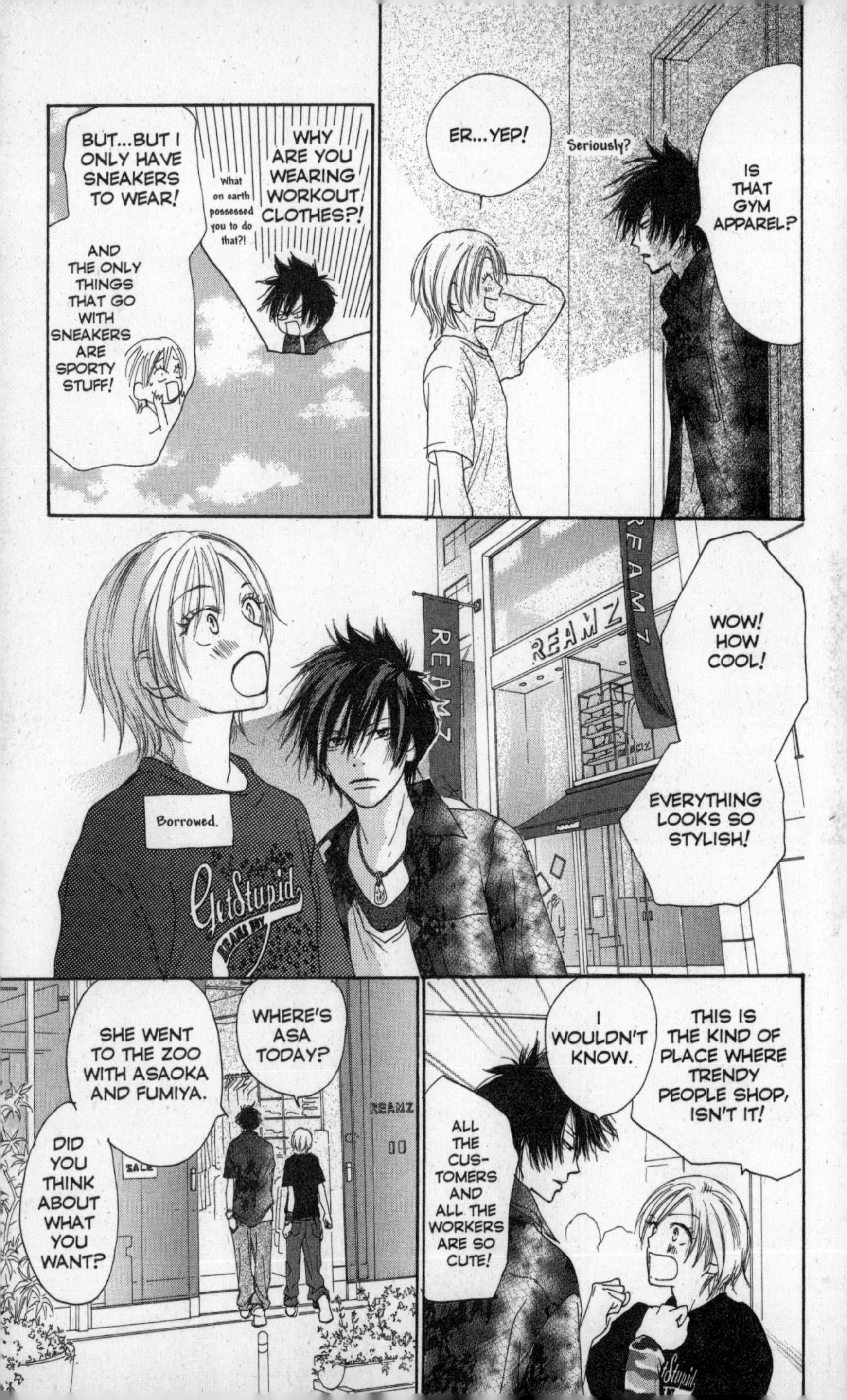
IS THAT GYM APPAREL?
Seriously?
ER...YEP!
WHY ARE YOU WEARING WORKOUT CLOTHES?!
What on earth possessed you to do that?!
BUT...BUT I ONLY HAVE SNEAKERS TO WEAR!
AND THE ONLY THINGS THAT GO WITH SNEAKERS ARE SPORTY STUFF!
WOW! HOW COOL!
EVERYTHING LOOKS SO STYLISH!
REAMZ
REAMZ
REAMZ
Borrowed.
GetStupid
THIS IS THE KIND OF PLACE WHERE TRENDY PEOPLE SHOP, ISN'T IT!
I WOULDN'T KNOW.
ALL THE CUS-TOMERS AND ALL THE WORKERS ARE SO CUTE!
WHERE'S ASA TODAY?
SHE WENT TO THE ZOO WITH ASAOKA AND FUMIYA.
REAMZ
SALE
DID YOU THINK ABOUT WHAT YOU WANT?

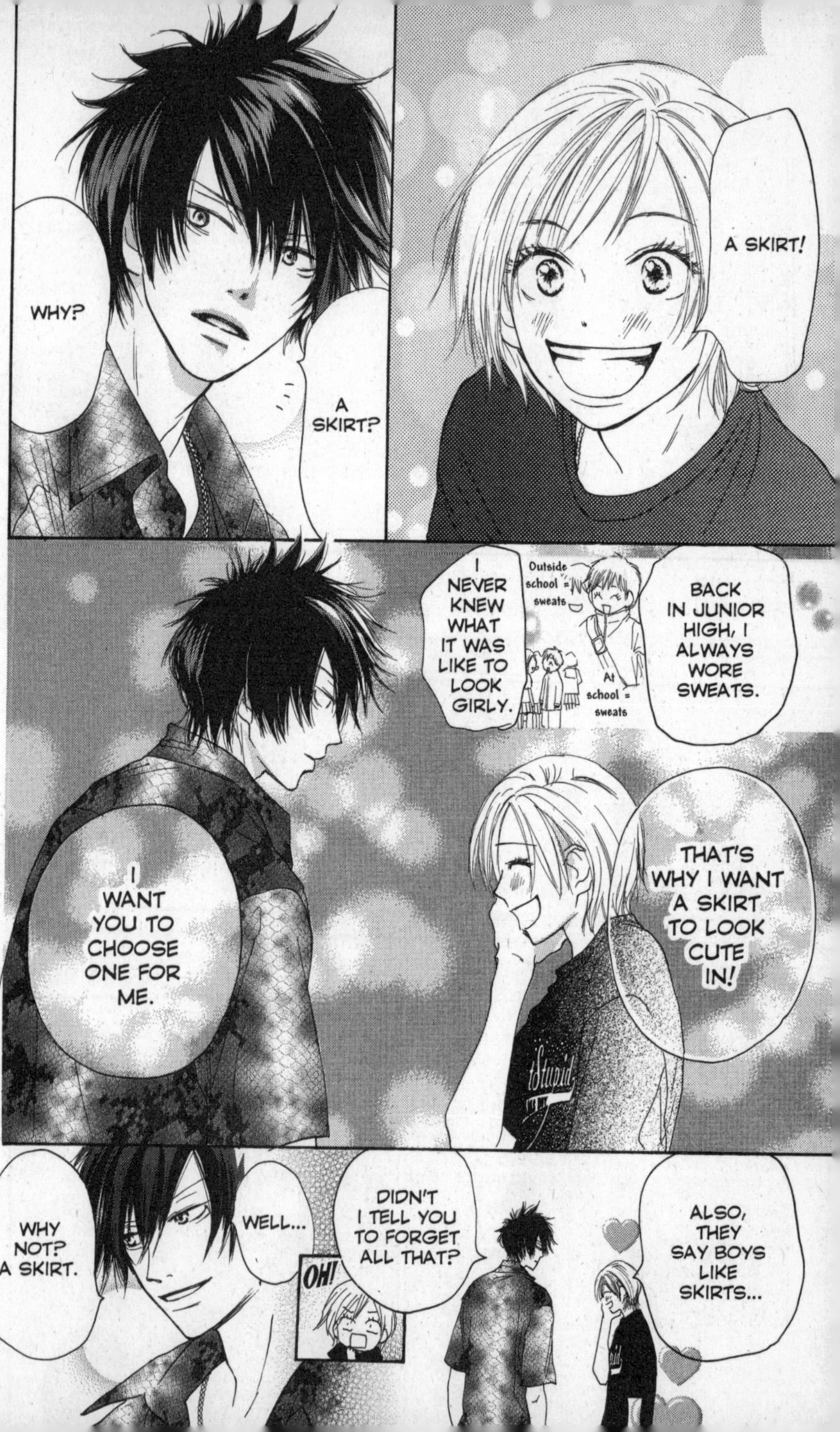
A SKIRT!
A SKIRT?
WHY?
BACK IN JUNIOR HIGH, I ALWAYS WORE SWEATS.
Outside school = sweats
At school = sweats
I NEVER KNEW WHAT IT WAS LIKE TO LOOK GIRLY.
THAT'S WHY I WANT A SKIRT TO LOOK CUTE IN!
I WANT YOU TO CHOOSE ONE FOR ME.
ALSO, THEY SAY BOYS LIKE SKIRTS...
DIDN'T I TELL YOU TO FORGET ALL THAT?
OH!
WELL...
WHY NOT? A SKIRT.

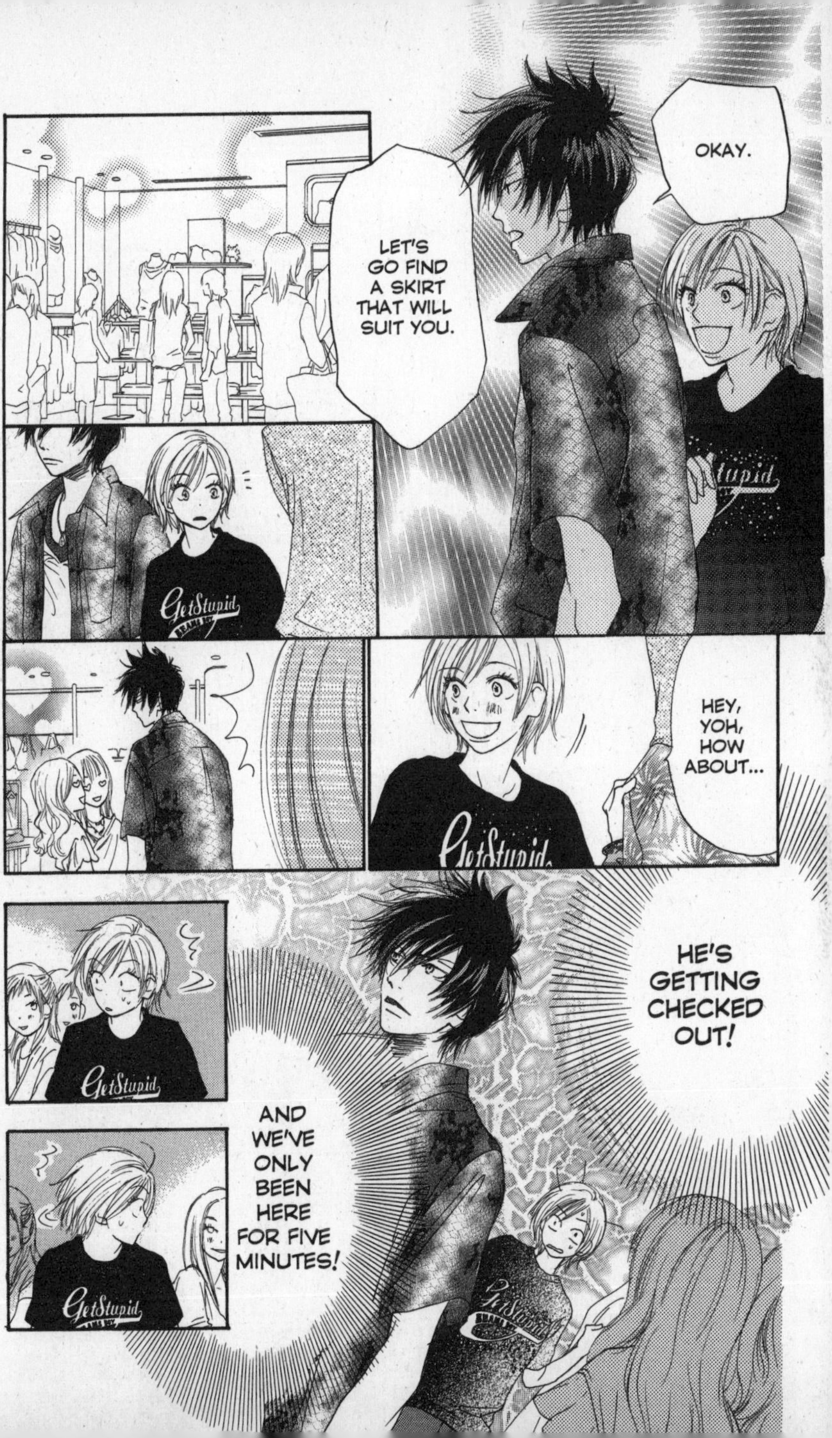
OKAY.
LET'S GO FIND A SKIRT THAT WILL SUIT YOU.
HEY, YOH, HOW ABOUT...
HE'S GETTING CHECKED OUT!
AND WE'VE ONLY BEEN HERE FOR FIVE MINUTES!

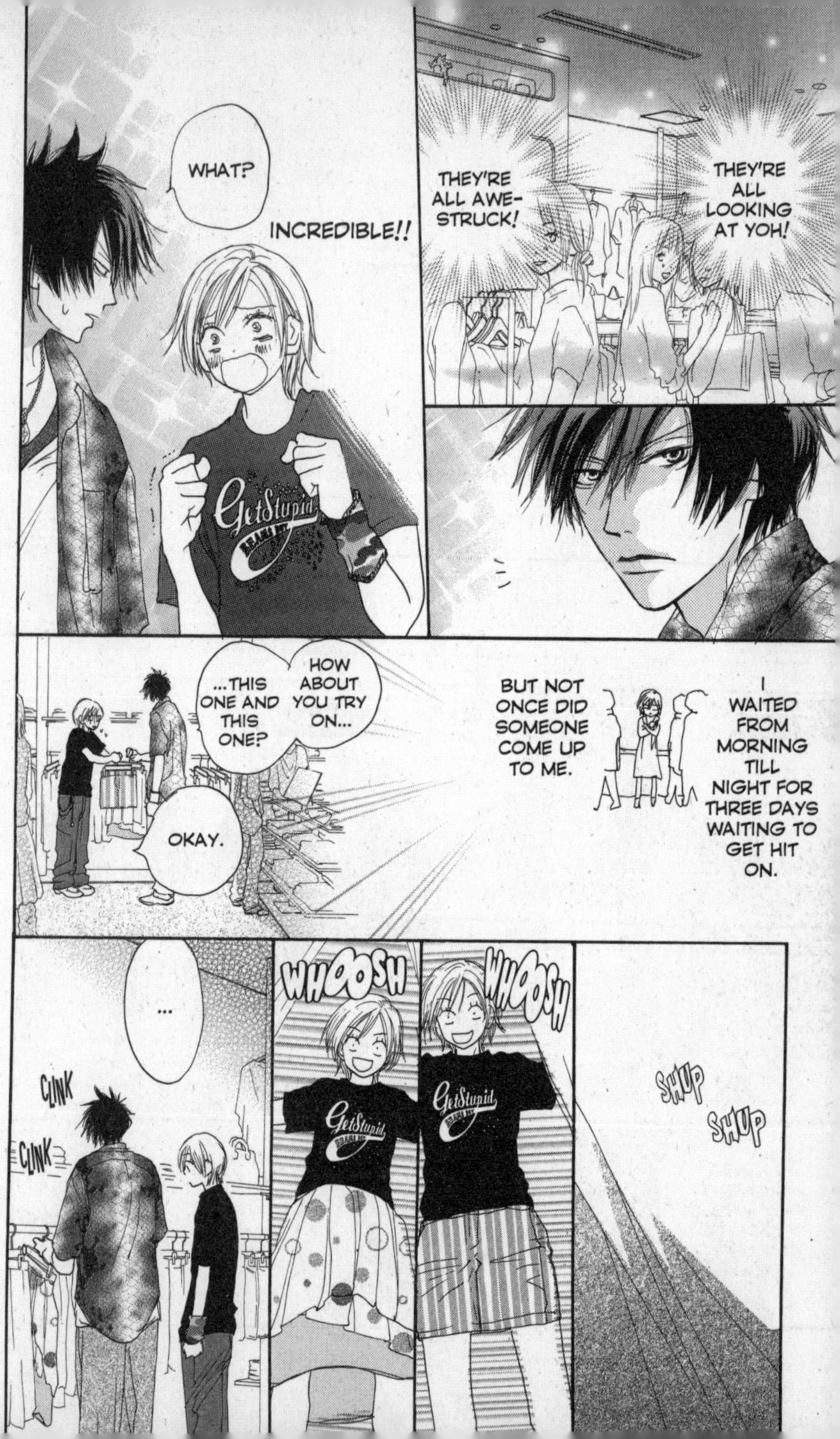
THEY'RE ALL LOOKING AT YOH!
THEY'RE ALL AWE-STRUCK!
WHAT?
INCREDIBLE!!
I WAITED FROM MORNING TILL NIGHT FOR THREE DAYS WAITING TO GET HIT ON.
BUT NOT ONCE DID SOMEONE COME UP TO ME.
HOW ABOUT YOU TRY ON...
...THIS ONE AND THIS ONE?
OKAY.
SHUP
SHUP
WHOOSH
WHOOSH
...
CLINK
CLINK

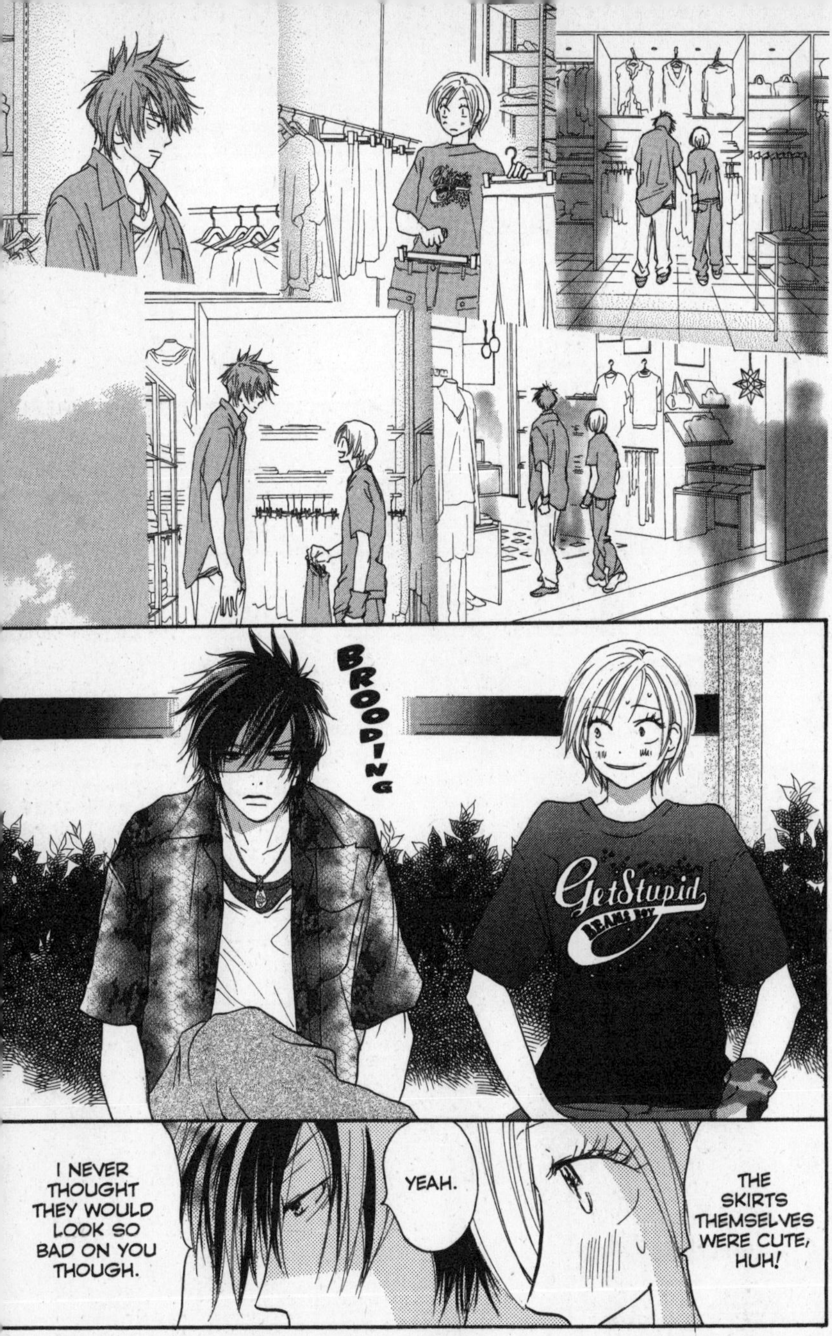
BROODING
GetStupid
BEAMS BOY
THE SKIRTS THEMSELVES WERE CUTE, HUH!
YEAH.
I NEVER THOUGHT THEY WOULD LOOK SO BAD ON YOU THOUGH.

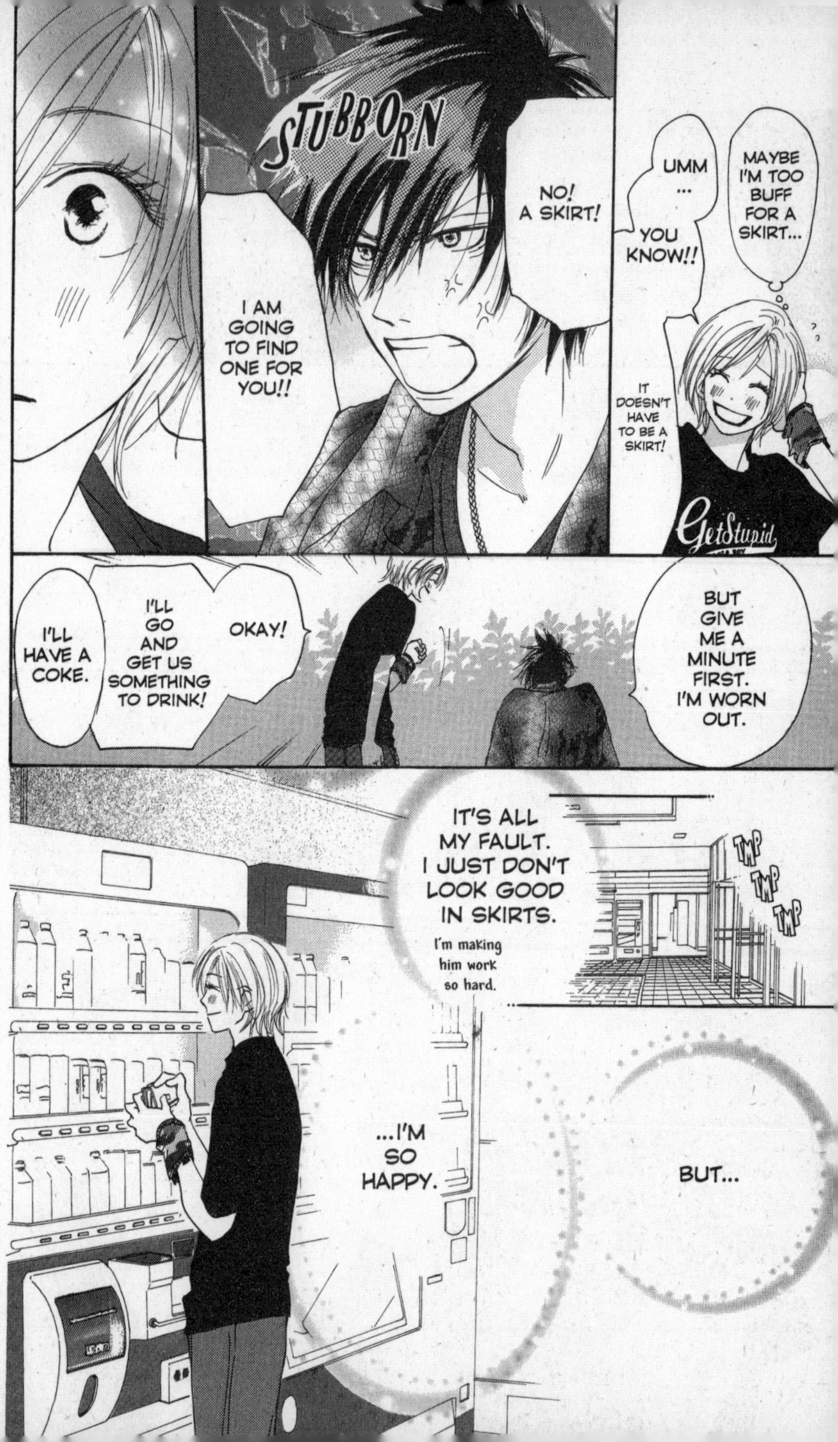
MAYBE I'M TOO BUFF FOR A SKIRT...
UMM ... YOU KNOW!!
IT DOESN'T HAVE TO BE A SKIRT!
STUBBORN
NO! A SKIRT!
I AM GOING TO FIND ONE FOR YOU!!
BUT GIVE ME A MINUTE FIRST. I'M WORN OUT.
OKAY!
I'LL GO AND GET US SOMETHING TO DRINK!
I'LL HAVE A COKE.
TMP TMP TMP
IT'S ALL MY FAULT. I JUST DON'T LOOK GOOD IN SKIRTS.
I'm making him work so hard.
BUT...
...I'M SO HAPPY.

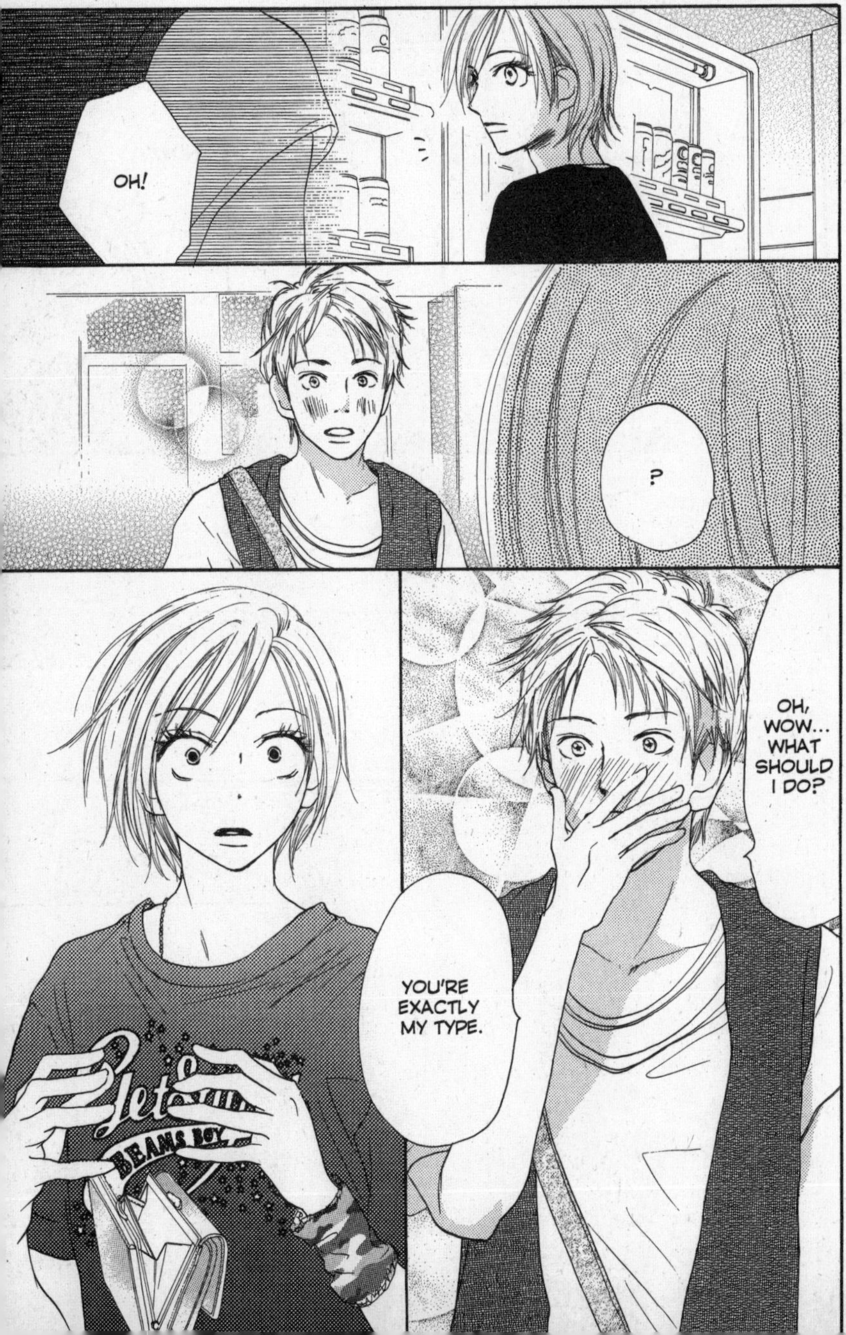
OH!
?
OH, WOW... WHAT SHOULD I DO?
YOU'RE EXACTLY MY TYPE.
BEAMS BOY

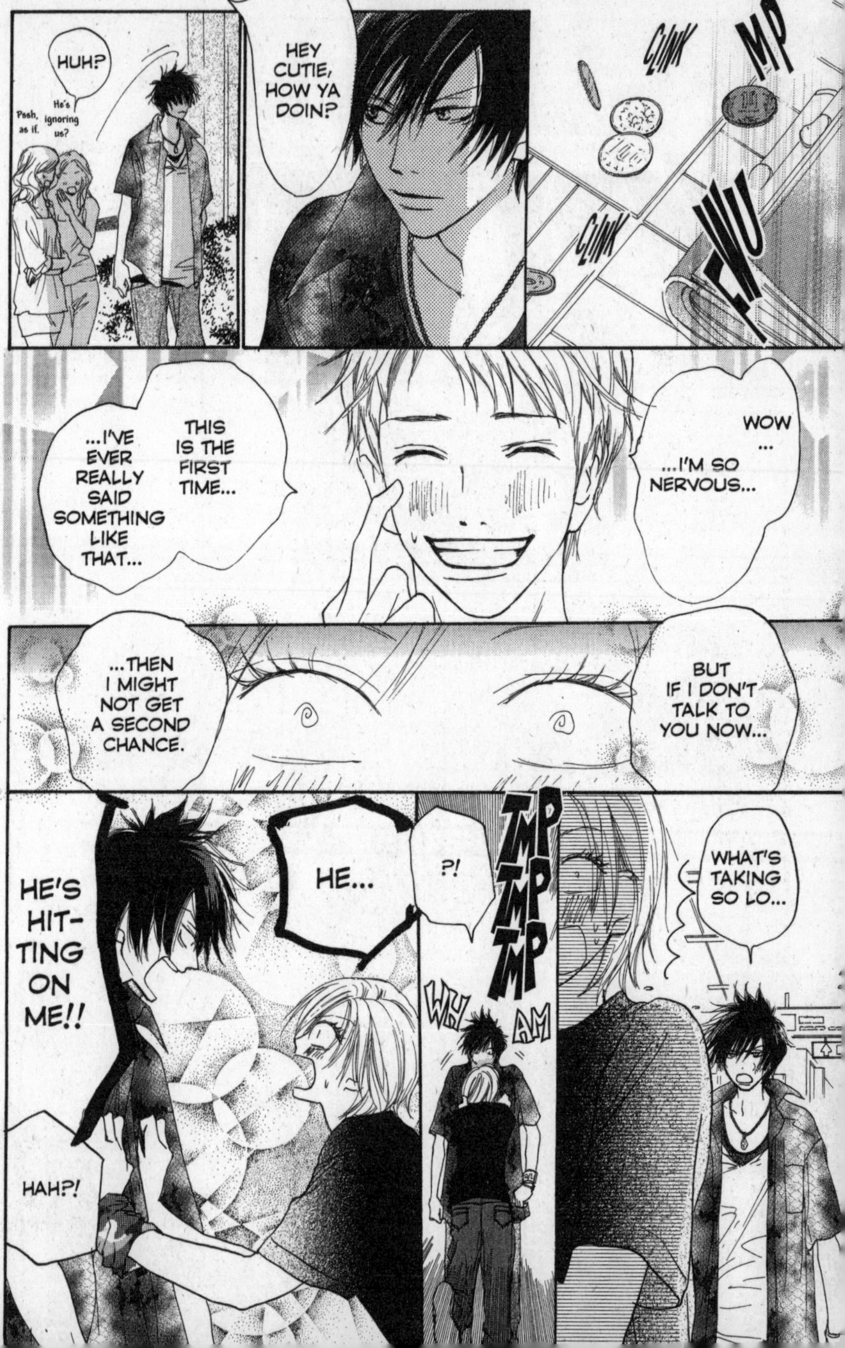
CLINK
MP
CLINK
WHU
HEY CUTIE, HOW YA DOIN?
HUH?
He's ignoring us?
Pssh, as if.
WOW ... ...I'M SO NERVOUS...
THIS IS THE FIRST TIME...
...I'VE EVER REALLY SAID SOMETHING LIKE THAT...
BUT IF I DON'T TALK TO YOU NOW...
...THEN I MIGHT NOT GET A SECOND CHANCE.
WHAT'S TAKING SO LO...
TMP TMP TMP
?!
WH AM
HE...
HE'S HIT-TING ON ME!!
HAH?!

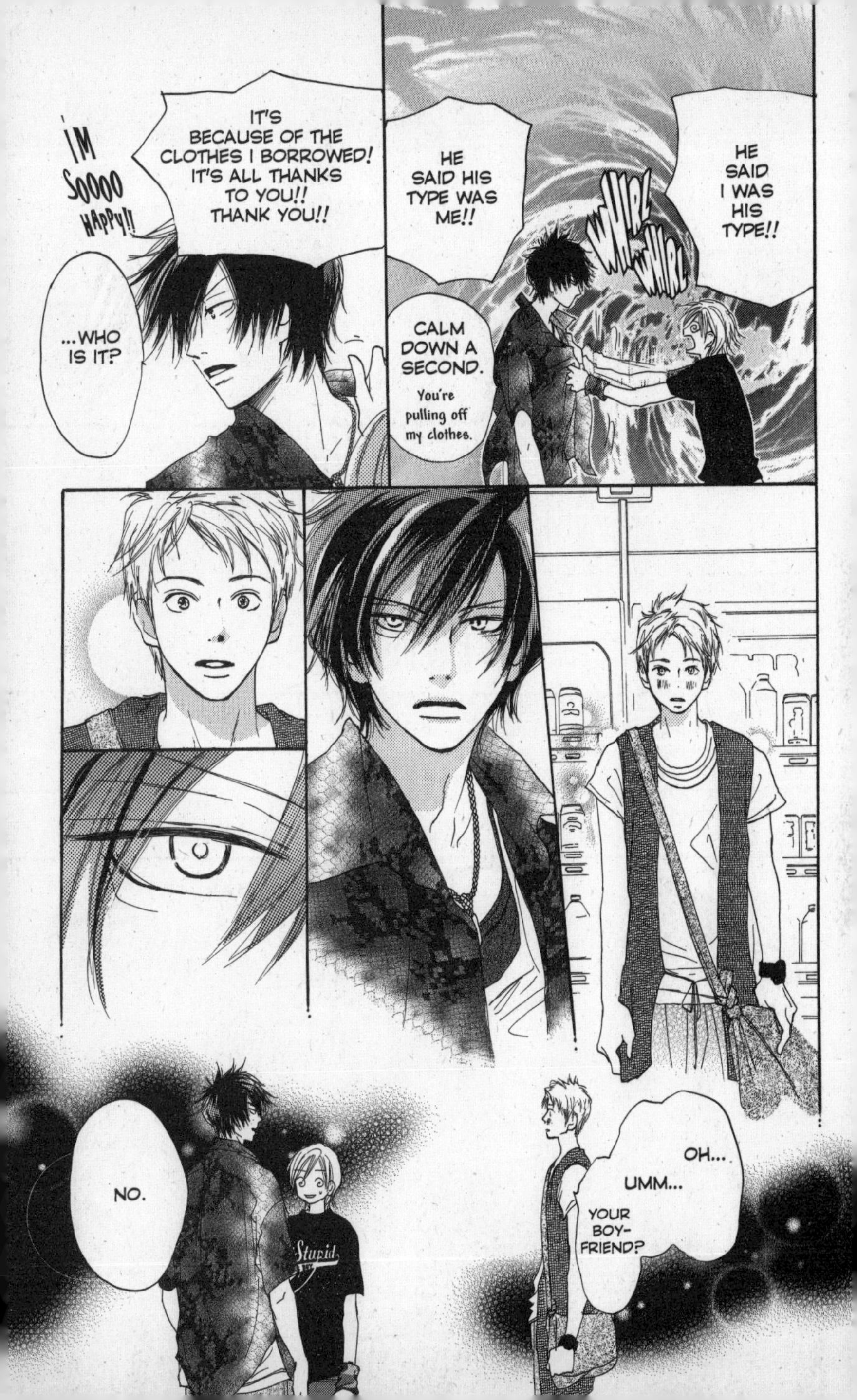
HE SAID I WAS HIS TYPE!!
WHIRL WHIRL
HE SAID HIS TYPE WAS ME!!
CALM DOWN A SECOND.
You're pulling off my clothes.
IT'S BECAUSE OF THE CLOTHES I BORROWED! IT'S ALL THANKS TO YOU!! THANK YOU!!
I'M SOOOO HAPPY!!
...WHO IS IT?
OH...
UMM...
YOUR BOY-FRIEND?
NO.
Stupid

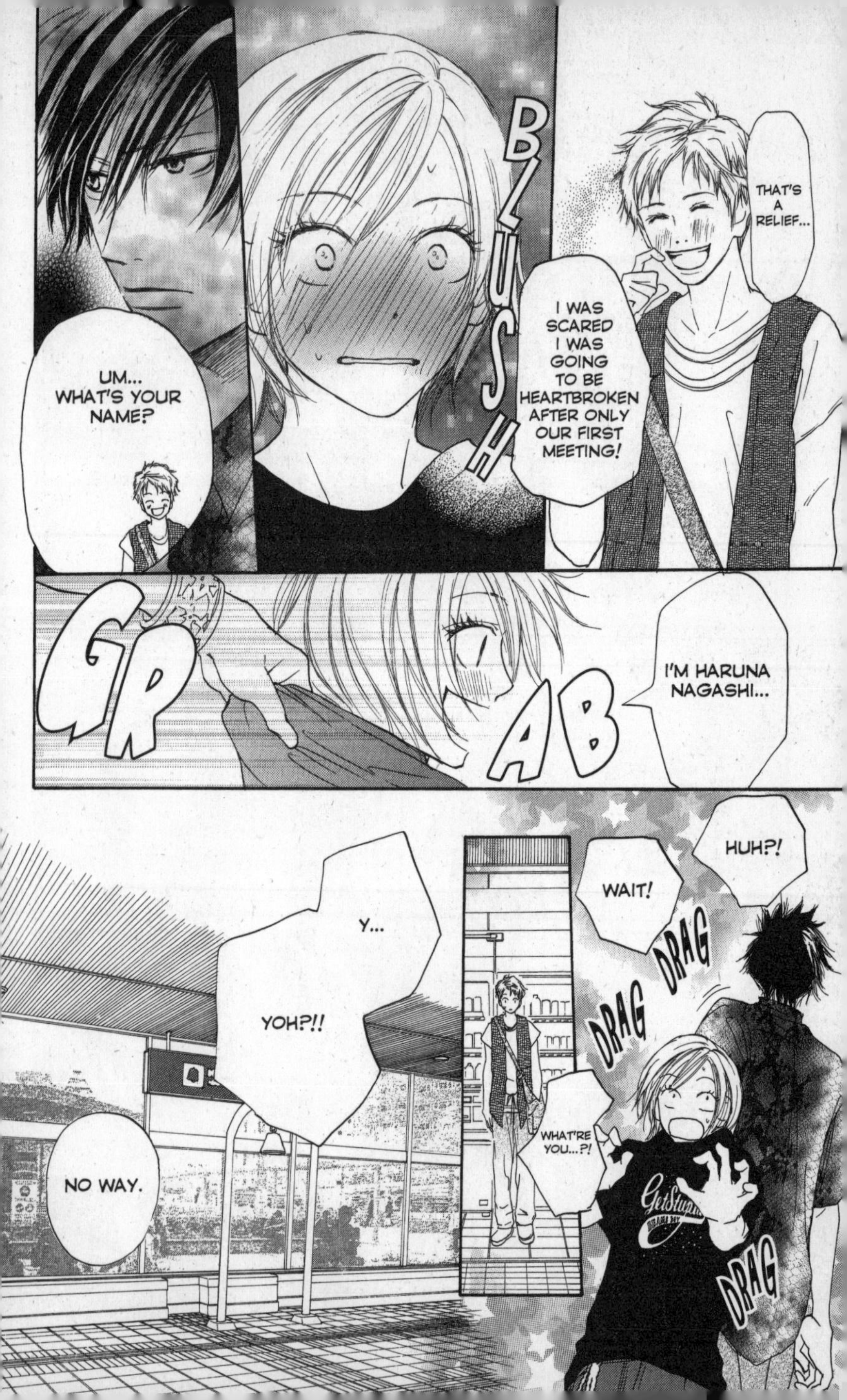
THAT'S A RELIEF...
I WAS SCARED I WAS GOING TO BE HEARTBROKEN AFTER ONLY OUR FIRST MEETING!
BLUSH
UM... WHAT'S YOUR NAME?
I'M HARUNA NAGASHI...
GRAB
HUH?!
WAIT!
DRAG
DRAG
WHAT'RE YOU...?!
DRAG
Y...
YOH?!!
NO WAY.

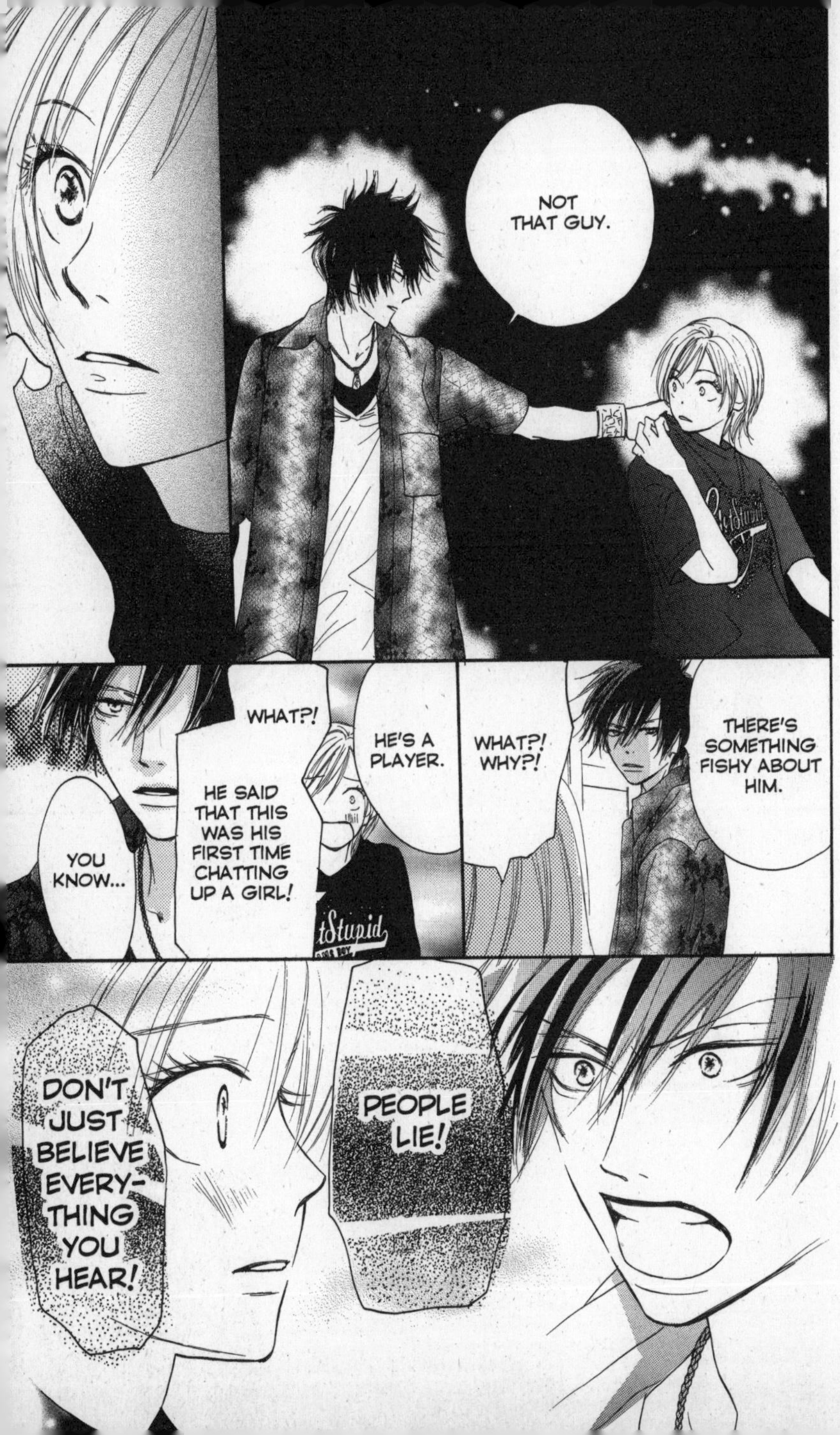
NOT THAT GUY.
THERE'S SOMETHING FISHY ABOUT HIM.
WHAT?! WHY?!
HE'S A PLAYER.
WHAT?!
HE SAID THAT THIS WAS HIS FIRST TIME CHATTING UP A GIRL!
YOU KNOW...
PEOPLE LIE!
DON'T JUST BELIEVE EVERY-THING YOU HEAR!

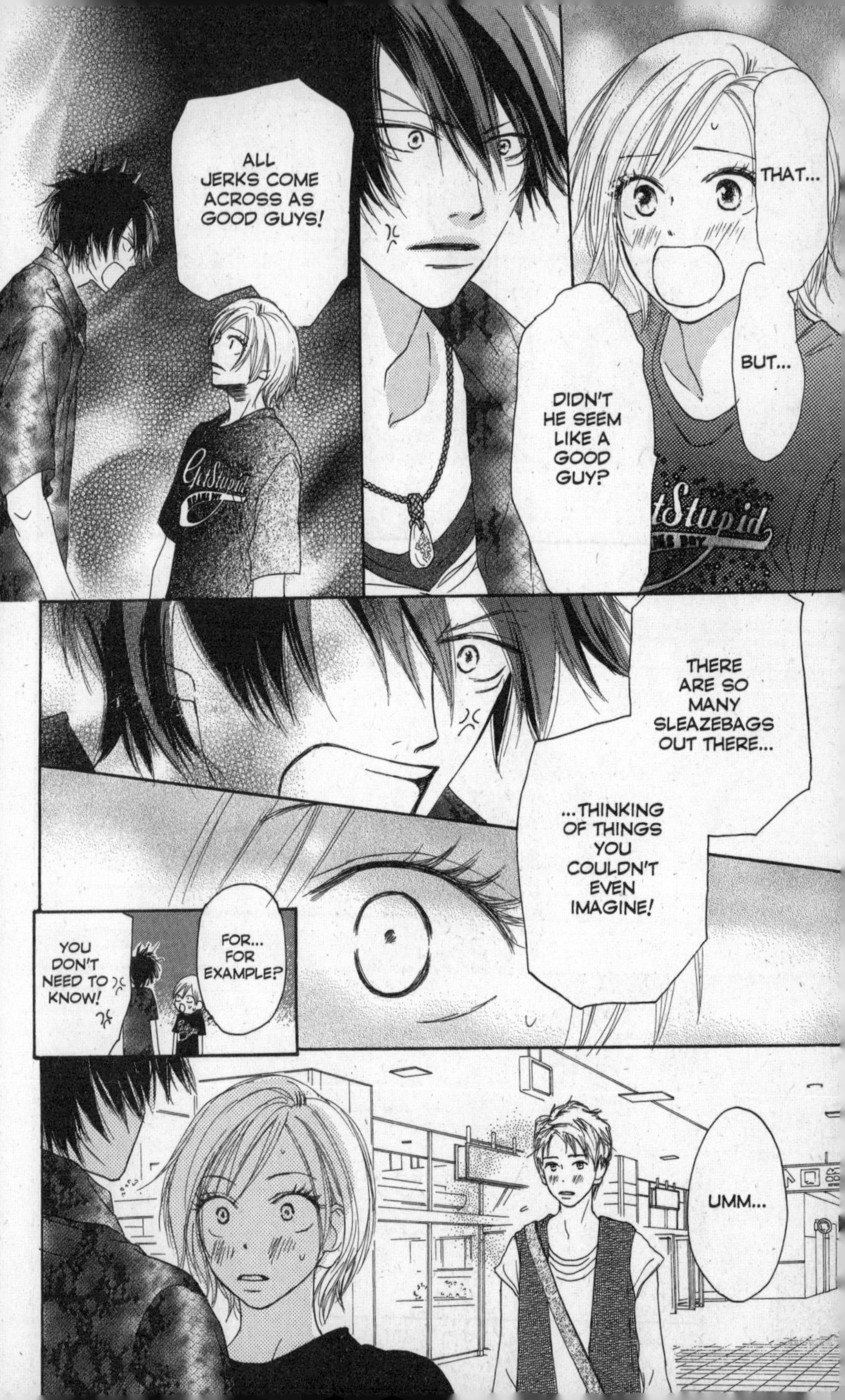
THAT...
BUT...
DIDN'T HE SEEM LIKE A GOOD GUY?
ALL JERKS COME ACROSS AS GOOD GUYS!
THERE ARE SO MANY SLEAZEBAGS OUT THERE...
...THINKING OF THINGS YOU COULDN'T EVEN IMAGINE!
FOR... FOR EXAMPLE?
YOU DON'T NEED TO KNOW!
UMM...

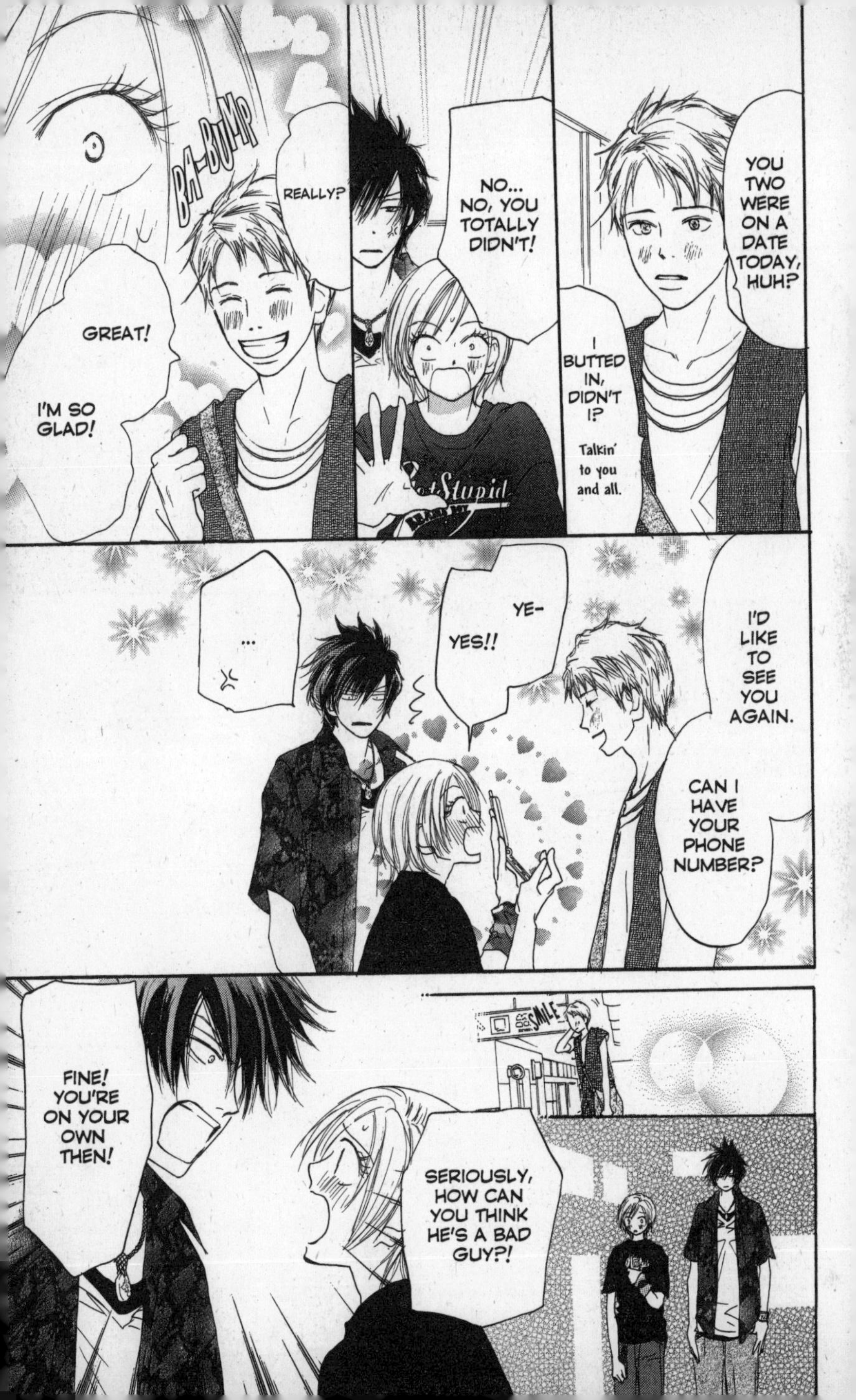
YOU TWO WERE ON A DATE TODAY, HUH?
I BUTTED IN, DIDN'T I?
Talkin' to you and all.
NO... NO, YOU TOTALLY DIDN'T!
REALLY?
BA-BUMP
GREAT!
I'M SO GLAD!
I'D LIKE TO SEE YOU AGAIN.
CAN I HAVE YOUR PHONE NUMBER?
YE- YES!!
...
SMILE
SERIOUSLY, HOW CAN YOU THINK HE'S A BAD GUY?!
FINE! YOU'RE ON YOUR OWN THEN!

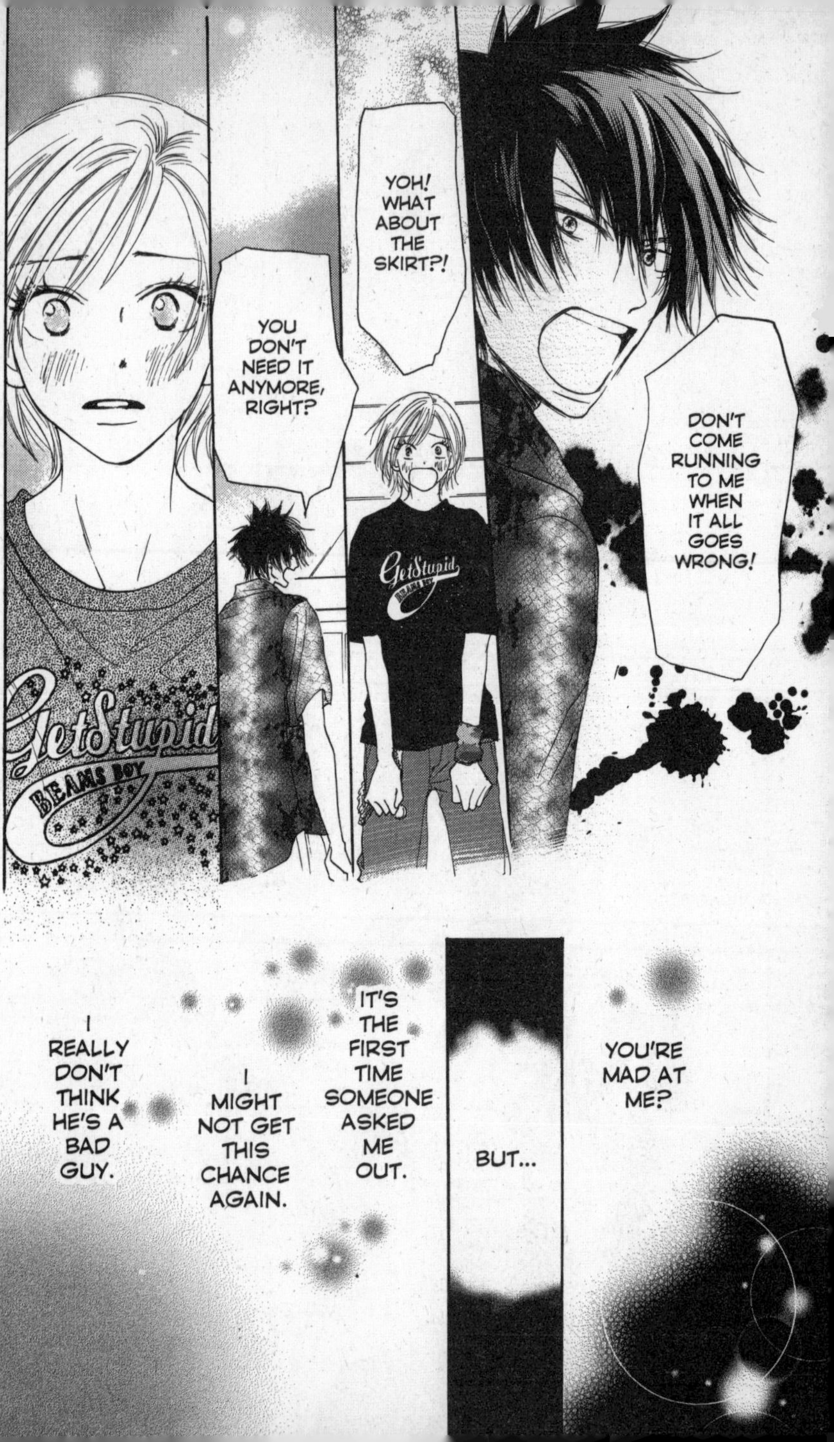
DON'T COME RUNNING TO ME WHEN IT ALL GOES WRONG!
YOH! WHAT ABOUT THE SKIRT?!
YOU DON'T NEED IT ANYMORE, RIGHT?
YOU'RE MAD AT ME?
BUT...
IT'S THE FIRST TIME SOMEONE ASKED ME OUT.
I MIGHT NOT GET THIS CHANCE AGAIN.
I REALLY DON'T THINK HE'S A BAD GUY.

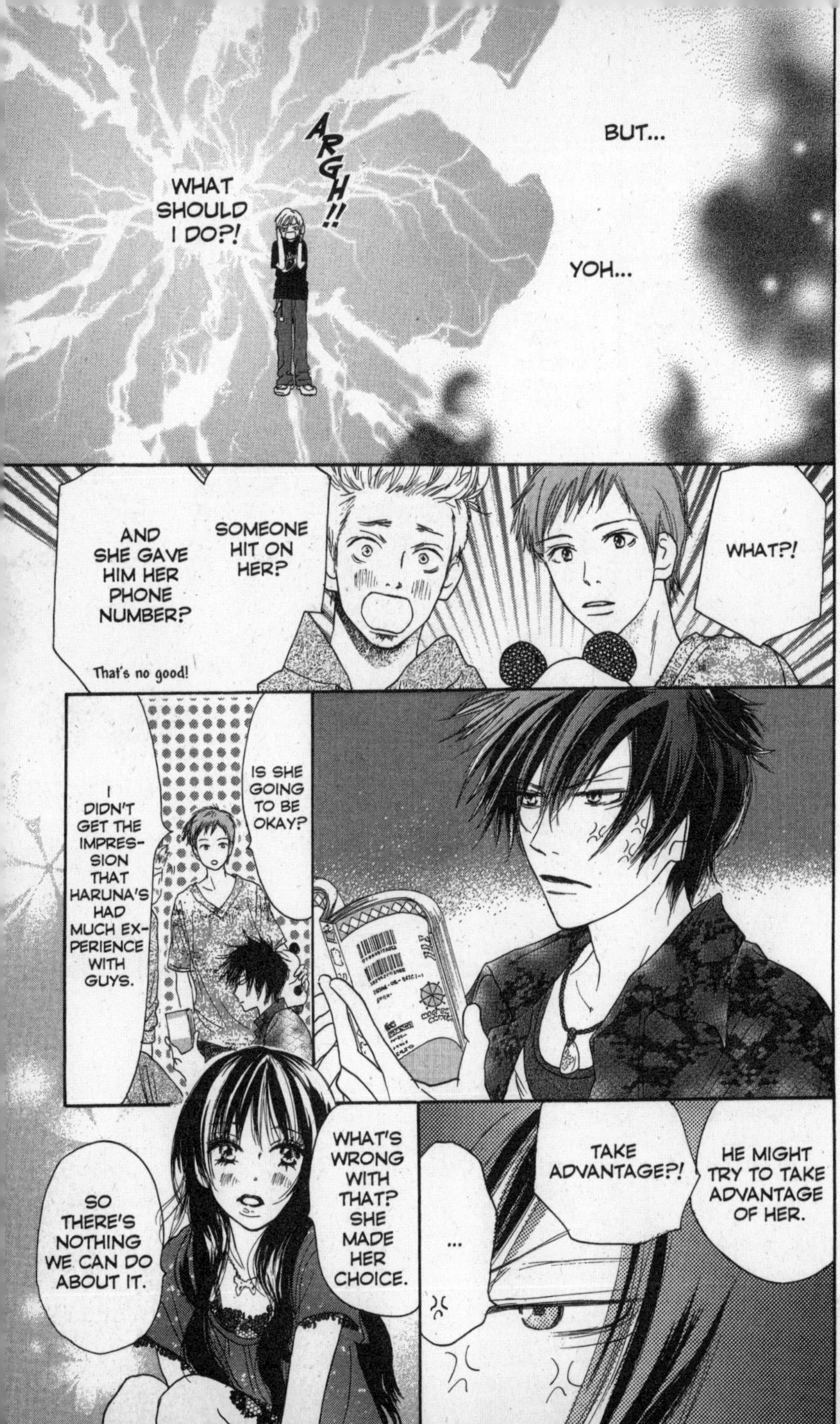

BUT...
YOH...
ARGH!!
WHAT SHOULD I DO?!
WHAT?!
SOMEONE HIT ON HER?
AND SHE GAVE HIM HER PHONE NUMBER?
That's no good!
IS SHE GOING TO BE OKAY?
I DIDN'T GET THE IMPRESSION THAT HARUNA'S HAD MUCH EXPERIENCE WITH GUYS.
HE MIGHT TRY TO TAKE ADVANTAGE OF HER.
TAKE ADVANTAGE?!
...
WHAT'S WRONG WITH THAT? SHE MADE HER CHOICE.
SO THERE'S NOTHING WE CAN DO ABOUT IT.

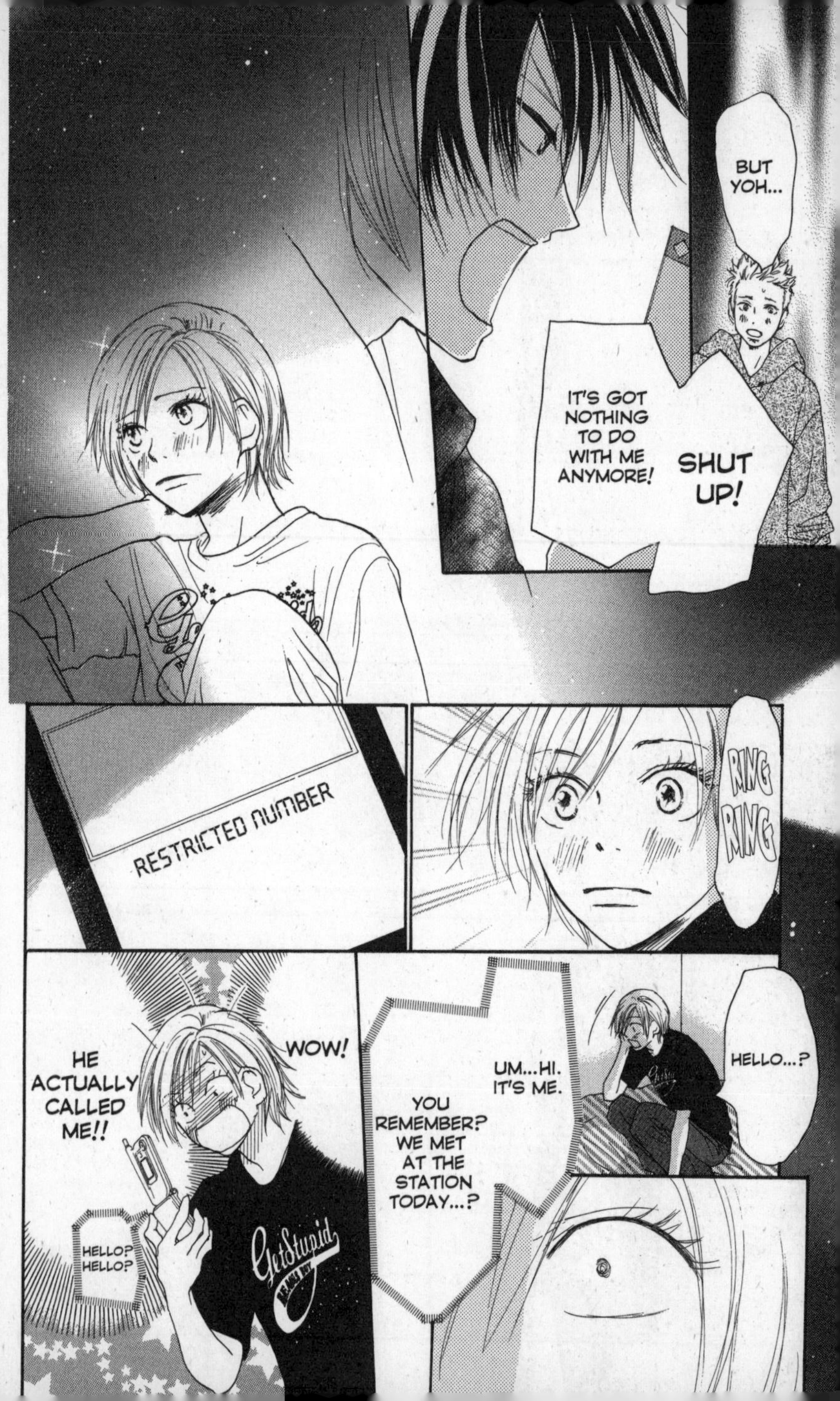
BUT YOH...
SHUT UP!
IT'S GOT NOTHING TO DO WITH ME ANYMORE!
RING RING
RESTRICTED NUMBER
HELLO...?
UM...HI. IT'S ME.
YOU REMEMBER? WE MET AT THE STATION TODAY...?
WOW!
HE ACTUALLY CALLED ME!!
HELLO? HELLO?

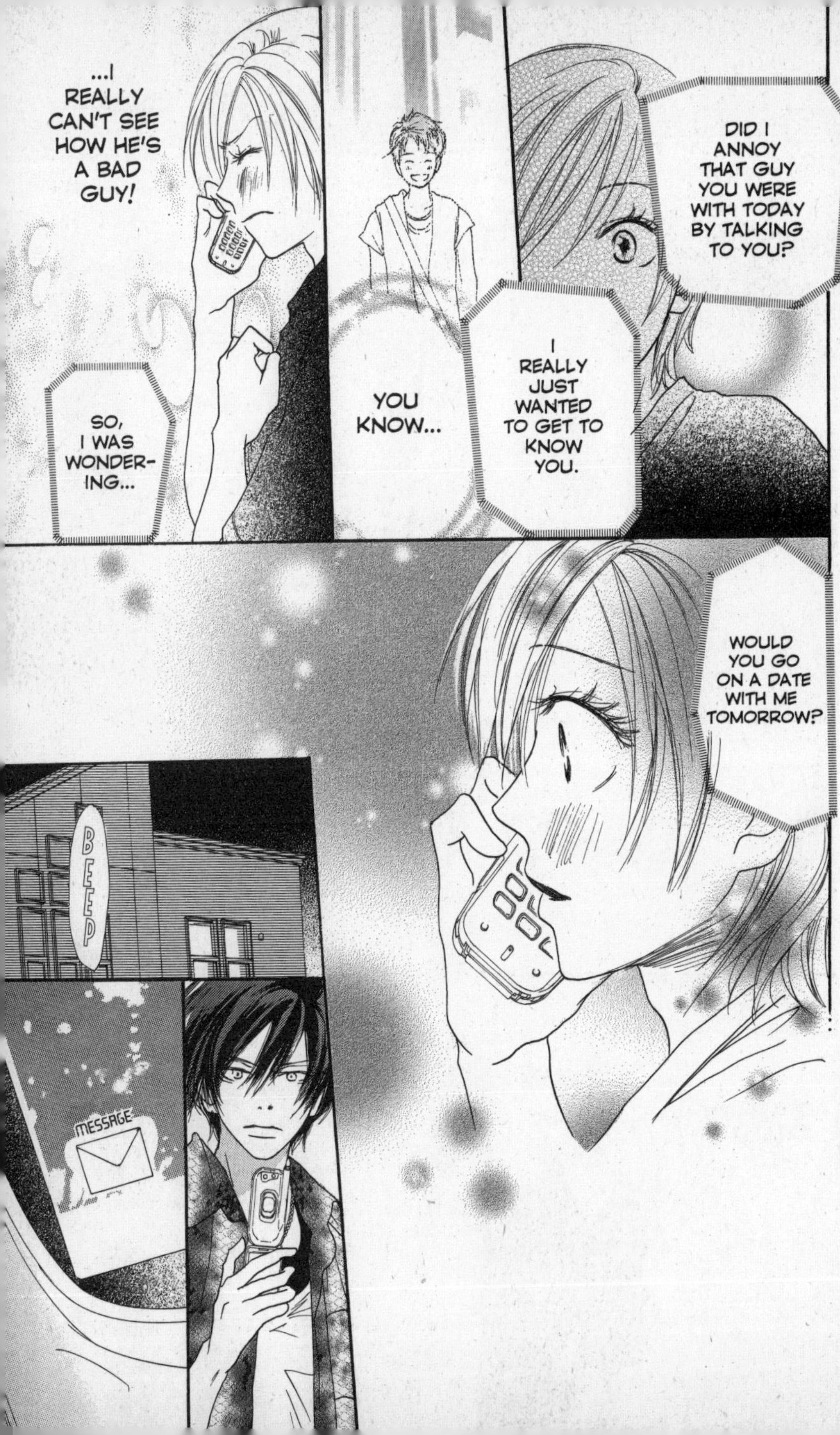
DID I ANNOY THAT GUY YOU WERE WITH TODAY BY TALKING TO YOU?
I REALLY JUST WANTED TO GET TO KNOW YOU.
YOU KNOW...
...I REALLY CAN'T SEE HOW HE'S A BAD GUY!
SO, I WAS WONDER-ING...
WOULD YOU GO ON A DATE WITH ME TOMORROW?
BEEP
MESSAGE

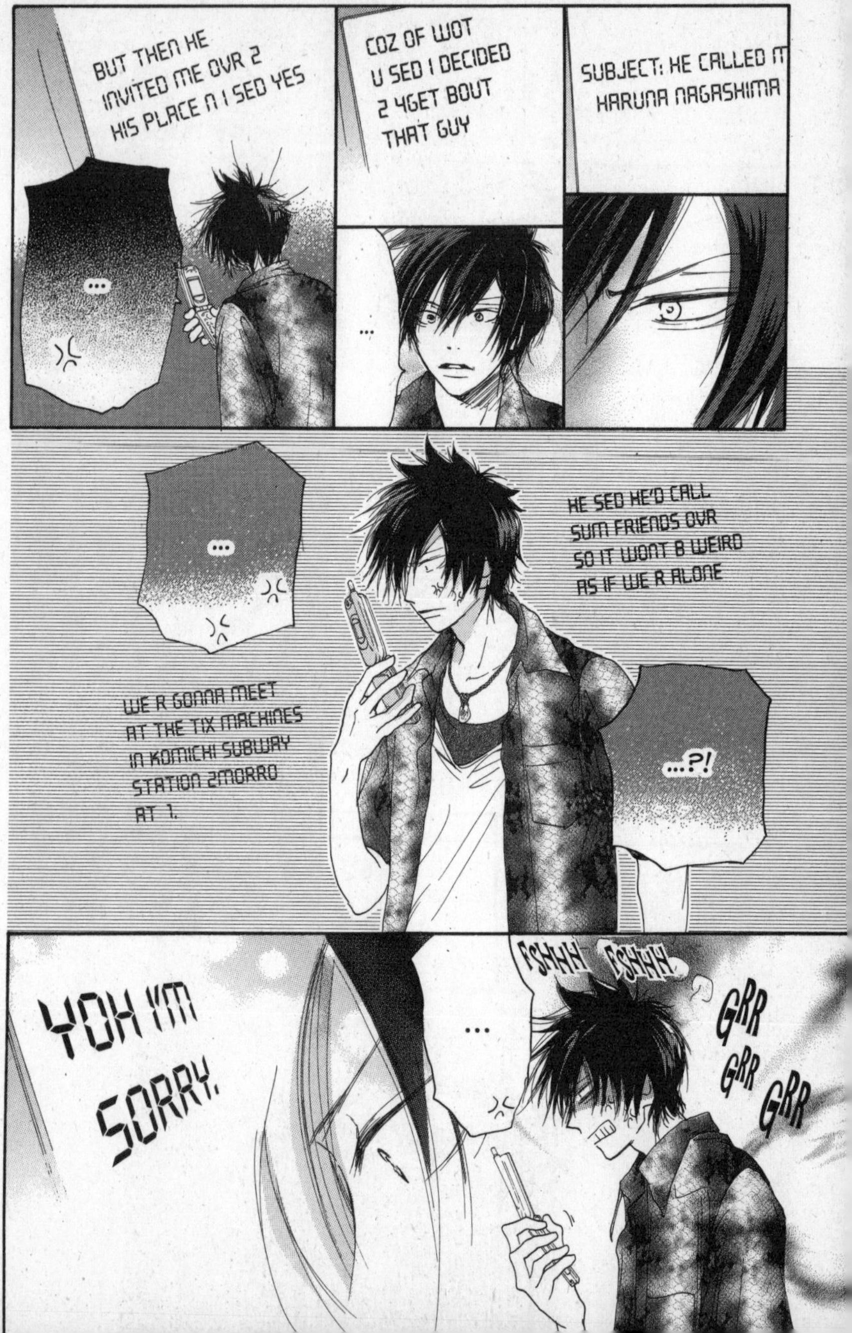
SUBJECT: HE CALLED M
HARUNA NAGASHIMA
COZ OF WOT U SED I DECIDED 2 4GET BOUT THAT GUY
...
BUT THEN HE INVITED ME OVR 2 HIS PLACE N I SED YES
...
HE SED HE'D CALL SUM FRIENDS OVR SO IT WONT B WEIRD AS IF WE R ALONE
...
WE R GONNA MEET AT THE TIX MACHINES IN KOMICHI SUBWAY STATION 2MORRO AT 1.
...?!
FSHHH FSHHH
GRR GRR GRR
...
YOH I'M SORRY.

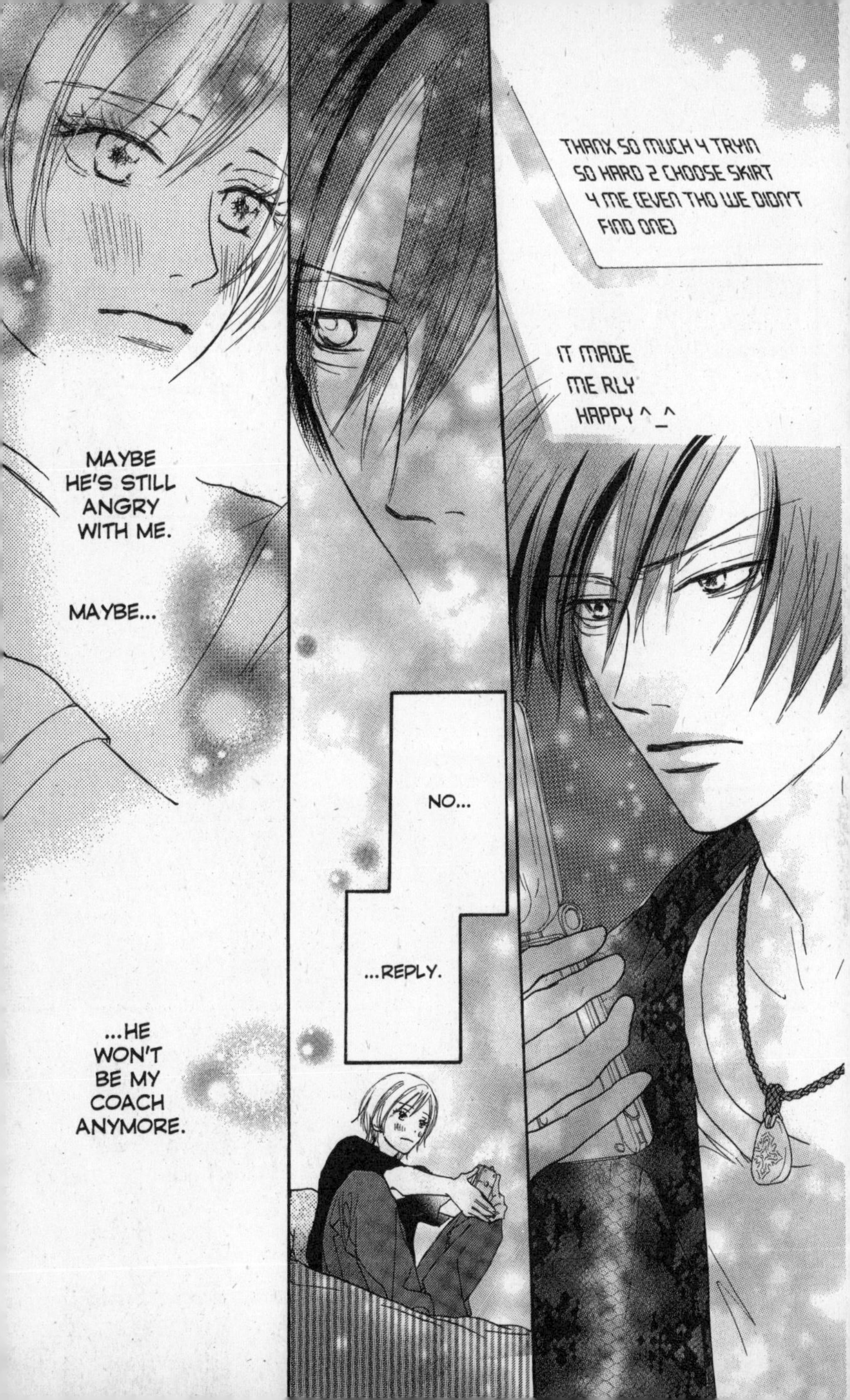
THANX SO MUCH 4 TRYIN SO HARD 2 CHOOSE SKIRT 4 ME (EVEN THO WE DIDN'T FIND ONE)
IT MADE ME RLY HAPPY ^_^
NO...
...REPLY.
MAYBE HE'S STILL ANGRY WITH ME.
MAYBE...
...HE WON'T BE MY COACH ANYMORE.

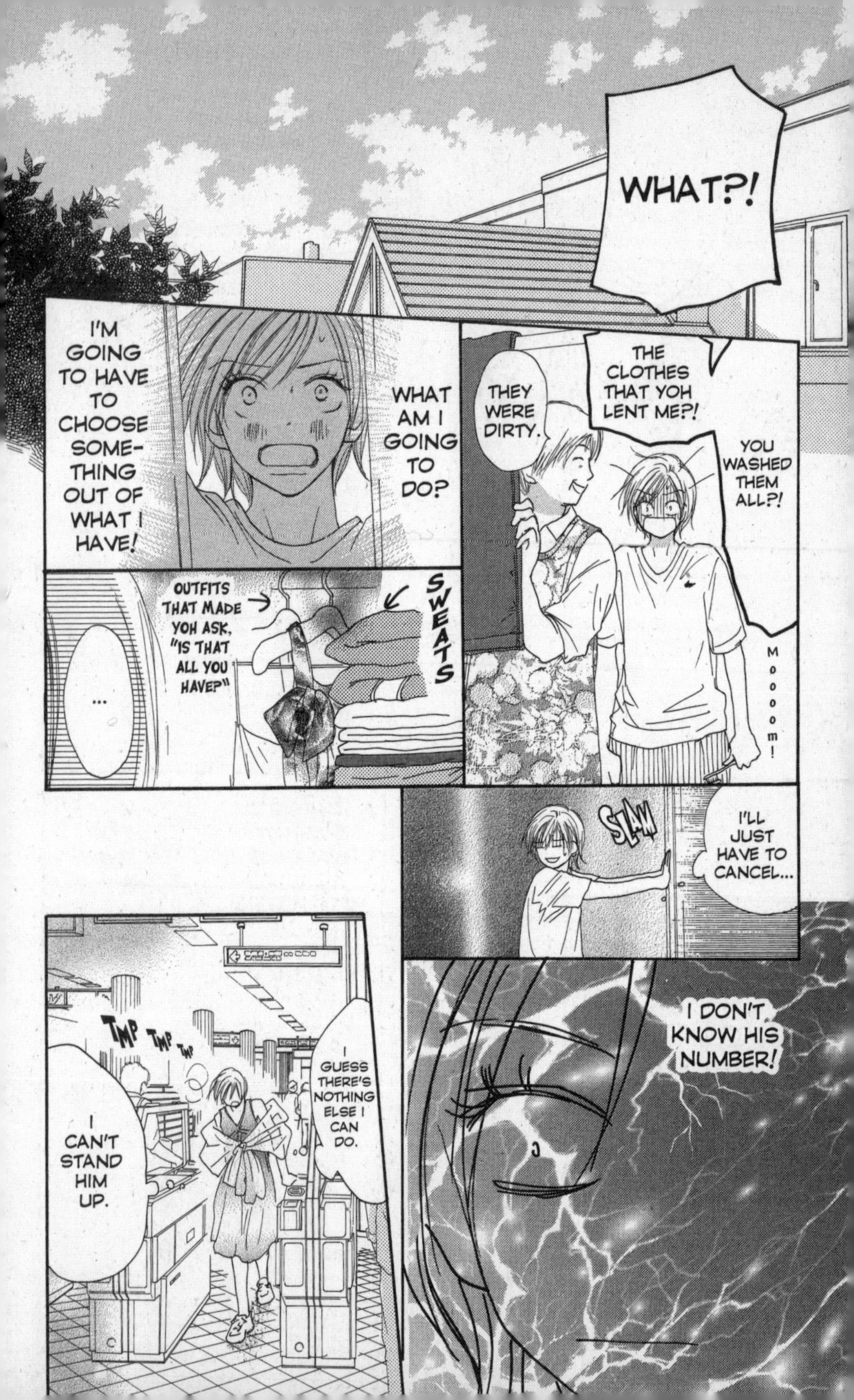
WHAT?!
THE CLOTHES THAT YOH LENT ME?!
THEY WERE DIRTY.
YOU WASHED THEM ALL?!
Mooooom!
WHAT AM I GOING TO DO?
I'M GOING TO HAVE TO CHOOSE SOME-THING OUT OF WHAT I HAVE!
SWEATS
OUTFITS THAT MADE YOH ASK, "IS THAT ALL YOU HAVE?"
...
SLAM
I'LL JUST HAVE TO CANCEL...
I DON'T KNOW HIS NUMBER!
I GUESS THERE'S NOTHING ELSE I CAN DO.
TMP TMP TMP
I CAN'T STAND HIM UP.

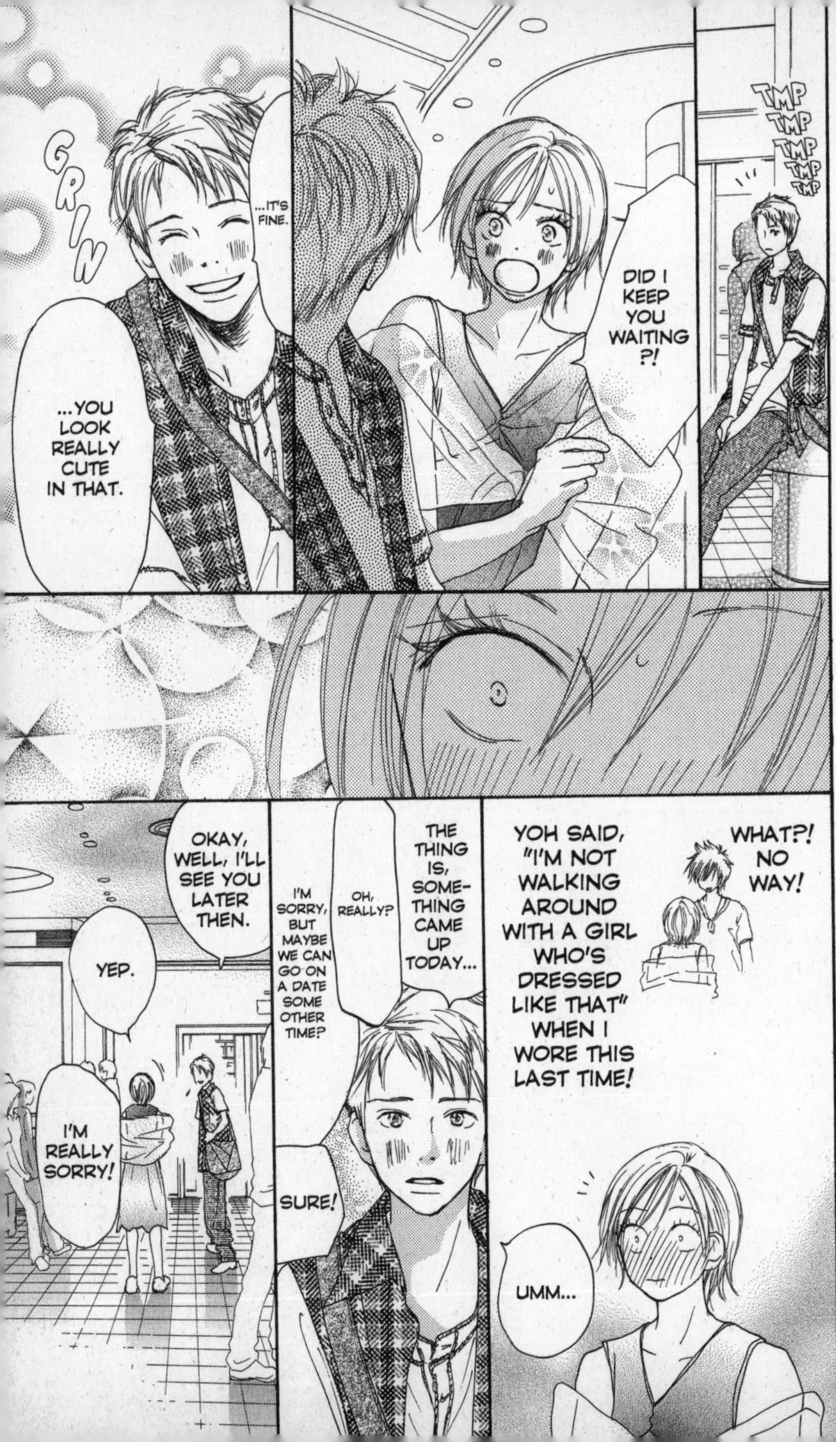

TMP TMP TMP TMP TMP
DID I KEEP YOU WAITING?!
...IT'S FINE.
GRIN
...YOU LOOK REALLY CUTE IN THAT.
WHAT?! NO WAY!
YOH SAID, "I'M NOT WALKING AROUND WITH A GIRL WHO'S DRESSED LIKE THAT" WHEN I WORE THIS LAST TIME!
UMM...
THE THING IS, SOME-THING CAME UP TODAY...
OH, REALLY?
I'M SORRY, BUT MAYBE WE CAN GO ON A DATE SOME OTHER TIME?
SURE!
OKAY, WELL, I'LL SEE YOU LATER THEN.
YEP.
I'M REALLY SORRY!

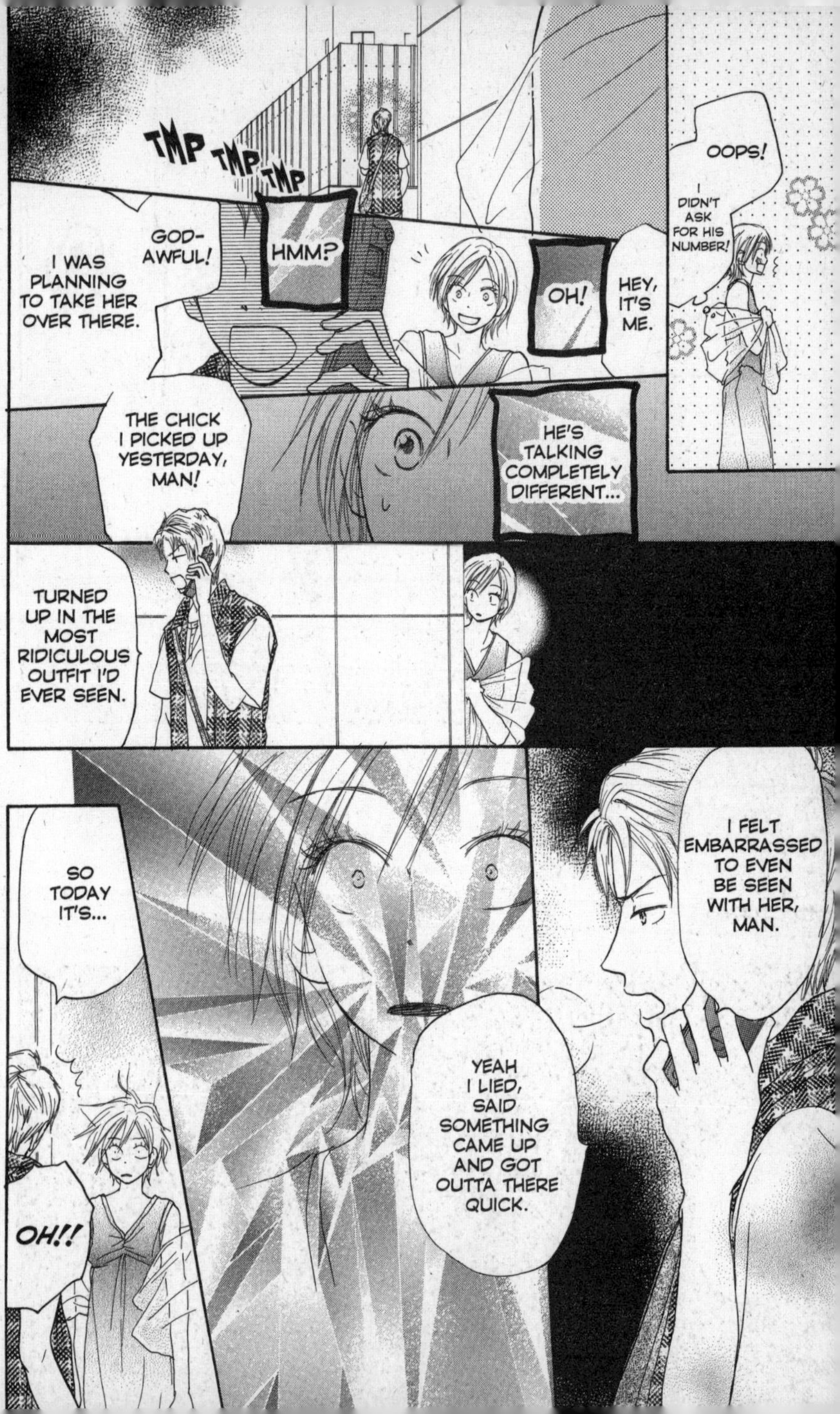
OOPS!
I DIDN'T ASK FOR HIS NUMBER!
TMP TMP TMP
HEY, IT'S ME.
OH!
HMM?
GOD-AWFUL!
I WAS PLANNING TO TAKE HER OVER THERE.
HE'S TALKING COMPLETELY DIFFERENT...
THE CHICK I PICKED UP YESTERDAY, MAN!
TURNED UP IN THE MOST RIDICULOUS OUTFIT I'D EVER SEEN.
I FELT EMBARRASSED TO EVEN BE SEEN WITH HER, MAN.
YEAH I LIED, SAID SOMETHING CAME UP AND GOT OUTTA THERE QUICK.
SO TODAY IT'S...
OH!!

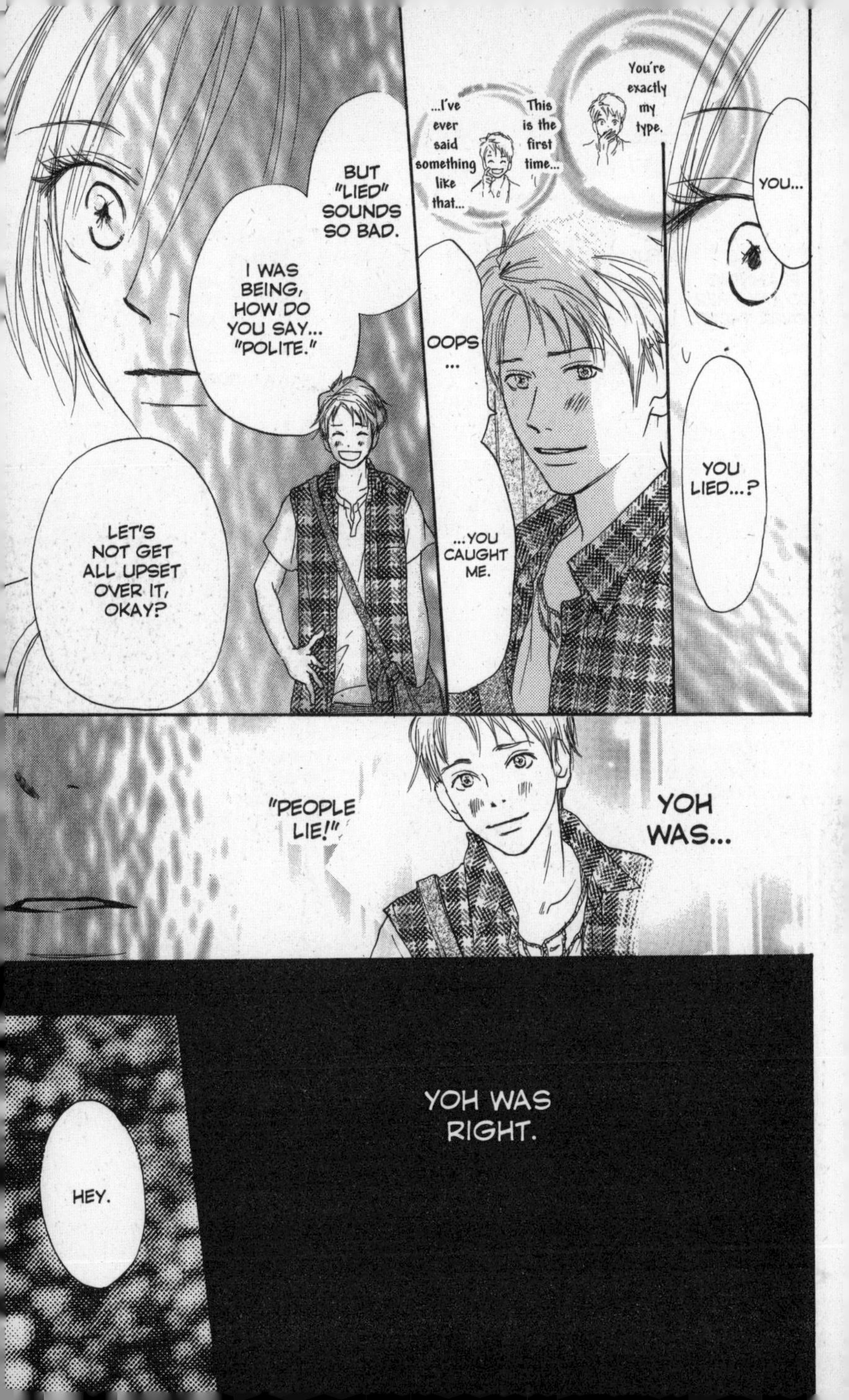
YOU...
YOU LIED...?
You're exactly my type.
This is the first time...
...I've ever said something like that...
OOPS...
...YOU CAUGHT ME.
BUT "LIED" SOUNDS SO BAD.
I WAS BEING, HOW DO YOU SAY... "POLITE."
LET'S NOT GET ALL UPSET OVER IT, OKAY?
YOH WAS...
"PEOPLE LIE!"
YOH WAS RIGHT.
HEY.

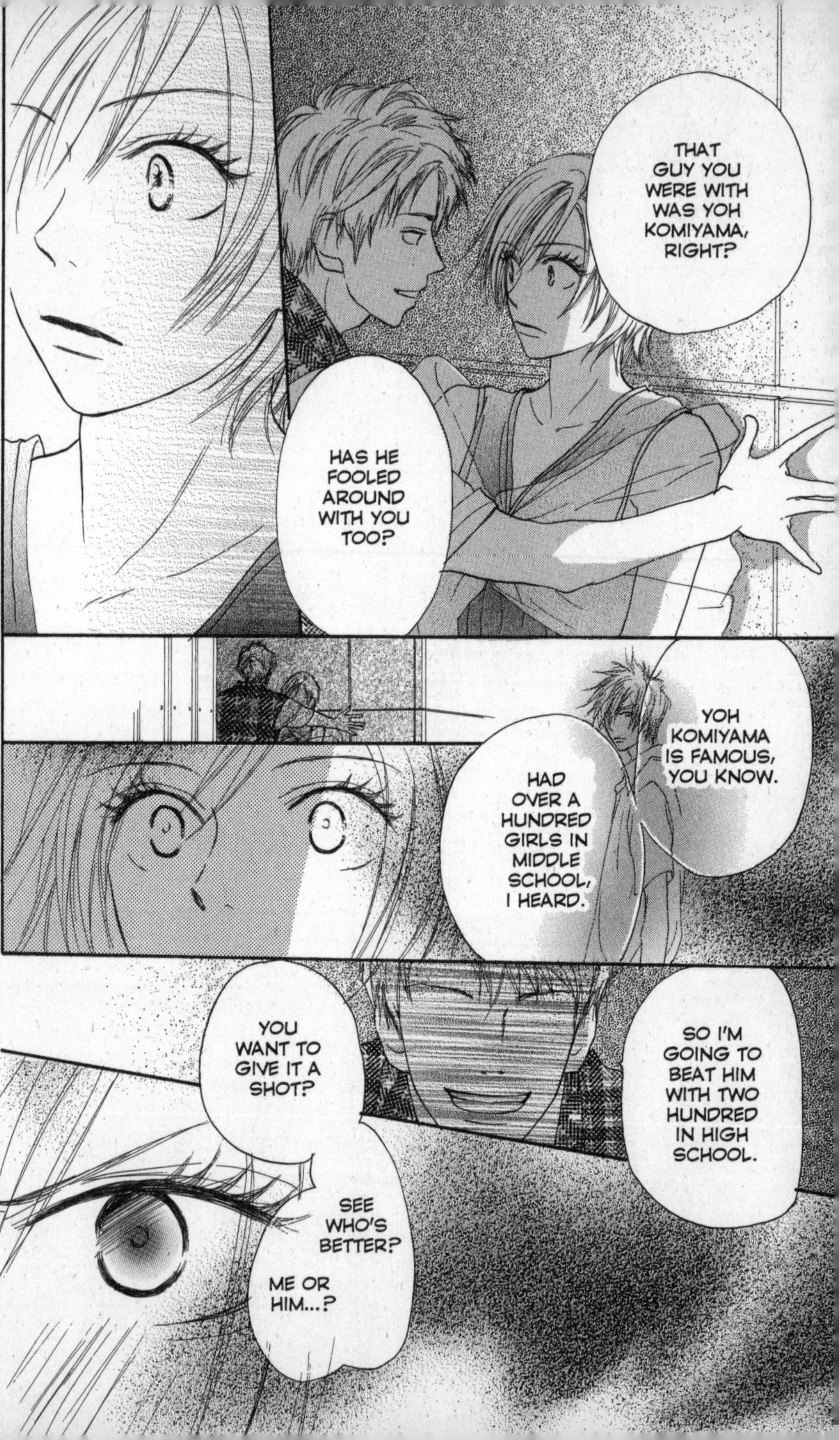
THAT GUY YOU WERE WITH WAS YOH KOMIYAMA, RIGHT?
HAS HE FOOLED AROUND WITH YOU TOO?
YOH KOMIYAMA IS FAMOUS, YOU KNOW.
HAD OVER A HUNDRED GIRLS IN MIDDLE SCHOOL, I HEARD.
SO I'M GOING TO BEAT HIM WITH TWO HUNDRED IN HIGH SCHOOL.
YOU WANT TO GIVE IT A SHOT?
SEE WHO'S BETTER?
ME OR HIM...?

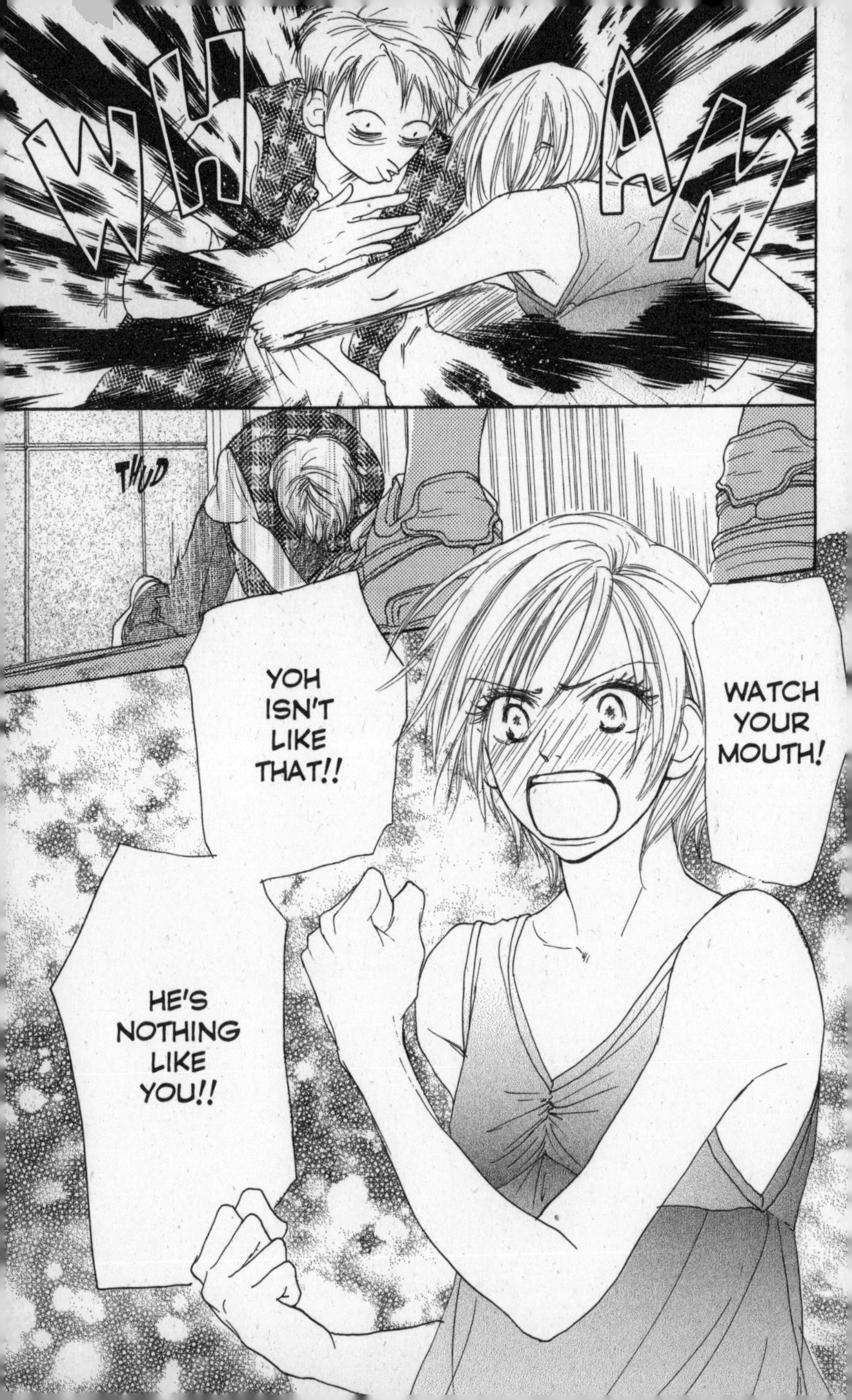
WHAM
THUD
WATCH YOUR MOUTH!
YOH ISN'T LIKE THAT!!
HE'S NOTHING LIKE YOU!!

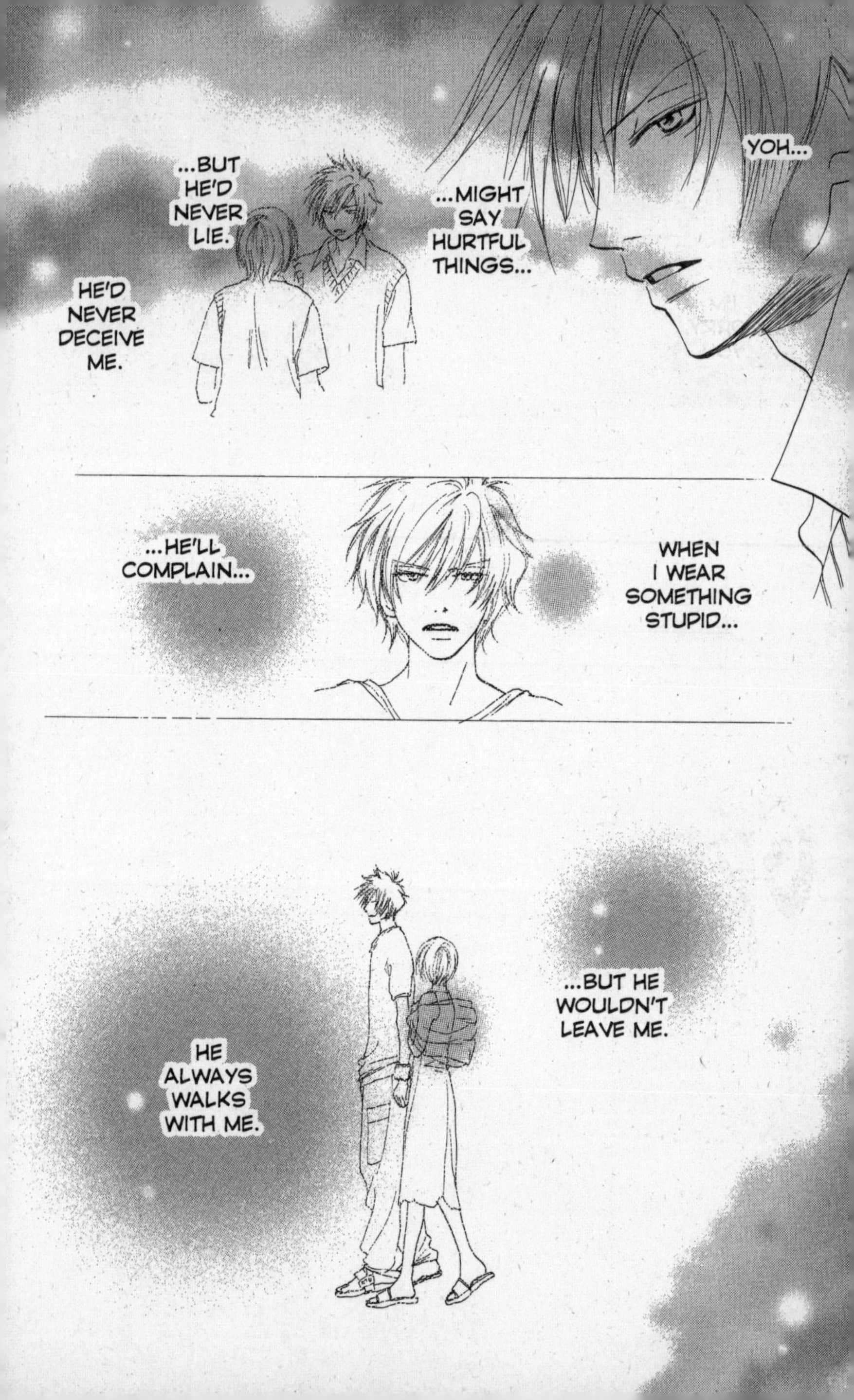
YOH...
...MIGHT SAY HURTFUL THINGS...
...BUT HE'D NEVER LIE.
HE'D NEVER DECEIVE ME.
WHEN I WEAR SOMETHING STUPID...
...HE'LL COMPLAIN...
...BUT HE WOULDN'T LEAVE ME.
HE ALWAYS WALKS WITH ME.

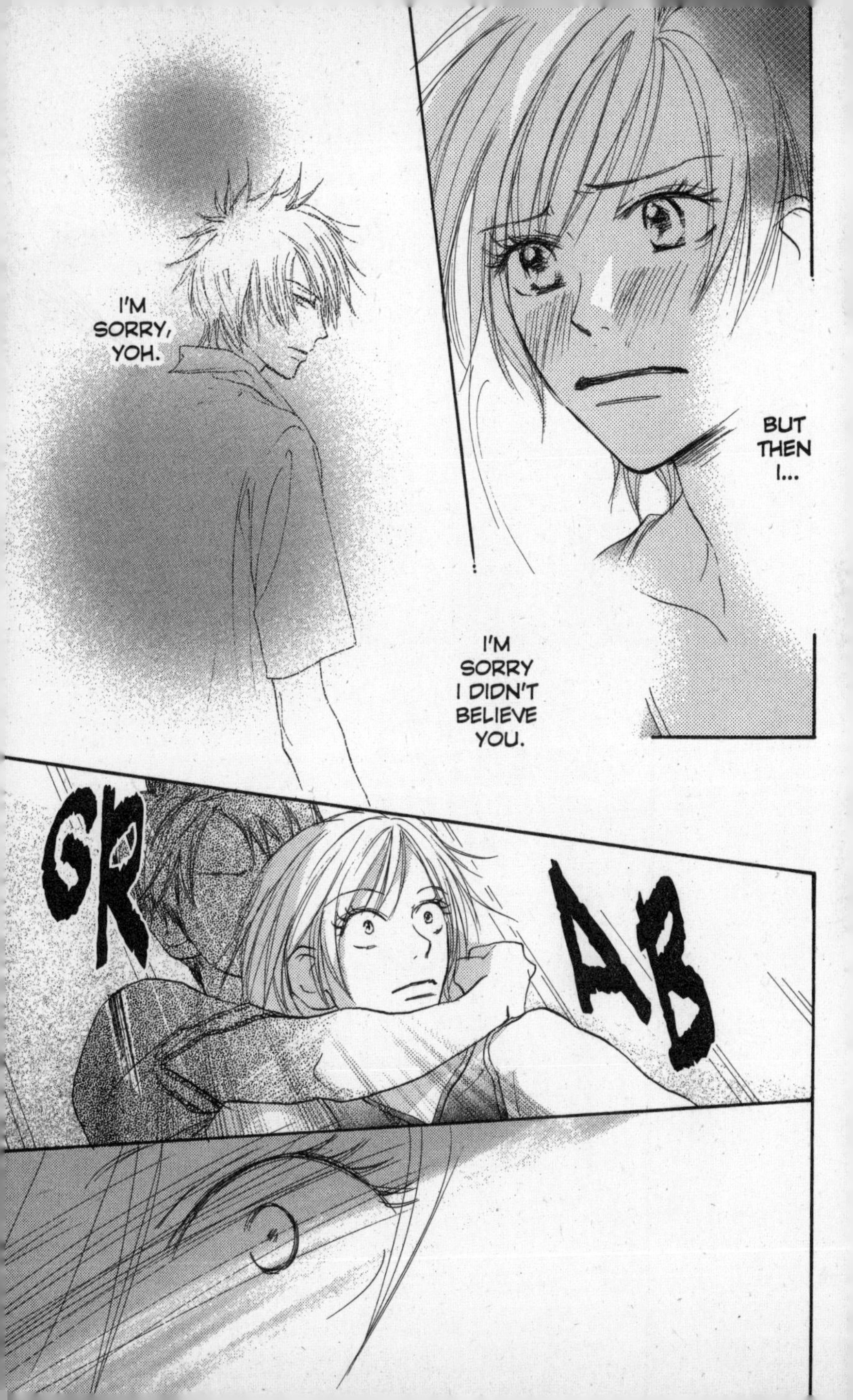
BUT THEN I...
I'M SORRY I DIDN'T BELIEVE YOU.
I'M SORRY, YOH.
GRAB

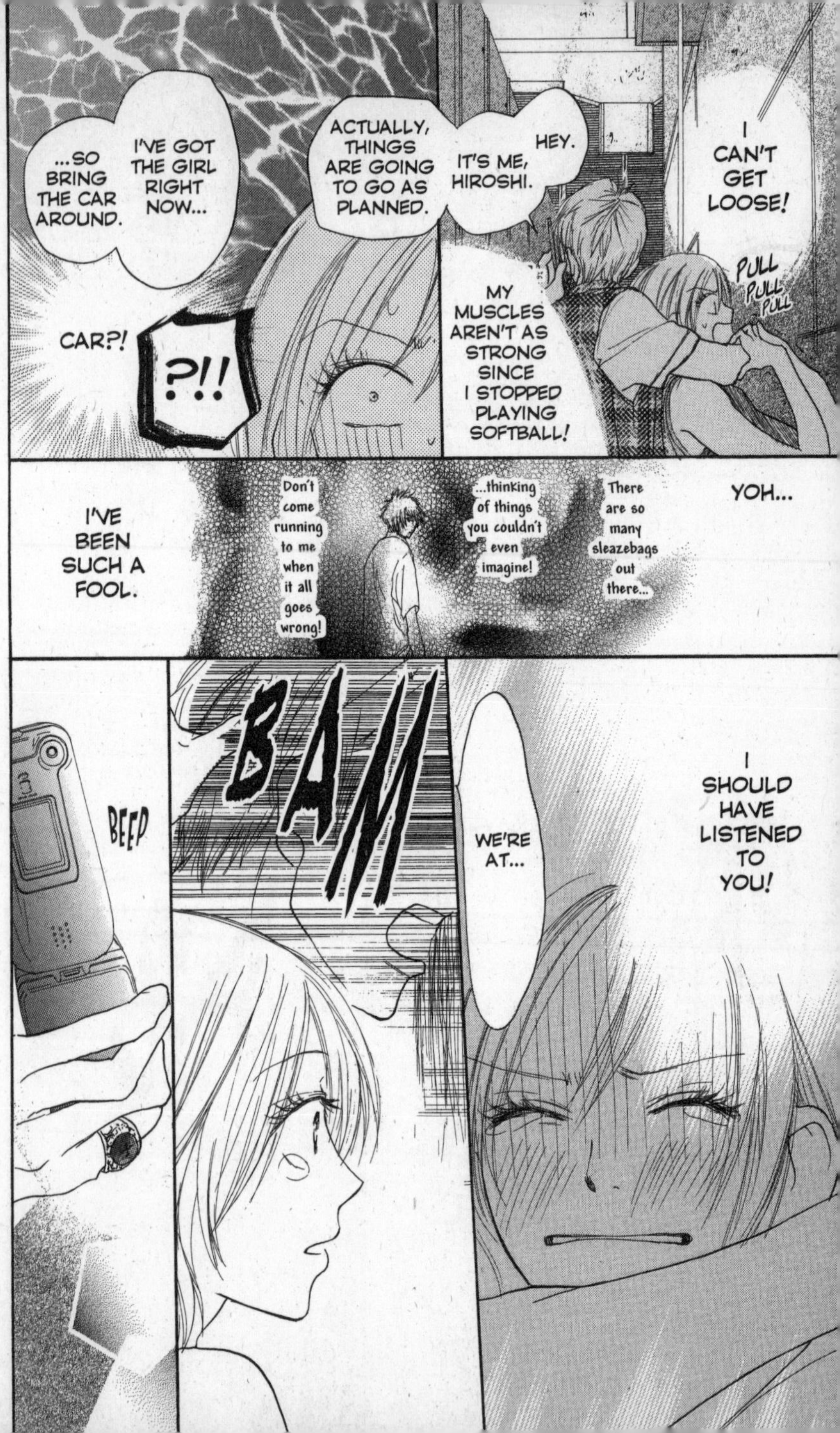
I CAN'T GET LOOSE!
PULL PULL PULL
HEY.
IT'S ME, HIROSHI.
MY MUSCLES AREN'T AS STRONG SINCE I STOPPED PLAYING SOFTBALL!
ACTUALLY, THINGS ARE GOING TO GO AS PLANNED.
I'VE GOT THE GIRL RIGHT NOW...
...SO BRING THE CAR AROUND.
?!!
CAR?!
YOH...
There are so many sleazebags out there...
...thinking of things you couldn't even imagine!
Don't come running to me when it all goes wrong!
I'VE BEEN SUCH A FOOL.
I SHOULD HAVE LISTENED TO YOU!
WE'RE AT...
BAM
BEEP

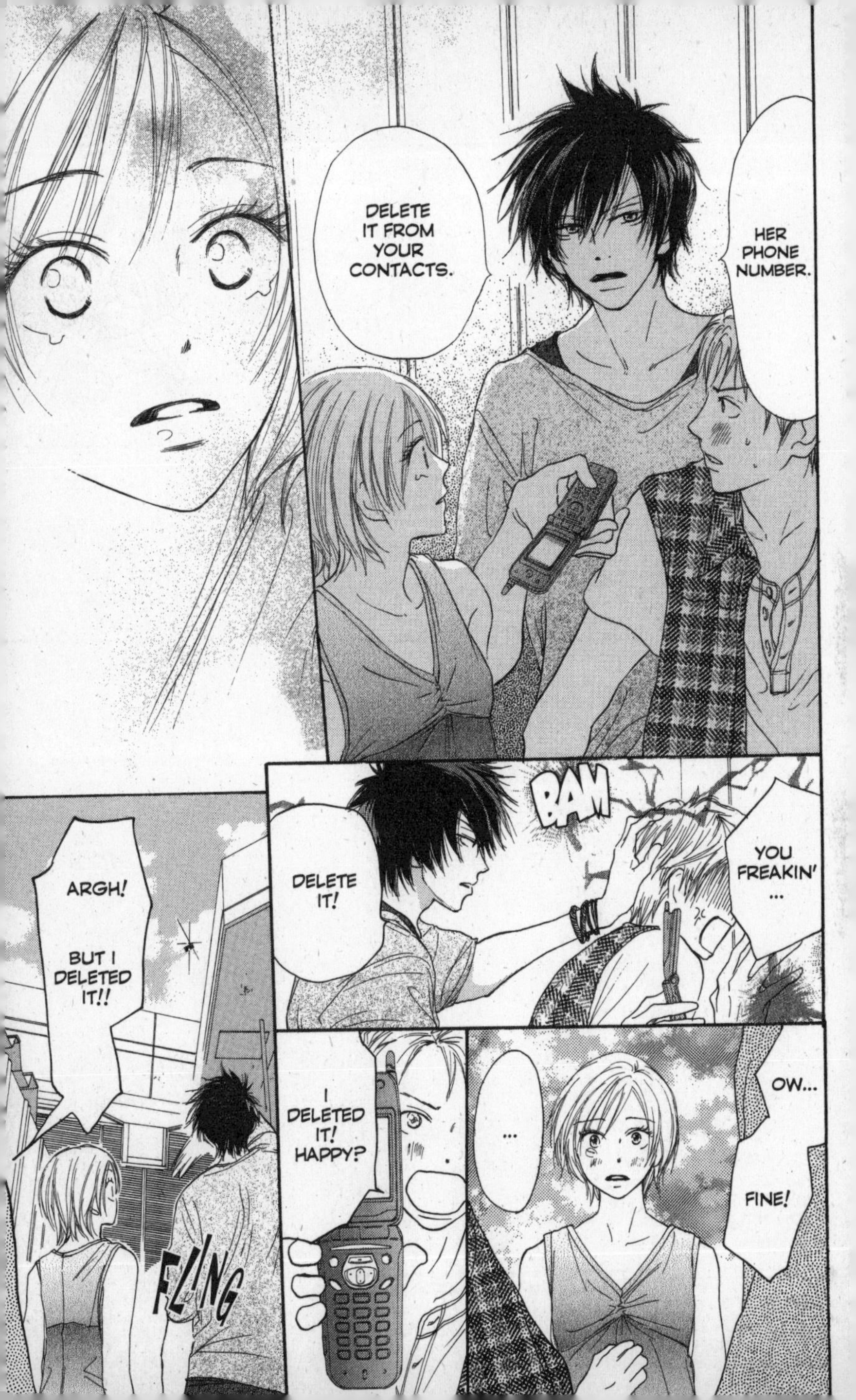
HER PHONE NUMBER.
DELETE IT FROM YOUR CONTACTS.
YOU FREAKIN' ...
BAM
DELETE IT!
OW...
FINE!
...
I DELETED IT! HAPPY?
ARGH!
BUT I DELETED IT!!
FLING

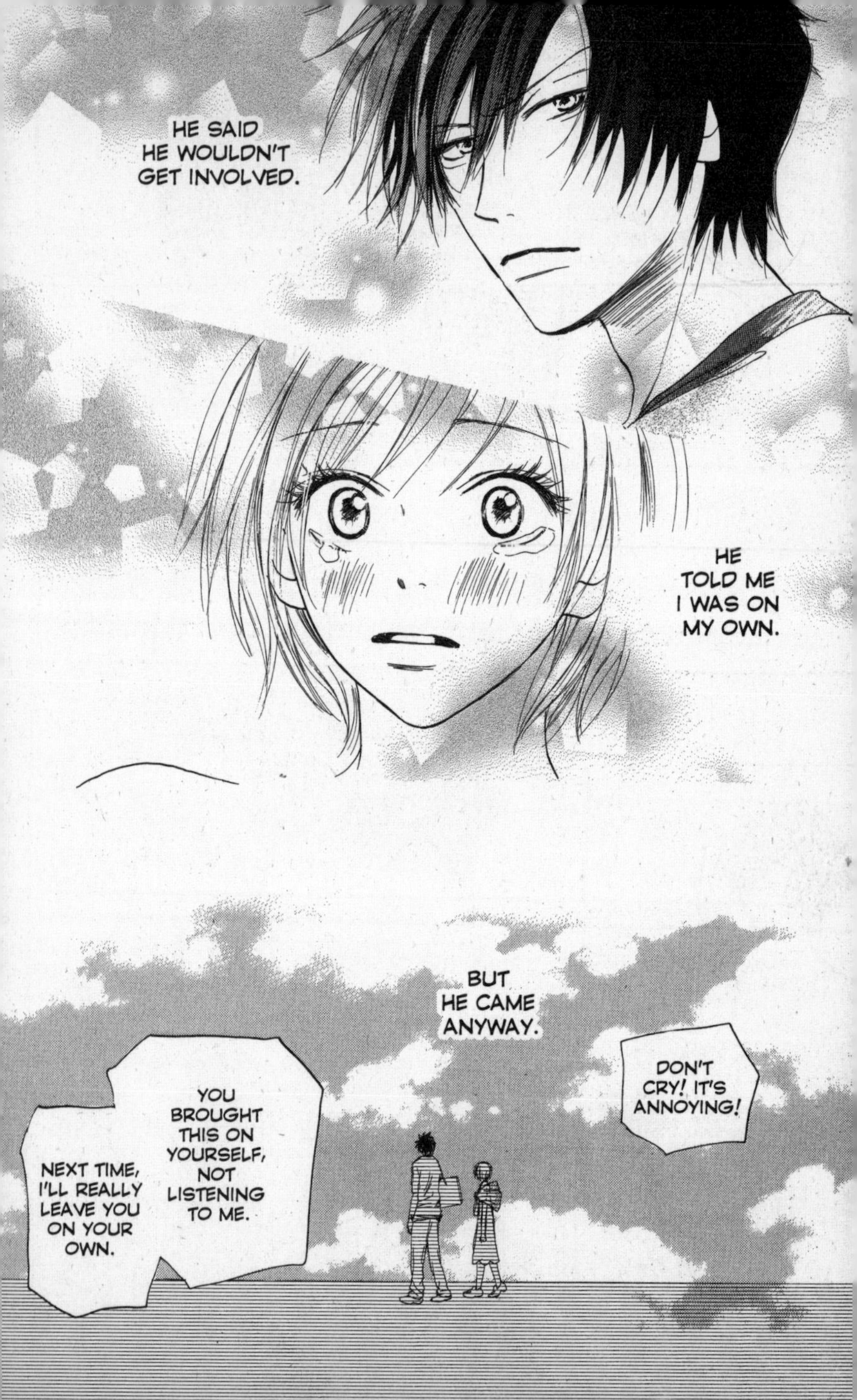
HE SAID HE WOULDN'T GET INVOLVED.
HE TOLD ME I WAS ON MY OWN.
BUT HE CAME ANYWAY.
DON'T CRY! IT'S ANNOYING!
YOU BROUGHT THIS ON YOURSELF, NOT LISTENING TO ME.
NEXT TIME, I'LL REALLY LEAVE YOU ON YOUR OWN.

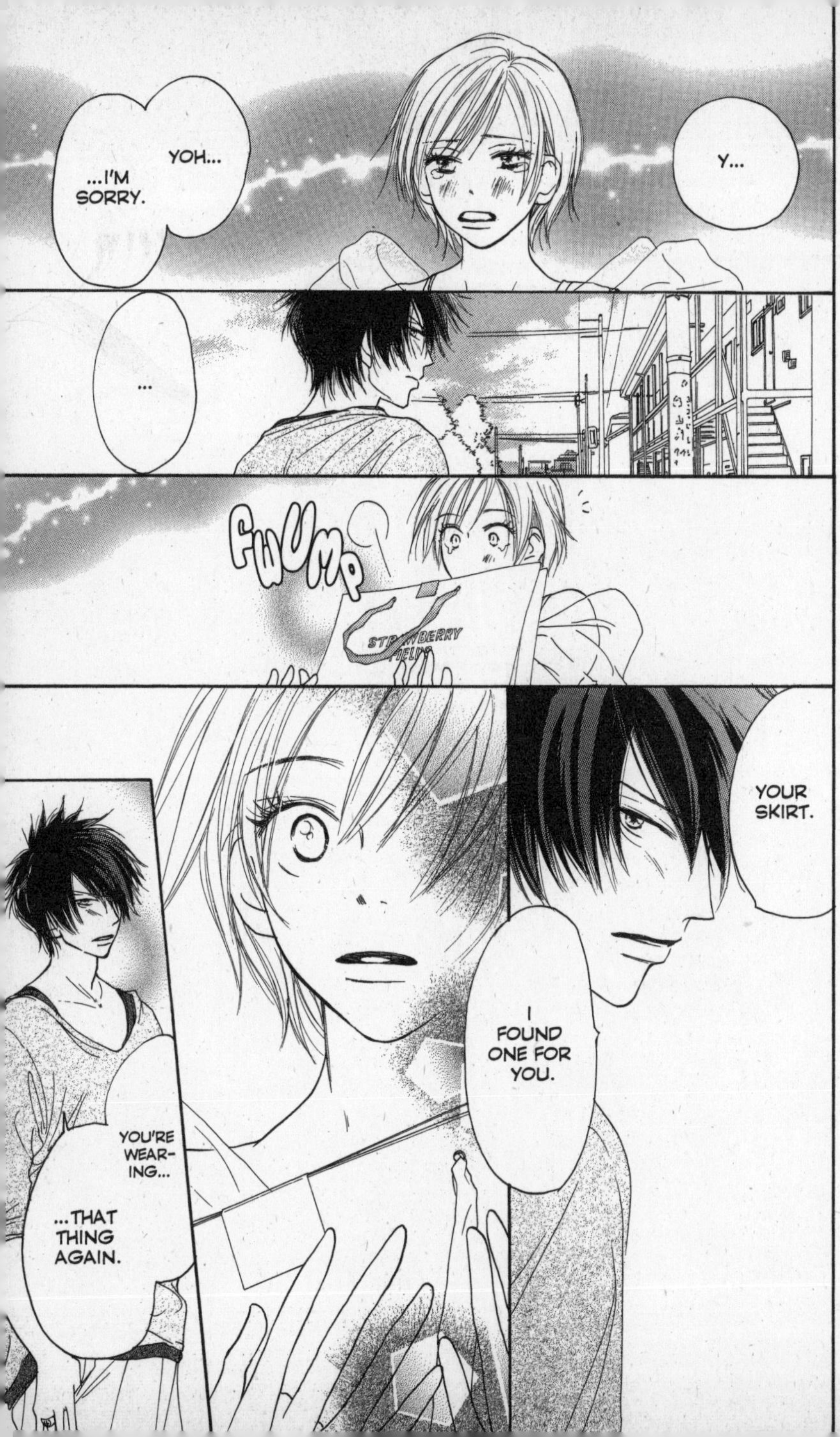
Y...
YOH...
...I'M SORRY.
...
FWUMP
YOUR SKIRT.
I FOUND ONE FOR YOU.
YOU'RE WEARING...
...THAT THING AGAIN.

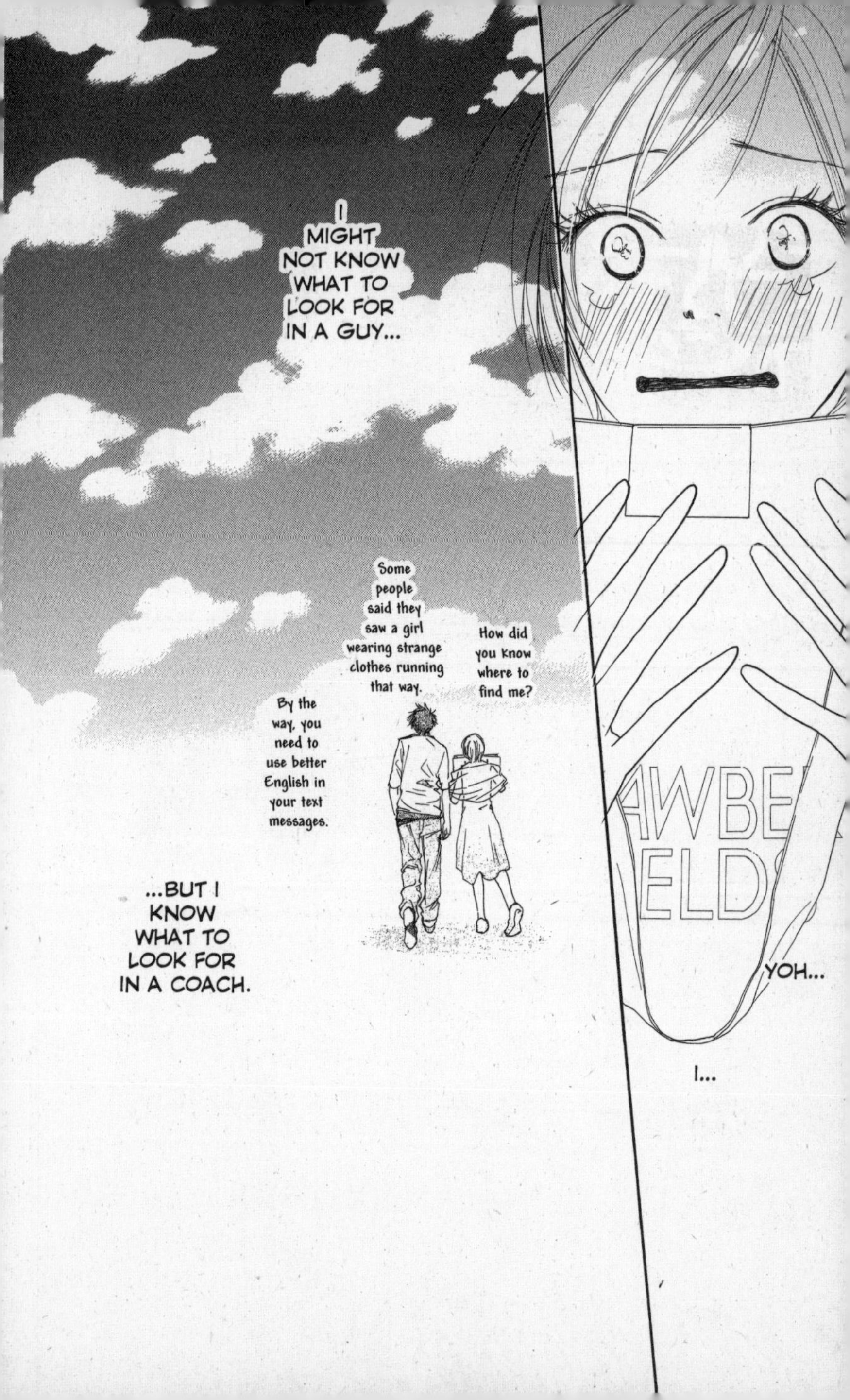
YOH...
I...
I MIGHT NOT KNOW WHAT TO LOOK FOR IN A GUY...
How did you know where to find me?
Some people said they saw a girl wearing strange clothes running that way.
By the way, you need to use better English in your text messages.
...BUT I KNOW WHAT TO LOOK FOR IN A COACH.

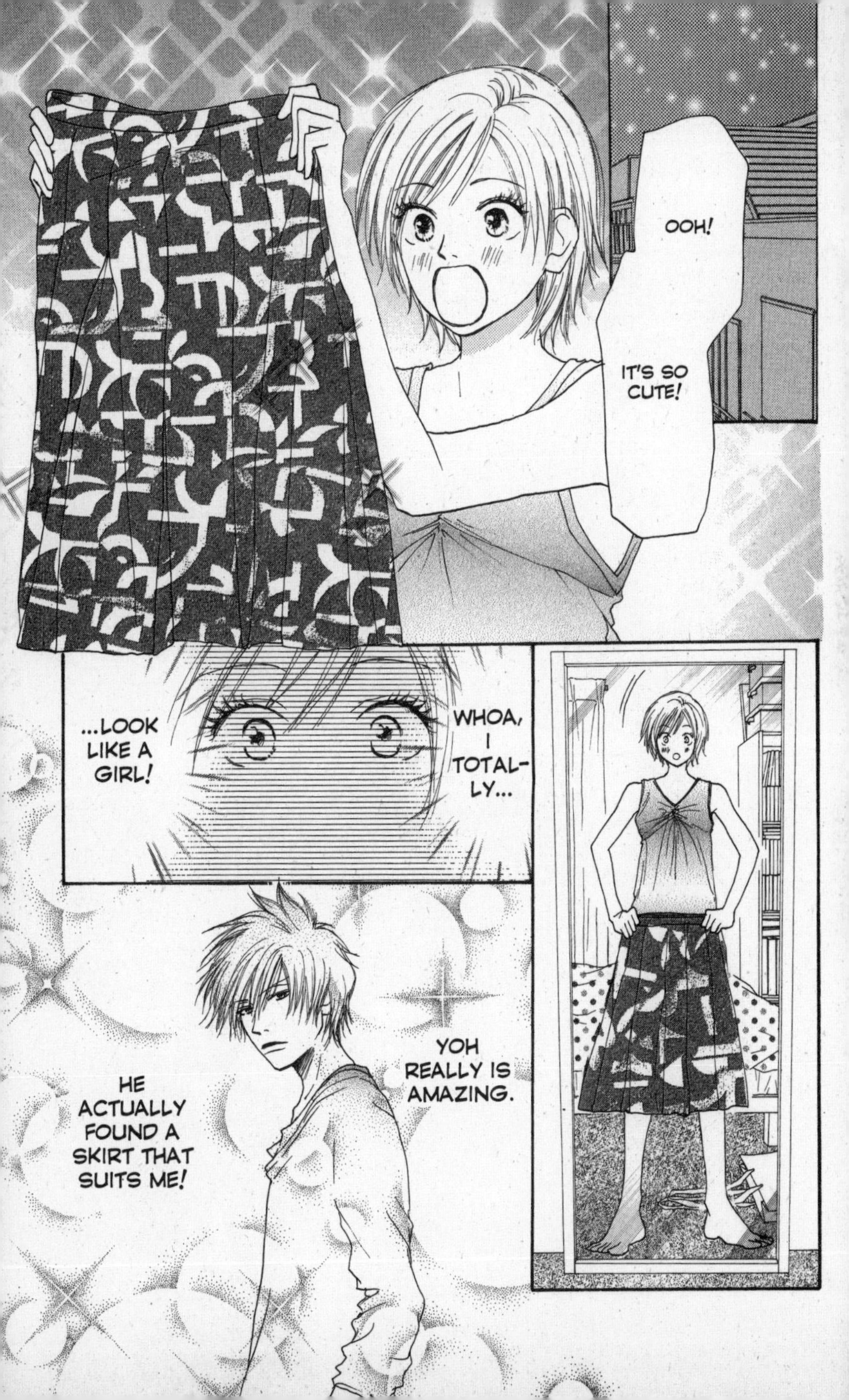
OOH!
IT'S SO CUTE!
WHOA, I TOTAL-LY...
...LOOK LIKE A GIRL!
YOH REALLY IS AMAZING.
HE ACTUALLY FOUND A SKIRT THAT SUITS ME!

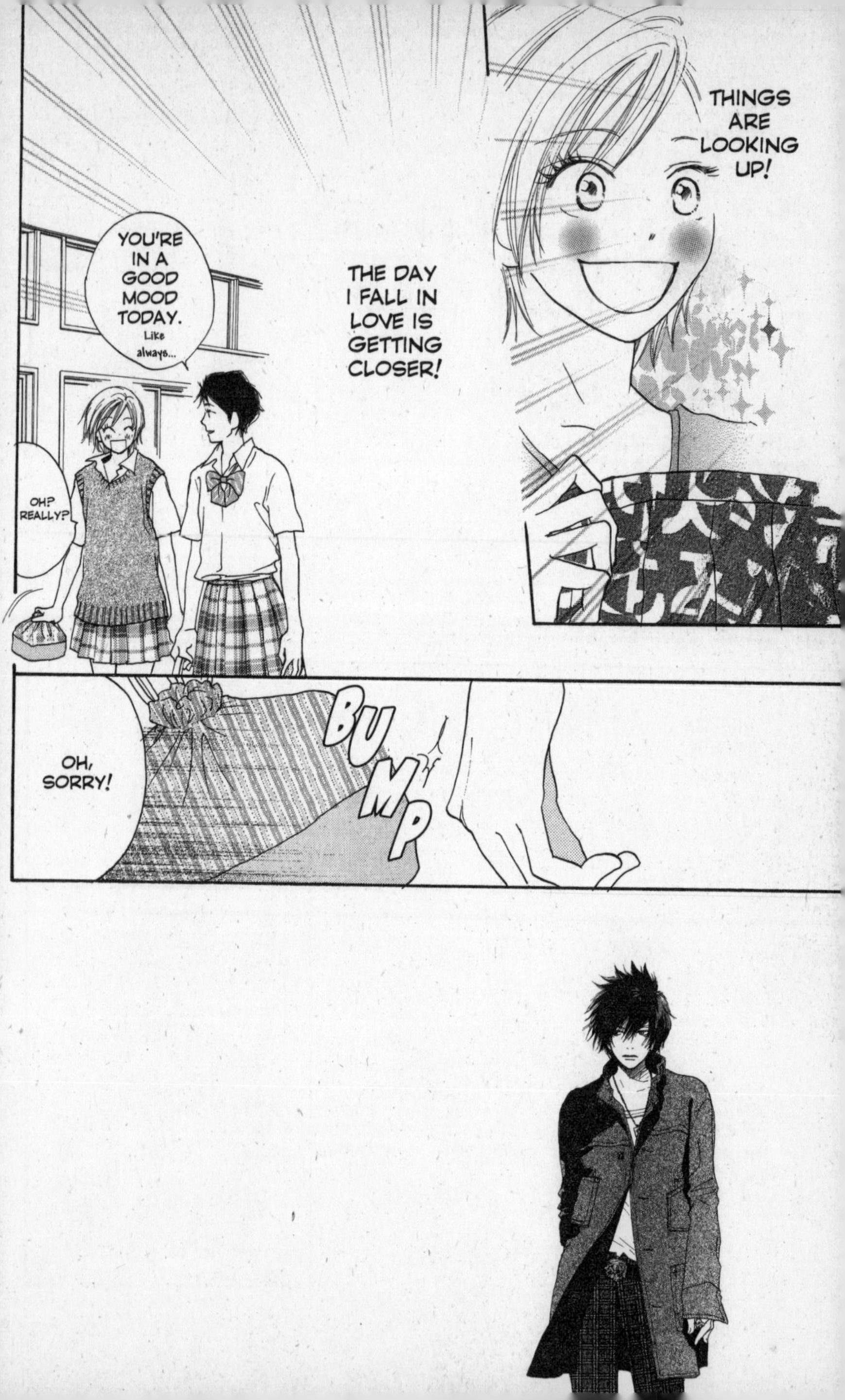
THINGS ARE LOOKING UP!
THE DAY I FALL IN LOVE IS GETTING CLOSER!
YOU'RE IN A GOOD MOOD TODAY.
Like always...
OH? REALLY?
BUMP
OH, SORRY!

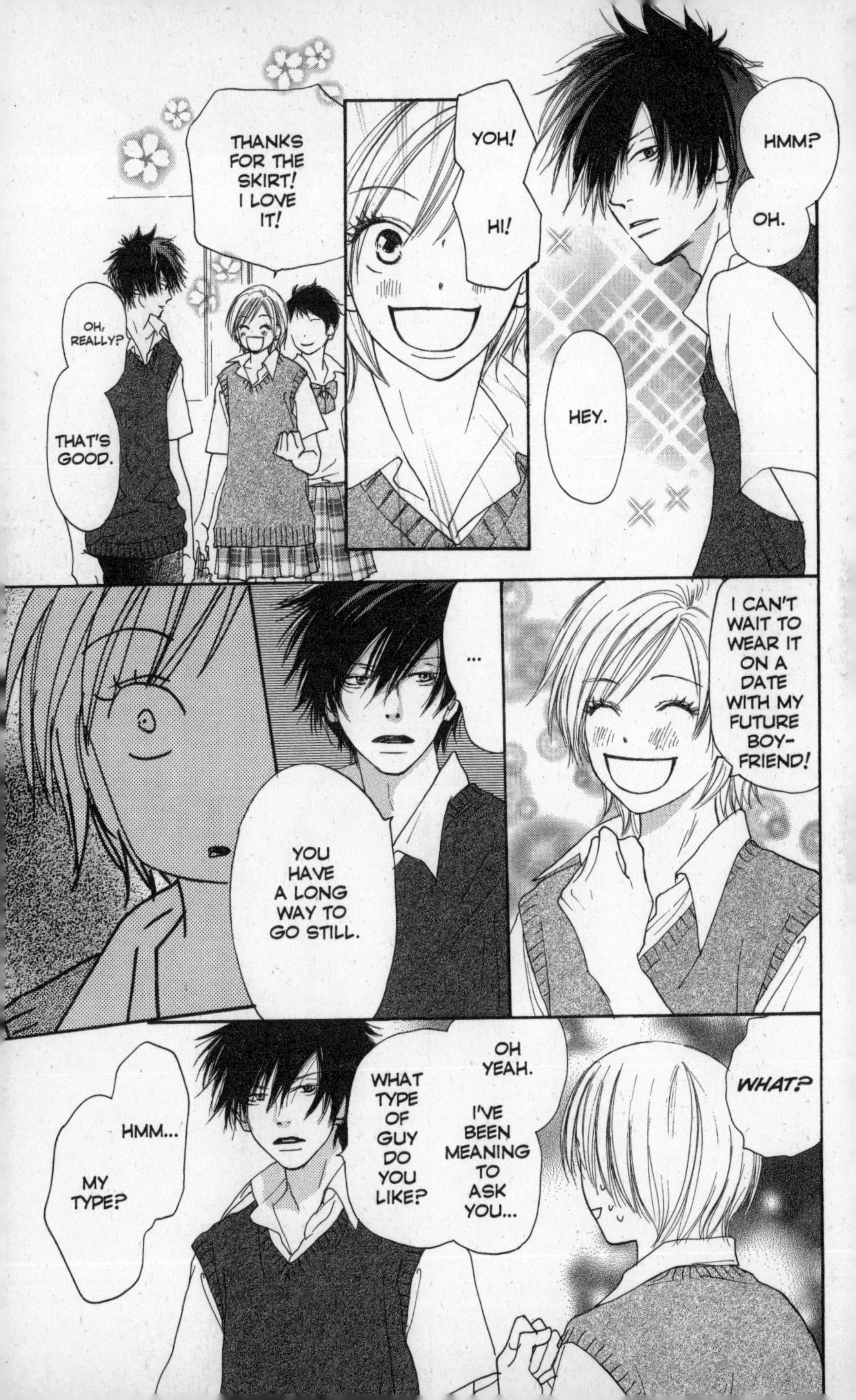
HMM?
OH.
HEY.
YOH!
HI!
THANKS FOR THE SKIRT! I LOVE IT!
OH, REALLY?
THAT'S GOOD.
I CAN'T WAIT TO WEAR IT ON A DATE WITH MY FUTURE BOY-FRIEND!
...
YOU HAVE A LONG WAY TO GO STILL.
WHAT?
OH YEAH.
I'VE BEEN MEANING TO ASK YOU...
WHAT TYPE OF GUY DO YOU LIKE?
HMM...
MY TYPE?

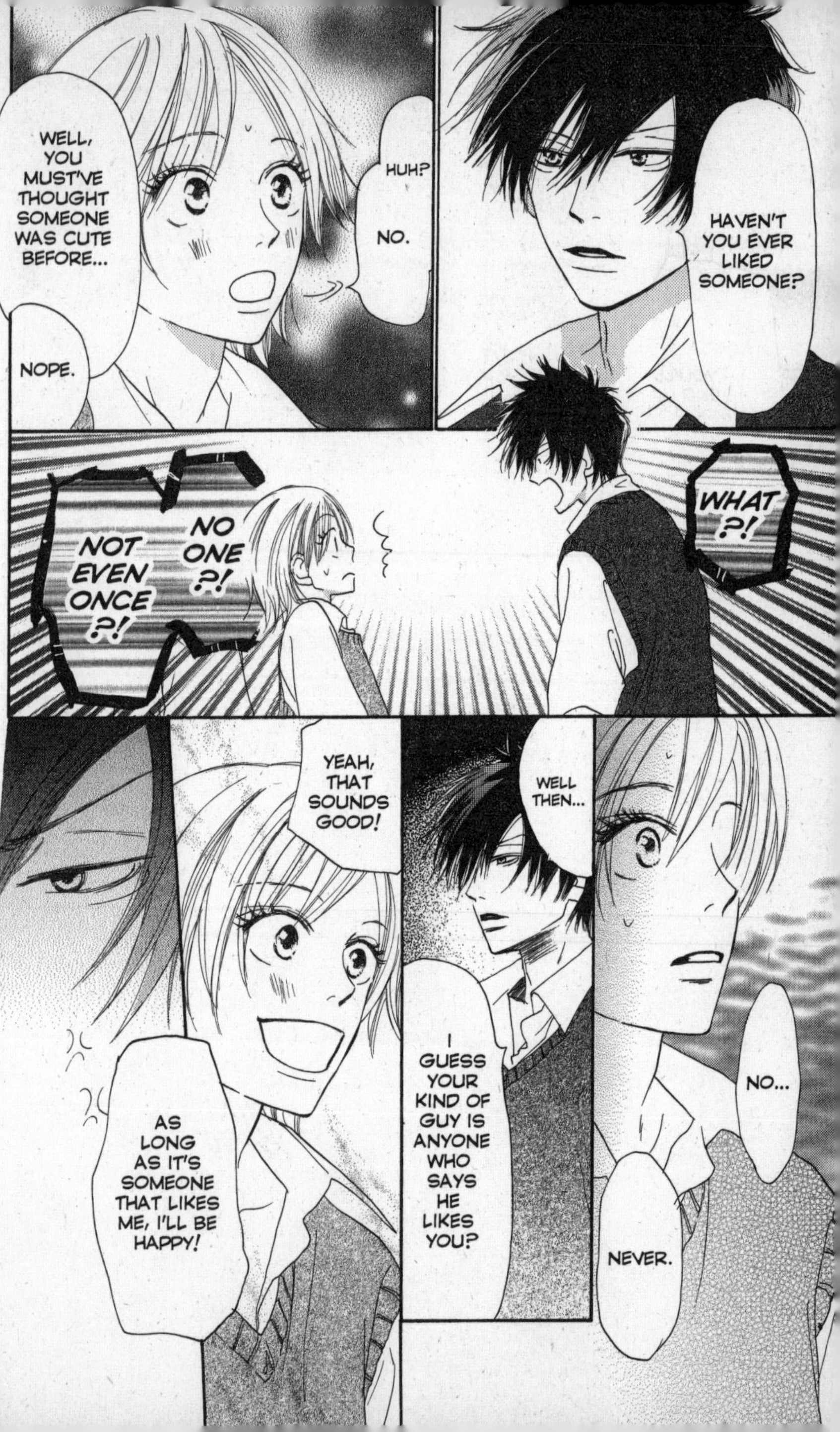
HAVEN'T YOU EVER LIKED SOMEONE?
HUH?
NO.
WELL, YOU MUST'VE THOUGHT SOMEONE WAS CUTE BEFORE...
NOPE.
WHAT?!
NO ONE?!
NOT EVEN ONCE?!
NO...
NEVER.
WELL THEN...
I GUESS YOUR KIND OF GUY IS ANYONE WHO SAYS HE LIKES YOU?
YEAH, THAT SOUNDS GOOD!
AS LONG AS IT'S SOMEONE THAT LIKES ME, I'LL BE HAPPY!

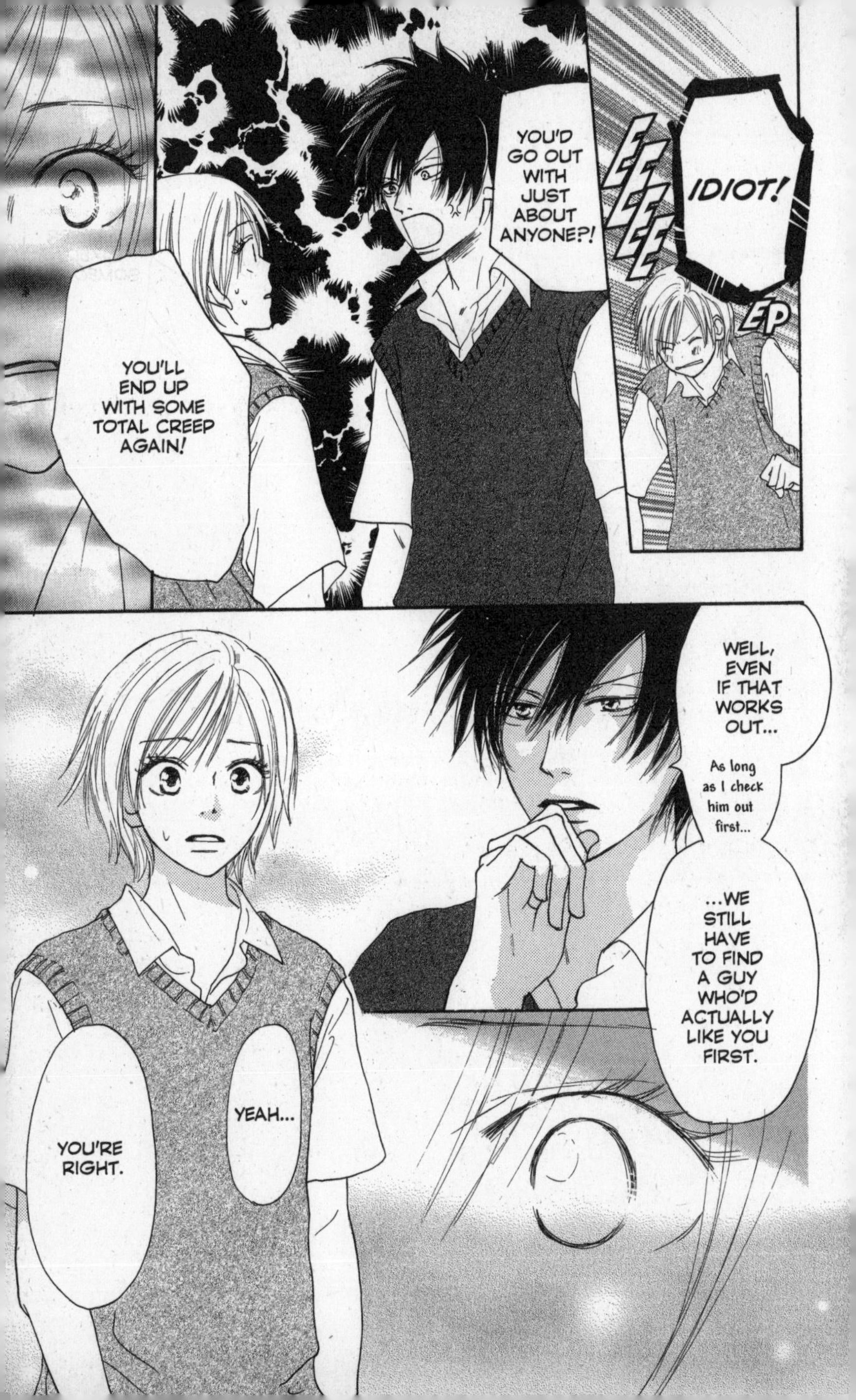
EEEE
IDIOT!
EP
YOU'D GO OUT WITH JUST ABOUT ANYONE?!
YOU'LL END UP WITH SOME TOTAL CREEP AGAIN!
WELL, EVEN IF THAT WORKS OUT...
As long as I check him out first...
...WE STILL HAVE TO FIND A GUY WHO'D ACTUALLY LIKE YOU FIRST.
YEAH...
YOU'RE RIGHT.

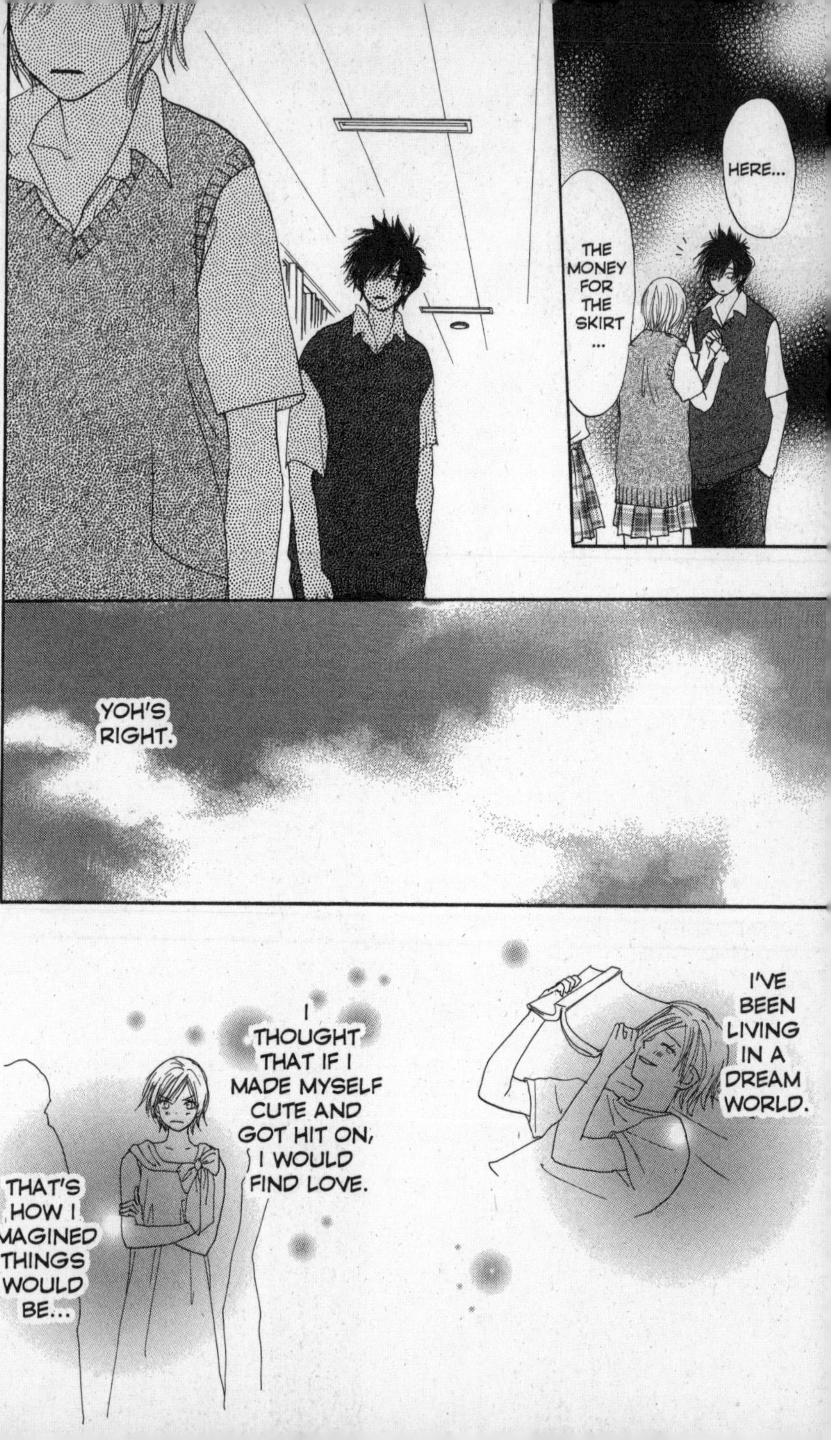
HERE...
THE MONEY FOR THE SKIRT...
YOH'S RIGHT.
I'VE BEEN LIVING IN A DREAM WORLD.
I THOUGHT THAT IF I MADE MYSELF CUTE AND GOT HIT ON, I WOULD FIND LOVE.
THAT'S HOW I IMAGINED THINGS WOULD BE...

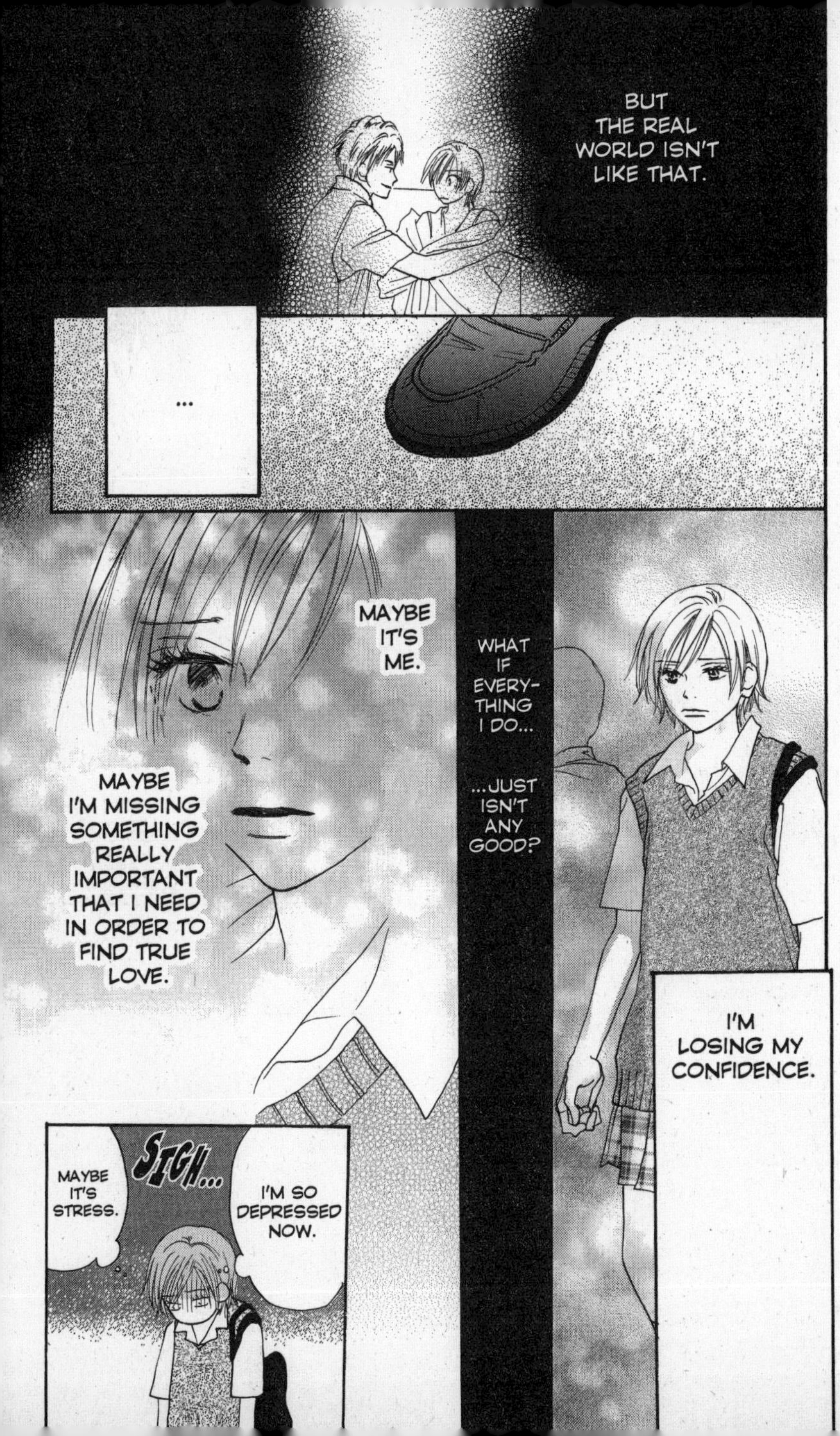
BUT THE REAL WORLD ISN'T LIKE THAT.
...
WHAT IF EVERYTHING I DO...
...JUST ISN'T ANY GOOD?
I'M LOSING MY CONFIDENCE.
MAYBE IT'S ME.
MAYBE I'M MISSING SOMETHING REALLY IMPORTANT THAT I NEED IN ORDER TO FIND TRUE LOVE.
SIGH...
I'M SO DEPRESSED NOW.
MAYBE IT'S STRESS.

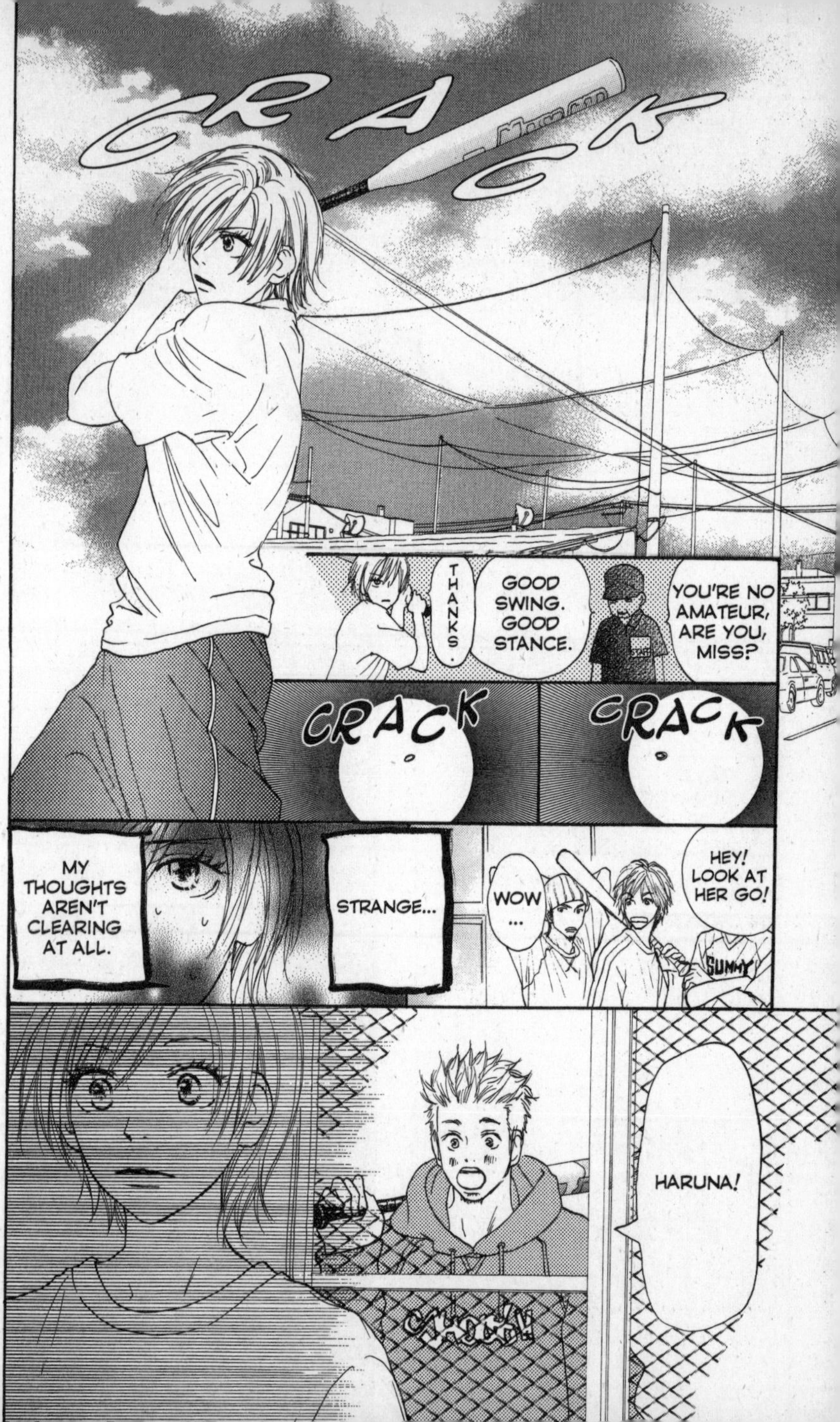
CRACK
YOU'RE NO AMATEUR, ARE YOU, MISS?
GOOD SWING. GOOD STANCE.
THANKS.
CRACK
CRACK
HEY! LOOK AT HER GO!
WOW...
STRANGE...
MY THOUGHTS AREN'T CLEARING AT ALL.
HARUNA!

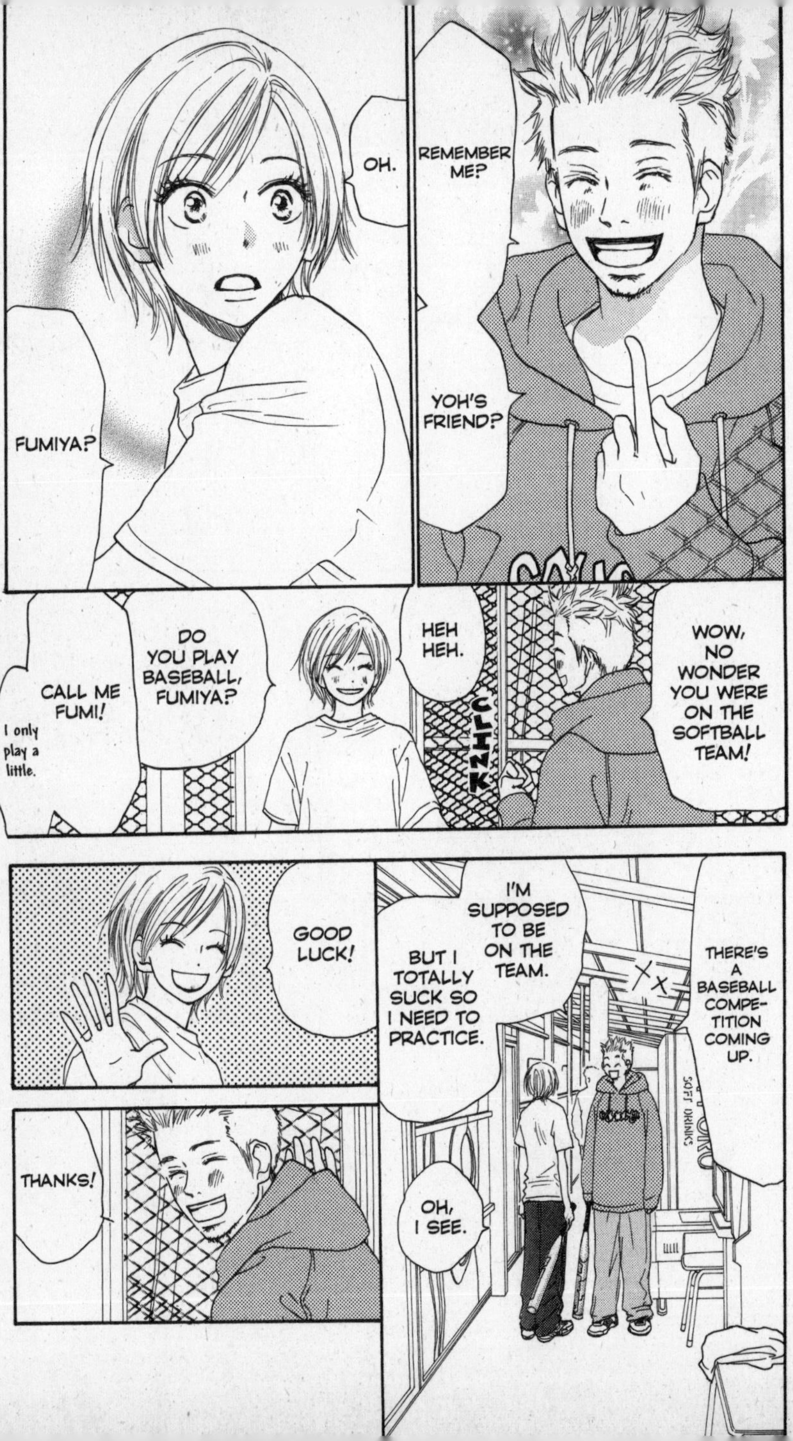
REMEMBER ME?
YOH'S FRIEND?
OH.
FUMIYA?
WOW, NO WONDER YOU WERE ON THE SOFTBALL TEAM!
CLINK
HEH HEH.
DO YOU PLAY BASEBALL, FUMIYA?
CALL ME FUMI!
I only play a little.
THERE'S A BASEBALL COMPE-TITION COMING UP.
SOFT DRINKS
I'M SUPPOSED TO BE ON THE TEAM.
BUT I TOTALLY SUCK SO I NEED TO PRACTICE.
OH, I SEE.
GOOD LUCK!
THANKS!

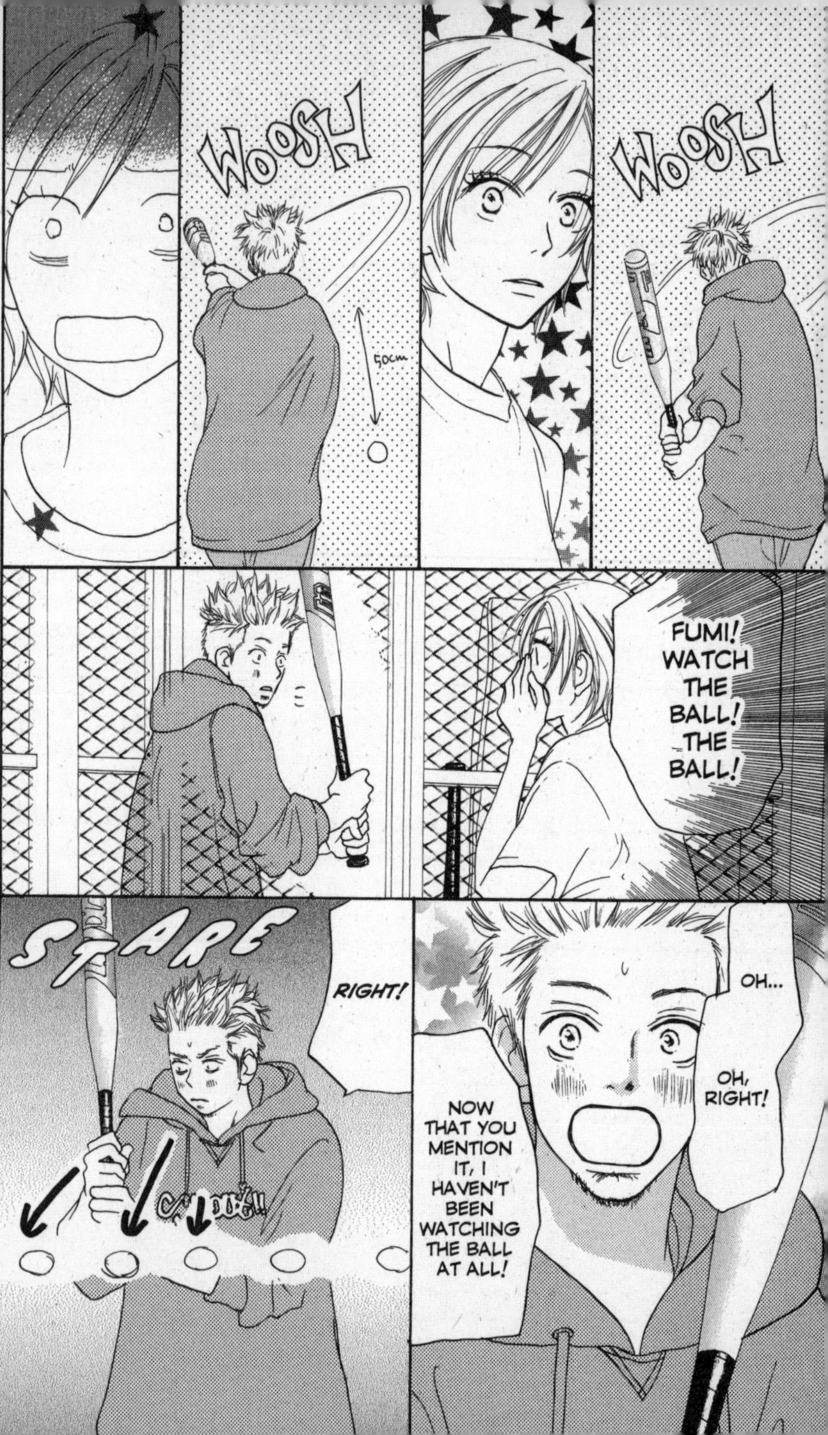
WOOSH
WOOSH
50cm
FUMI! WATCH THE BALL! THE BALL!
OH...
OH, RIGHT!
NOW THAT YOU MENTION IT, I HAVEN'T BEEN WATCHING THE BALL AT ALL!
RIGHT!
STARE

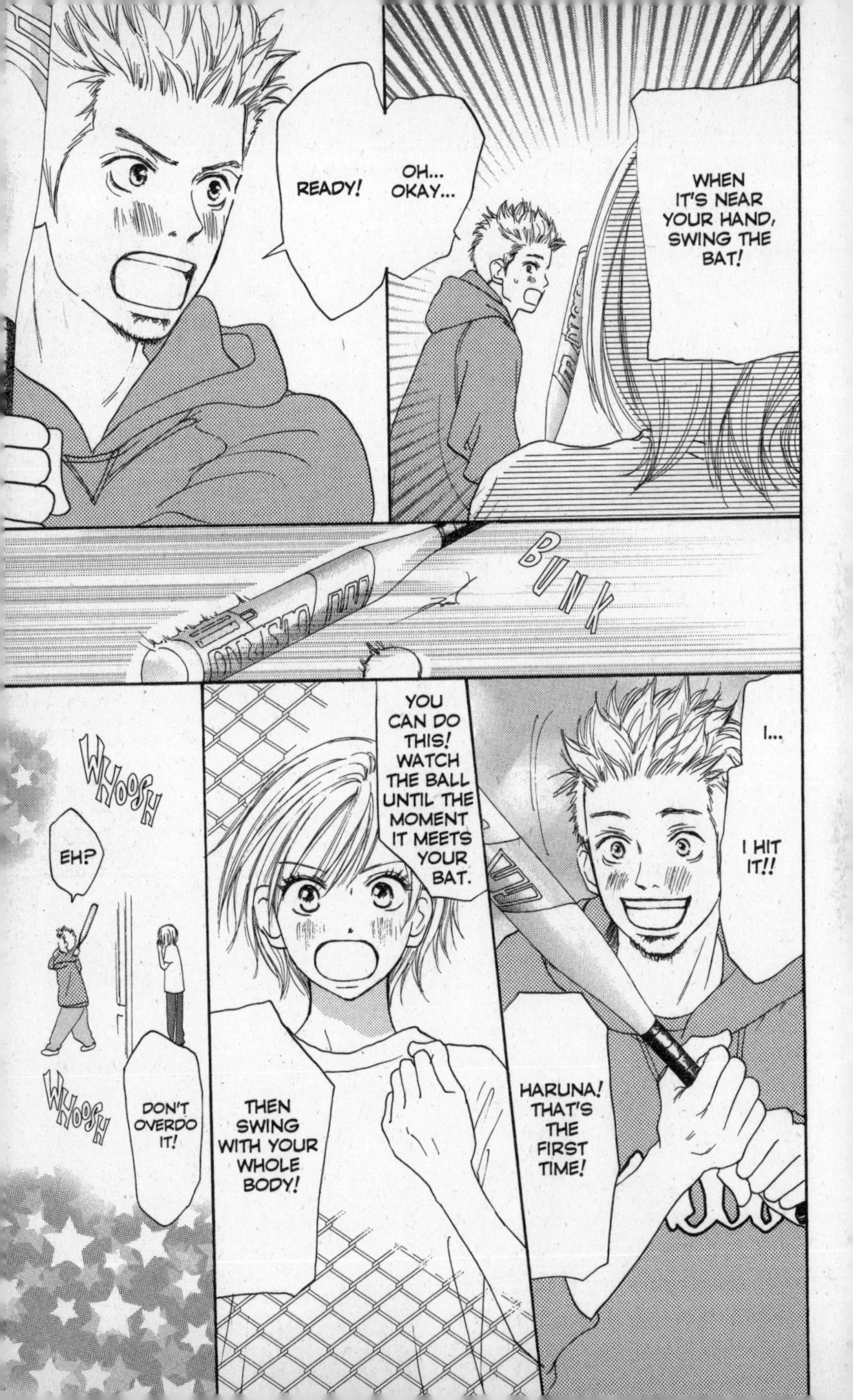
WHEN IT'S NEAR YOUR HAND, SWING THE BAT!
OH... OKAY...
READY!
BUNK
I...
I HIT IT!!
HARUNA! THAT'S THE FIRST TIME!
YOU CAN DO THIS! WATCH THE BALL UNTIL THE MOMENT IT MEETS YOUR BAT.
THEN SWING WITH YOUR WHOLE BODY!
WHOOSH
EH?
WHOOSH
DON'T OVERDO IT!

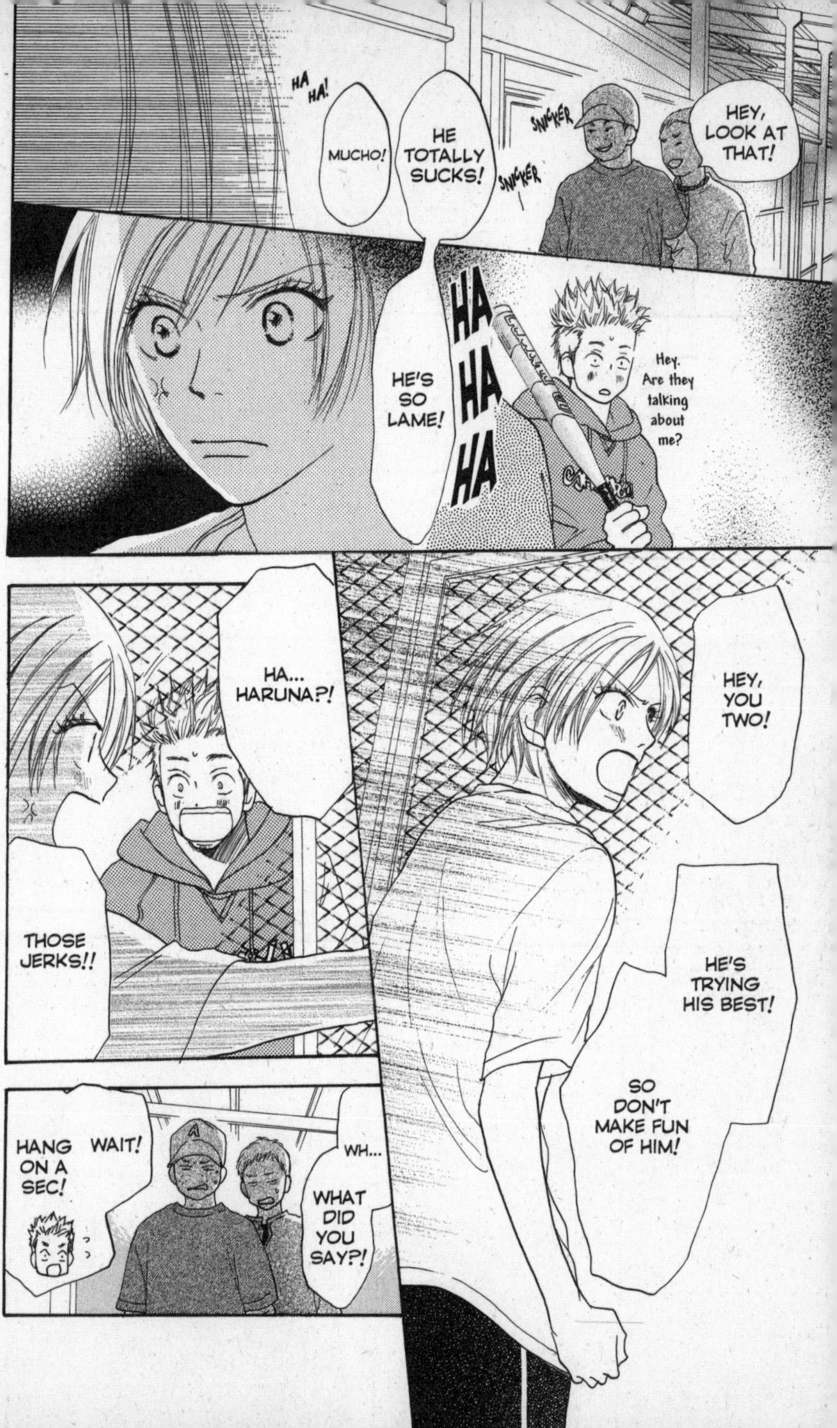
HEY, LOOK AT THAT!
SNICKER
SNICKER
HE TOTALLY SUCKS!
MUCHO!
HA HA!
Hey. Are they talking about me?
HA HA HA
HE'S SO LAME!
HEY, YOU TWO!
HE'S TRYING HIS BEST!
SO DON'T MAKE FUN OF HIM!
HA... HARUNA?!
THOSE JERKS!!
WH...
WHAT DID YOU SAY?!
WAIT!
HANG ON A SEC!

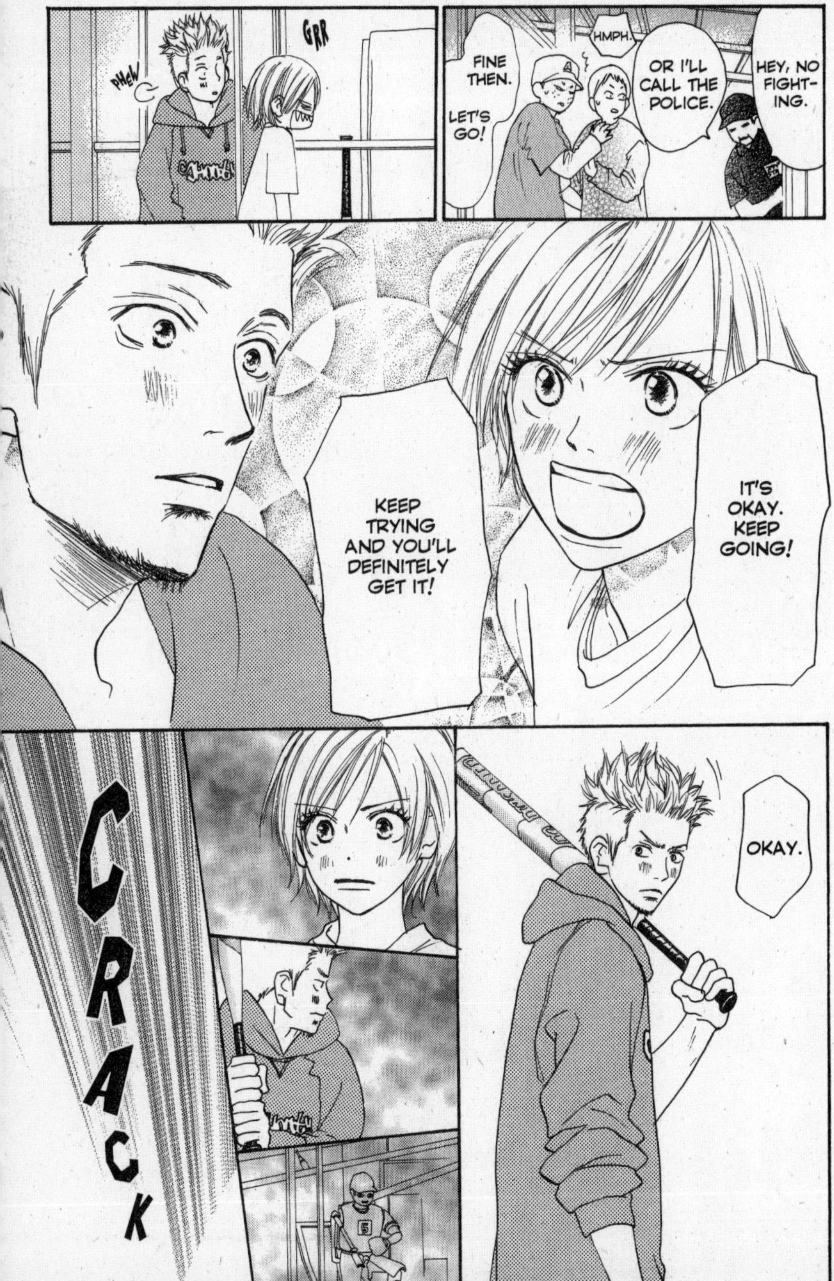
HEY, NO FIGHT-ING.
OR I'LL CALL THE POLICE.
HMPH.
FINE THEN.
LET'S GO!
GRR
PHEW
IT'S OKAY. KEEP GOING!
KEEP TRYING AND YOU'LL DEFINITELY GET IT!
OKAY.
CRACK

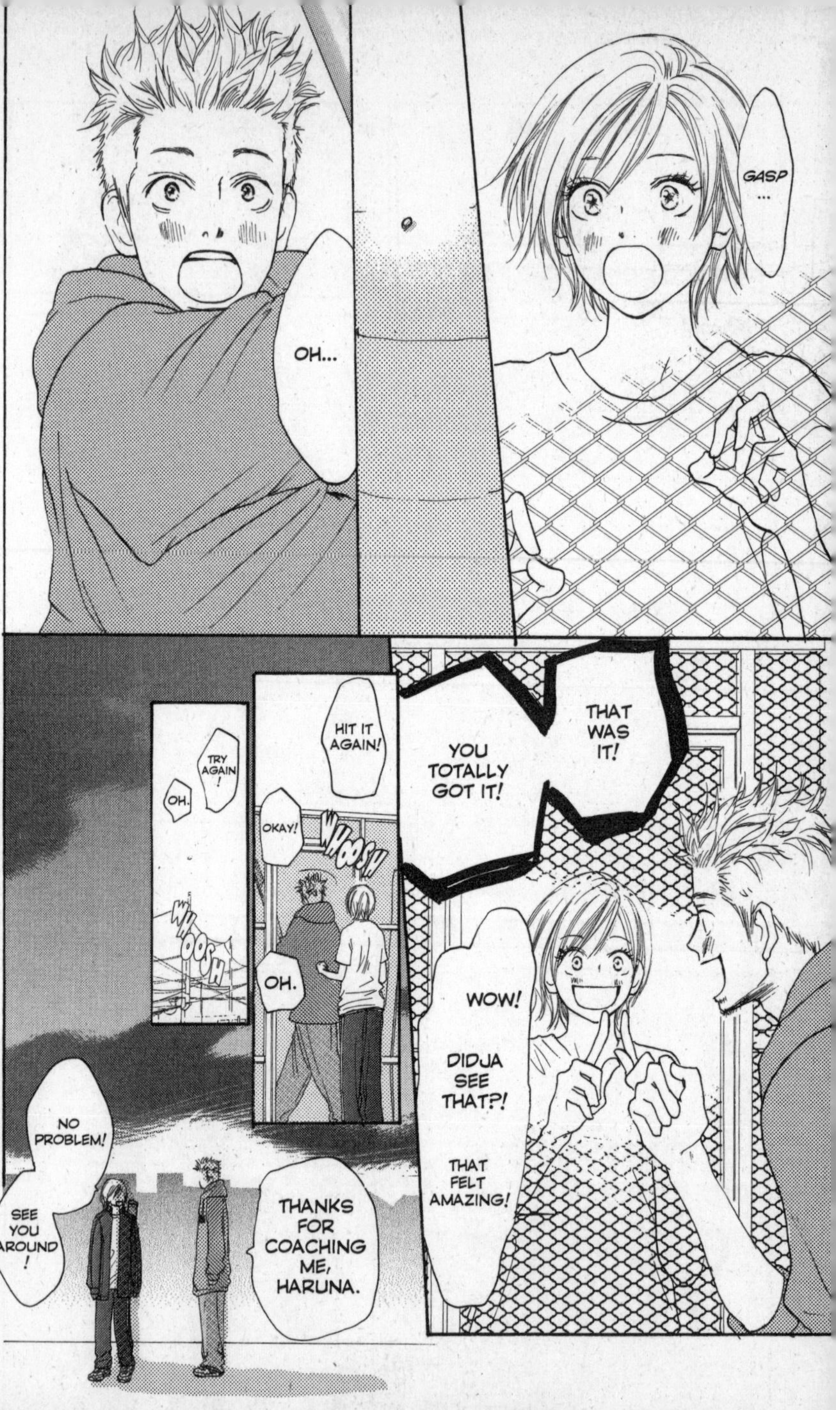
GASP ...
OH...
THAT WAS IT!
YOU TOTALLY GOT IT!
WOW!
DIDJA SEE THAT?!
THAT FELT AMAZING!
HIT IT AGAIN!
OKAY!
WHOOSH
OH.
TRY AGAIN!
OH.
WHOOSH
THANKS FOR COACHING ME, HARUNA.
NO PROBLEM!
SEE YOU AROUND!

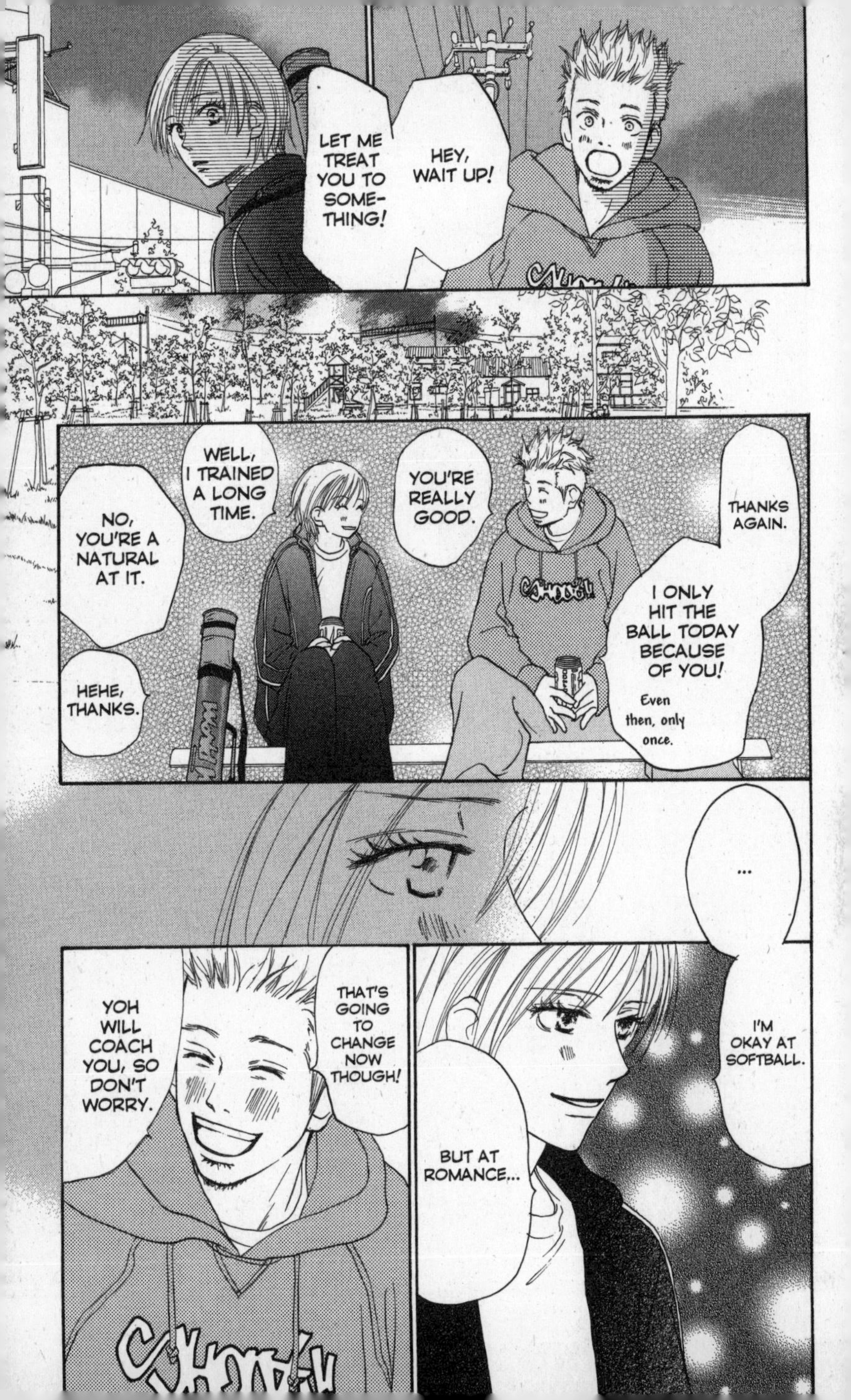
HEY, WAIT UP!
LET ME TREAT YOU TO SOME-THING!
THANKS AGAIN.
I ONLY HIT THE BALL TODAY BECAUSE OF YOU!
Even then, only once.
YOU'RE REALLY GOOD.
WELL, I TRAINED A LONG TIME.
NO, YOU'RE A NATURAL AT IT.
HEHE, THANKS.
...
I'M OKAY AT SOFTBALL.
BUT AT ROMANCE...
THAT'S GOING TO CHANGE NOW THOUGH!
YOH WILL COACH YOU, SO DON'T WORRY.

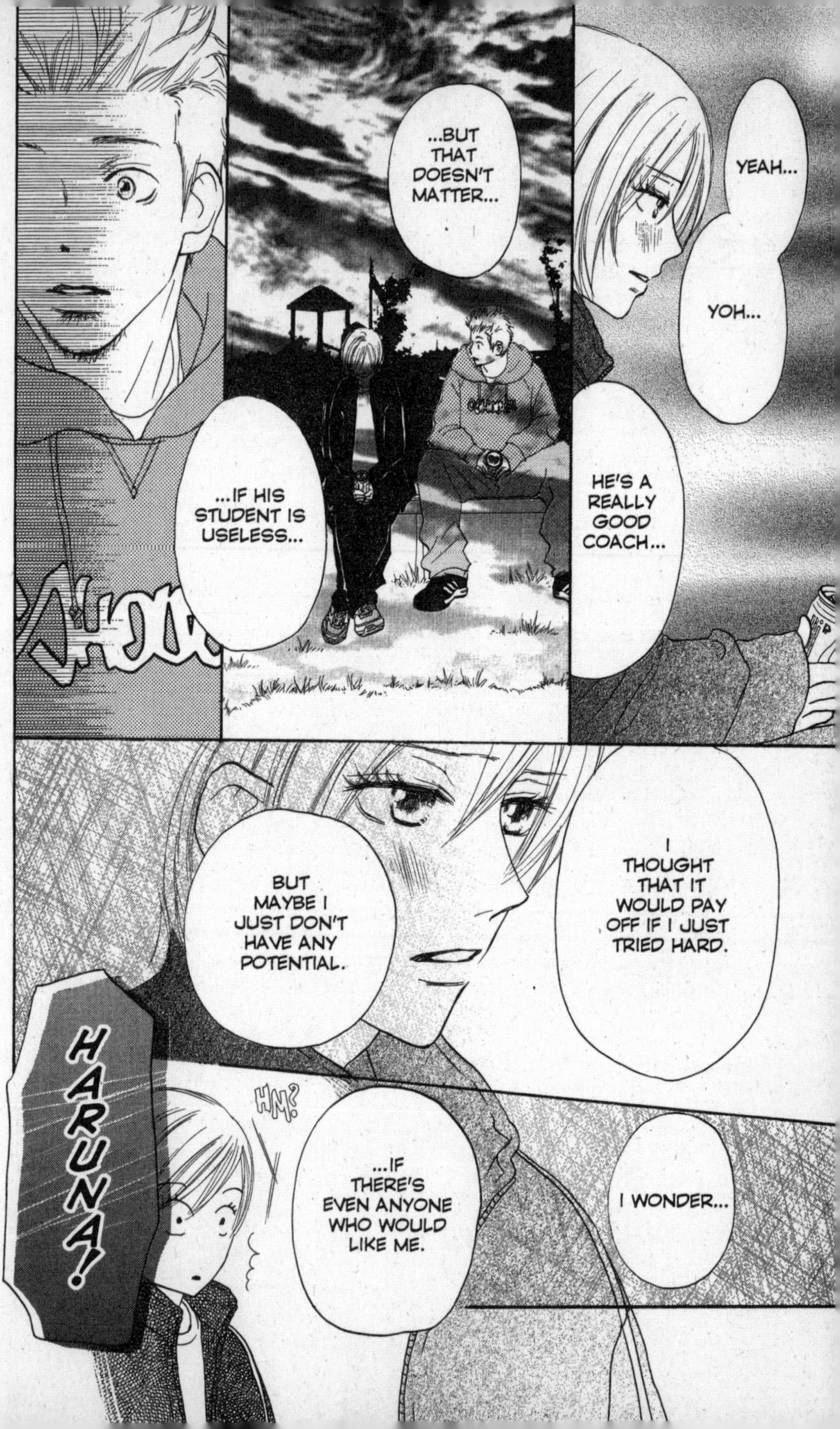
YEAH...
YOH...
HE'S A REALLY GOOD COACH...
...BUT THAT DOESN'T MATTER...
...IF HIS STUDENT IS USELESS...
I THOUGHT THAT IT WOULD PAY OFF IF I JUST TRIED HARD.
BUT MAYBE I JUST DON'T HAVE ANY POTENTIAL.
I WONDER...
...IF THERE'S EVEN ANYONE WHO WOULD LIKE ME.
HM?
HARUNA!

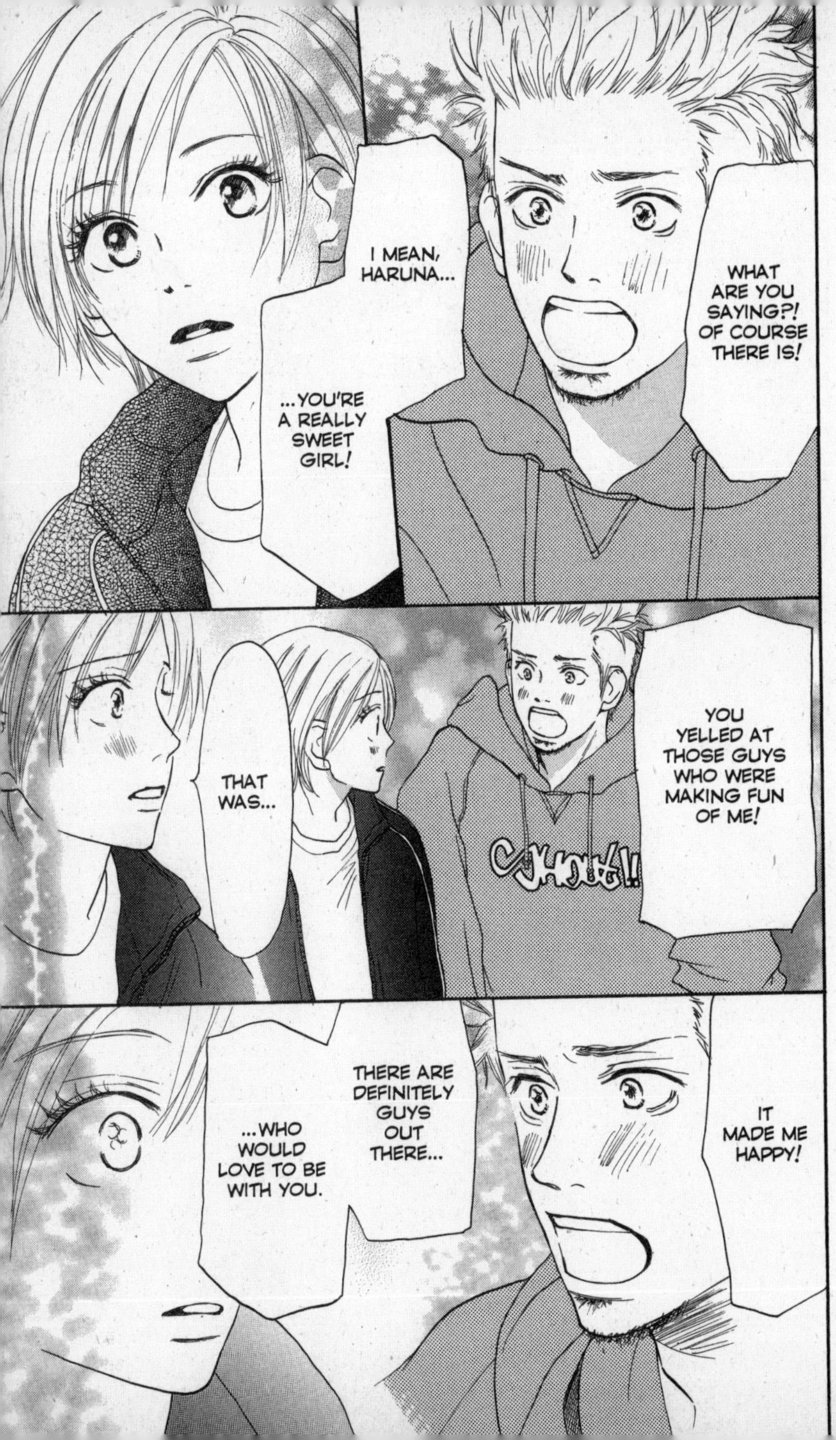
WHAT ARE YOU SAYING?! OF COURSE THERE IS!
I MEAN, HARUNA...
...YOU'RE A REALLY SWEET GIRL!
YOU YELLED AT THOSE GUYS WHO WERE MAKING FUN OF ME!
THAT WAS...
IT MADE ME HAPPY!
THERE ARE DEFINITELY GUYS OUT THERE...
...WHO WOULD LOVE TO BE WITH YOU.

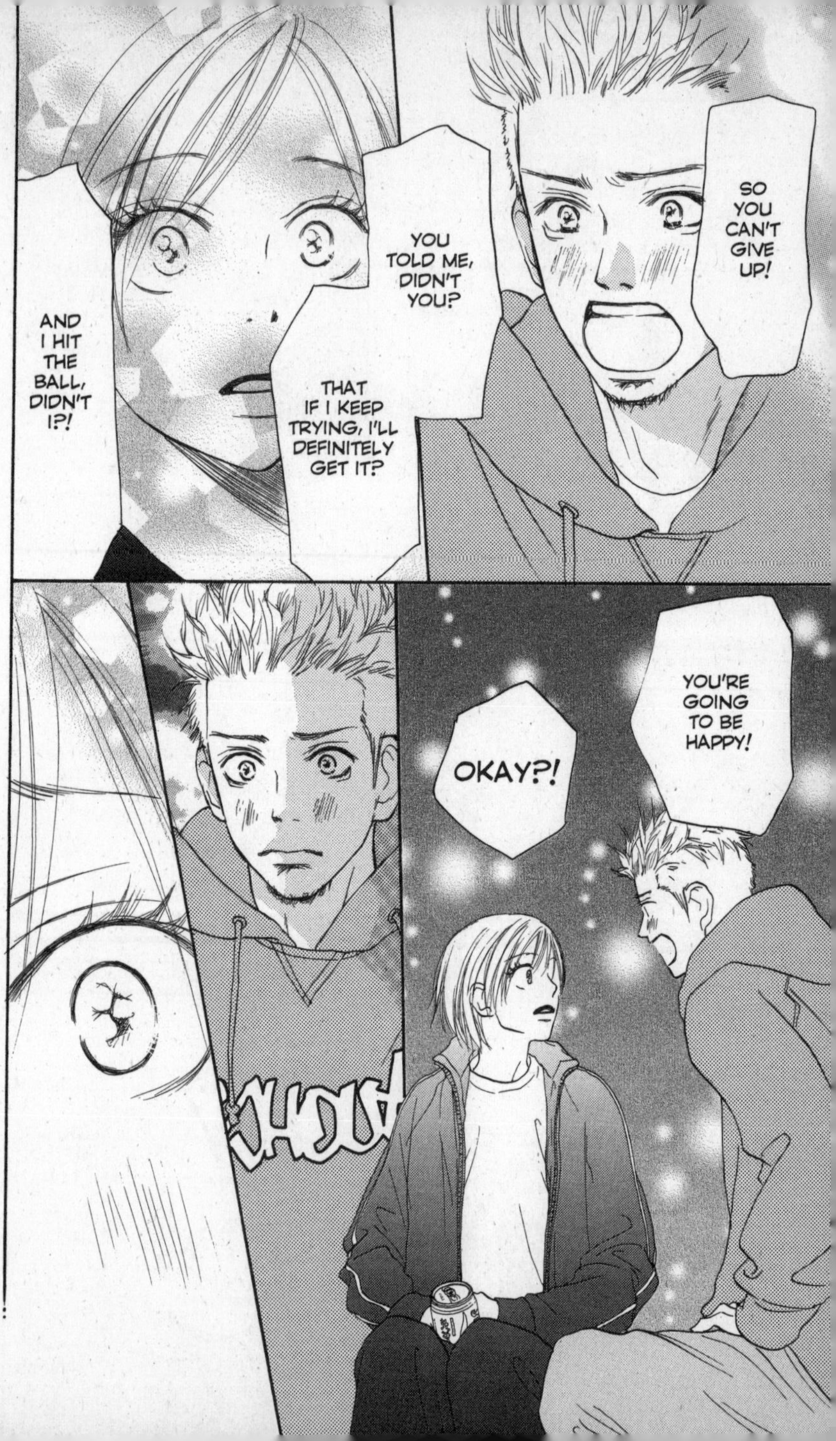
SO YOU CAN'T GIVE UP!
YOU TOLD ME, DIDN'T YOU?
THAT IF I KEEP TRYING, I'LL DEFINITELY GET IT?
AND I HIT THE BALL, DIDN'T I?!
YOU'RE GOING TO BE HAPPY!
OKAY?!

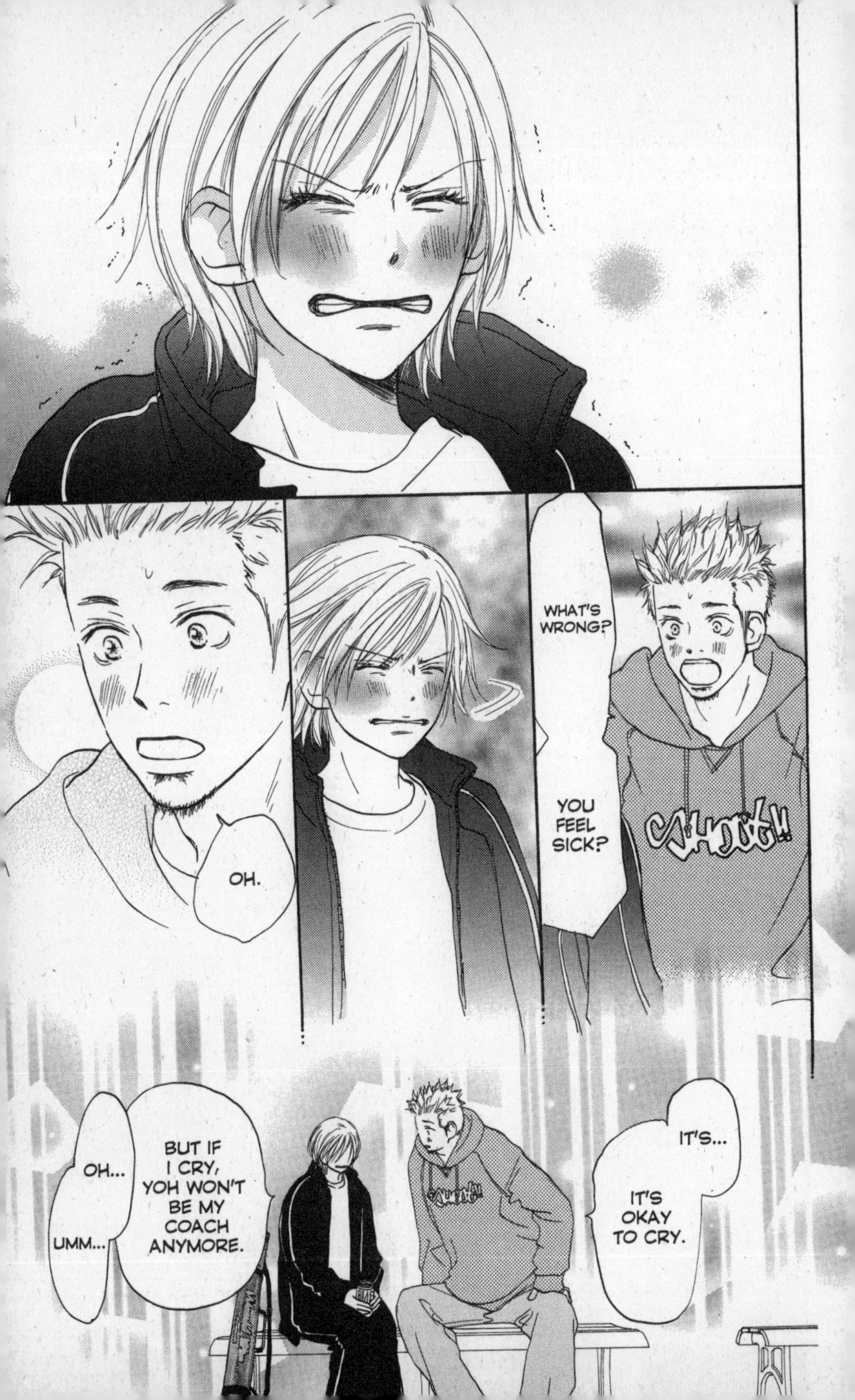
WHAT'S WRONG?
YOU FEEL SICK?
OH.
IT'S...
IT'S OKAY TO CRY.
BUT IF I CRY, YOH WON'T BE MY COACH ANYMORE.
OH...
UMM...

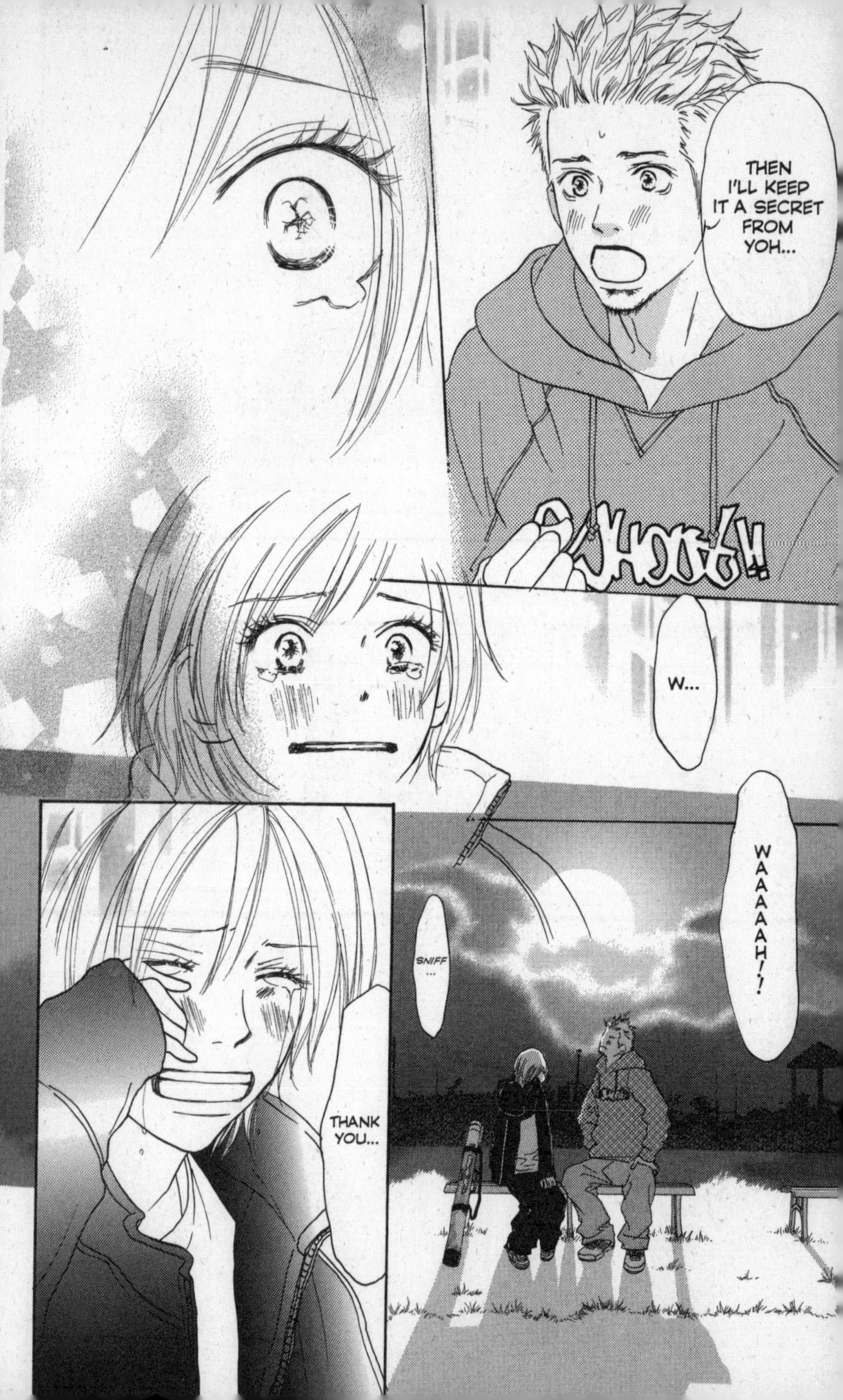
THEN I'LL KEEP IT A SECRET FROM YOH...
W...
WAAAAAH!!
SNIFF...
THANK YOU...

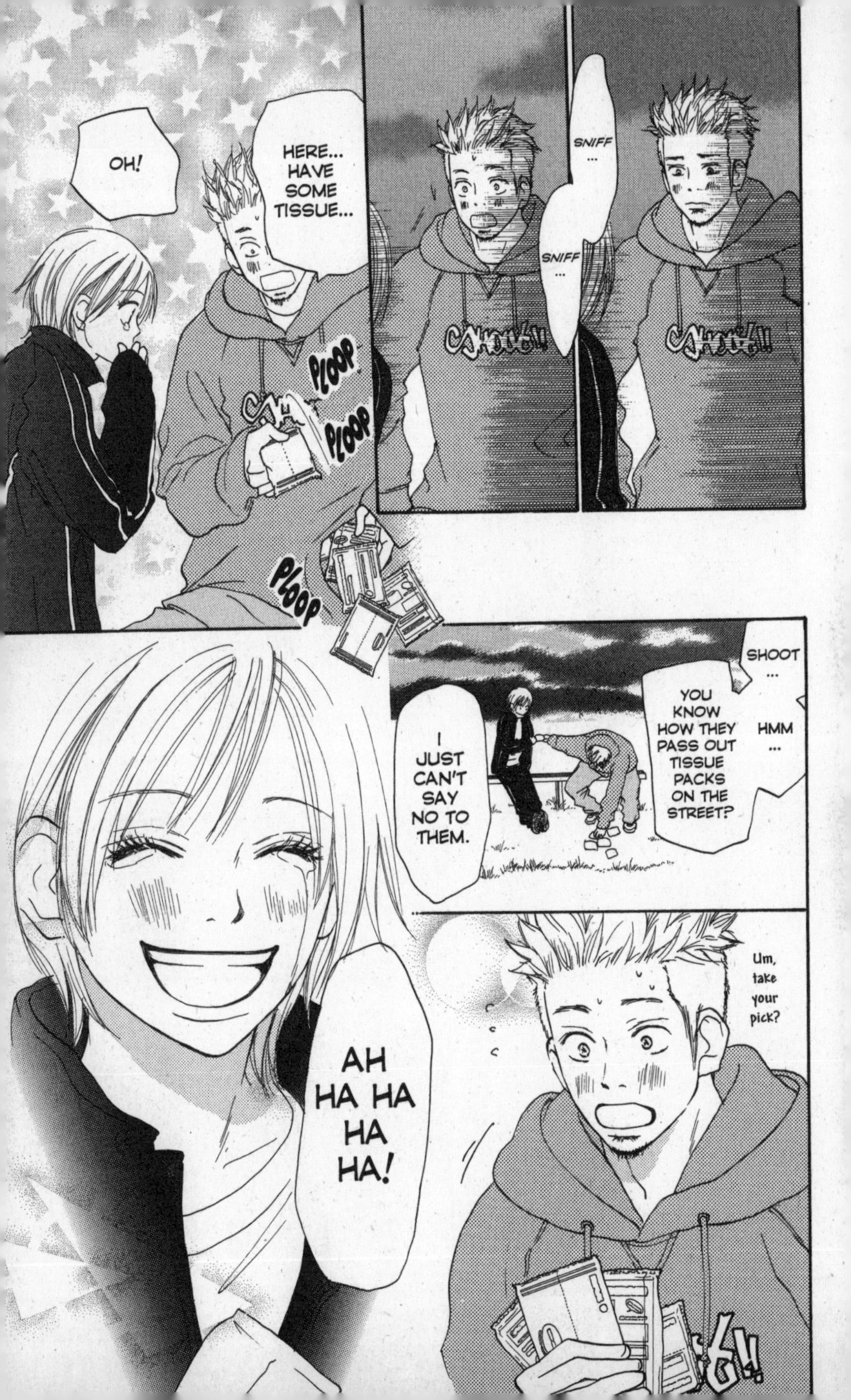
SNIFF ...
SNIFF ...
HERE... HAVE SOME TISSUE...
OH!
PLOOP
PLOOP
PLOOP
SHOOT ...
HMM ...
YOU KNOW HOW THEY PASS OUT TISSUE PACKS ON THE STREET?
I JUST CAN'T SAY NO TO THEM.
Um, take your pick?
AH HA HA HA HA!

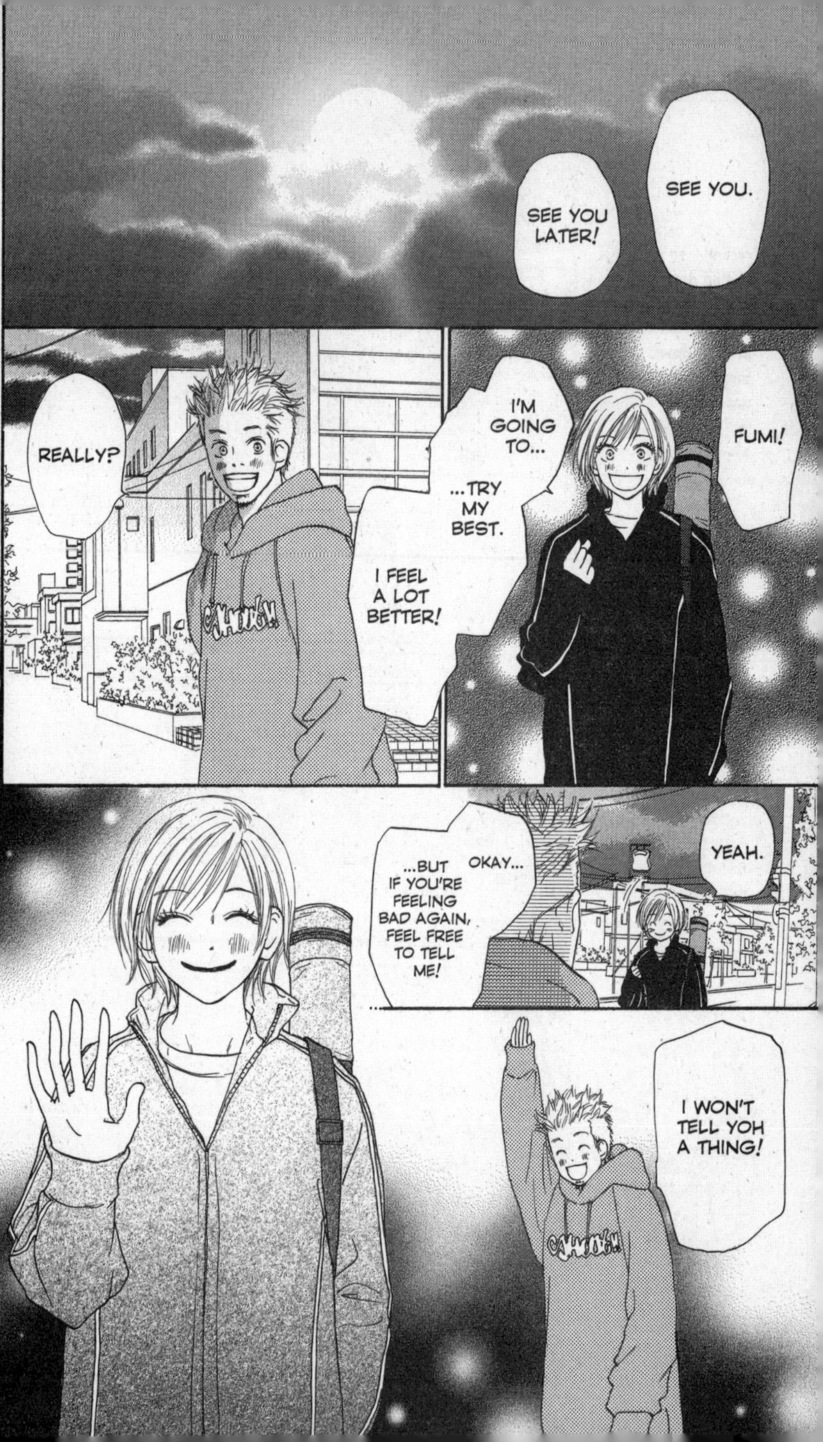
SEE YOU.
SEE YOU LATER!
FUMI!
I'M GOING TO...
...TRY MY BEST.
I FEEL A LOT BETTER!
REALLY?
YEAH.
OKAY...
...BUT IF YOU'RE FEELING BAD AGAIN, FEEL FREE TO TELL ME!
I WON'T TELL YOH A THING!

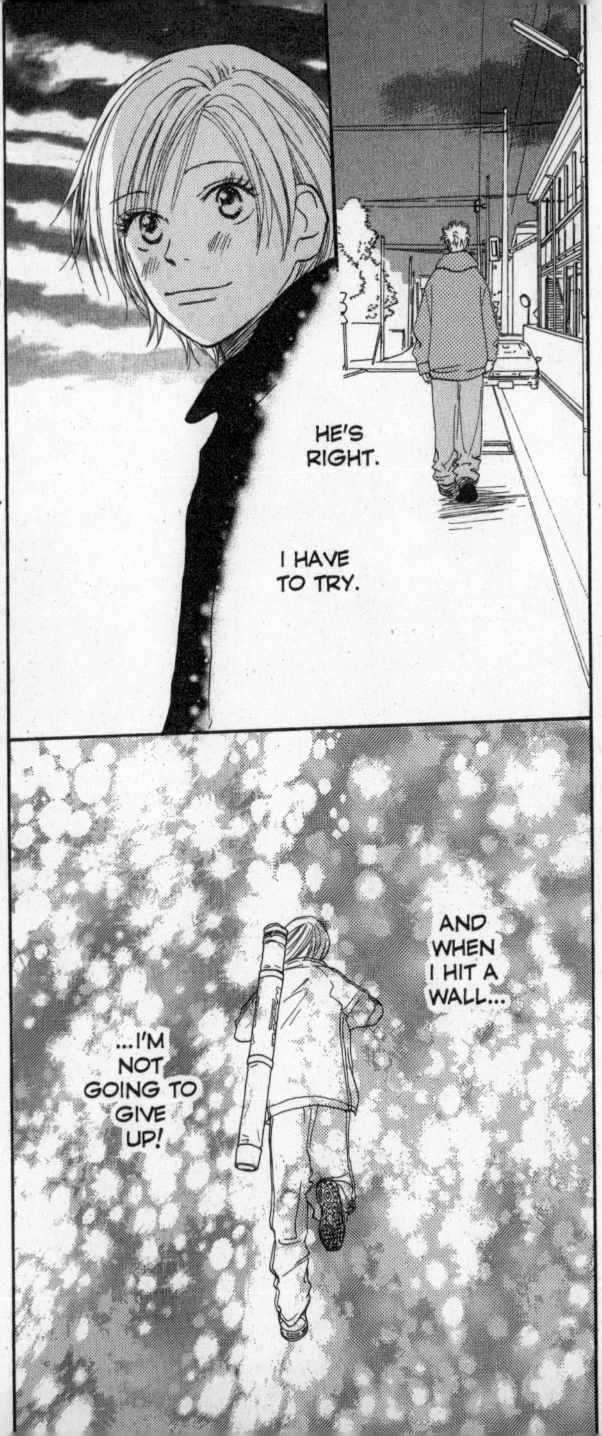
HE'S RIGHT.
I HAVE TO TRY.
AND WHEN I HIT A WALL...
...I'M NOT GOING TO GIVE UP!

3

I've been forgetful recently, so I've been writing down everything that I think of. But then I forget that I wrote it down. Or I forget what the note was about. So it hasn't really turned out to be much of a solution.

When I was a student, I must have had tests and stuff like that. But I can't remember how I managed to memorize everything. Maybe that's why I hate tests so much...because I'm so bad at them! I still dream that I've done badly on a test sometimes. Often right before a deadline. I wonder if my brain links the stress somehow. Or maybe not.

Because I'm so forgetful, people I work with often have to remind me of stuff.

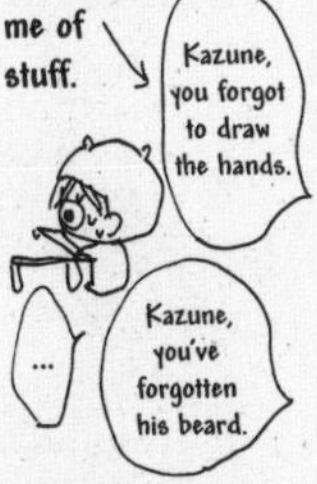
Kazune, you forgot to draw the hands.
Kazune, you've forgotten his beard.
...

Thank you so much, everyone!

See you in the next volume!

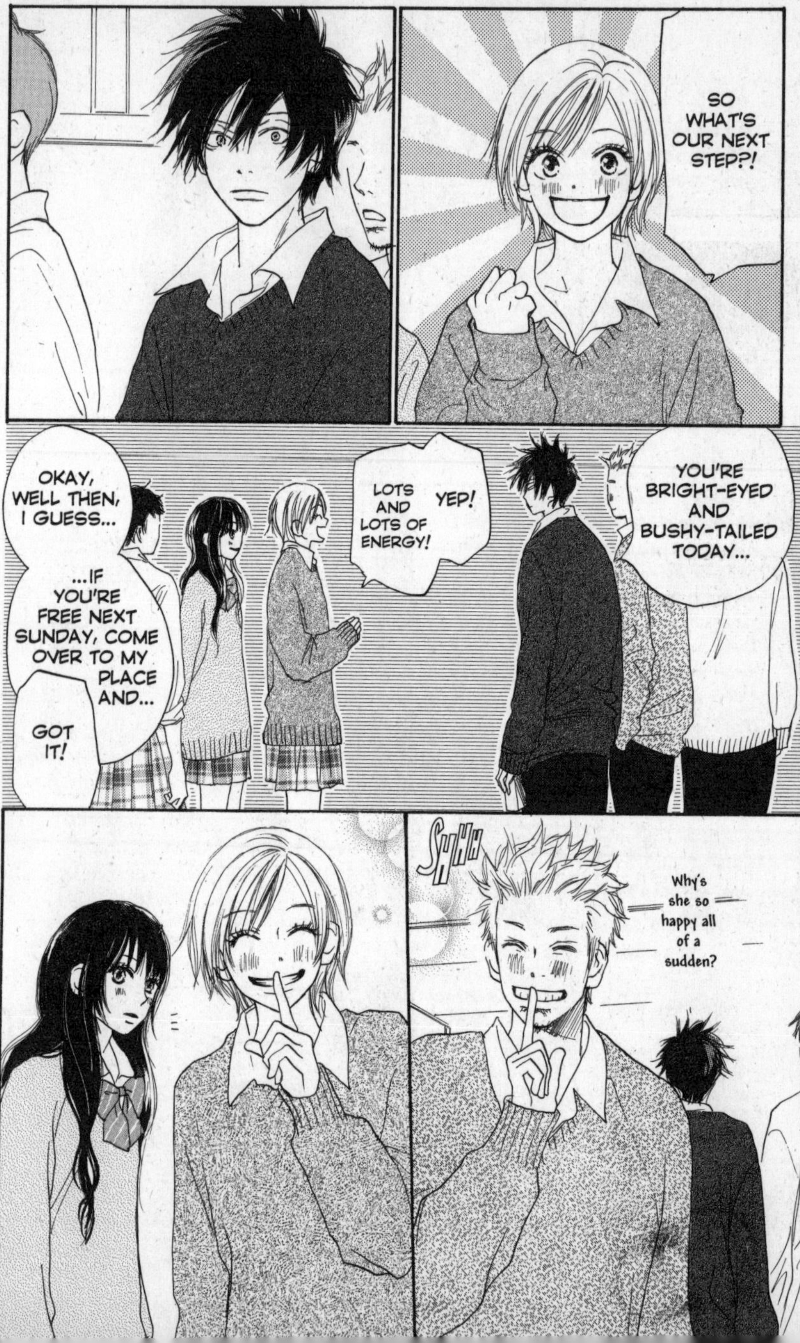
SO WHAT'S OUR NEXT STEP?!
YOU'RE BRIGHT-EYED AND BUSHY-TAILED TODAY...
YEP!
LOTS AND LOTS OF ENERGY!
OKAY, WELL THEN, I GUESS...
...IF YOU'RE FREE NEXT SUNDAY, COME OVER TO MY PLACE AND...
GOT IT!
SHHH
Why's she so happy all of a sudden?

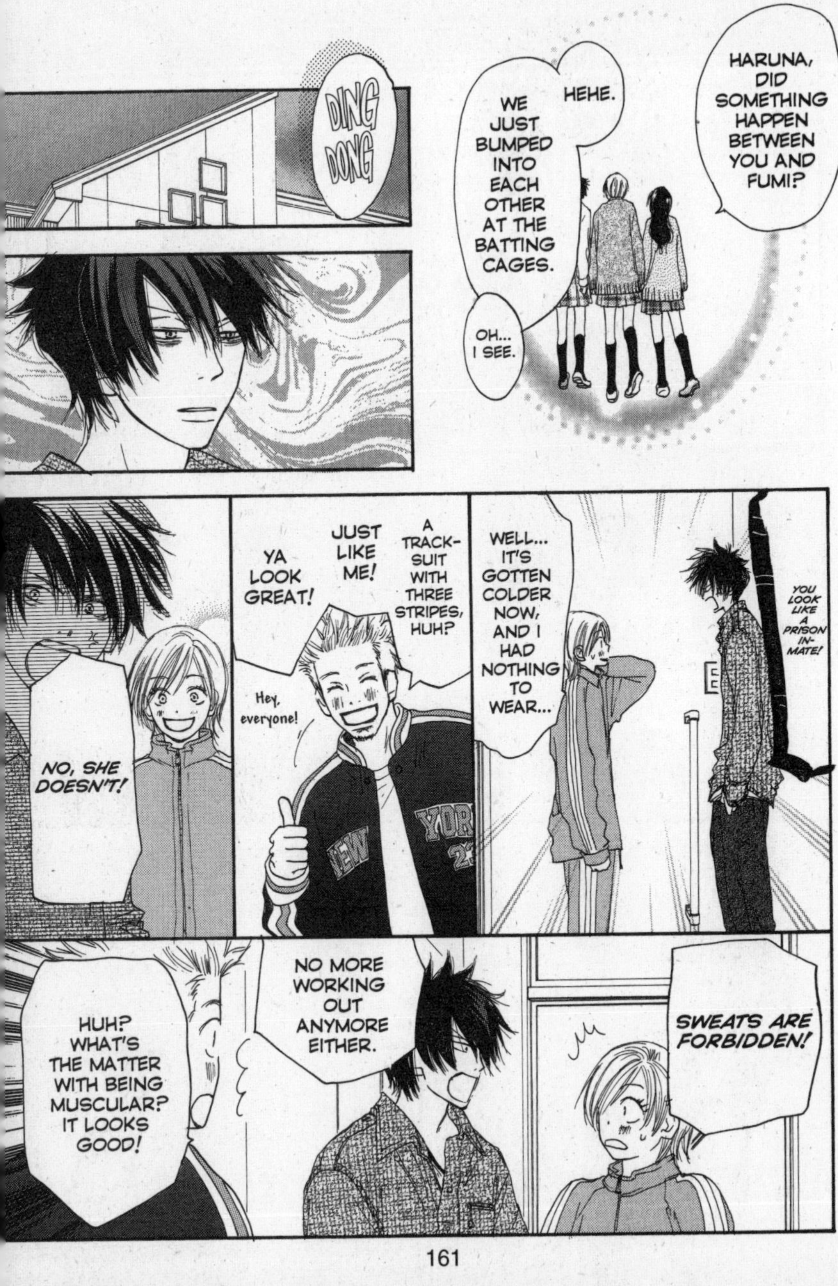
HARUNA, DID SOMETHING HAPPEN BETWEEN YOU AND FUMI?
HEHE.
WE JUST BUMPED INTO EACH OTHER AT THE BATTING CAGES.
OH... I SEE.
DING DONG
YOU LOOK LIKE A PRISON INMATE!
WELL... IT'S GOTTEN COLDER NOW, AND I HAD NOTHING TO WEAR...
A TRACK-SUIT WITH THREE STRIPES, HUH?
JUST LIKE ME!
YA LOOK GREAT!
Hey, everyone!
NO, SHE DOESN'T!
SWEATS ARE FORBIDDEN!
NO MORE WORKING OUT ANYMORE EITHER.
HUH? WHAT'S THE MATTER WITH BEING MUSCULAR? IT LOOKS GOOD!

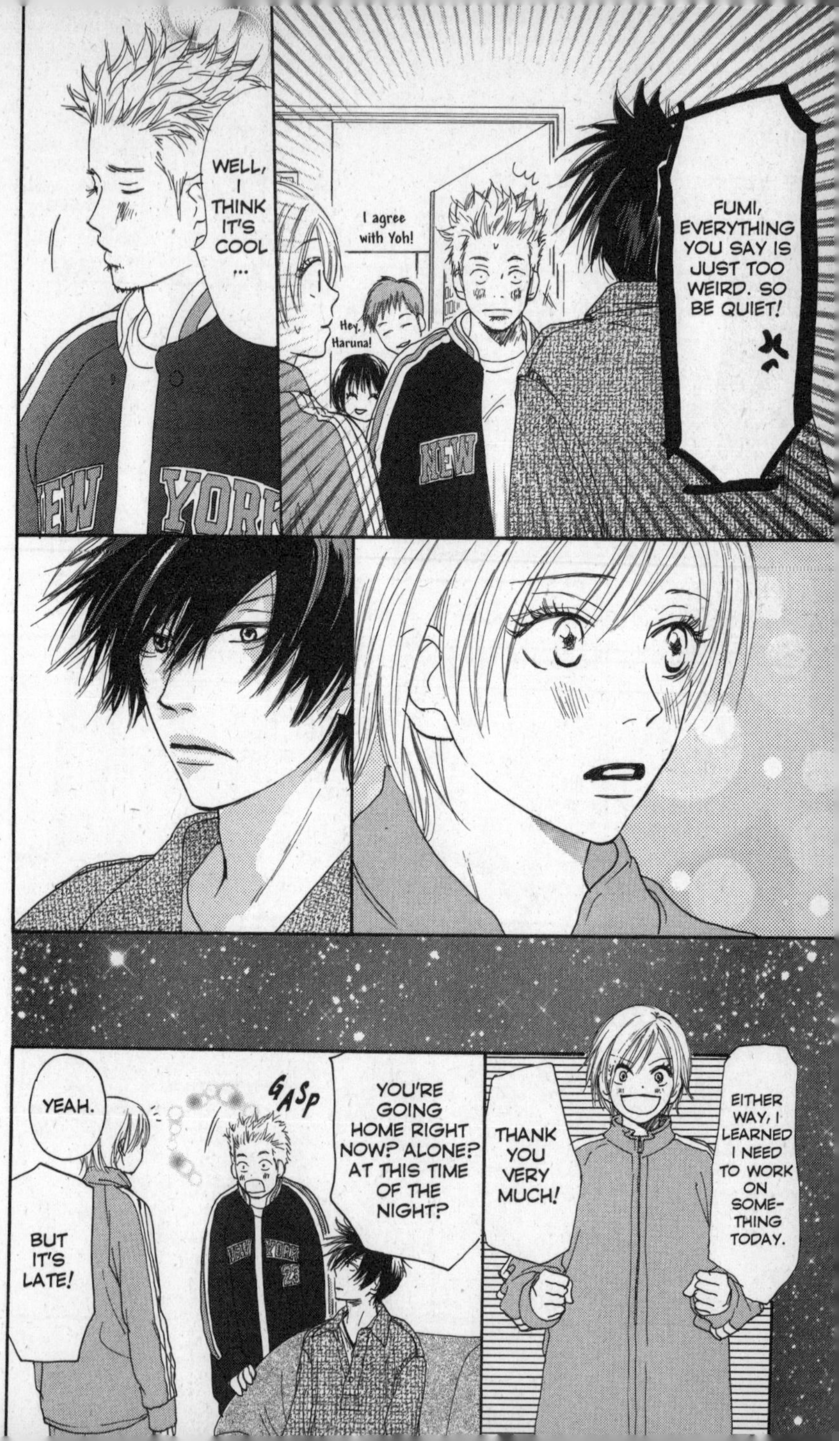
FUMI, EVERYTHING YOU SAY IS JUST TOO WEIRD. SO BE QUIET!
I agree with Yoh!
Hey, Haruna!
WELL, I THINK IT'S COOL...
EITHER WAY, I LEARNED I NEED TO WORK ON SOMETHING TODAY.
THANK YOU VERY MUCH!
YOU'RE GOING HOME RIGHT NOW? ALONE? AT THIS TIME OF THE NIGHT?
GASP
YEAH.
BUT IT'S LATE!

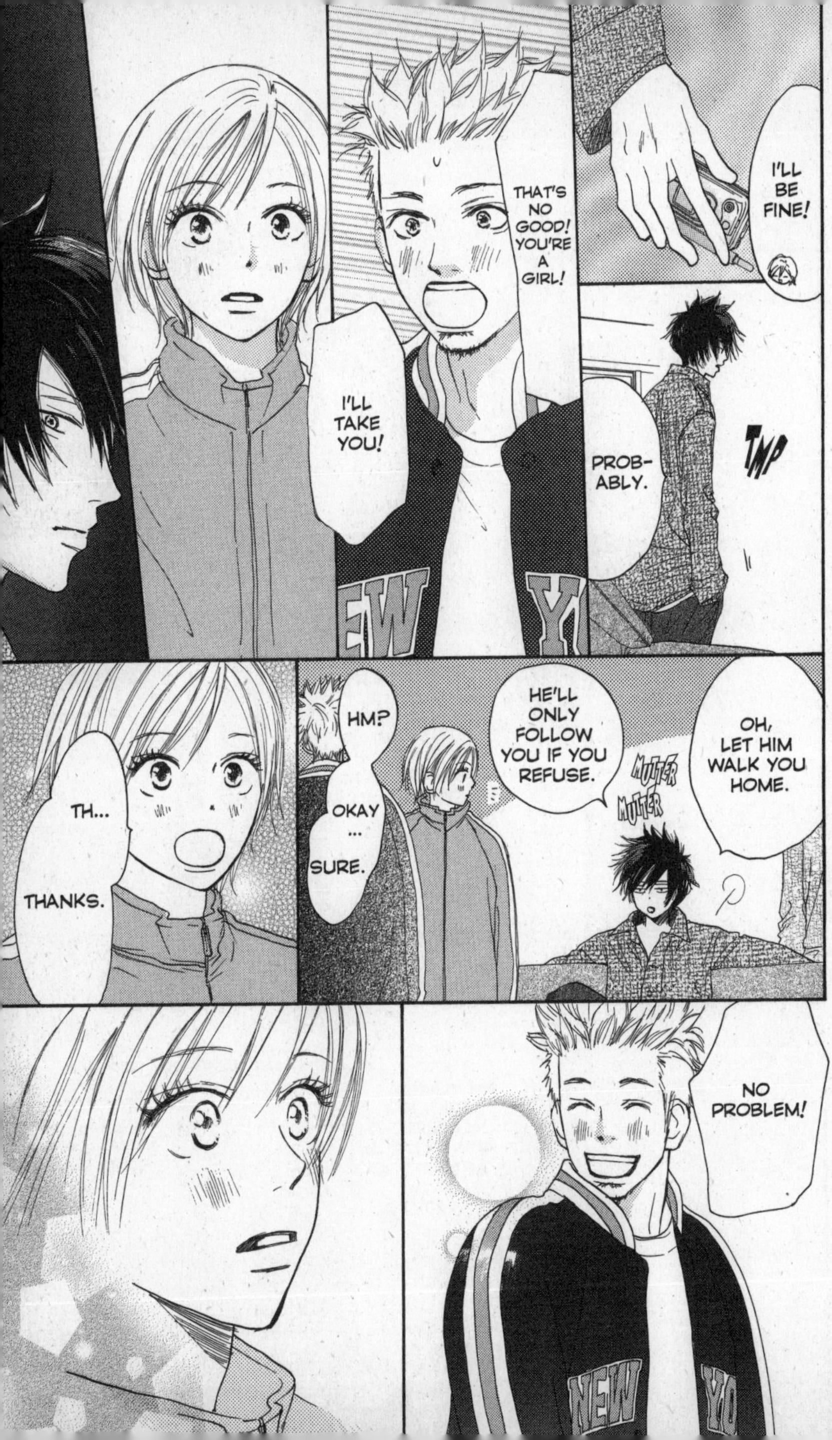
I'LL BE FINE!
PROB-ABLY.
TMP
THAT'S NO GOOD! YOU'RE A GIRL!
I'LL TAKE YOU!
OH, LET HIM WALK YOU HOME.
HE'LL ONLY FOLLOW YOU IF YOU REFUSE.
MUTTER MUTTER
HM?
OKAY ... SURE.
TH... THANKS.
NO PROBLEM!

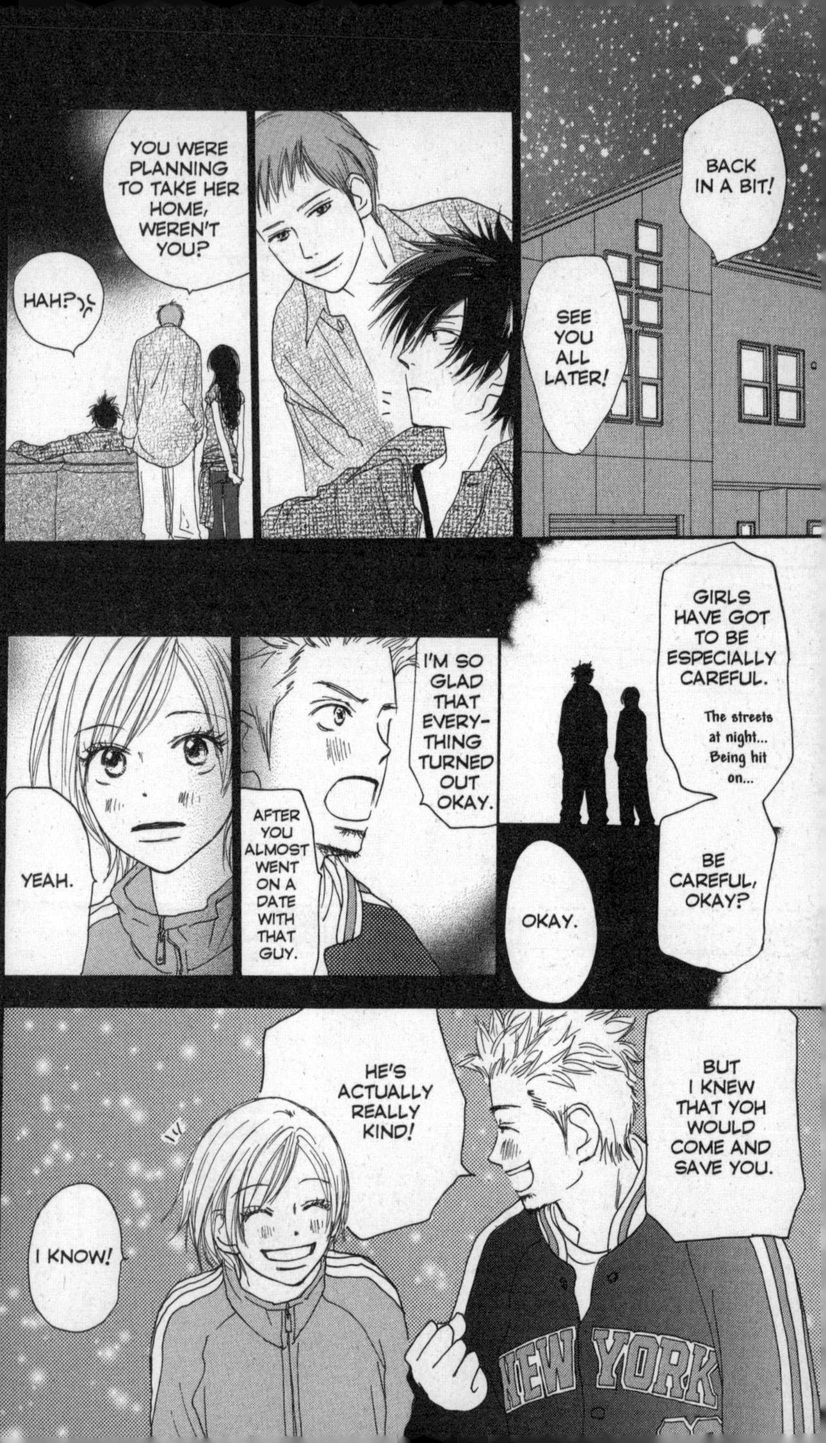
BACK IN A BIT!
SEE YOU ALL LATER!
YOU WERE PLANNING TO TAKE HER HOME, WEREN'T YOU?
HAH?
GIRLS HAVE GOT TO BE ESPECIALLY CAREFUL.
The streets at night... Being hit on...
BE CAREFUL, OKAY?
OKAY.
I'M SO GLAD THAT EVERY-THING TURNED OUT OKAY.
AFTER YOU ALMOST WENT ON A DATE WITH THAT GUY.
YEAH.
BUT I KNEW THAT YOH WOULD COME AND SAVE YOU.
HE'S ACTUALLY REALLY KIND!
I KNOW!
NEW YORK

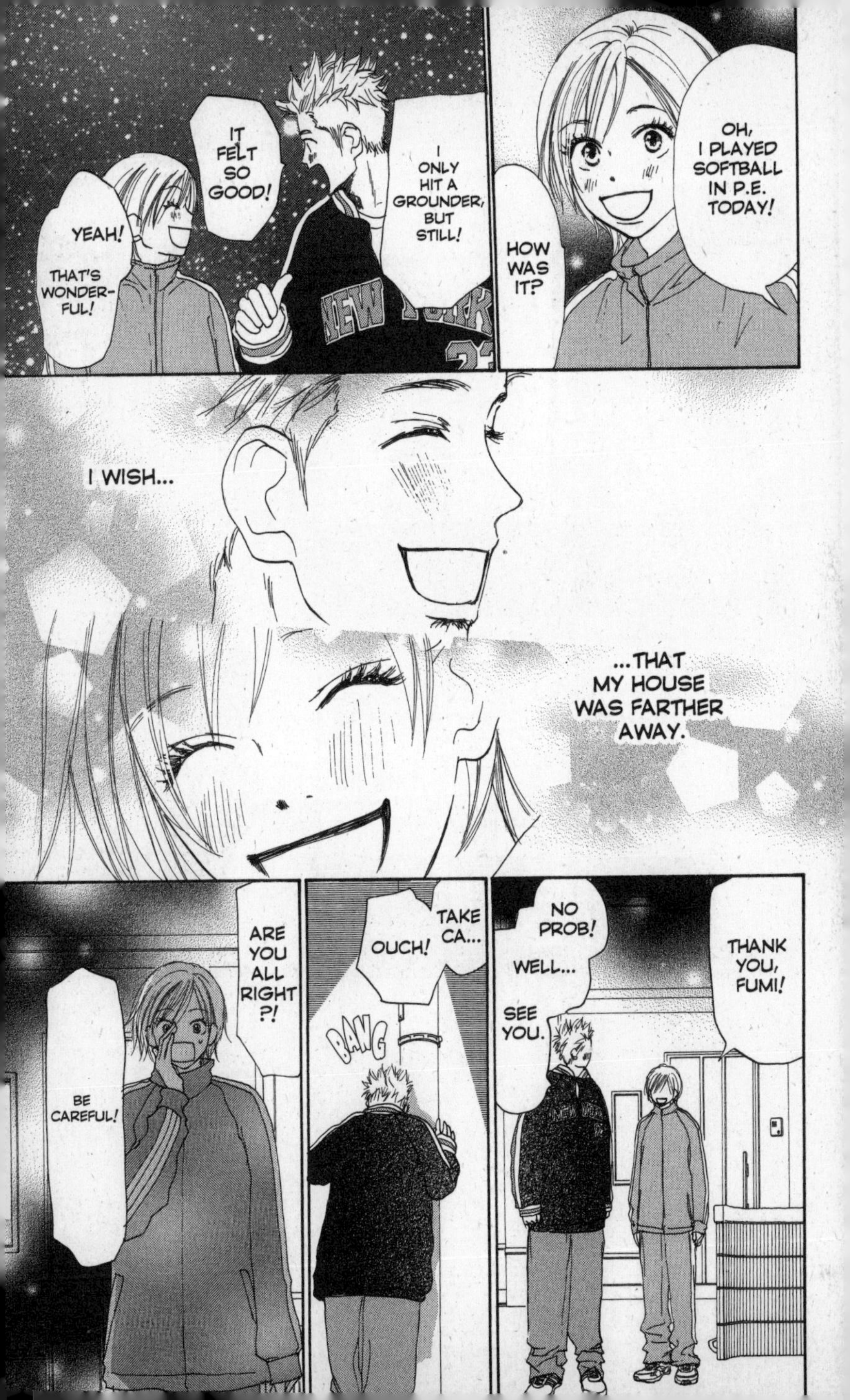
OH, I PLAYED SOFTBALL IN P.E. TODAY!
HOW WAS IT?
I ONLY HIT A GROUNDER, BUT STILL!
IT FELT SO GOOD!
YEAH!
THAT'S WONDER-FUL!
I WISH...
...THAT MY HOUSE WAS FARTHER AWAY.
THANK YOU, FUMI!
NO PROB!
WELL...
SEE YOU.
TAKE CA...
OUCH!
BANG
ARE YOU ALL RIGHT?!
BE CAREFUL!

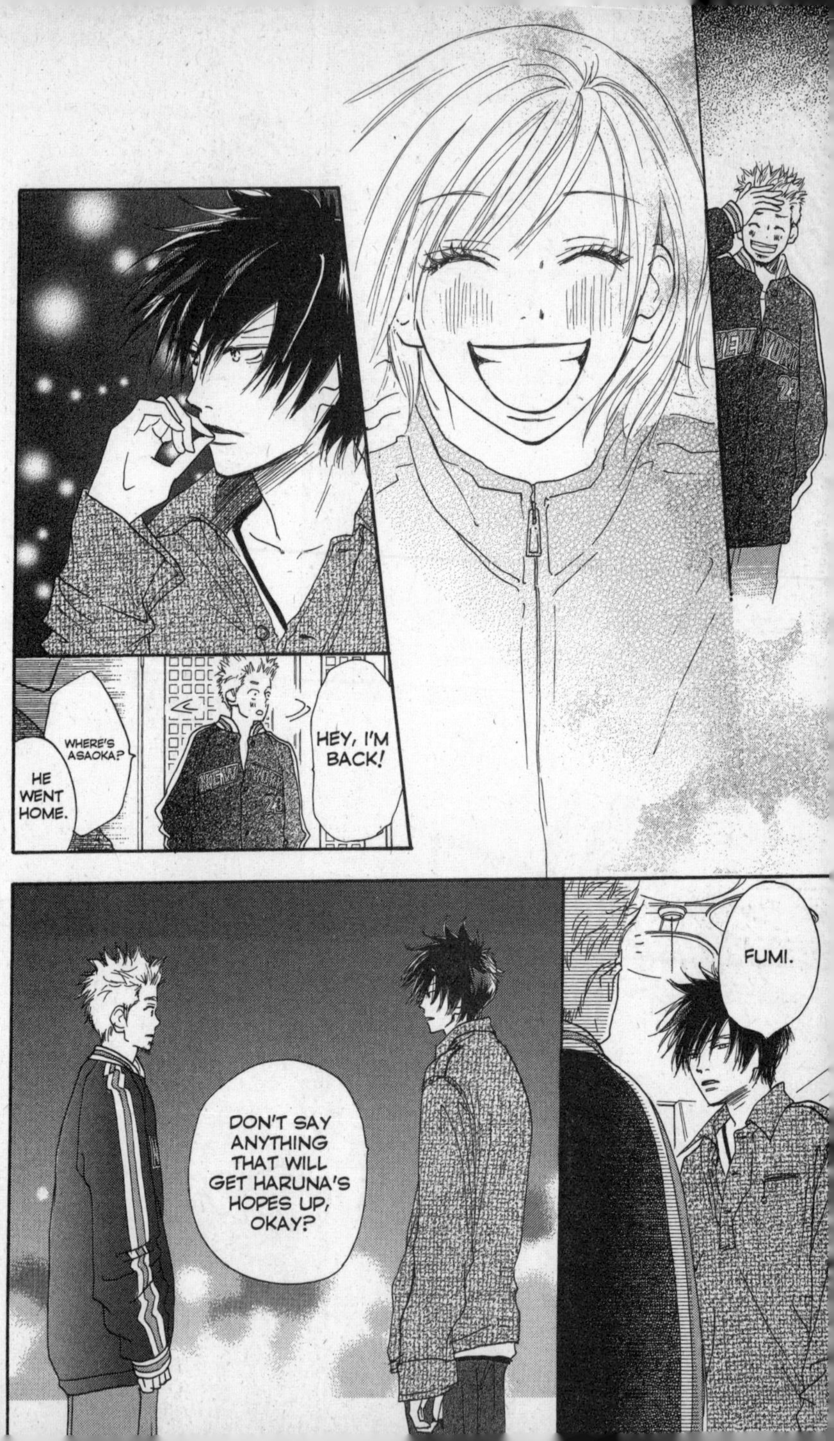
HEY, I'M BACK!
WHERE'S ASAOKA?
HE WENT HOME.
FUMI.
DON'T SAY ANYTHING THAT WILL GET HARUNA'S HOPES UP, OKAY?

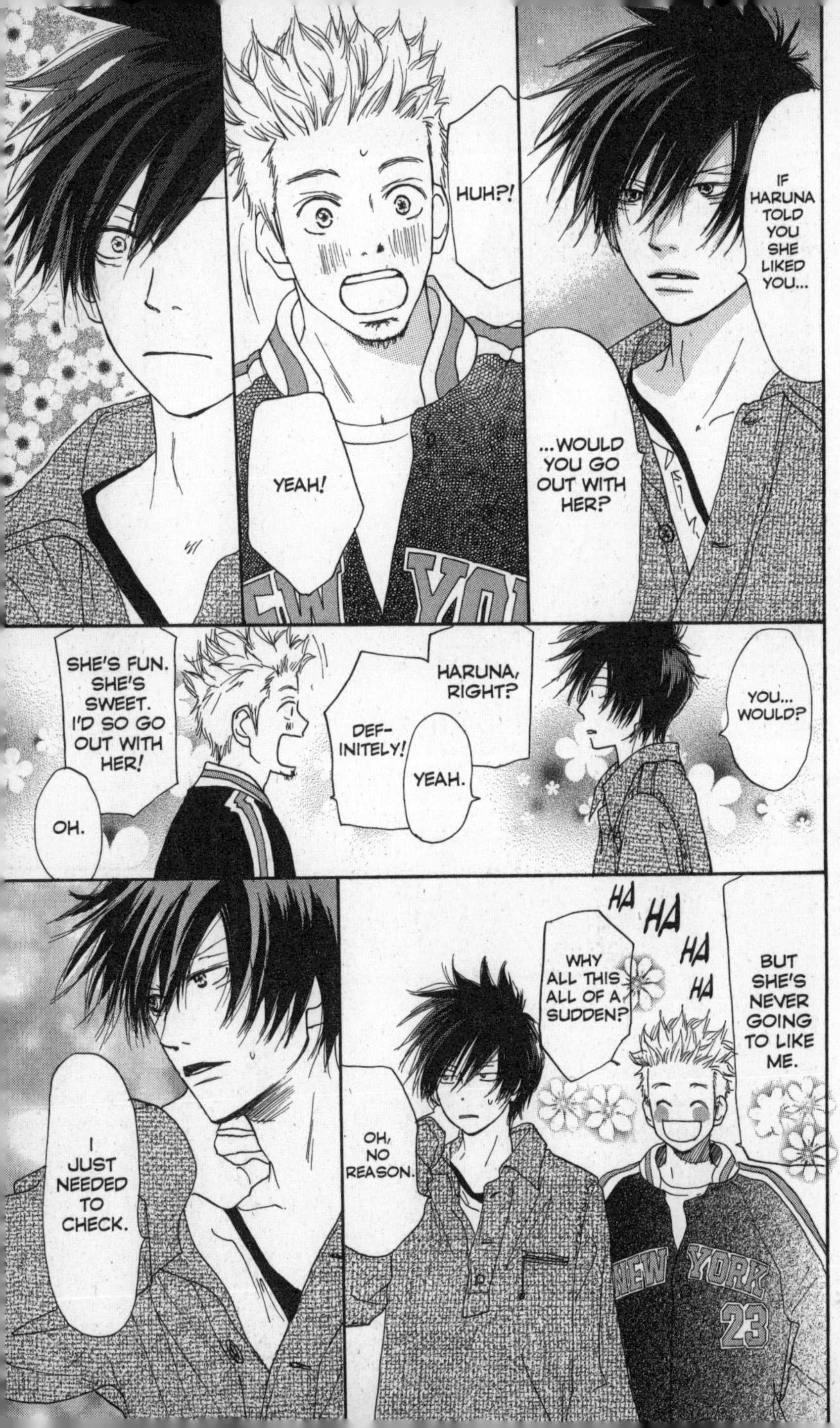
IF HARUNA TOLD YOU SHE LIKED YOU...
...WOULD YOU GO OUT WITH HER?
HUH?!
YEAH!
YOU... WOULD?
HARUNA, RIGHT?
DEF-INITELY!
YEAH.
SHE'S FUN. SHE'S SWEET. I'D SO GO OUT WITH HER!
OH.
BUT SHE'S NEVER GOING TO LIKE ME.
HA HA HA HA
WHY ALL THIS ALL OF A SUDDEN?
OH, NO REASON.
I JUST NEEDED TO CHECK.

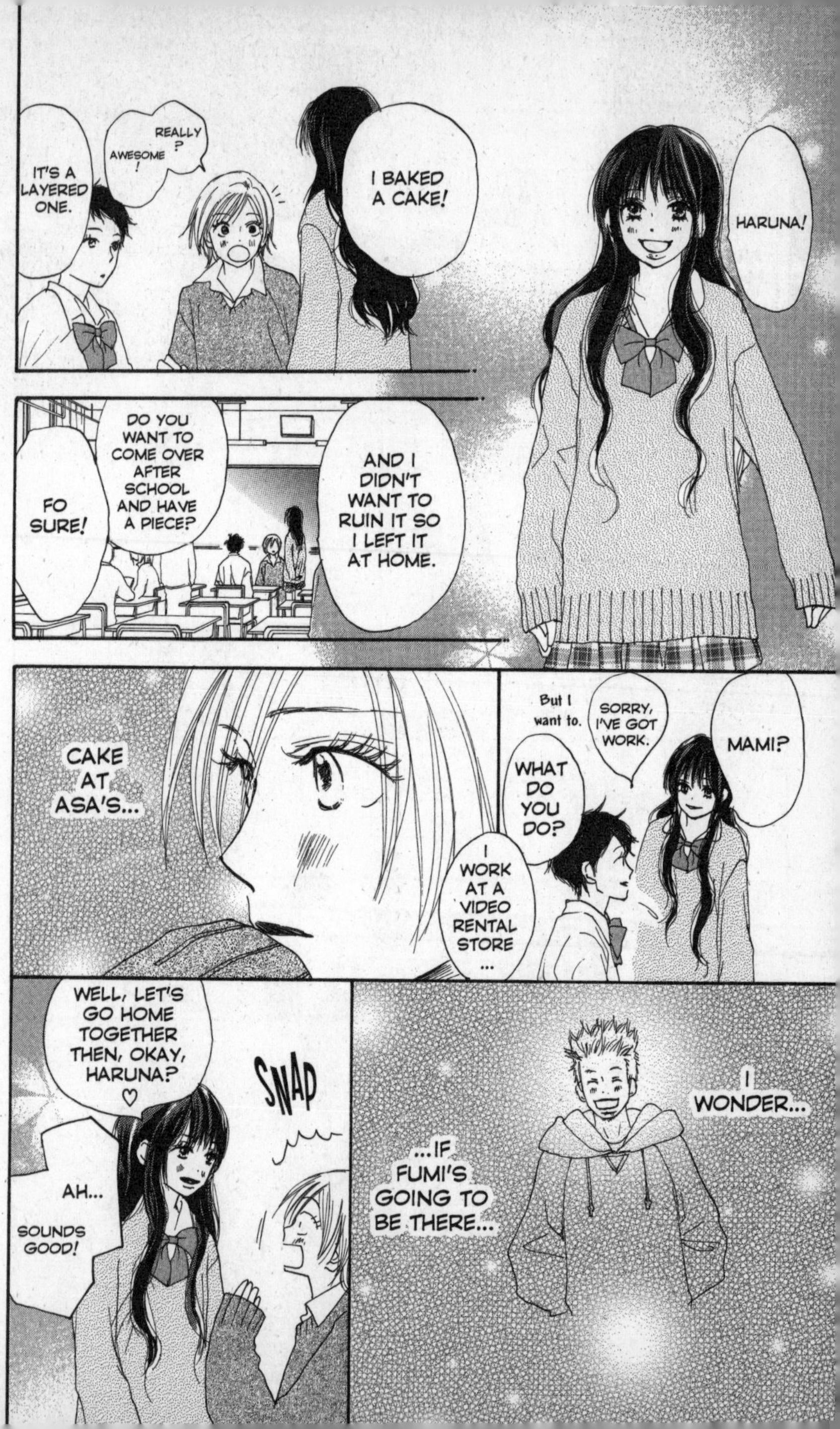
HARUNA!
I BAKED A CAKE!
REALLY?
AWESOME!
IT'S A LAYERED ONE.
AND I DIDN'T WANT TO RUIN IT SO I LEFT IT AT HOME.
DO YOU WANT TO COME OVER AFTER SCHOOL AND HAVE A PIECE?
FO SURE!
MAMI?
SORRY, I'VE GOT WORK.
But I want to.
WHAT DO YOU DO?
I WORK AT A VIDEO RENTAL STORE ...
CAKE AT ASA'S...
I WONDER...
...IF FUMI'S GOING TO BE THERE...
WELL, LET'S GO HOME TOGETHER THEN, OKAY, HARUNA? ♡
SNAP
AH...
SOUNDS GOOD!

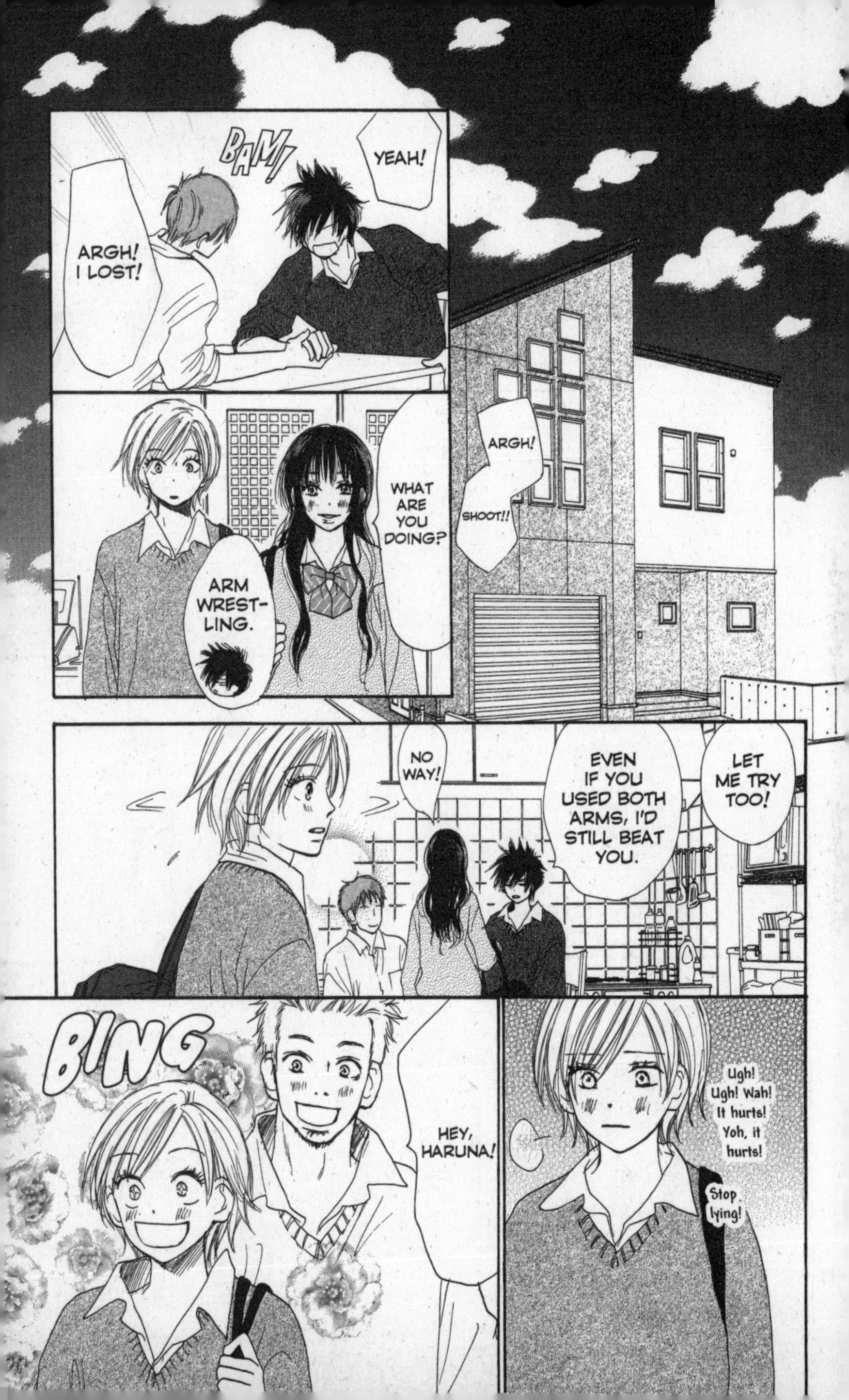
ARGH!
SHOOT!!
YEAH!
BAM!
ARGH! I LOST!
WHAT ARE YOU DOING?
ARM WRESTLING.
LET ME TRY TOO!
EVEN IF YOU USED BOTH ARMS, I'D STILL BEAT YOU.
NO WAY!
Ugh! Ugh! Wah! It hurts! Yoh, it hurts!
Stop lying!
HEY, HARUNA!
BING

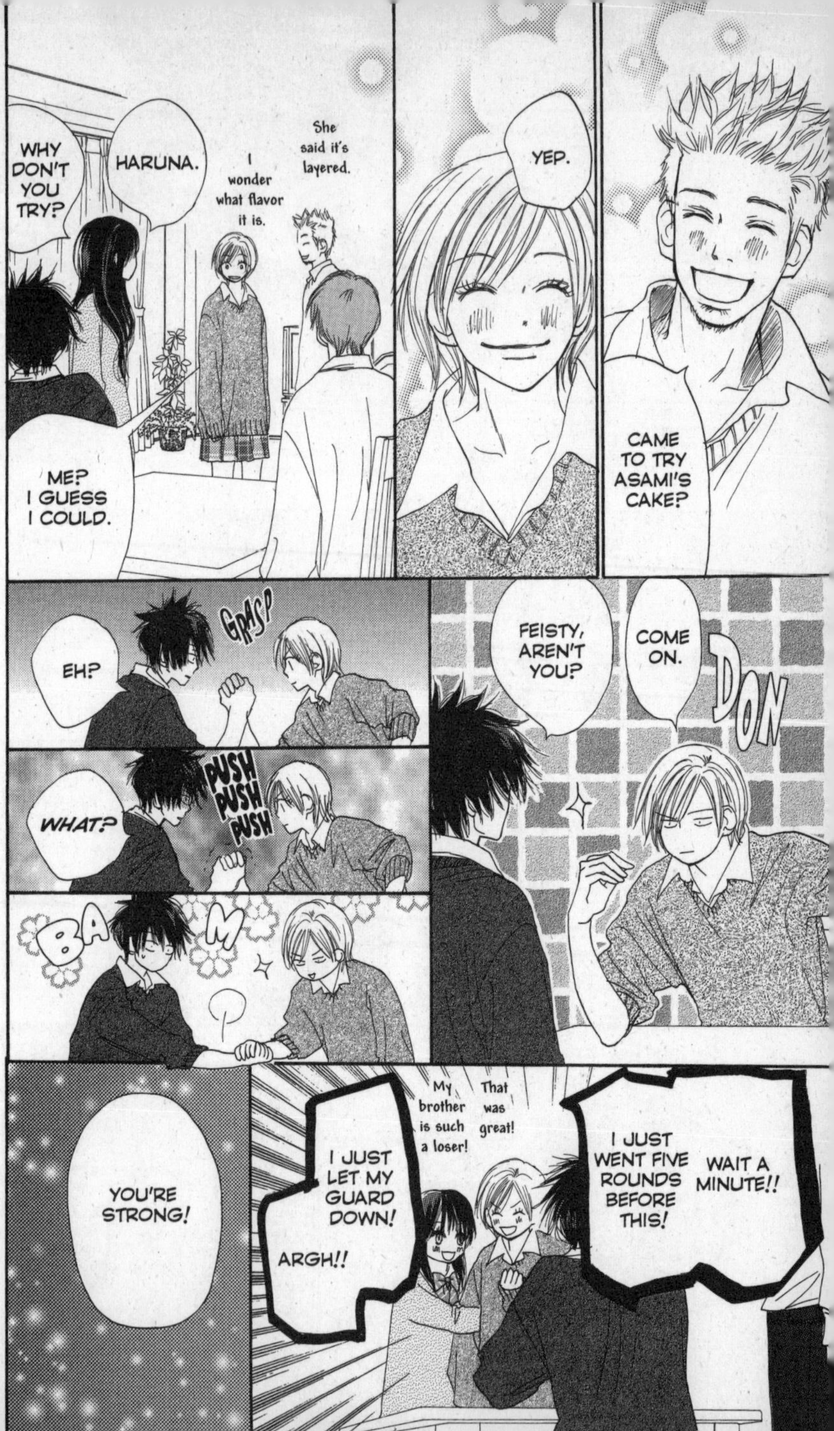
CAME TO TRY ASAMI'S CAKE?
YEP.
She said it's layered.
I wonder what flavor it is.
HARUNA.
WHY DON'T YOU TRY?
ME? I GUESS I COULD.
COME ON.
DON
FEISTY, AREN'T YOU?
GRASP
EH?
PUSH PUSH PUSH
WHAT?
BAM
WAIT A MINUTE!!
I JUST WENT FIVE ROUNDS BEFORE THIS!
That was great!
My brother is such a loser!
I JUST LET MY GUARD DOWN!
ARGH!!
YOU'RE STRONG!

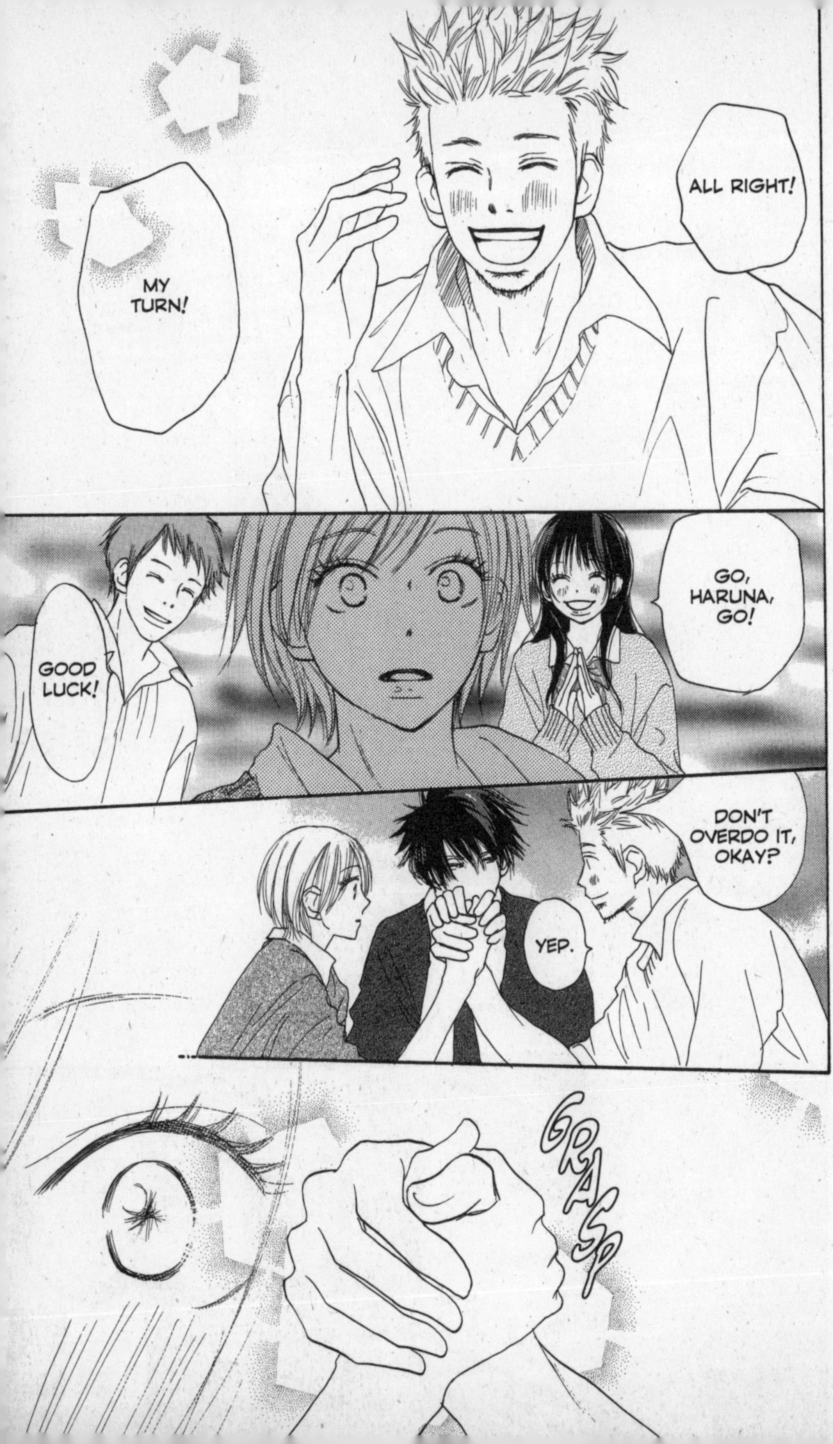
ALL RIGHT!
MY TURN!
GO, HARUNA, GO!
GOOD LUCK!
DON'T OVERDO IT, OKAY?
YEP.
GRASP

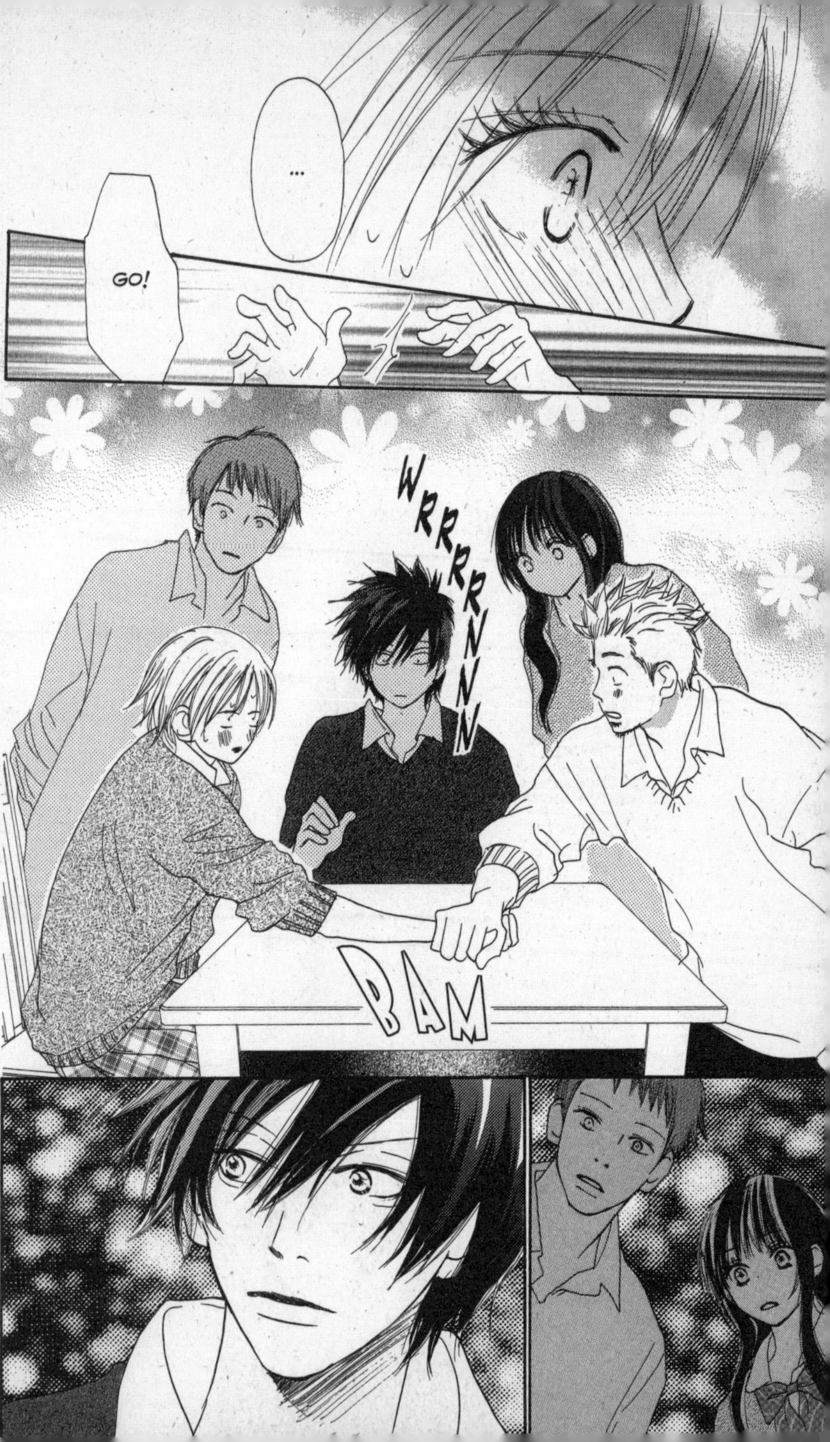
...
GO!
WRRRRRNNNN
BAM

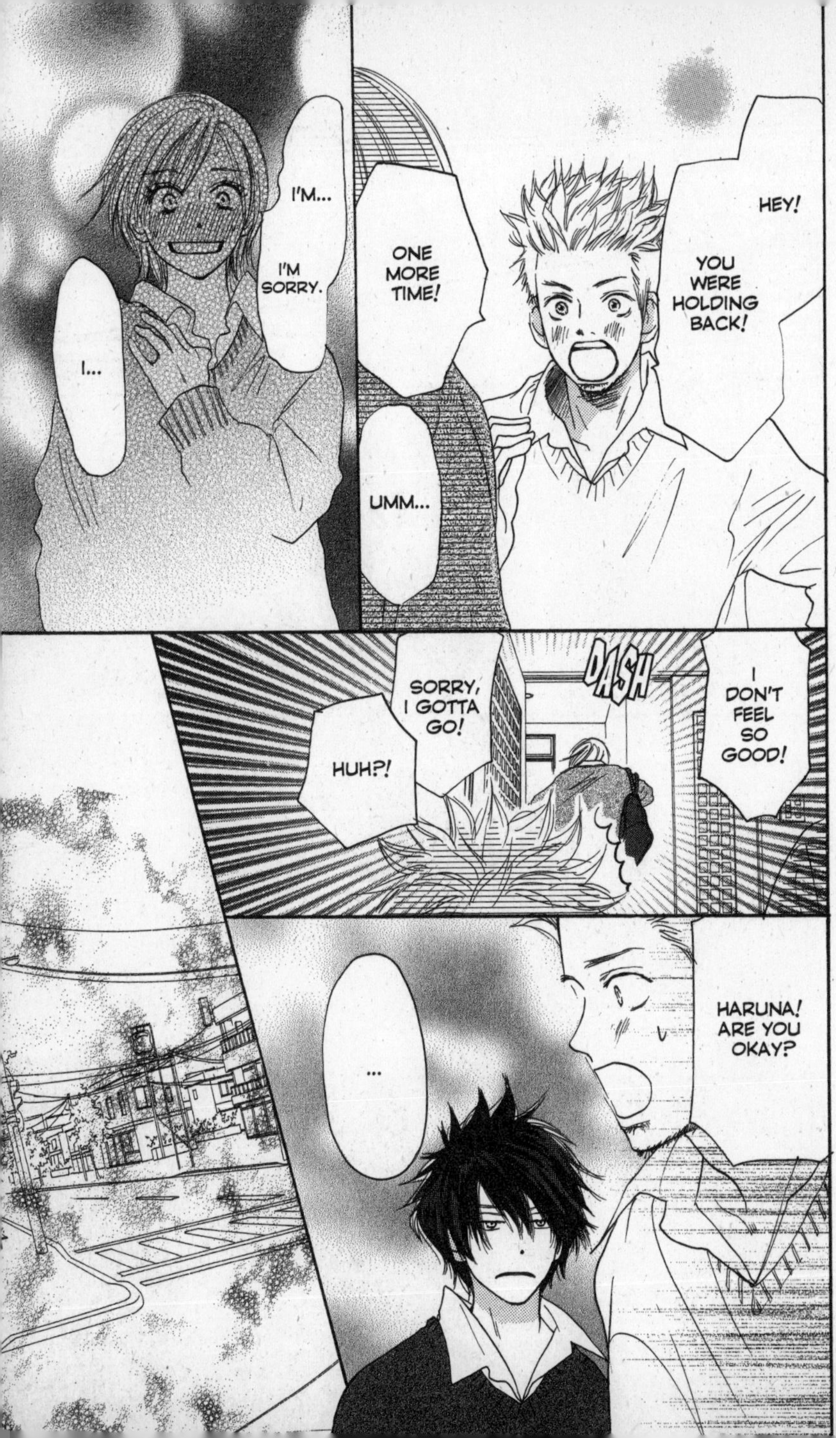
HEY!
YOU WERE HOLDING BACK!
ONE MORE TIME!
UMM...
I'M...
I'M SORRY.
I...
I DON'T FEEL SO GOOD!
DASH
SORRY, I GOTTA GO!
HUH?!
HARUNA! ARE YOU OKAY?
...

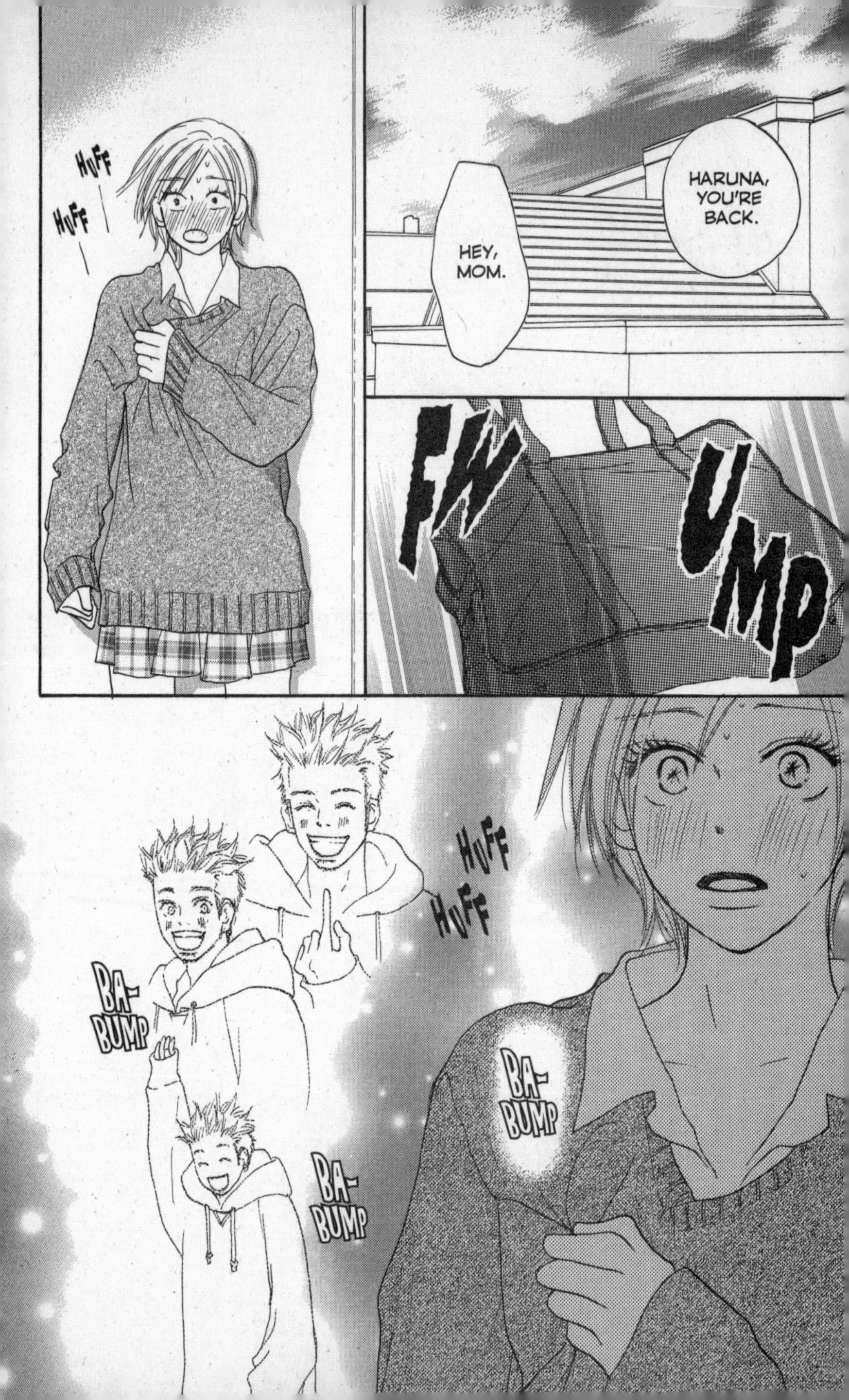
HARUNA, YOU'RE BACK.
HEY, MOM.
FWUMP
HUFF
HUFF
HUFF
HUFF
BA-BUMP
BA-BUMP
BA-BUMP

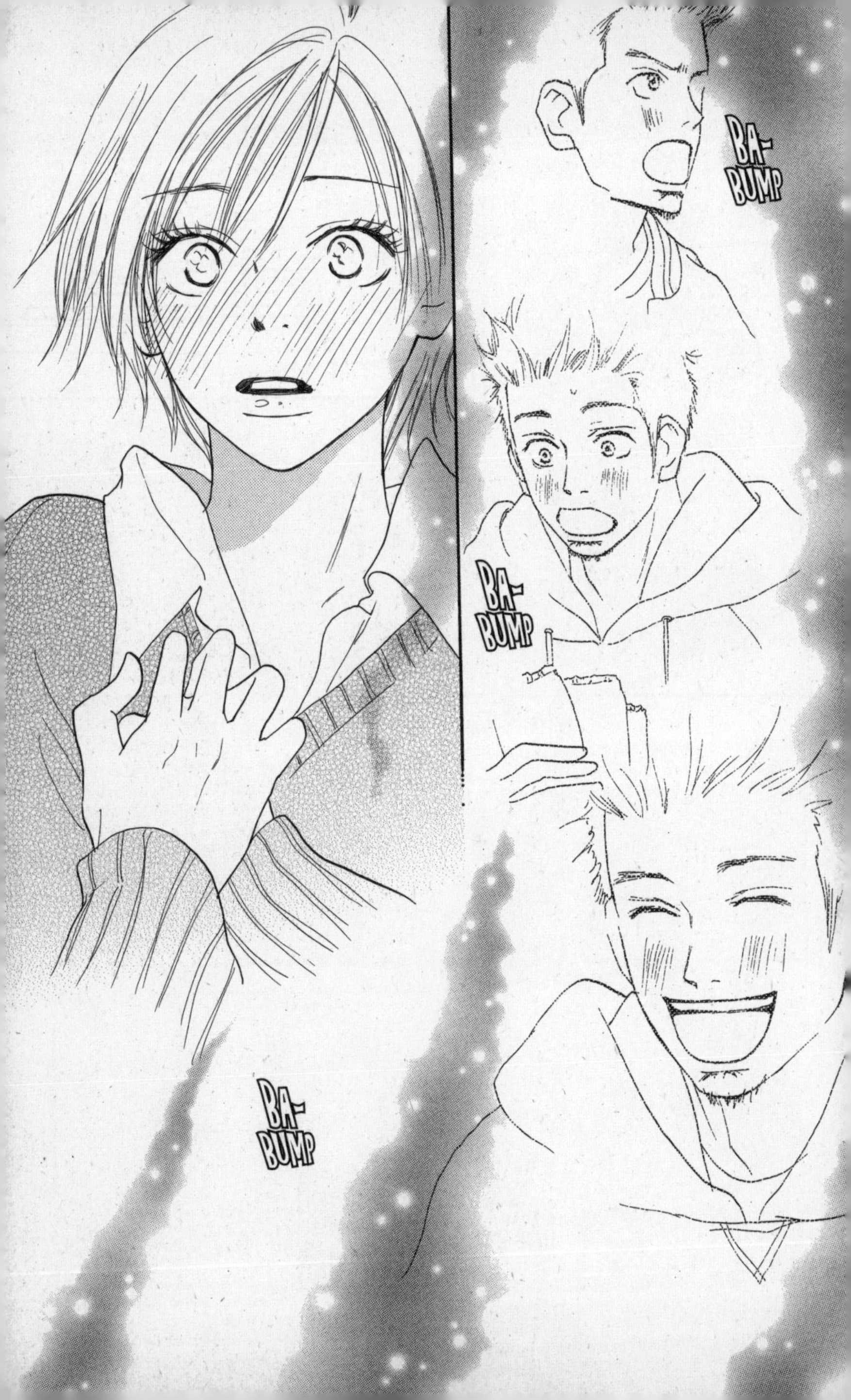
BA-BUMP
BA-BUMP
BA-BUMP

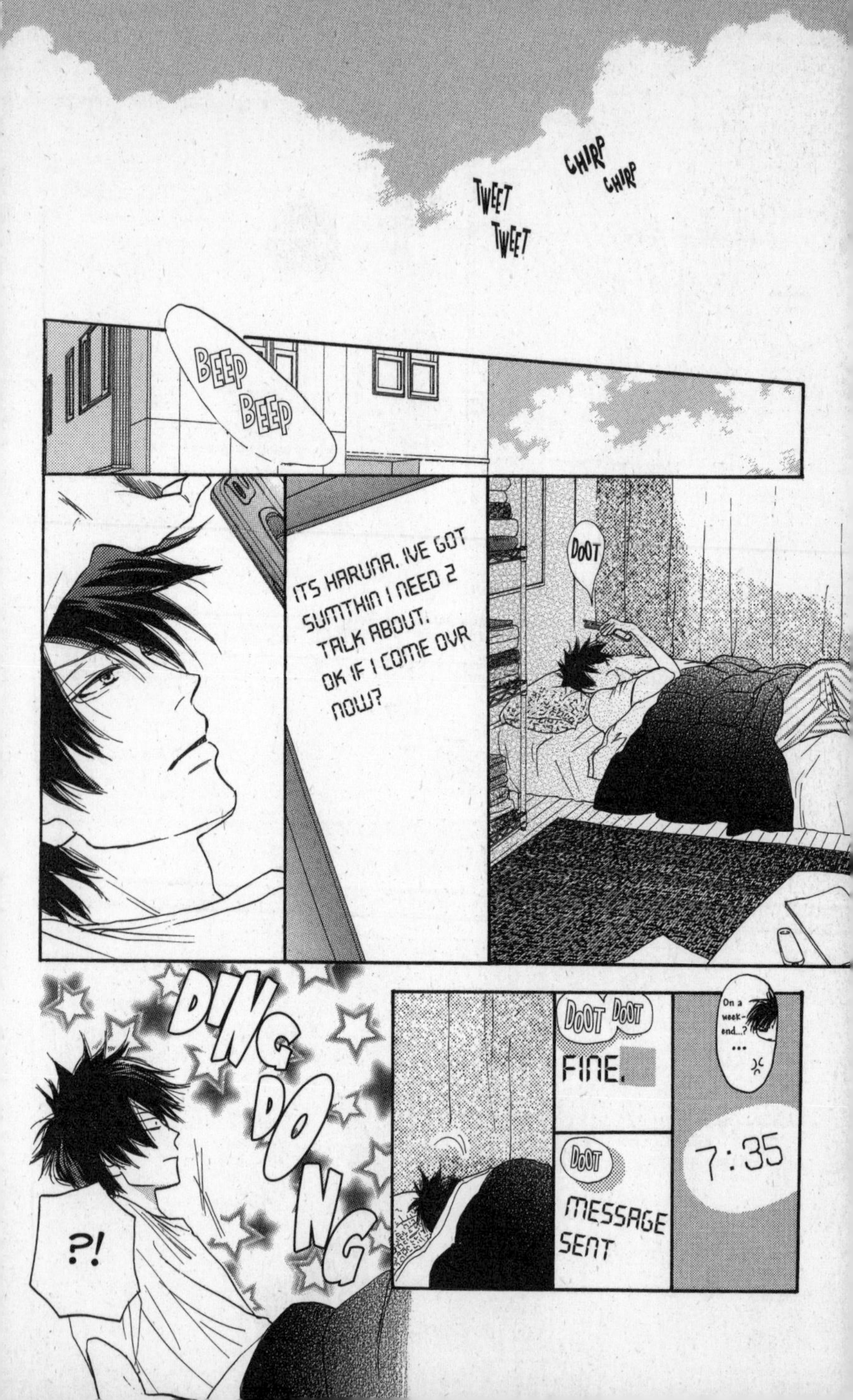
CHIRP CHIRP
TWEET TWEET
BEEP BEEP
DOOT
ITS HARUNA. IVE GOT SUMTHIN I NEED 2 TALK ABOUT. OK IF I COME OVR NOW?
On a week-end...?
...
7:35
DOOT DOOT
FINE.
DOOT
MESSAGE SENT
DING DONG
?!

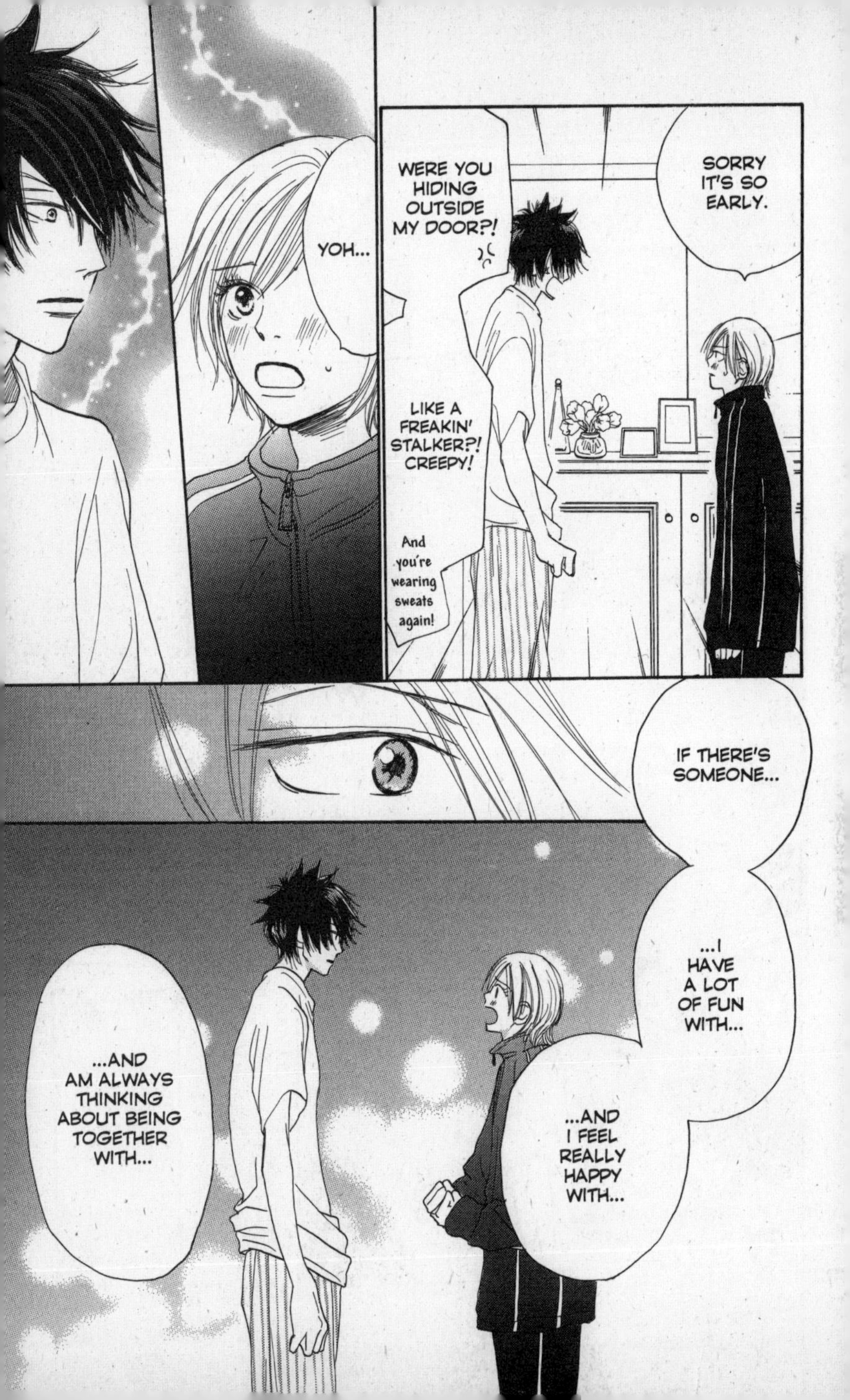
SORRY IT'S SO EARLY.
WERE YOU HIDING OUTSIDE MY DOOR?!
LIKE A FREAKIN' STALKER?! CREEPY!
And you're wearing sweats again!
YOH...
IF THERE'S SOMEONE...
...I HAVE A LOT OF FUN WITH...
...AND I FEEL REALLY HAPPY WITH...
...AND AM ALWAYS THINKING ABOUT BEING TOGETHER WITH...

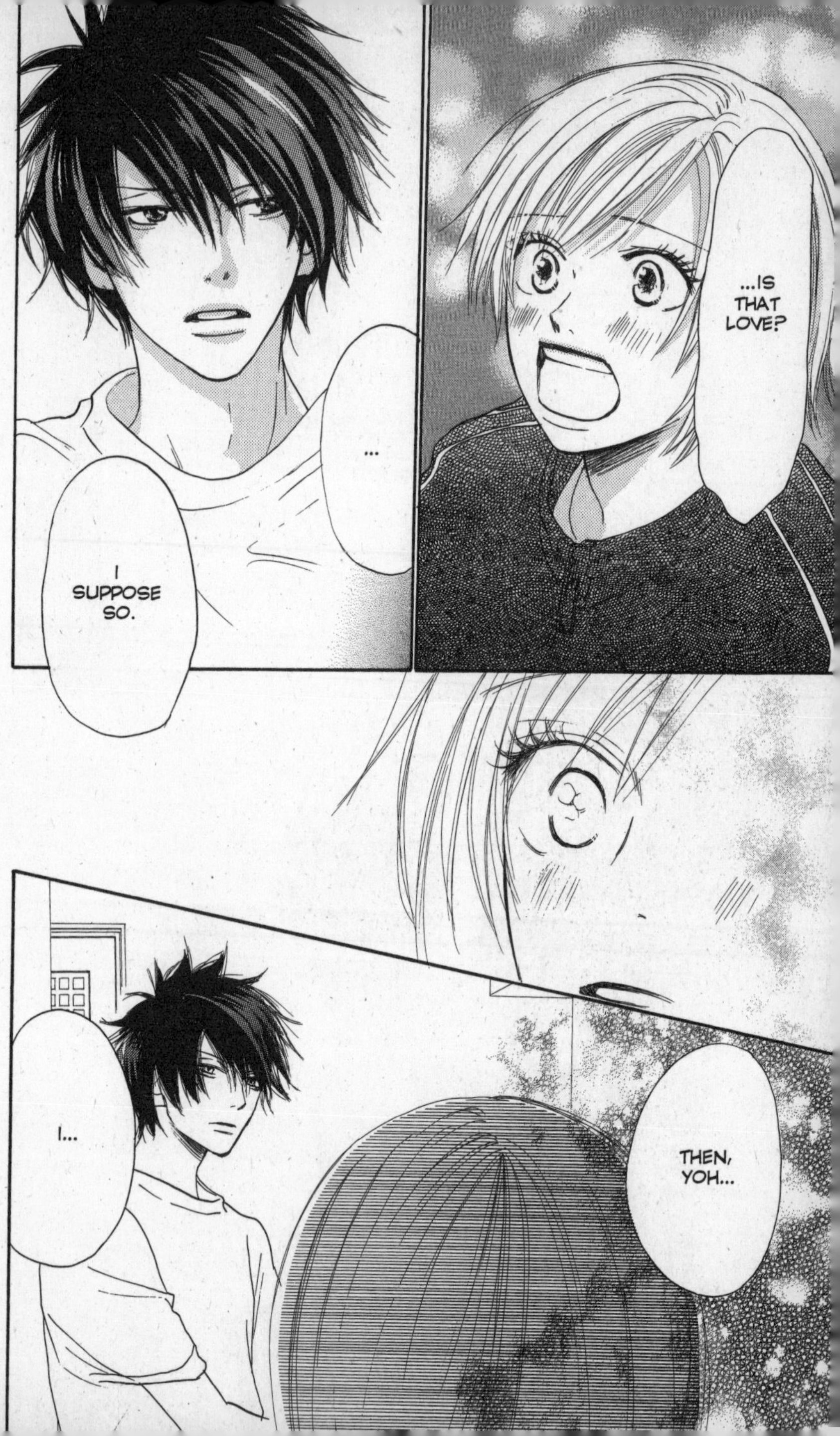
...IS THAT LOVE?
...
I SUPPOSE SO.
THEN, YOH...
I...

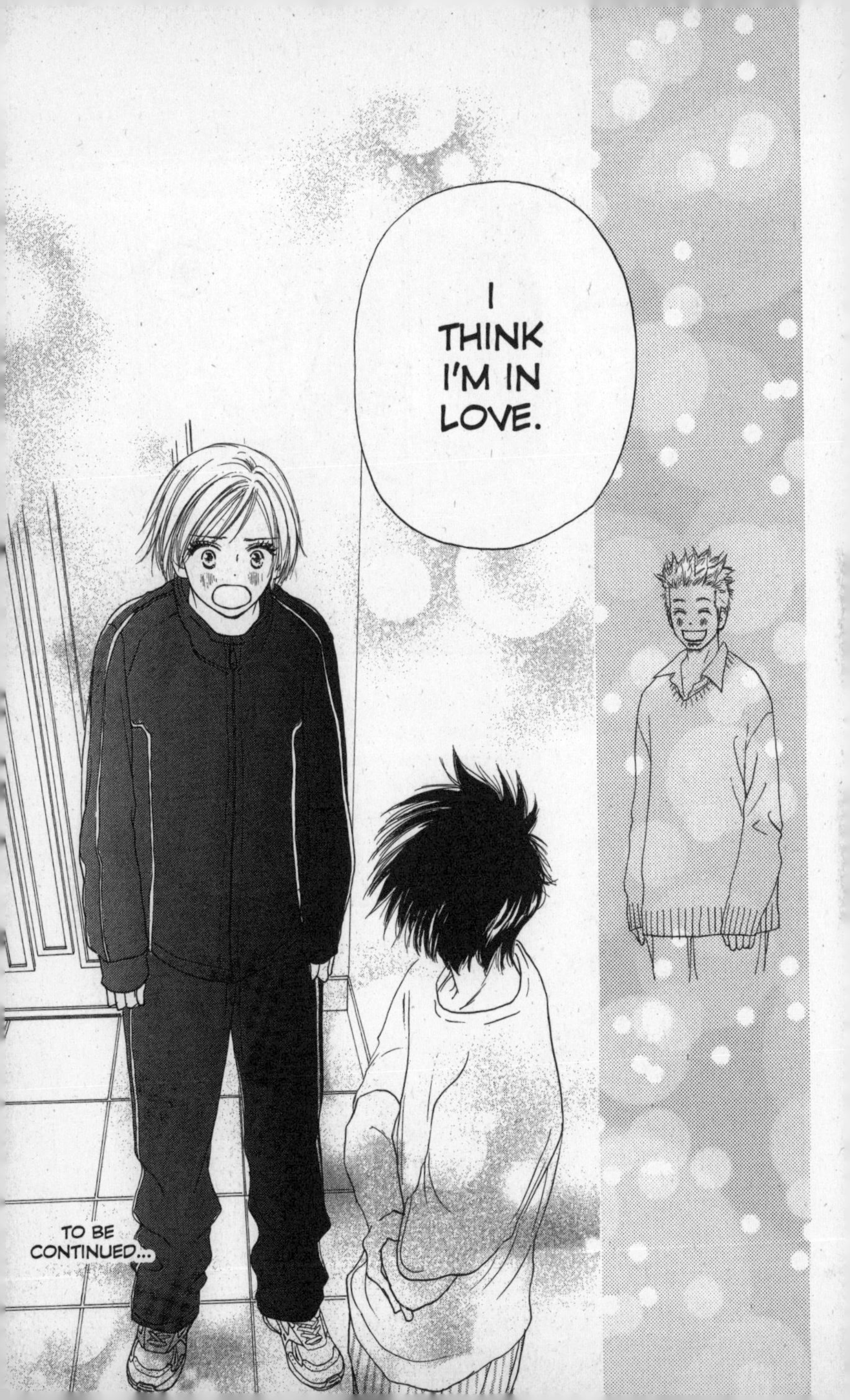
I THINK I'M IN LOVE.
TO BE CONTINUED...

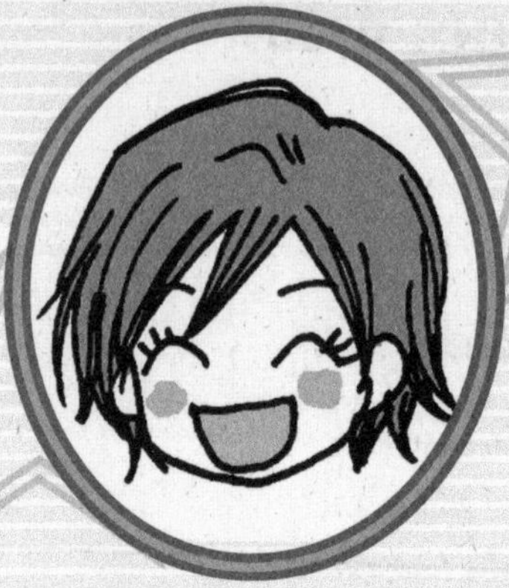

I must like psychological tests and personality diagnoses since every time I see one, I just have to take it. However, personality diagnoses are nothing but a self-evaluation, and psychological tests all just say "this will look deep into your psyche" and pose questions that make you think about something so much that you can't even give an answer anymore! So I don't think they help that much in the end.

– Kazune Kawahara

Kazune Kawahara is from Hokkaido prefecture in Japan and was born on March 11th (a Pisces!). She made her manga debut at age 18 with *Kare no Ichiban Sukina Hito* (His Most Favorite Person). Her other works include *Sensei!*, serialized in *Bessatsu Margaret* magazine. Her hobby is interior redecorating.

HIGH SCHOOL DEBUT
VOL. 1
Shojo Beat Edition

This manga volume contains material that was originally published in English in *Shojo Beat* magazine, December 2007 issue. Artwork in the magazine may have been slightly altered from that presented here.

STORY & ART BY
KAZUNE KAWAHARA

Translation & Adaptation/Translation By Design - Gemma Collinge
Touch-up Art & Lettering/Mark Griffin
Design/Izumi Hirayama
Editor/Amy Yu

First published in Japan in 2003 by SHUEISHA Inc., Tokyo.
English translation rights arranged by SHUEISHA Inc.

Printed in Canada

Published by VIZ Media, LLC
P.O. Box 77010
San Francisco, CA 94107

10 9 8 7 6 5
First printing, January 2008
Fifth printing, May 2011

www.viz.com www.shojobeat.com

PARENTAL ADVISORY
HIGH SCHOOL DEBUT is rated T for Teen and is recommended for ages 13 and up. This volume contains suggestive themes.
ratings.viz.com

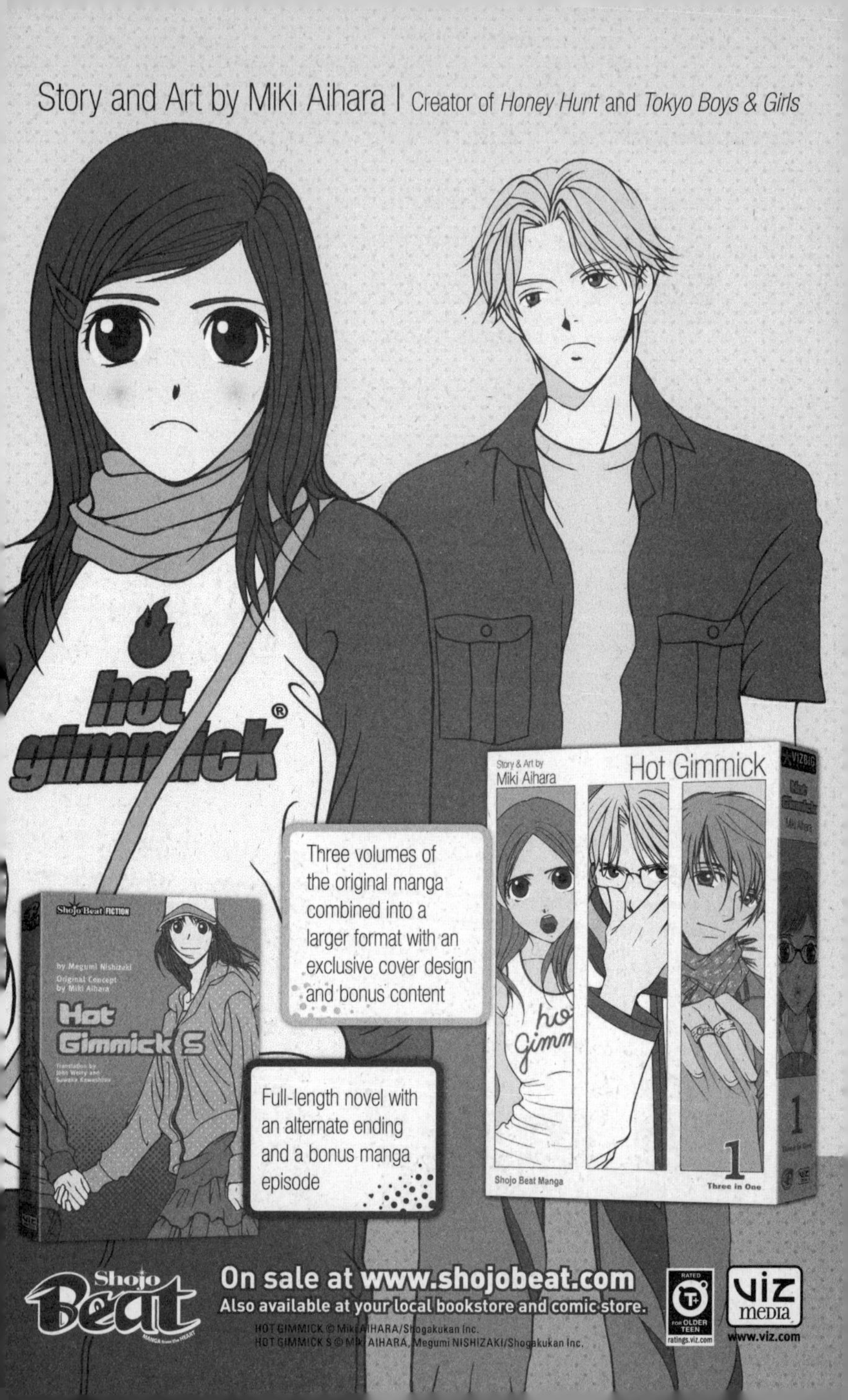
Story and Art by Miki Aihara | Creator of Honey Hunt and Tokyo Boys & Girls
hot gimmick®
Story & Art by Miki Aihara
Hot Gimmick
Shojo Beat Manga
1
Three in One
Three volumes of the original manga combined into a larger format with an exclusive cover design and bonus content
Shojo Beat FICTION
by Megumi Nishizaki
Original Concept by Miki Aihara
Hot Gimmick S
Full-length novel with an alternate ending and a bonus manga episode
Shojo Beat
On sale at www.shojobeat.com
Also available at your local bookstore and comic store.
HOT GIMMICK © Miki AIHARA/Shogakukan Inc.
HOT GIMMICK S © Miki AIHARA, Megumi NISHIZAKI/Shogakukan Inc.
RATED T+ FOR OLDER TEEN
ratings.viz.com
VIZ MEDIA
www.viz.com

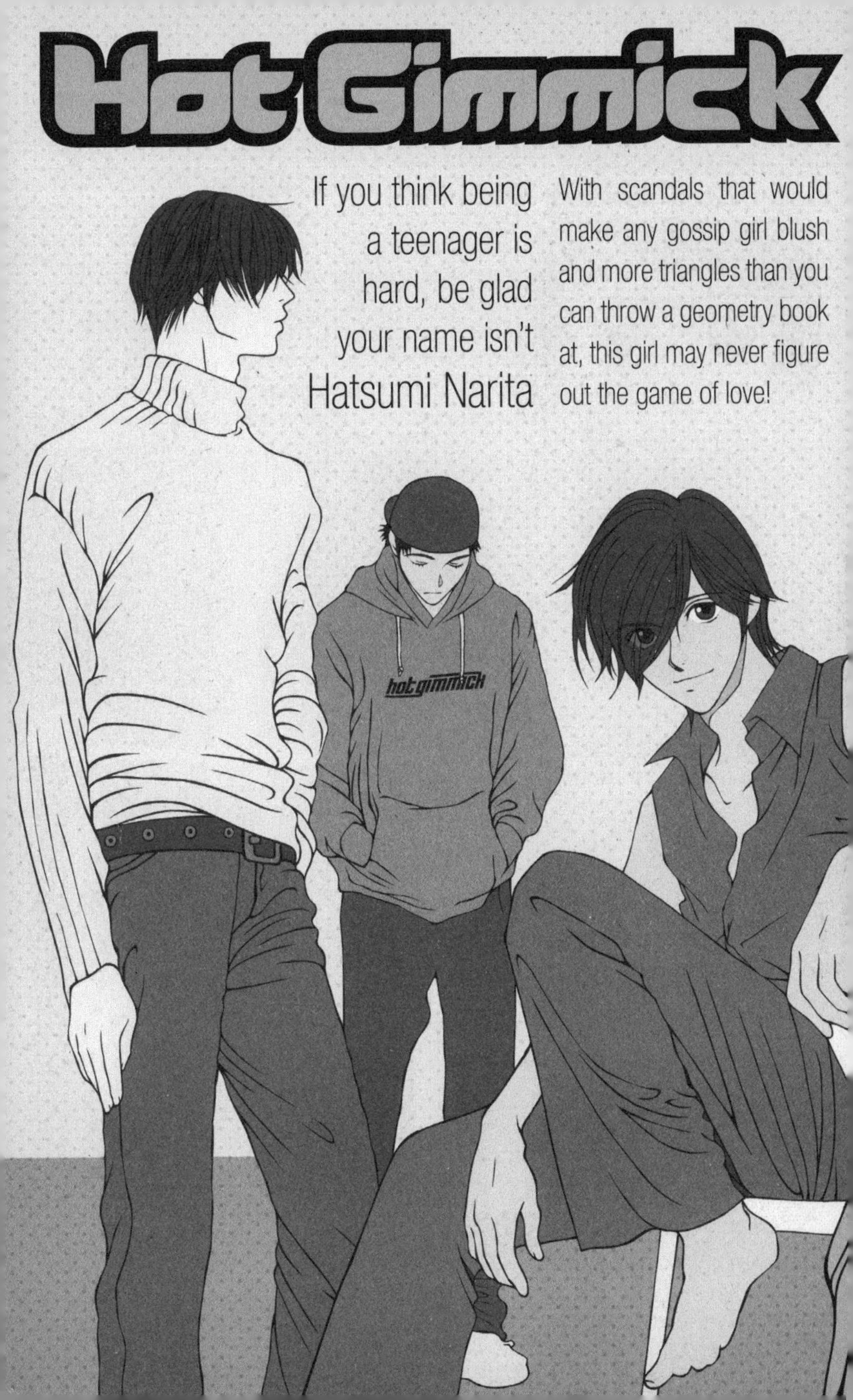

Hot Gimmick
If you think being a teenager is hard, be glad your name isn't Hatsumi Narita
With scandals that would make any gossip girl blush and more triangles than you can throw a geometry book at, this girl may never figure out the game of love!
hotgimmick

About the Authors

David Nyuol Vincent is one of the Lost Boys of Sudan. At the age of twelve he was trained as a child soldier in Ethiopia and lived as a refugee in Kenya until he was resettled in Australia when he was twenty-six. Since rebuilding his life here in Australia, David has become an advocate for the Sudanese community. He works with the Brotherhood of St Laurence, is a Victorian Human Rights Youth Ambassador, and in 2012 he received the honour of becoming one of forty People of Australia Ambassadors. He also helped to set up an all-Sudanese refugee football team, the Western Tigers, in the Brimbank soccer league. David champions the rights of refugees in Australia and is committed to achieving peace for his people in South Sudan.

Carol Nader is an award-winning journalist who worked for *The Age* for fifteen years. She is a former health editor and social policy editor and has written extensively on child protection and family law, race and ethnic affairs, the health system, abortion law reform, IVF laws, gay rights, mental health and medical research. She has been honoured in awards from the Victorian Law Foundation, Research Australia and the National Press Club.

the UN Office for the Coordination of Humanitarian Affairs; the Australian Department of Immigration and Citizenship; the Assessment and Evaluation Commission of the Republic of Sudan; Child Soldiers International; the Victorian Equal Opportunity and Human Rights Commission; UNICEF; warrants of arrest issued by the International Criminal Court; and the BBC.